I'll Give It My All... Tomorrow

BY SHUNJU AONO

1

Table of Contents

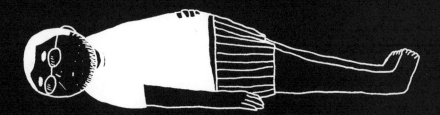

Kaleidoscope

FIGURE

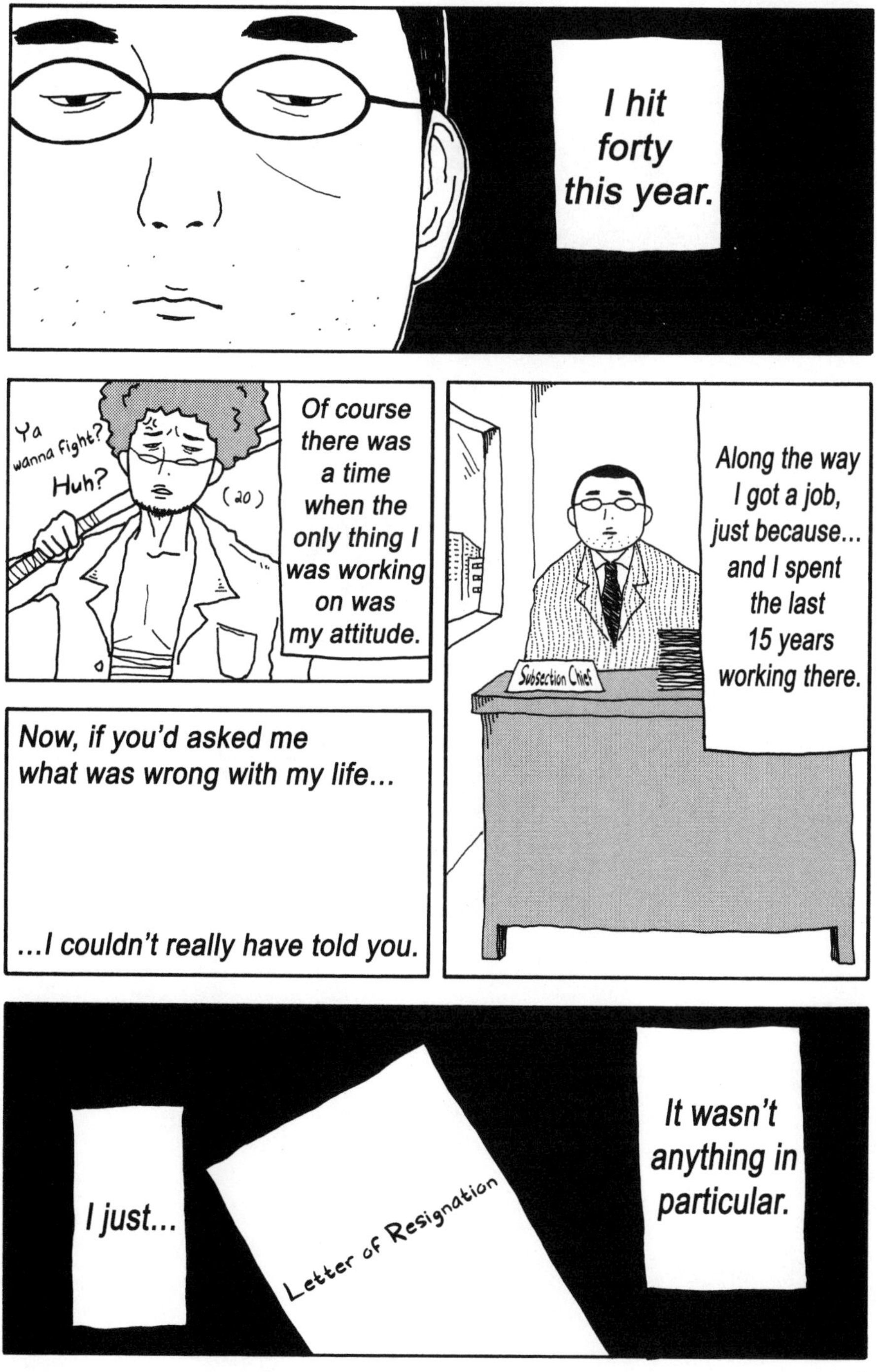
I hit forty this year.
Along the way I got a job, just because... and I spent the last 15 years working there.
Subsection Chief
Of course there was a time when the only thing I was working on was my attitude.
Ya wanna fight?
Huh?
(20)
Now, if you'd asked me what was wrong with my life...
...I couldn't really have told you.
It wasn't anything in particular.
Letter of Resignation
I just...

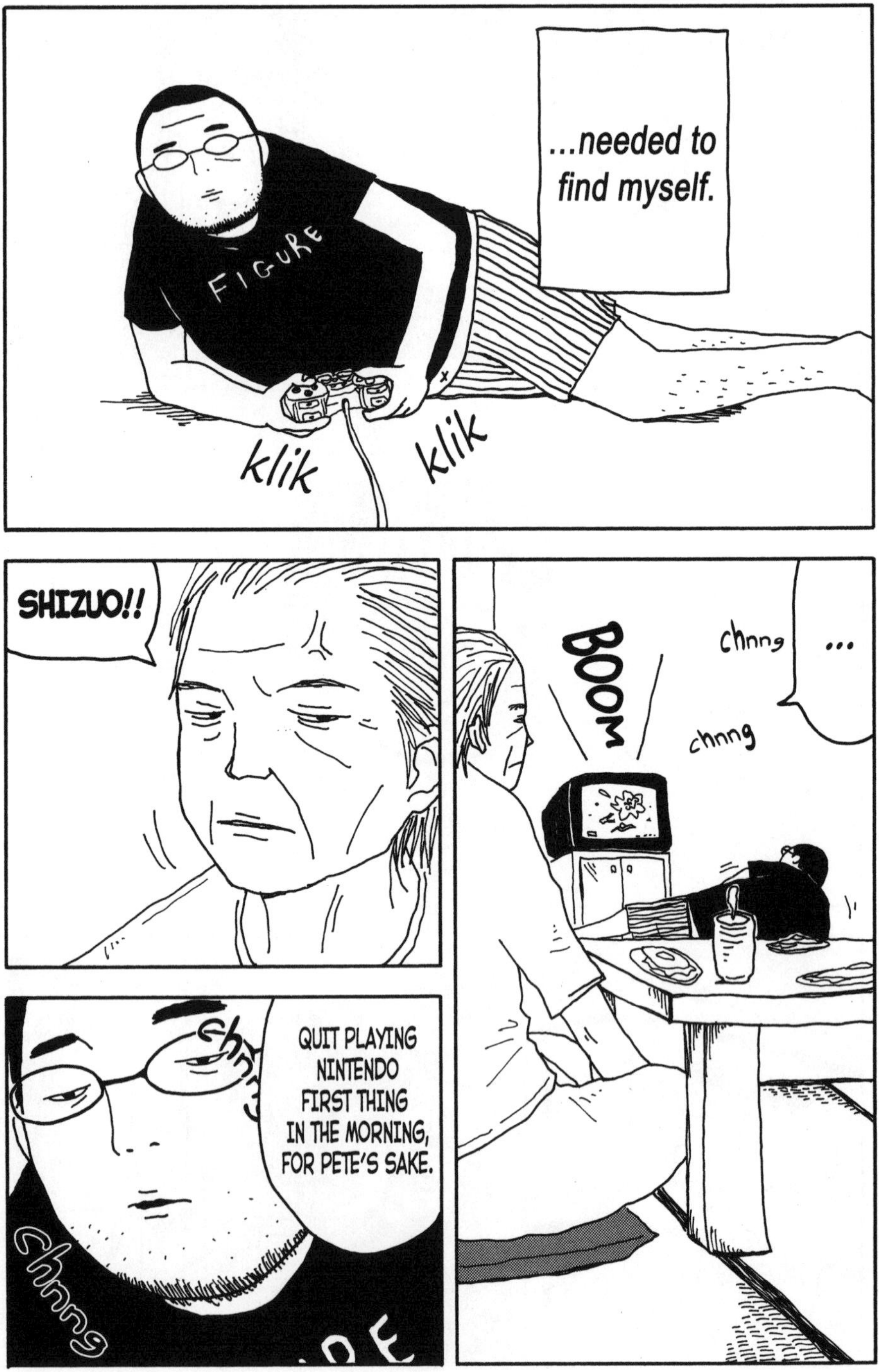
...needed to find myself.
klik
klik
BOOM
chnng
...
chnng
SHIZUO!!
chnng
QUIT PLAYING NINTENDO FIRST THING IN THE MORNING, FOR PETE'S SAKE.
chnng

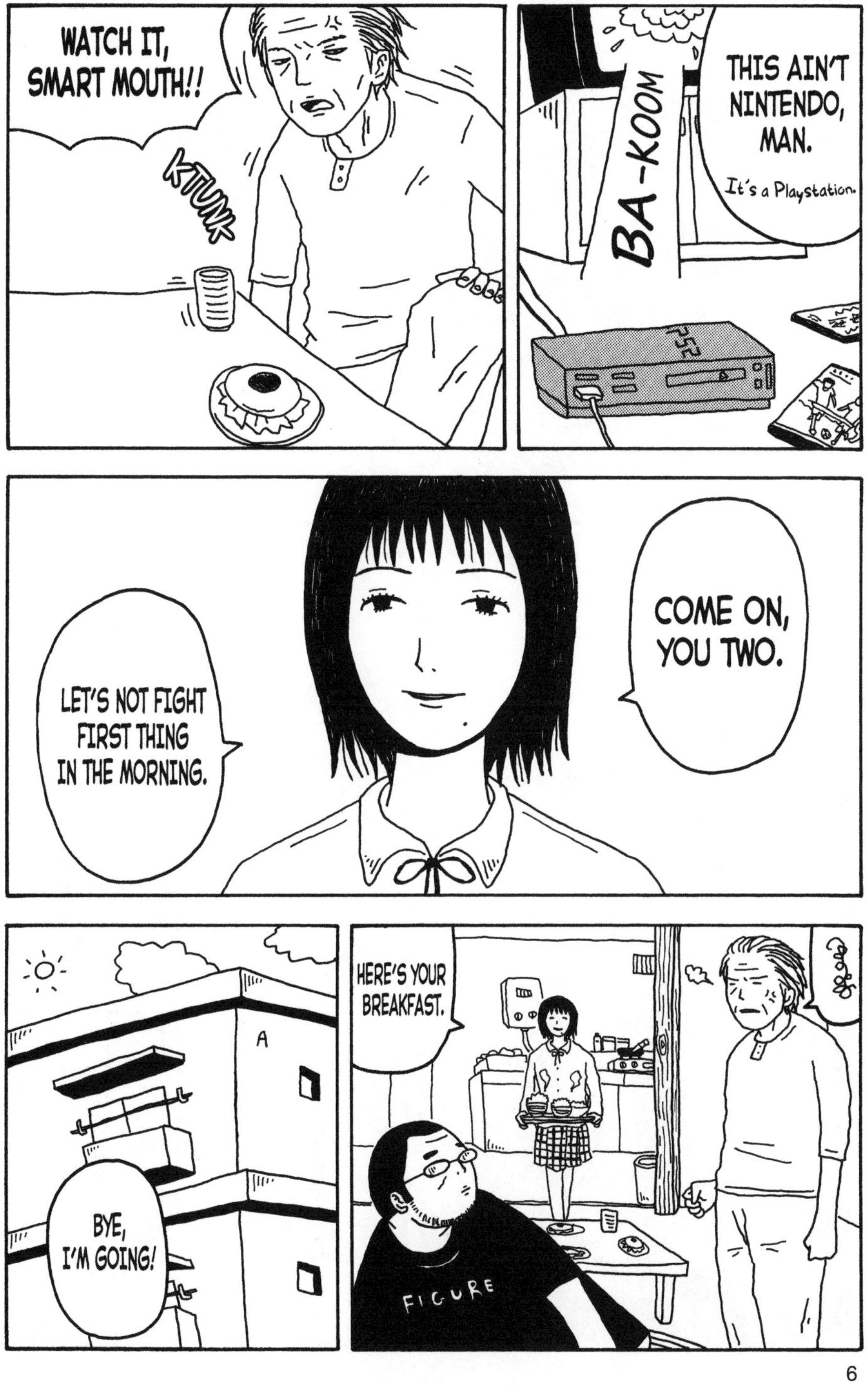
BA-KOOM
THIS AIN'T NINTENDO, MAN.
It's a Playstation.
WATCH IT, SMART MOUTH!!
KTUNK
COME ON, YOU TWO.
LET'S NOT FIGHT FIRST THING IN THE MORNING.
HERE'S YOUR BREAKFAST.
FIGURE
BYE, I'M GOING!

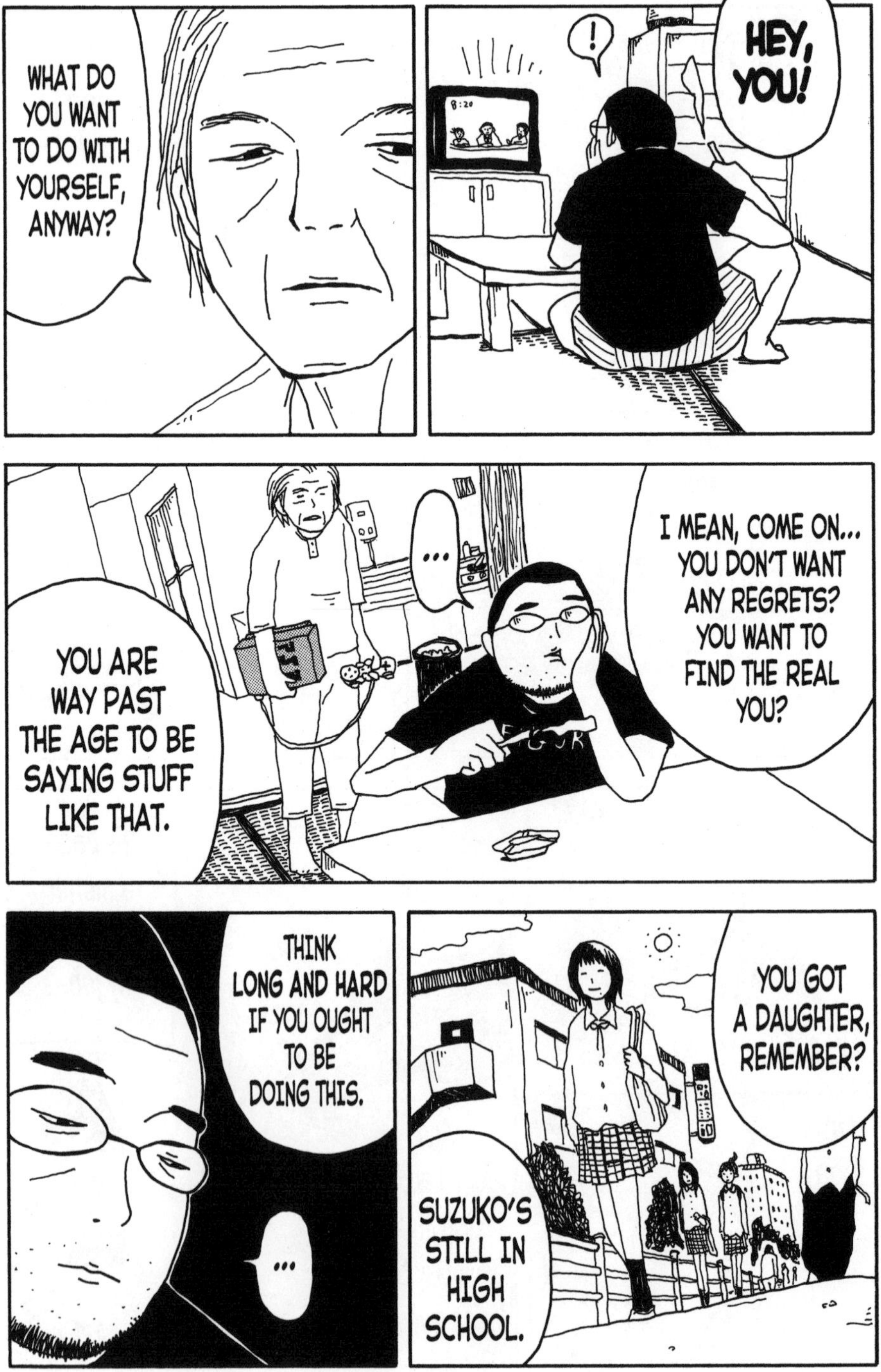
HEY, YOU!
!
WHAT DO YOU WANT TO DO WITH YOURSELF, ANYWAY?
I MEAN, COME ON... YOU DON'T WANT ANY REGRETS? YOU WANT TO FIND THE REAL YOU?
...
YOU ARE WAY PAST THE AGE TO BE SAYING STUFF LIKE THAT.
YOU GOT A DAUGHTER, REMEMBER?
SUZUKO'S STILL IN HIGH SCHOOL.
THINK LONG AND HARD IF YOU OUGHT TO BE DOING THIS.
...

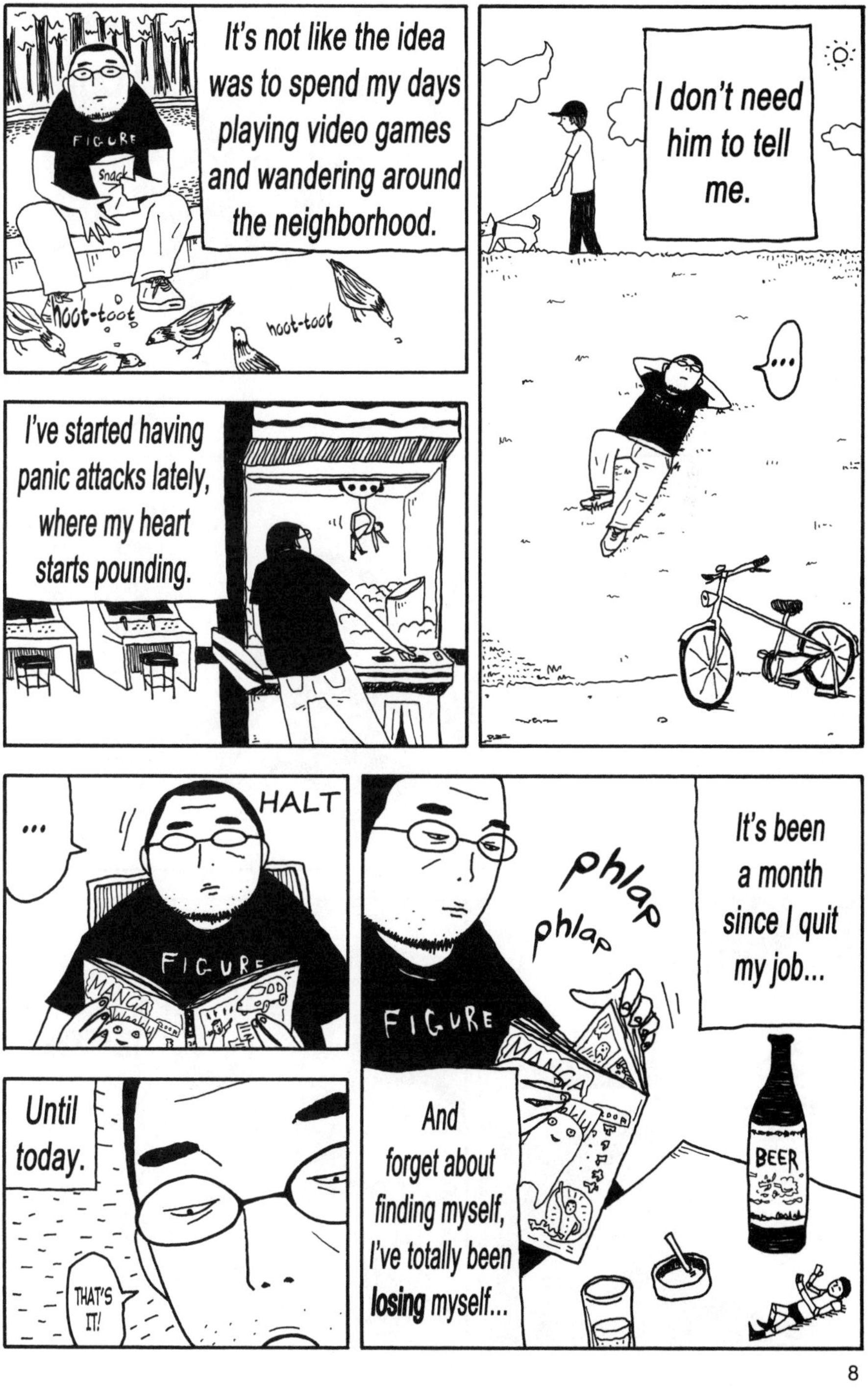
I don't need him to tell me.
...
It's not like the idea was to spend my days playing video games and wandering around the neighborhood.
Snack
FIGURE
hoot-toot
hoot-toot
I've started having panic attacks lately, where my heart starts pounding.
It's been a month since I quit my job...
phlap
phlap
FIGURE
MANGA
And forget about finding myself, I've totally been **losing** myself...
BEER
HALT
...
FIGURE
MANGA
Until today.
THAT'S IT!

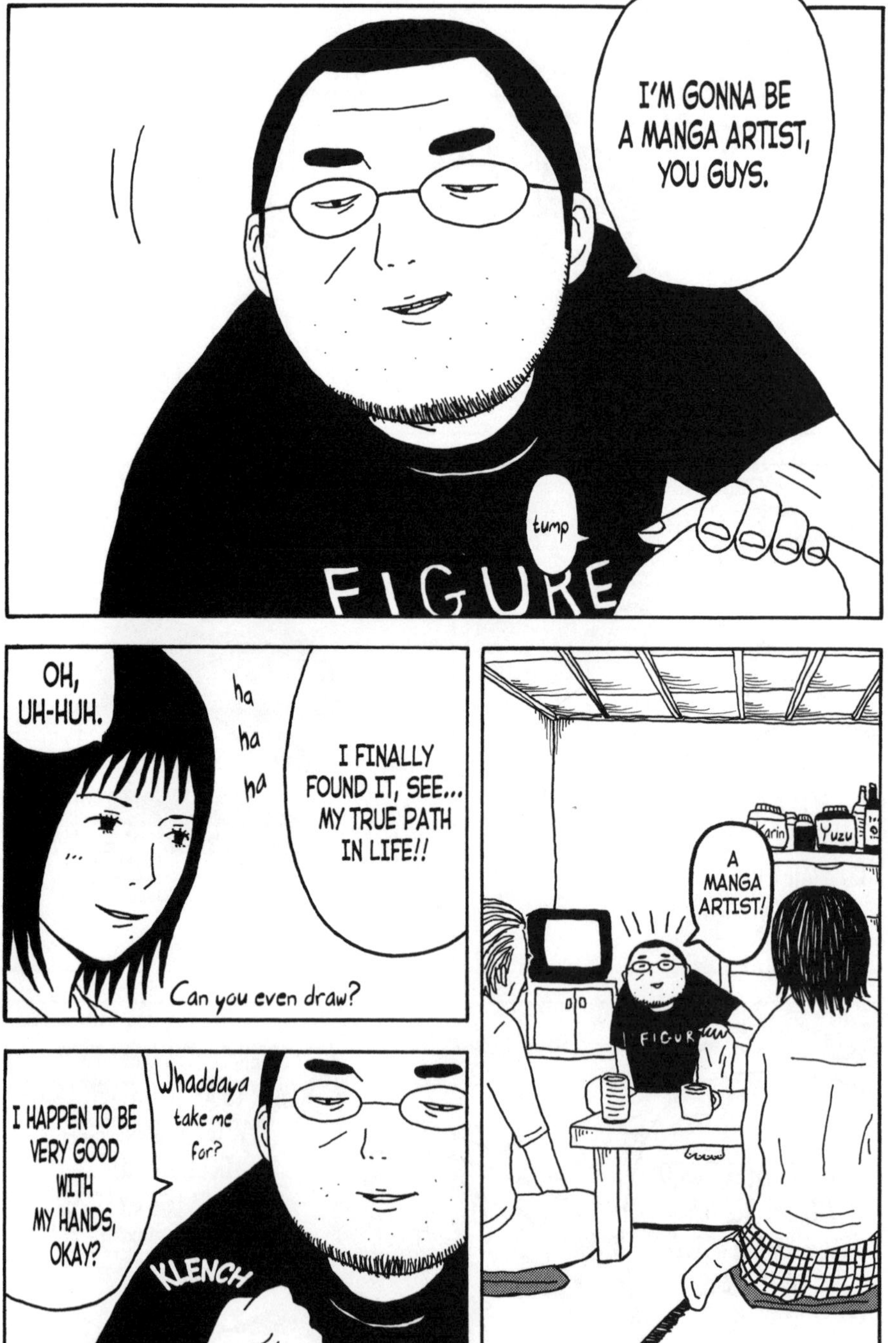

I'M GONNA BE A MANGA ARTIST, YOU GUYS.
tump
FIGURE
A MANGA ARTIST!
Karin
Yuzu
FIGUR
I FINALLY FOUND IT, SEE... MY TRUE PATH IN LIFE!!
ha ha ha
OH, UH-HUH.
Can you even draw?
Whaddaya take me for?
I HAPPEN TO BE VERY GOOD WITH MY HANDS, OKAY?
KLENCH

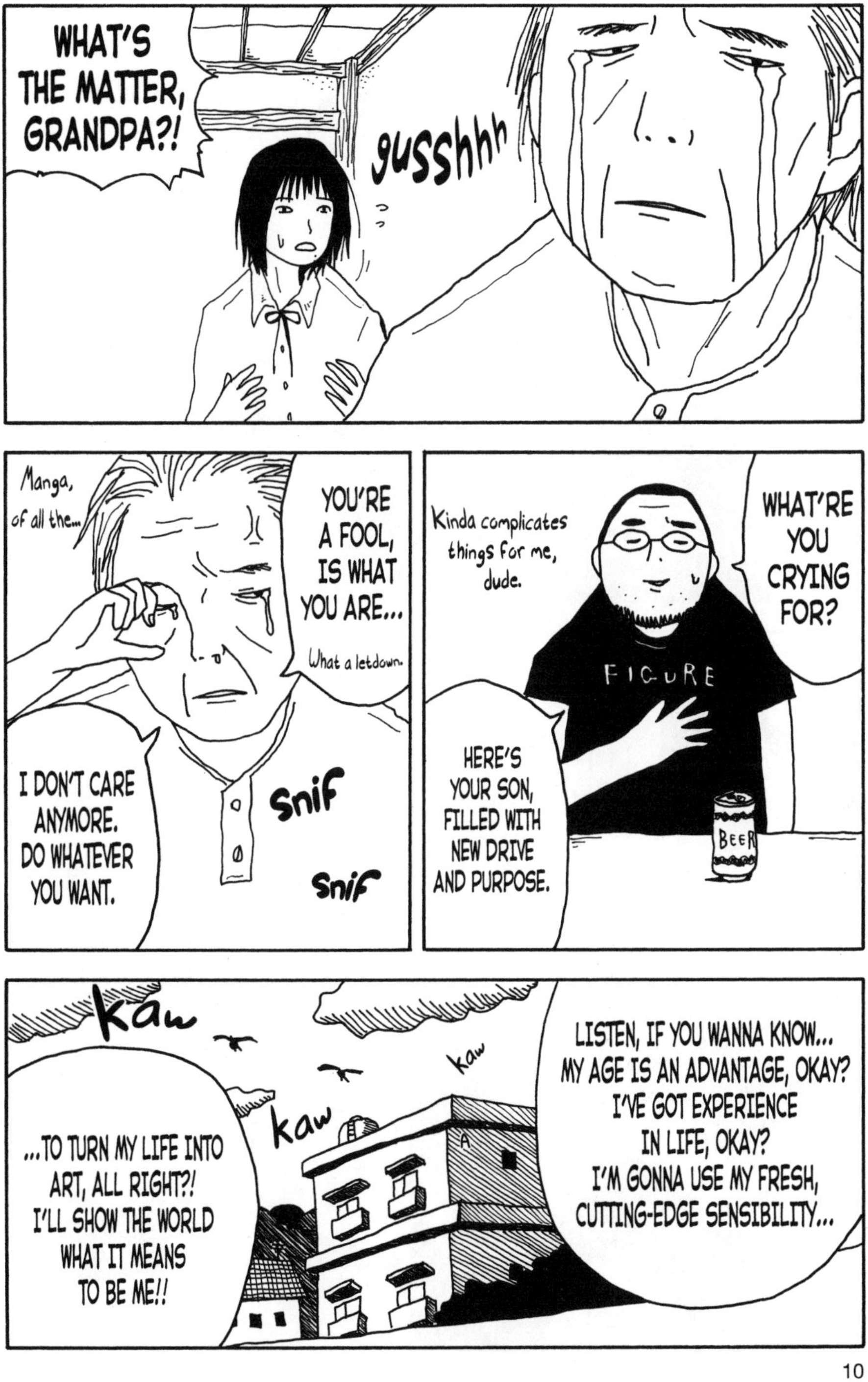
WHAT'S THE MATTER, GRANDPA?!
gusshhh
WHAT'RE YOU CRYING FOR?
Kinda complicates things for me, dude.
FIGURE
HERE'S YOUR SON, FILLED WITH NEW DRIVE AND PURPOSE.
BEER
YOU'RE A FOOL, IS WHAT YOU ARE...
What a letdown.
Manga, of all the...
Snif
I DON'T CARE ANYMORE. DO WHATEVER YOU WANT.
Snif
LISTEN, IF YOU WANNA KNOW... MY AGE IS AN ADVANTAGE, OKAY? I'VE GOT EXPERIENCE IN LIFE, OKAY? I'M GONNA USE MY FRESH, CUTTING-EDGE SENSIBILITY...
kaw
kaw
kaw
...TO TURN MY LIFE INTO ART, ALL RIGHT?! I'LL SHOW THE WORLD WHAT IT MEANS TO BE ME!!

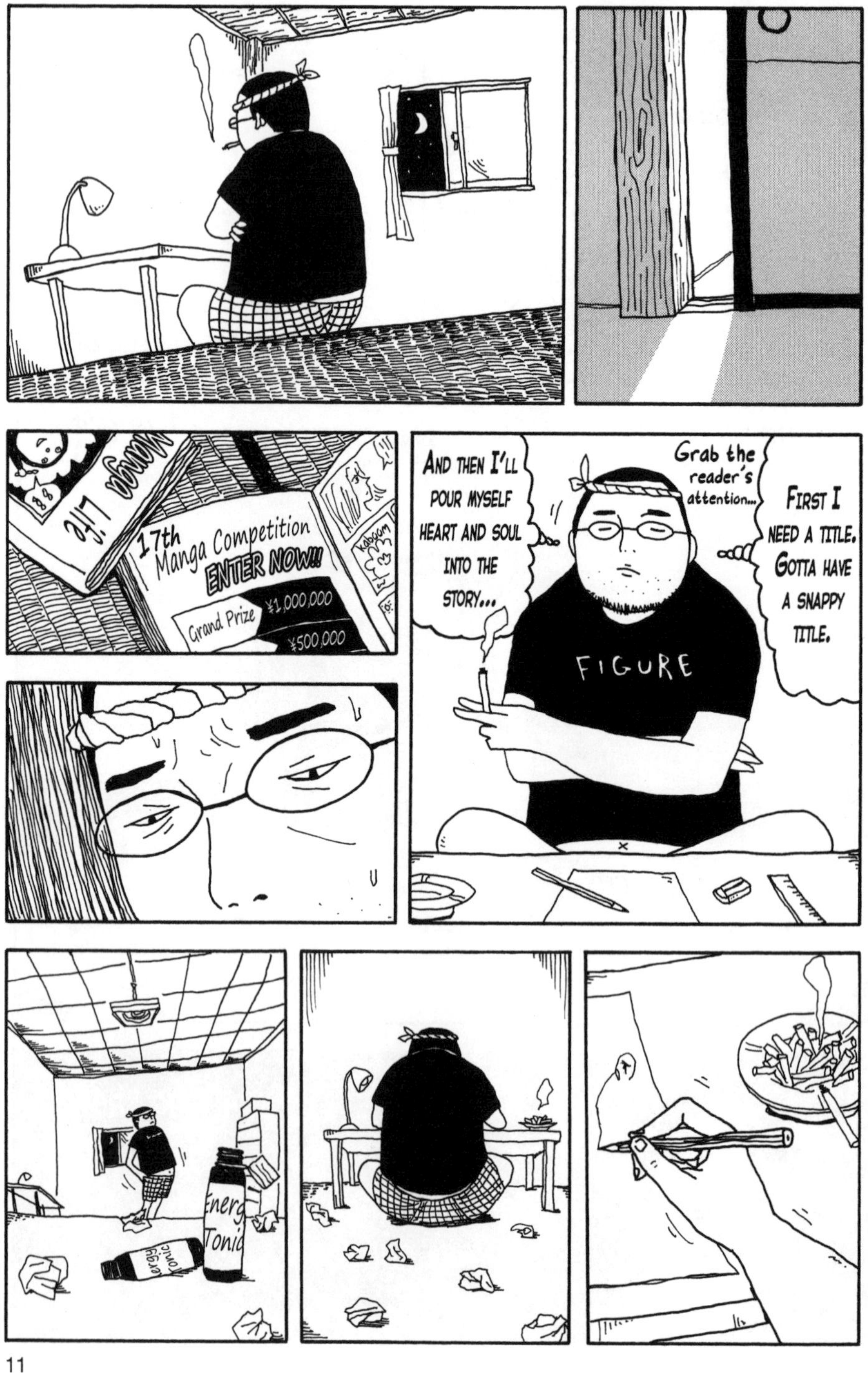
FIRST I NEED A TITLE. GOTTA HAVE A SNAPPY TITLE.
Grab the reader's attention...
AND THEN I'LL POUR MYSELF HEART AND SOUL INTO THE STORY...
FIGURE
Manga Life
17th Manga Competition
ENTER NOW!!
Grand Prize ¥1,000,000
¥500,000

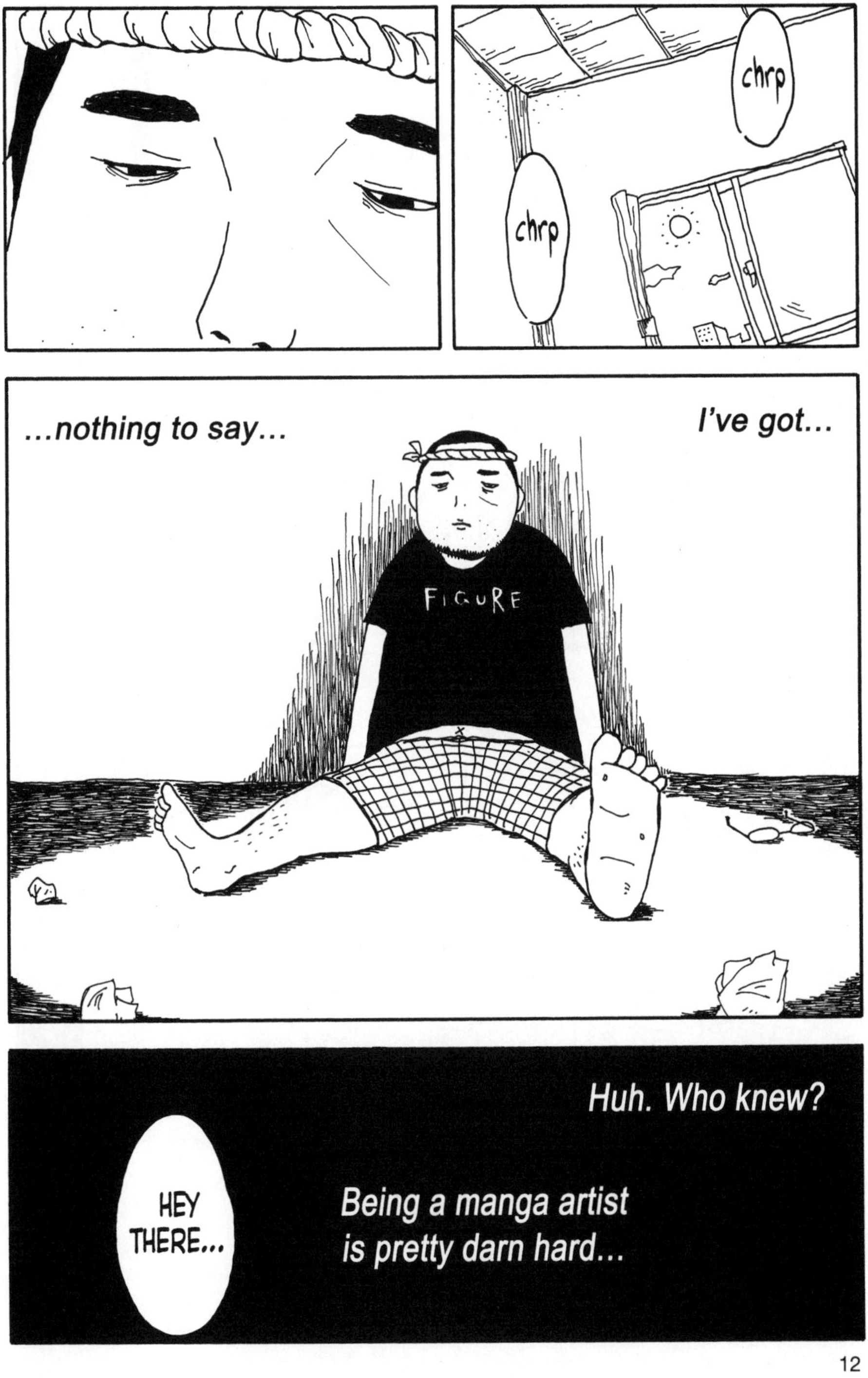
chrp
chrp
I've got...
...nothing to say...
FIGURE
Huh. Who knew?
Being a manga artist is pretty darn hard...
HEY THERE...

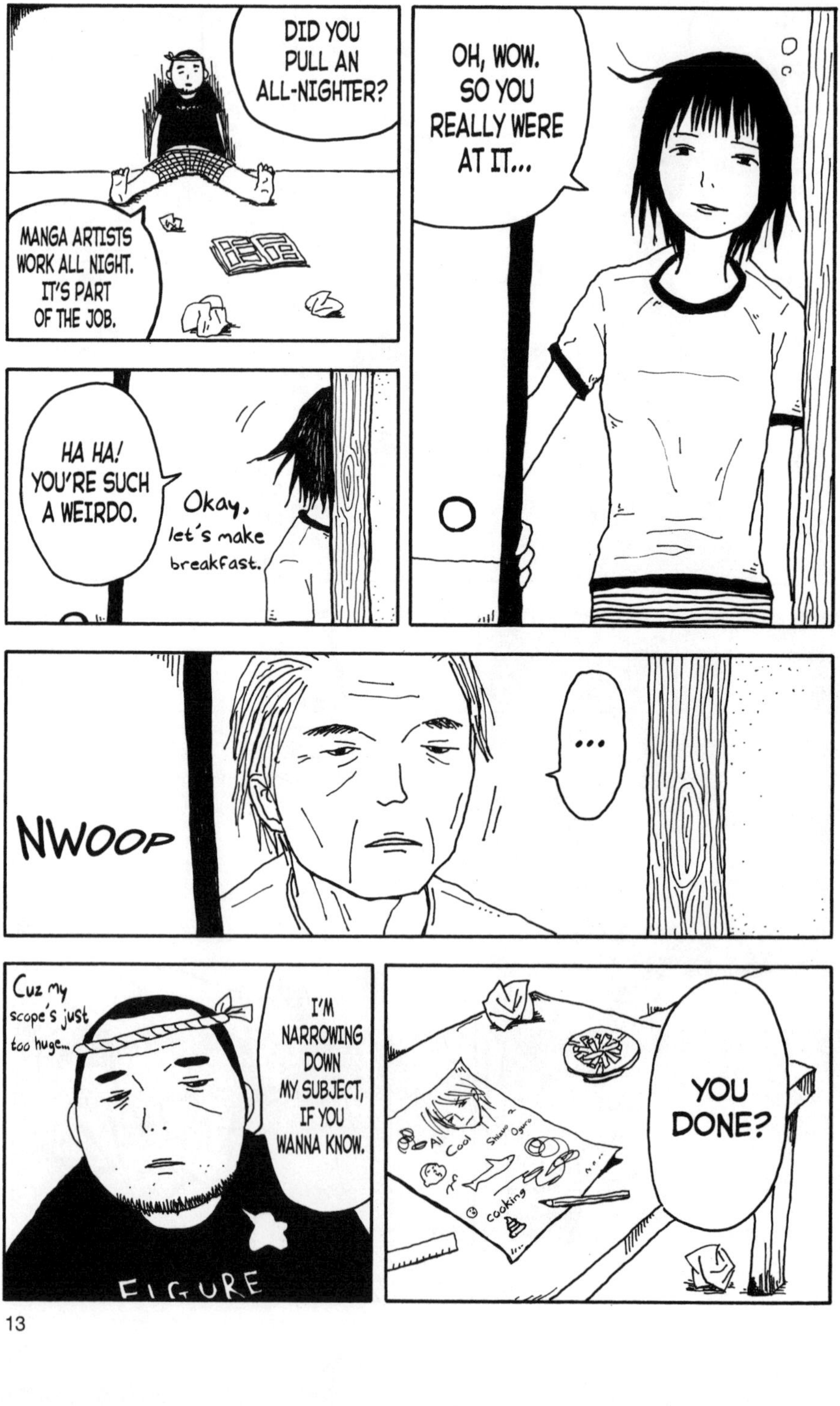
OH, WOW. SO YOU REALLY WERE AT IT...
DID YOU PULL AN ALL-NIGHTER?
MANGA ARTISTS WORK ALL NIGHT. IT'S PART OF THE JOB.
HA HA! YOU'RE SUCH A WEIRDO.
Okay, let's make breakfast.
...
NWOOP
YOU DONE?
I'M NARROWING DOWN MY SUBJECT, IF YOU WANNA KNOW.
Cuz my scope's just too huge...
FIGURE

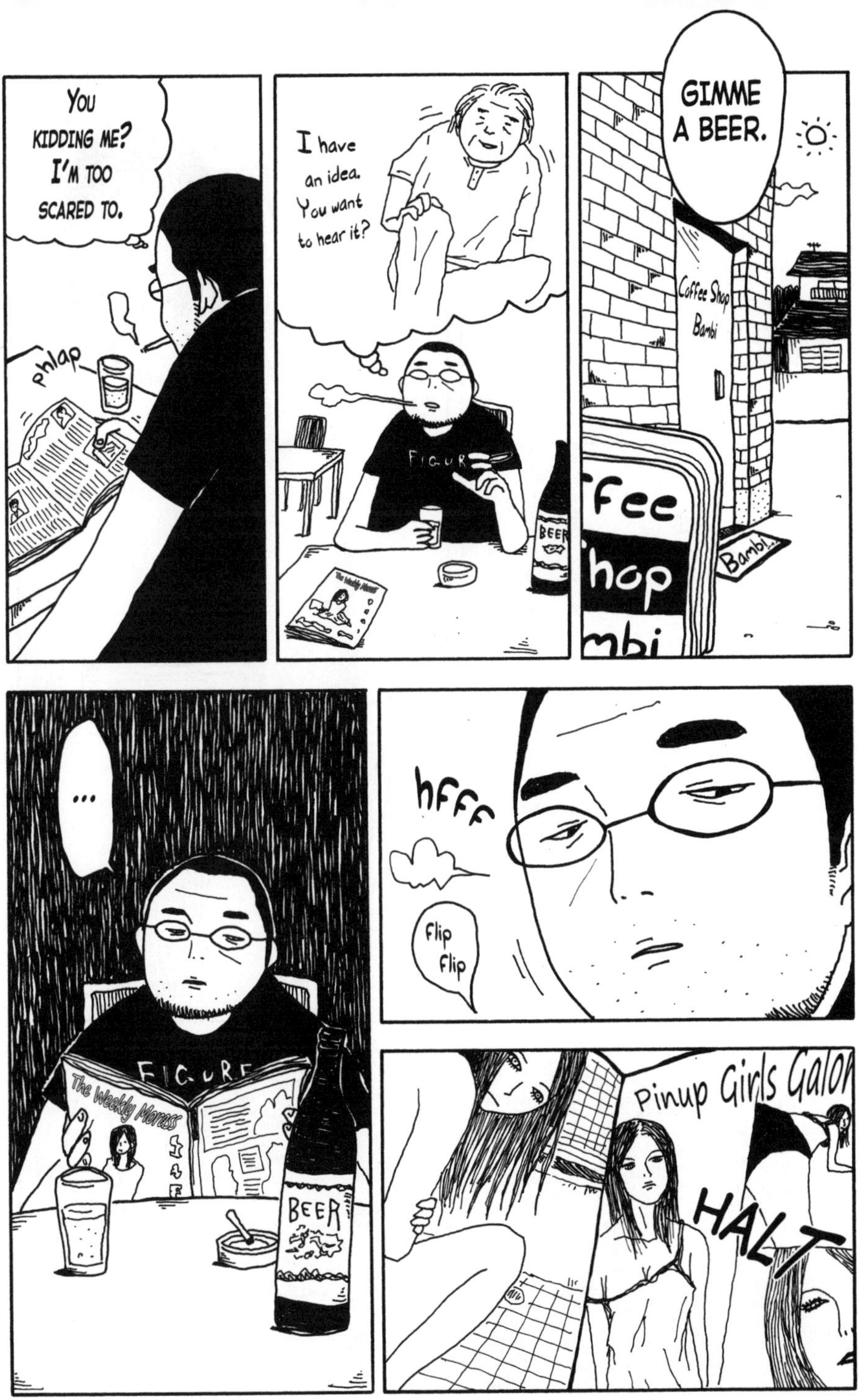
GIMME A BEER.
Coffee Shop Bambi
Bambi
I have an idea. You want to hear it?
FIGURE
BEER
YOU KIDDING ME? I'M TOO SCARED TO.
phlap
hfff
Flip flip
Pinup Girls Galor
HALT
...
FIGURE
BEER

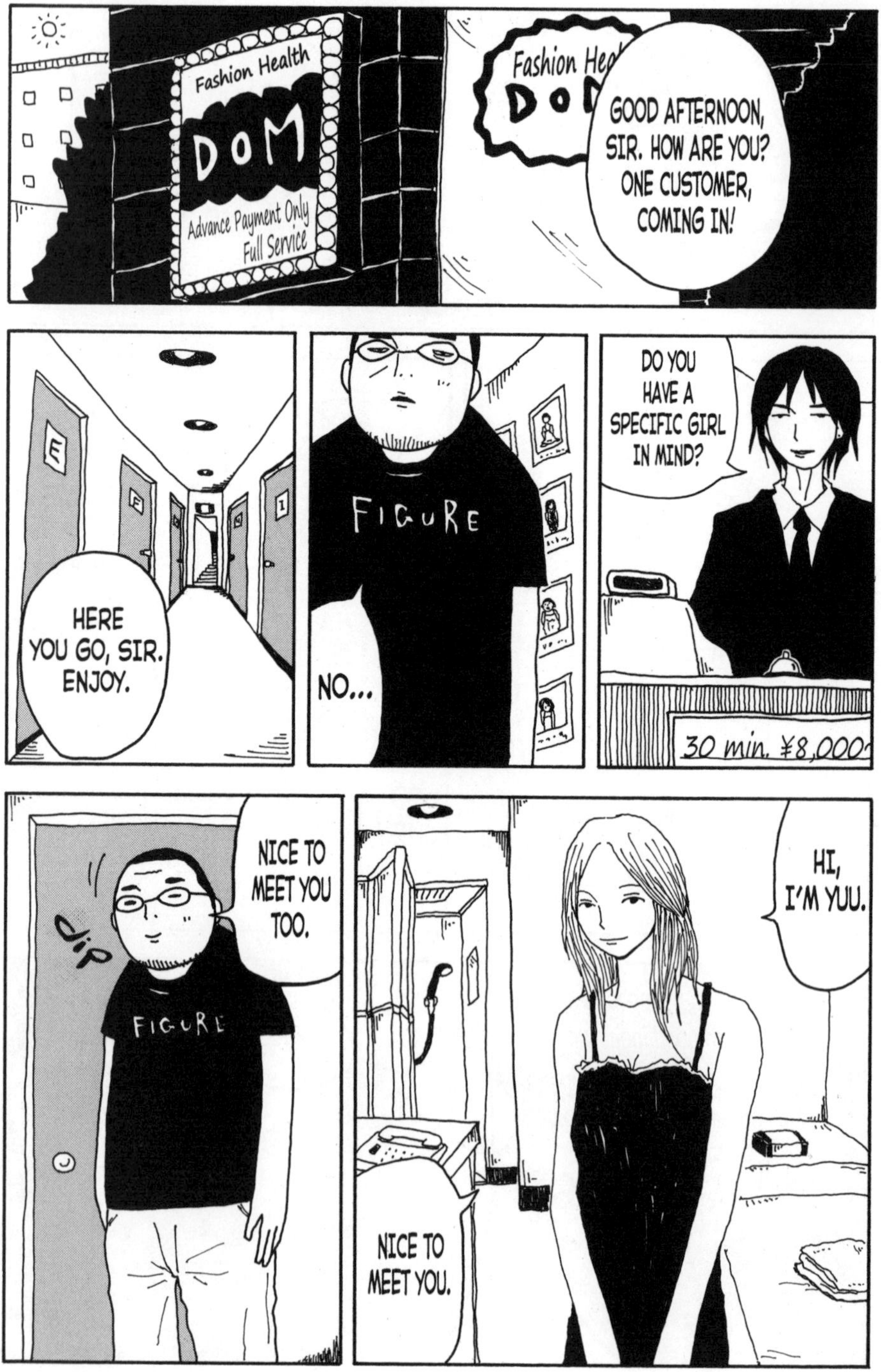
GOOD AFTERNOON, SIR. HOW ARE YOU? ONE CUSTOMER, COMING IN!
Fashion Health
DOM
Advance Payment Only
Full Service
DO YOU HAVE A SPECIFIC GIRL IN MIND?
30 min. ¥8,000~
FIGURE
NO...
HERE YOU GO, SIR. ENJOY.
HI, I'M YUU.
NICE TO MEET YOU.
NICE TO MEET YOU TOO.
clip
FIGURE

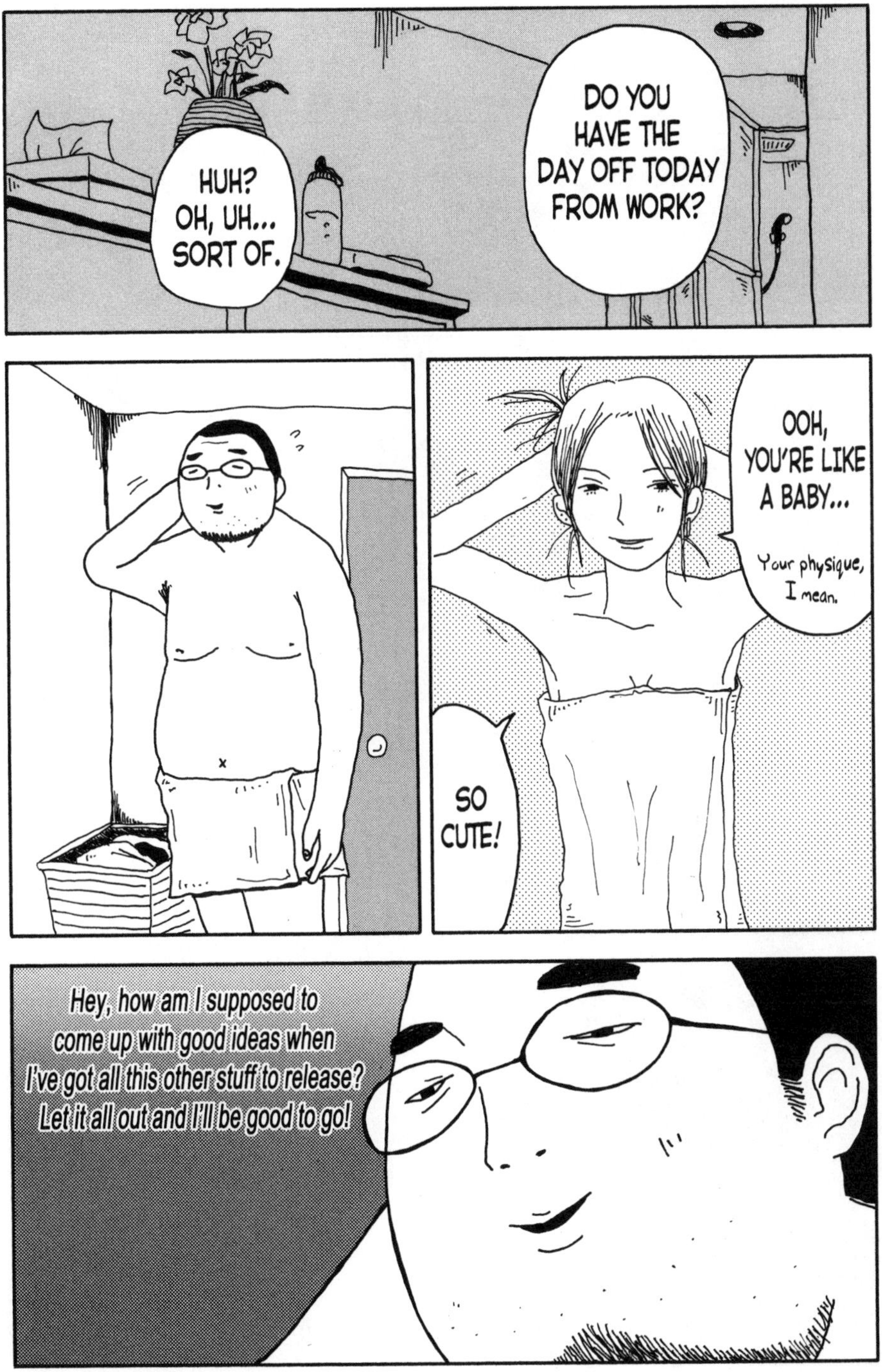
DO YOU HAVE THE DAY OFF TODAY FROM WORK?
HUH? OH, UH... SORT OF.
OOH, YOU'RE LIKE A BABY...
Your physique, I mean.
SO CUTE!
Hey, how am I supposed to come up with good ideas when I've got all this other stuff to release? Let it all out and I'll be good to go!

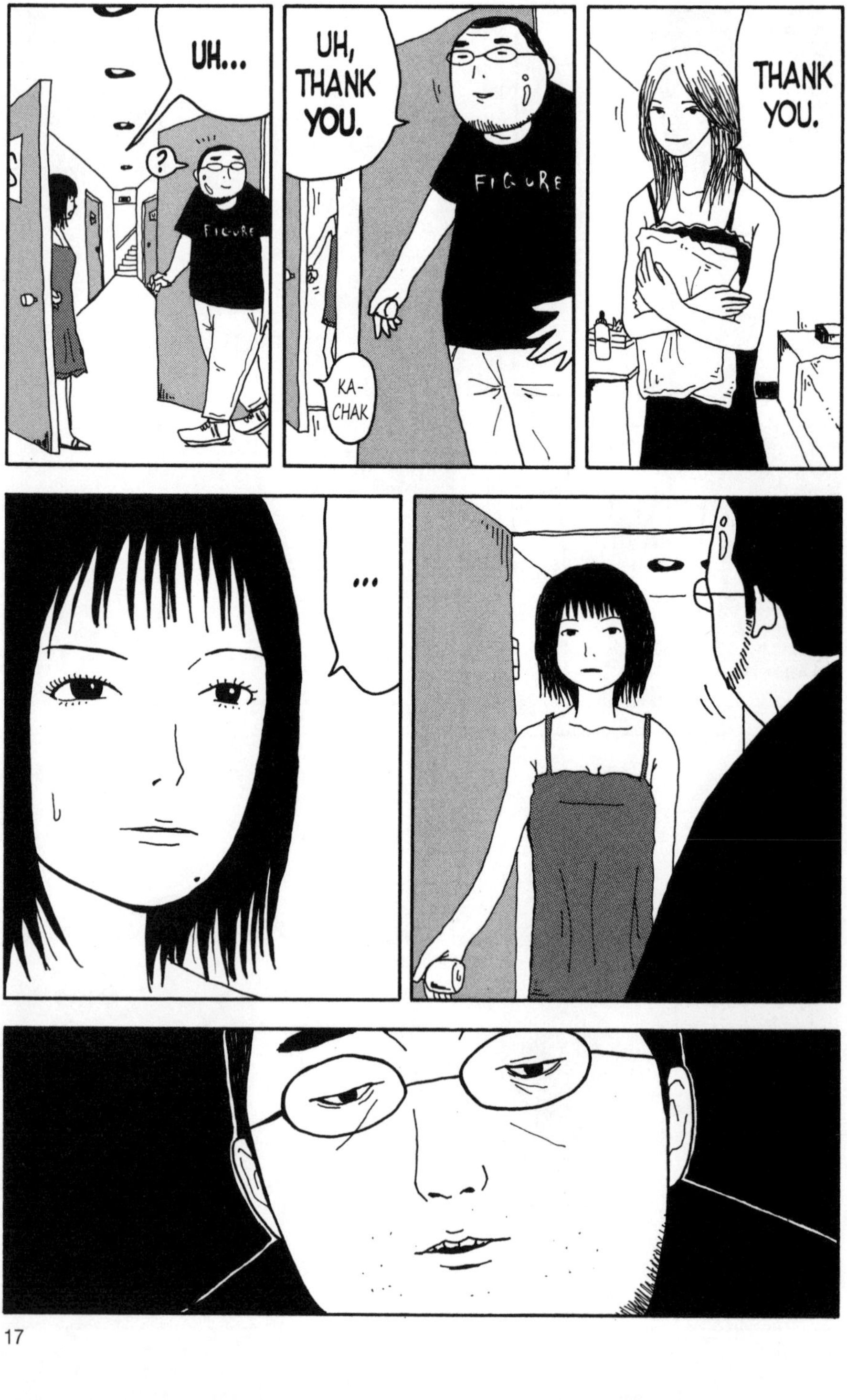
THANK YOU.
UH, THANK YOU.
KA-CHAK
UH...
?
...

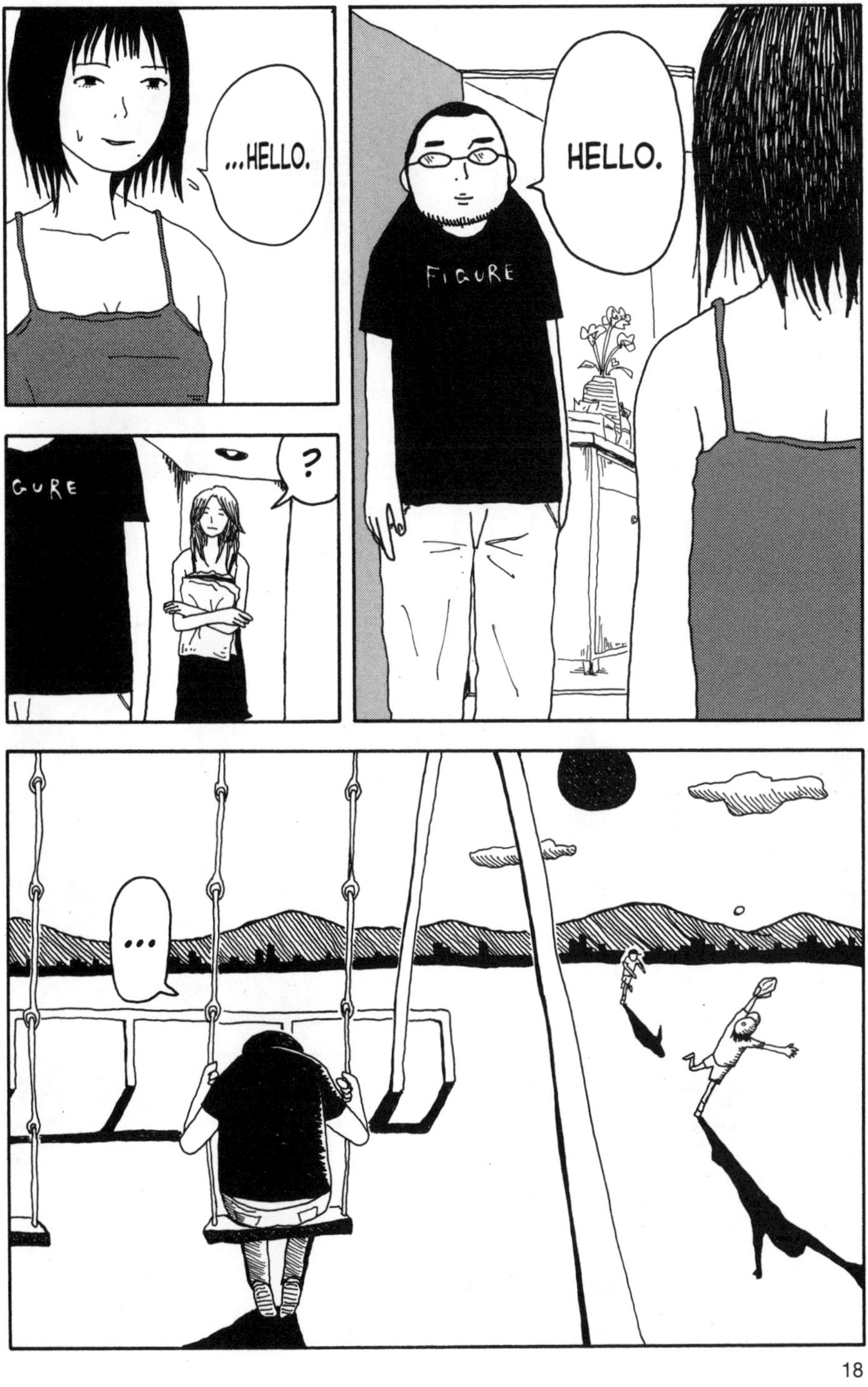
HELLO.
FIGURE
...HELLO.
GURE
?
...

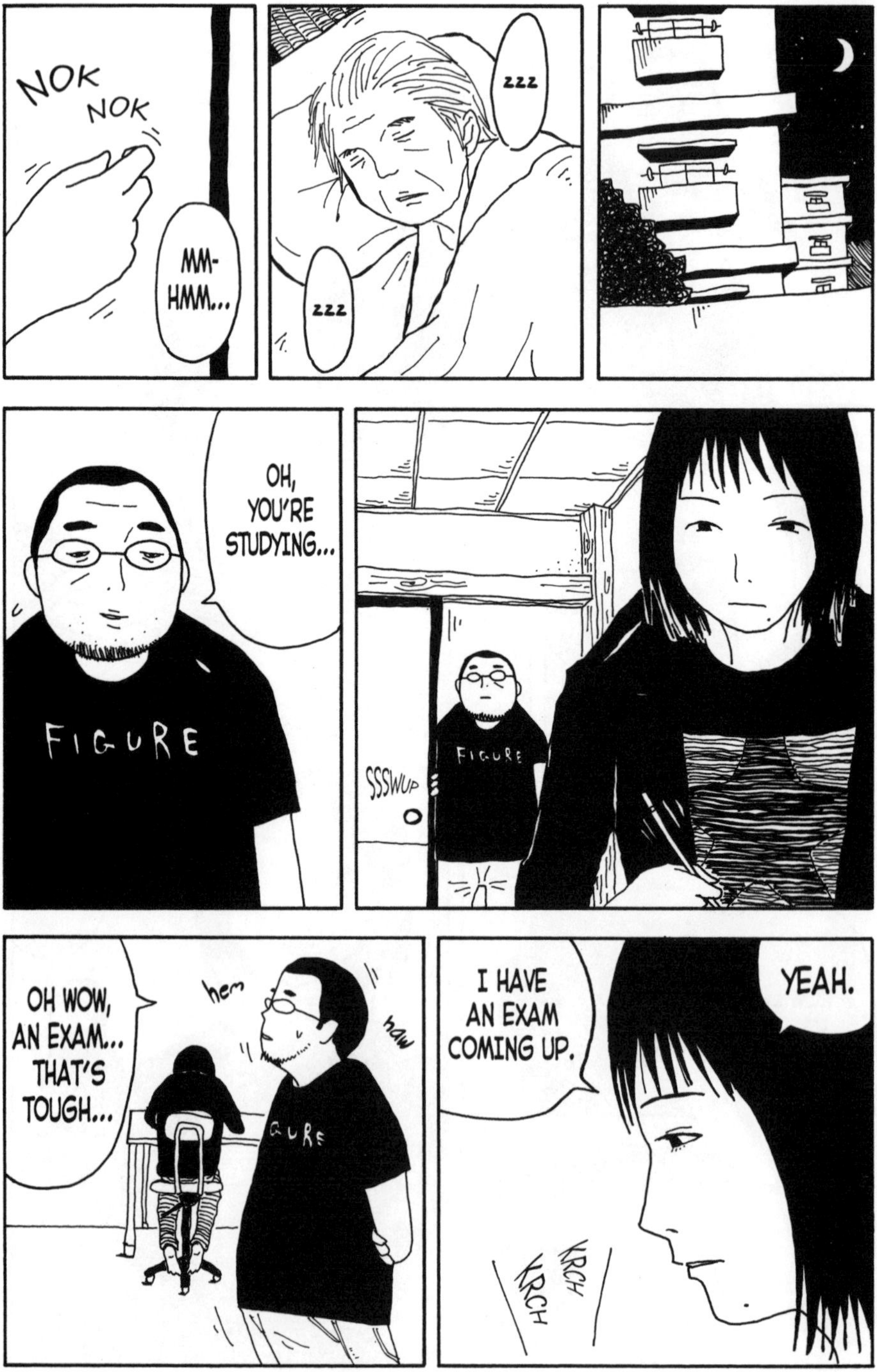
zzz
zzz
NOK NOK
MM-HMM...
SSSWUP
FIGURE
FIGURE
OH, YOU'RE STUDYING...
YEAH.
I HAVE AN EXAM COMING UP.
KRCH KRCH
haw
hem
OH WOW, AN EXAM... THAT'S TOUGH...

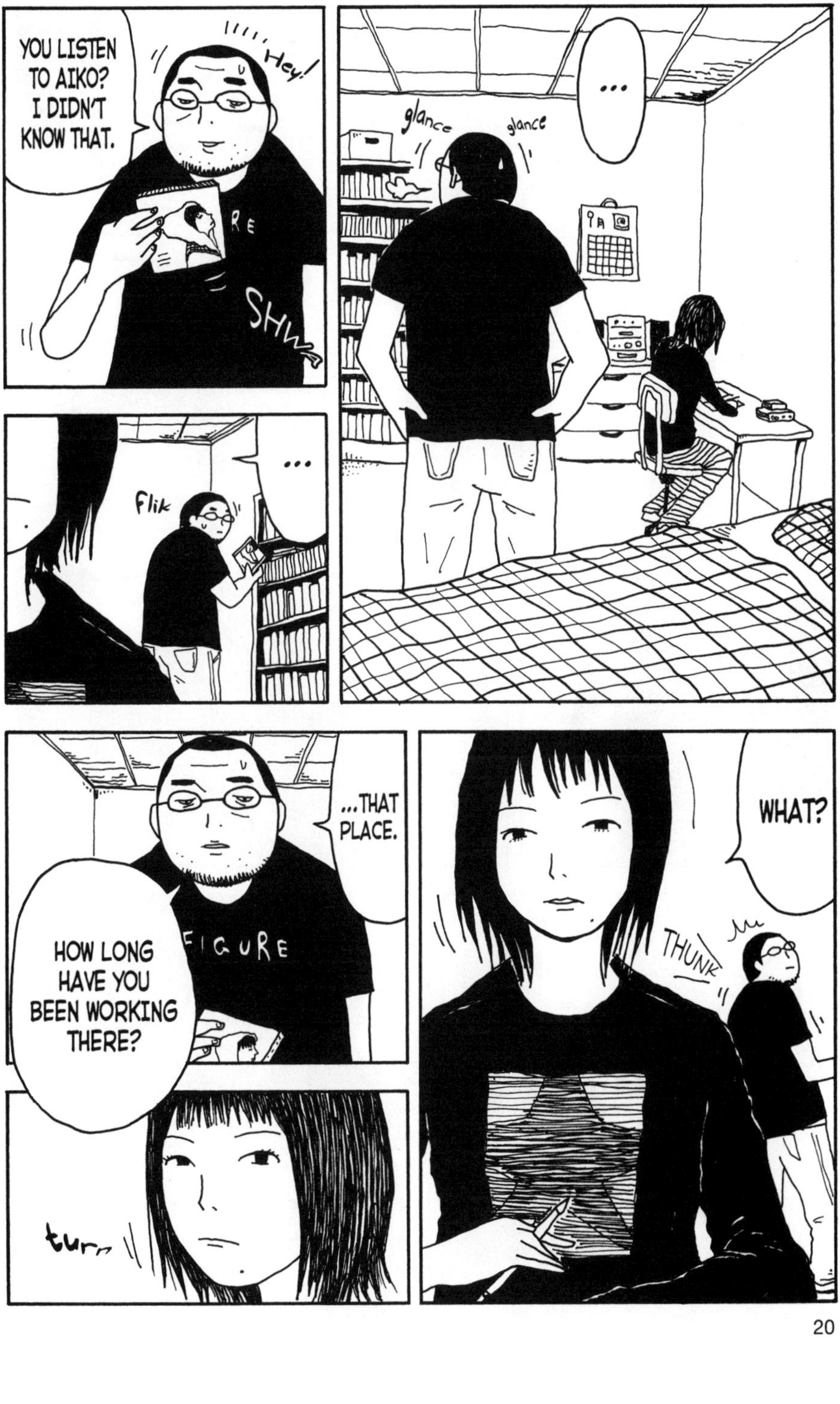
...
glance
glance
Hey!
YOU LISTEN TO AIKO? I DIDN'T KNOW THAT.
SHW
...
Flik
WHAT?
THUNK
...THAT PLACE.
HOW LONG HAVE YOU BEEN WORKING THERE?
turn

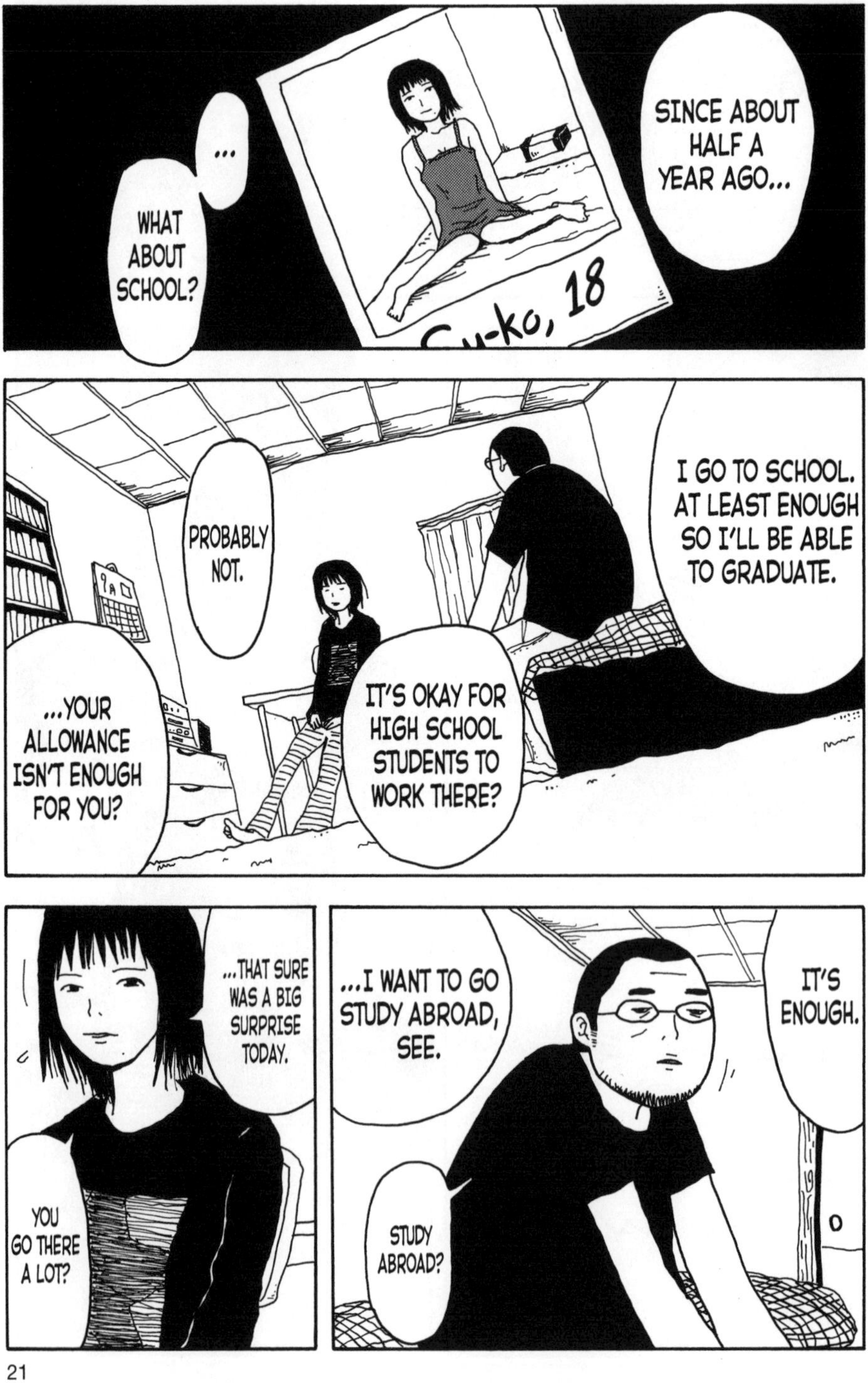
SINCE ABOUT HALF A YEAR AGO...
...
WHAT ABOUT SCHOOL?
Su-ko, 18
I GO TO SCHOOL. AT LEAST ENOUGH SO I'LL BE ABLE TO GRADUATE.
PROBABLY NOT.
IT'S OKAY FOR HIGH SCHOOL STUDENTS TO WORK THERE?
...YOUR ALLOWANCE ISN'T ENOUGH FOR YOU?
IT'S ENOUGH.
...I WANT TO GO STUDY ABROAD, SEE.
STUDY ABROAD?
...THAT SURE WAS A BIG SURPRISE TODAY.
YOU GO THERE A LOT?

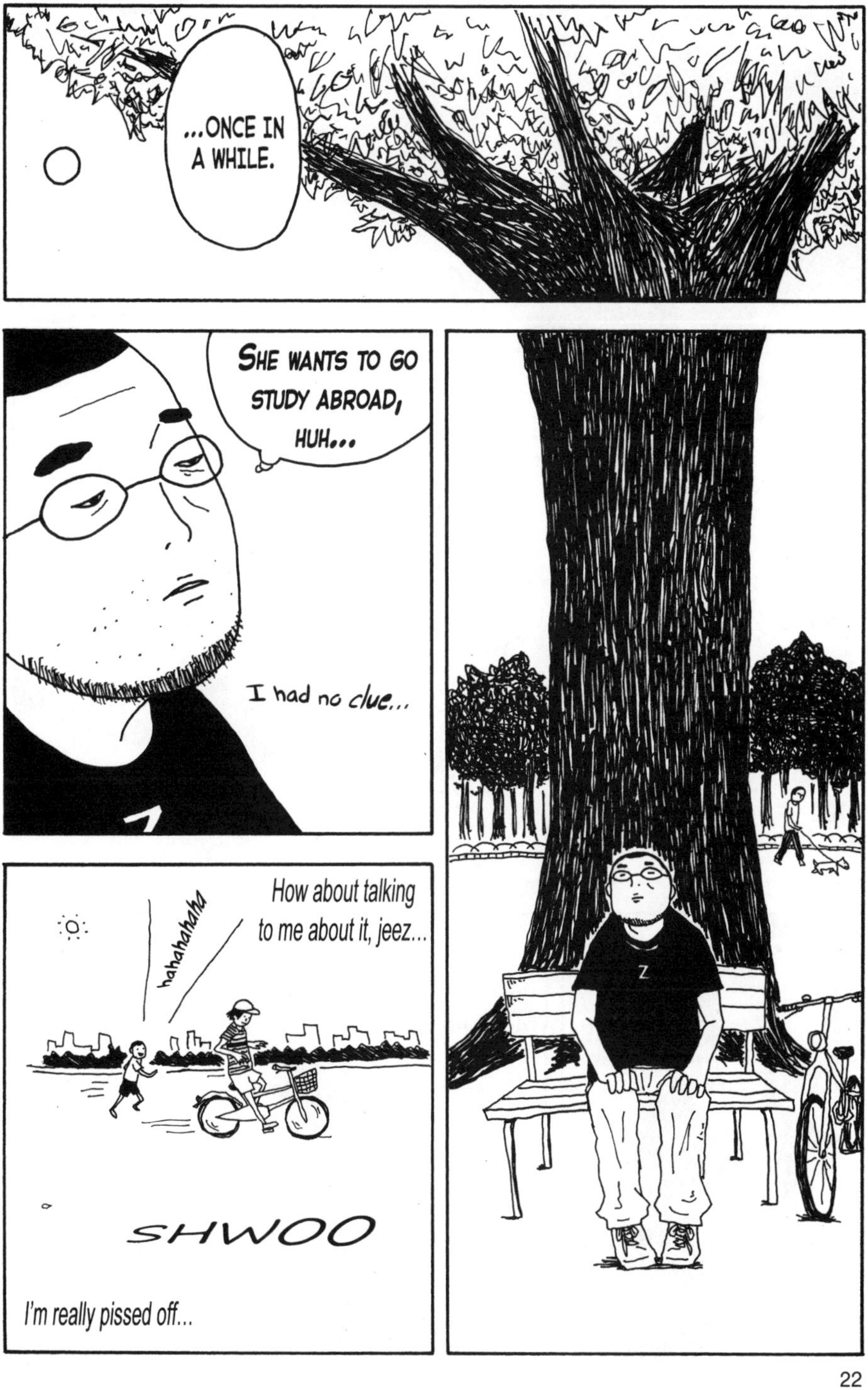
...ONCE IN A WHILE.
SHE WANTS TO GO STUDY ABROAD, HUH...
I had no clue...
How about talking to me about it, jeez...
hahahahaha
SHWOO
I'm really pissed off...

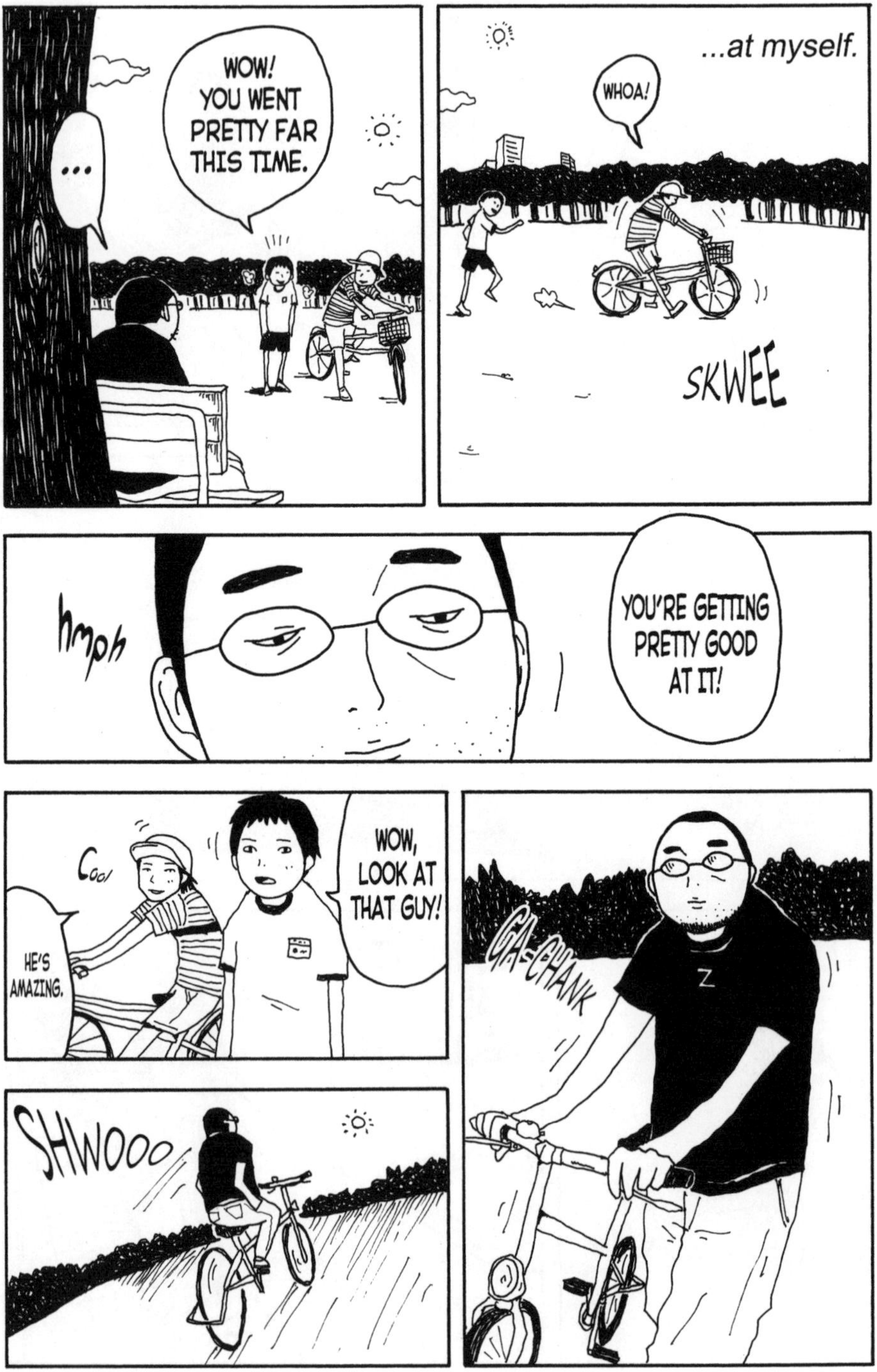
...at myself.
WHOA!
SKWEE
WOW! YOU WENT PRETTY FAR THIS TIME.
...
YOU'RE GETTING PRETTY GOOD AT IT!
hmph
GA-CHANK
WOW, LOOK AT THAT GUY!
Cool
HE'S AMAZING.
SHWOOO

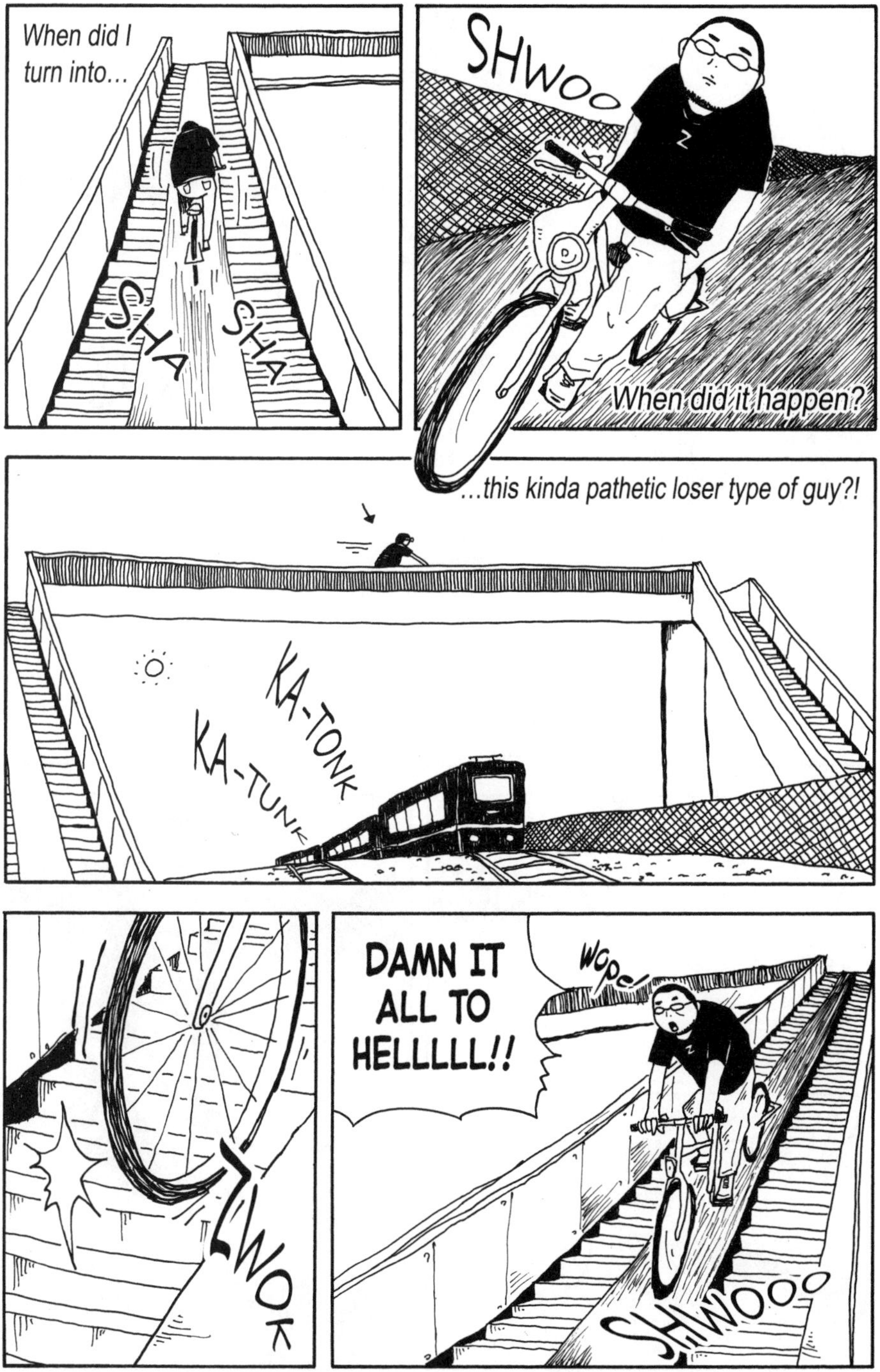
SHWOO
When did it happen?
When did I turn into...
SHA
SHA
...this kinda pathetic loser type of guy?!
KA-TONK
KA-TUNK
DAMN IT ALL TO HELLLLL!!
wope!
SHWOOO
ZWOK

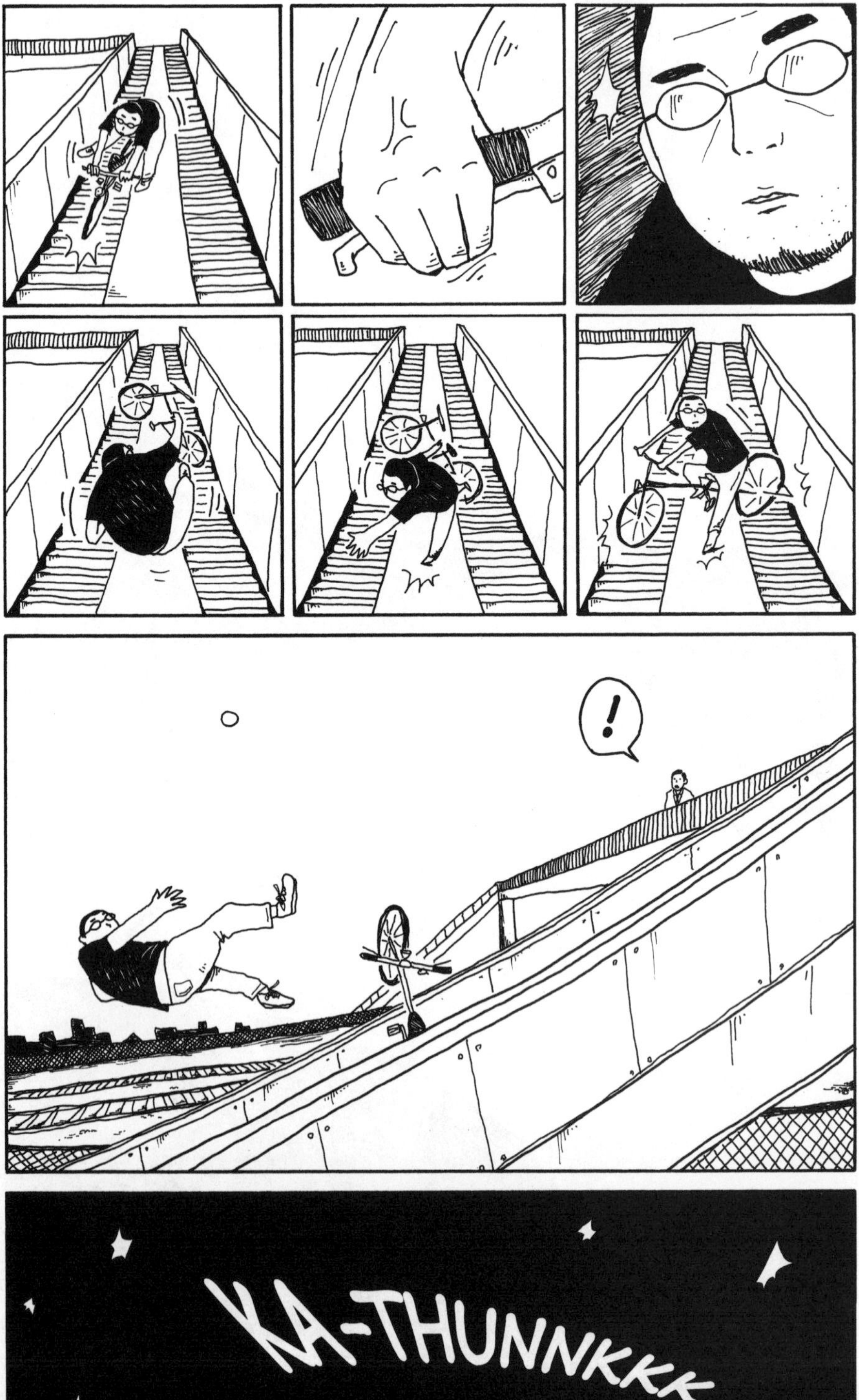
!
KA-THUNNKKK

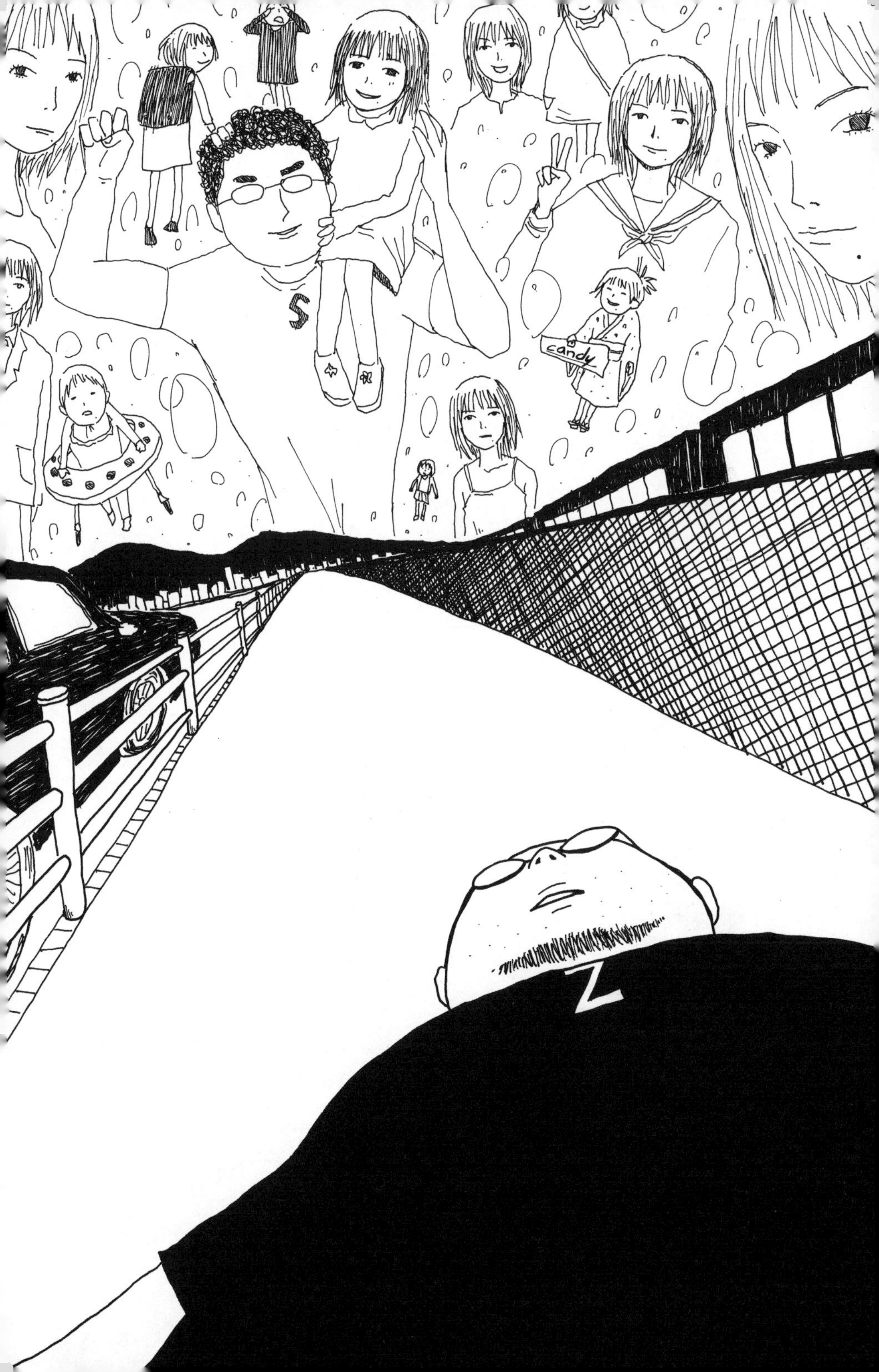
candy
S
Z

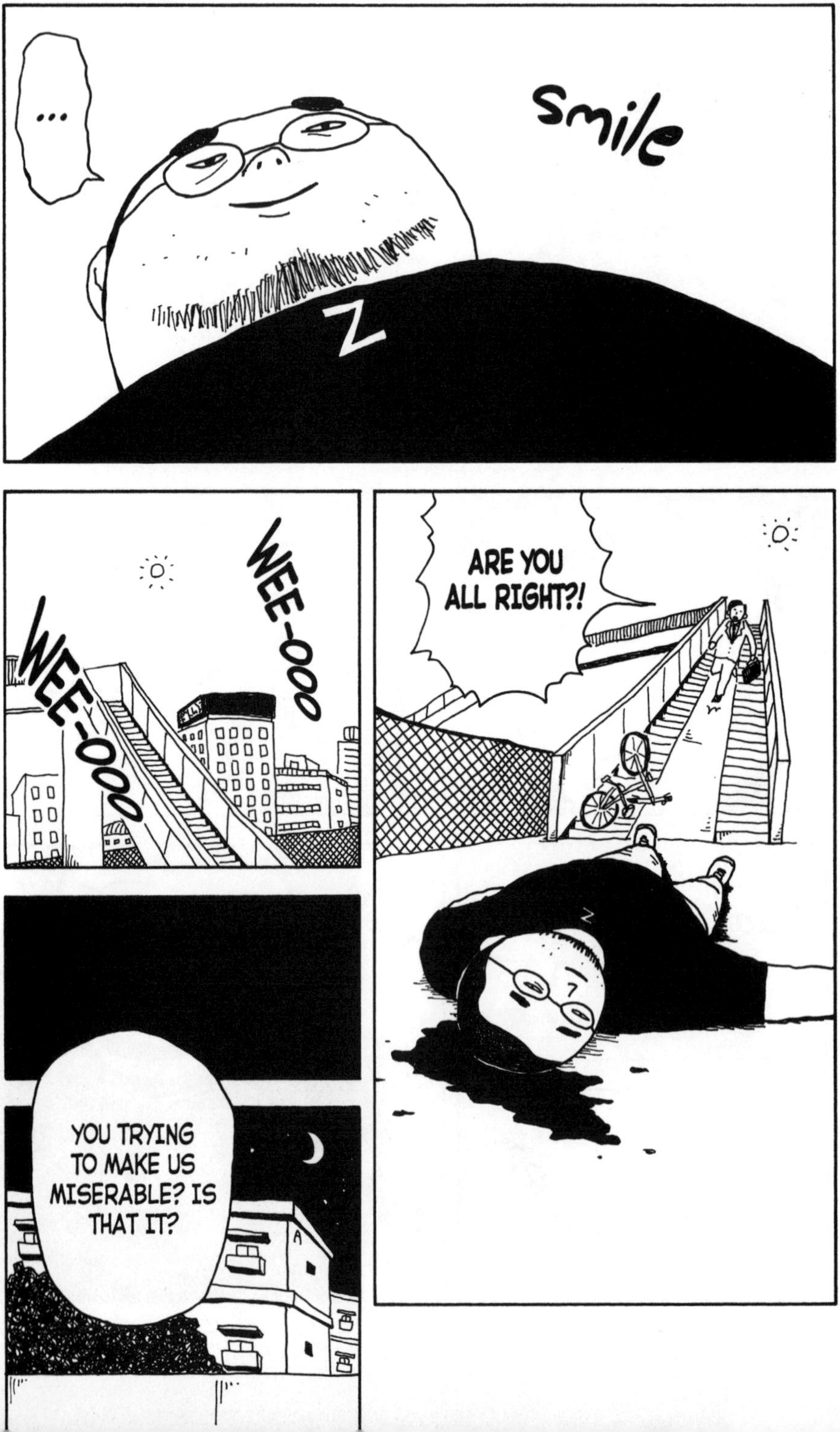
Smile
...
ARE YOU ALL RIGHT?!
WEE-OOO
WEE-OOO
YOU TRYING TO MAKE US MISERABLE? IS THAT IT?

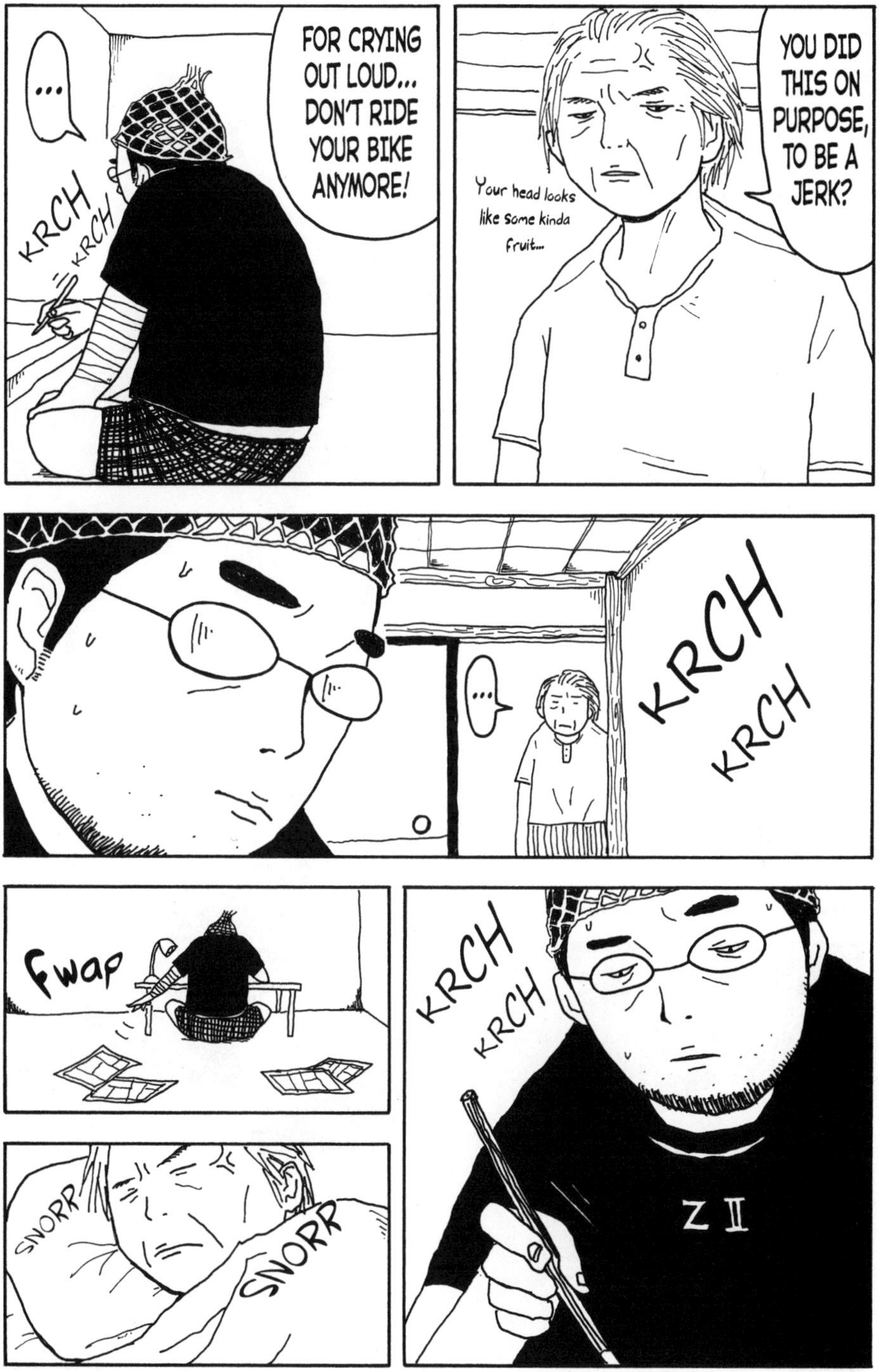
YOU DID THIS ON PURPOSE, TO BE A JERK?
Your head looks like some kinda fruit...
FOR CRYING OUT LOUD... DON'T RIDE YOUR BIKE ANYMORE!
...
KRCH
KRCH
KRCH
KRCH
...
KRCH
KRCH
Z II
Fwap
SNORR
SNORR

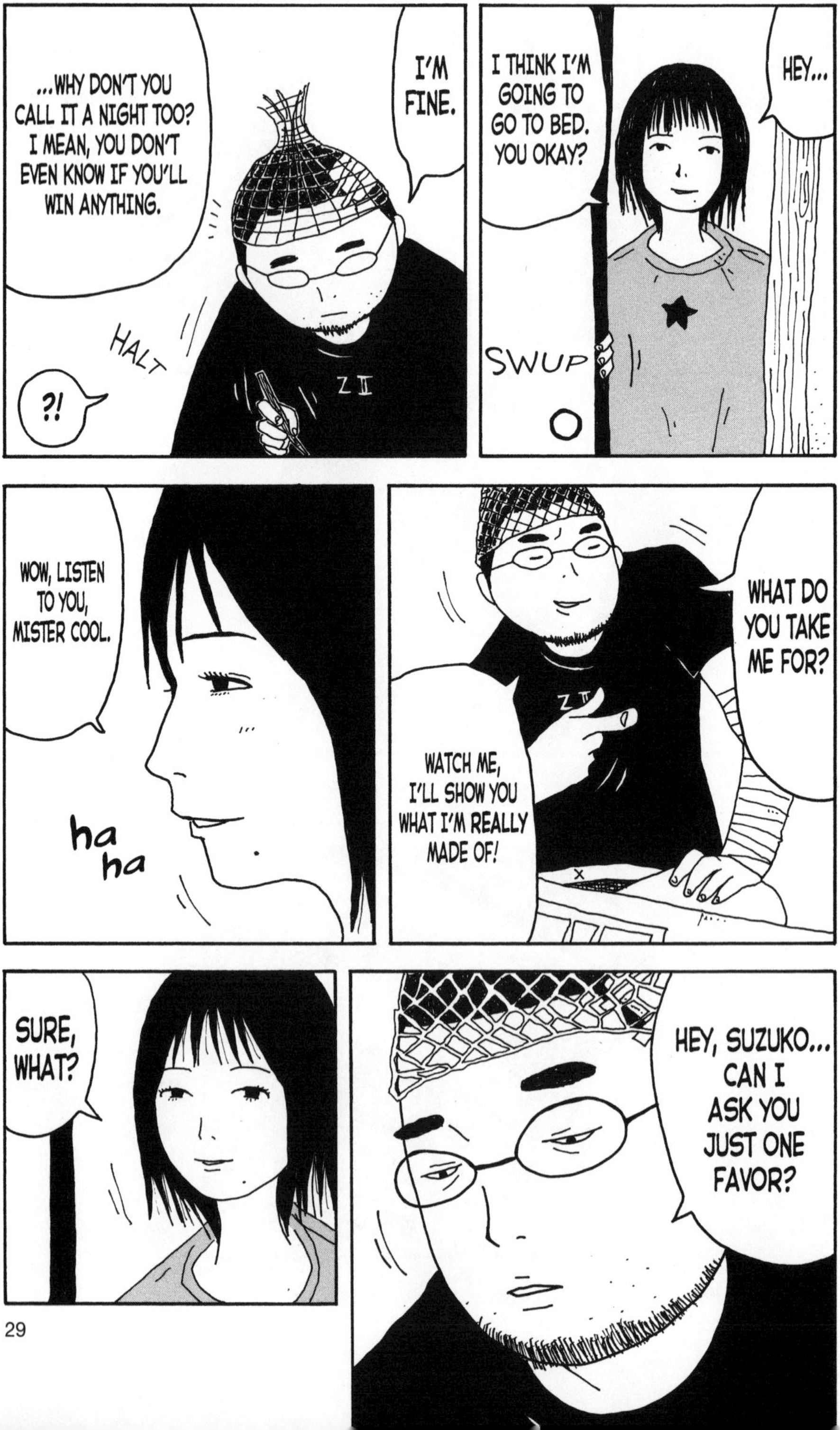
HEY...
I THINK I'M GOING TO GO TO BED. YOU OKAY?
SWUP
I'M FINE.
...WHY DON'T YOU CALL IT A NIGHT TOO? I MEAN, YOU DON'T EVEN KNOW IF YOU'LL WIN ANYTHING.
HALT
?!
WHAT DO YOU TAKE ME FOR?
WATCH ME, I'LL SHOW YOU WHAT I'M REALLY MADE OF!
WOW, LISTEN TO YOU, MISTER COOL.
ha ha
HEY, SUZUKO... CAN I ASK YOU JUST ONE FAVOR?
SURE, WHAT?

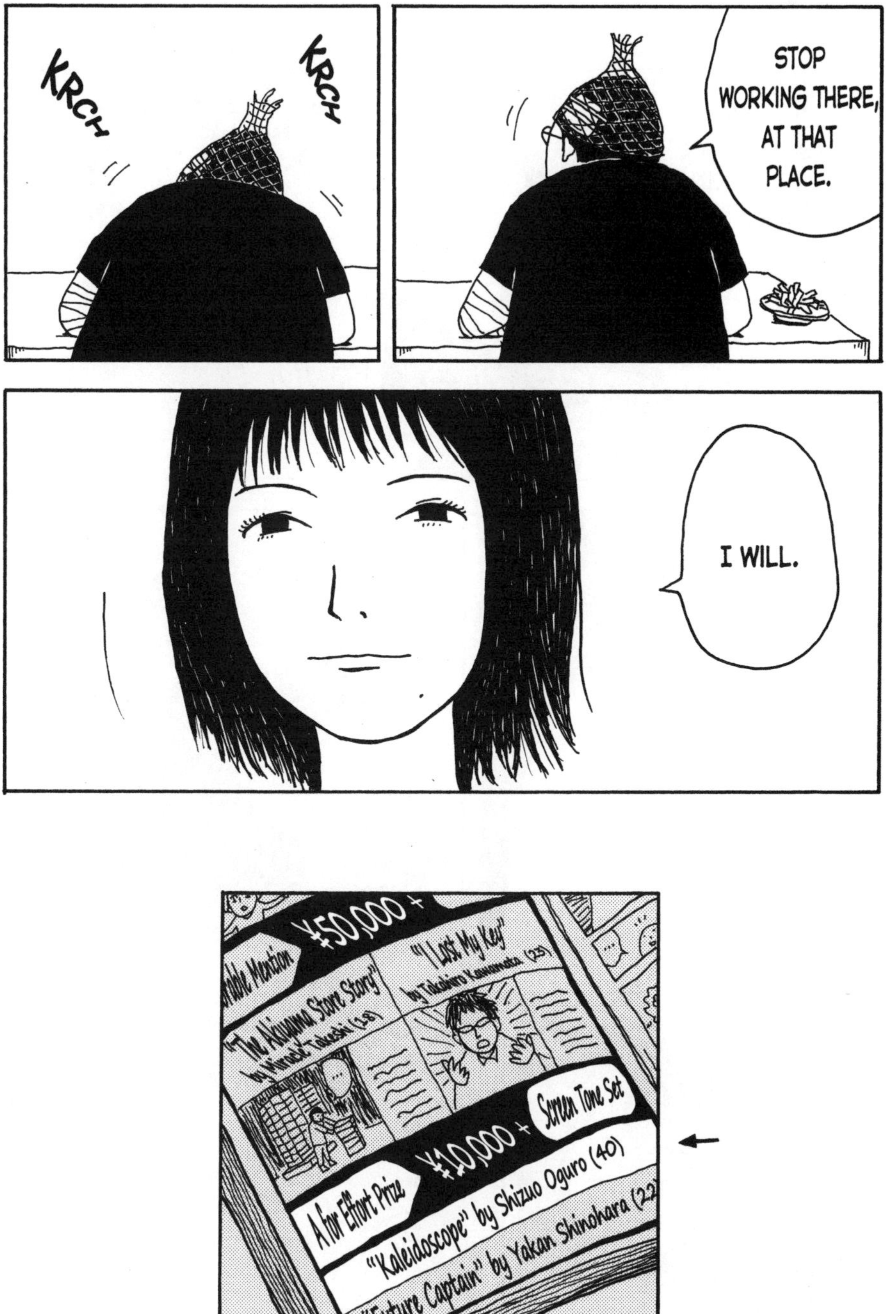
STOP WORKING THERE, AT THAT PLACE.
KRCH
KRCH
I WILL.
¥50,000 +
"I Lost My Key"
by Takahiro Kawamata (23)
"The Akiyama Store Story"
by Miracle Takeshi (18)
¥10,000 +
Screen Tone Set
A for Effort Prize
"Kaleidoscope" by Shizuo Oguro (40)
"Future Captain" by Yakan Shinohara (22
The End

I Just Haven't Gotten Serious Yet, That's All

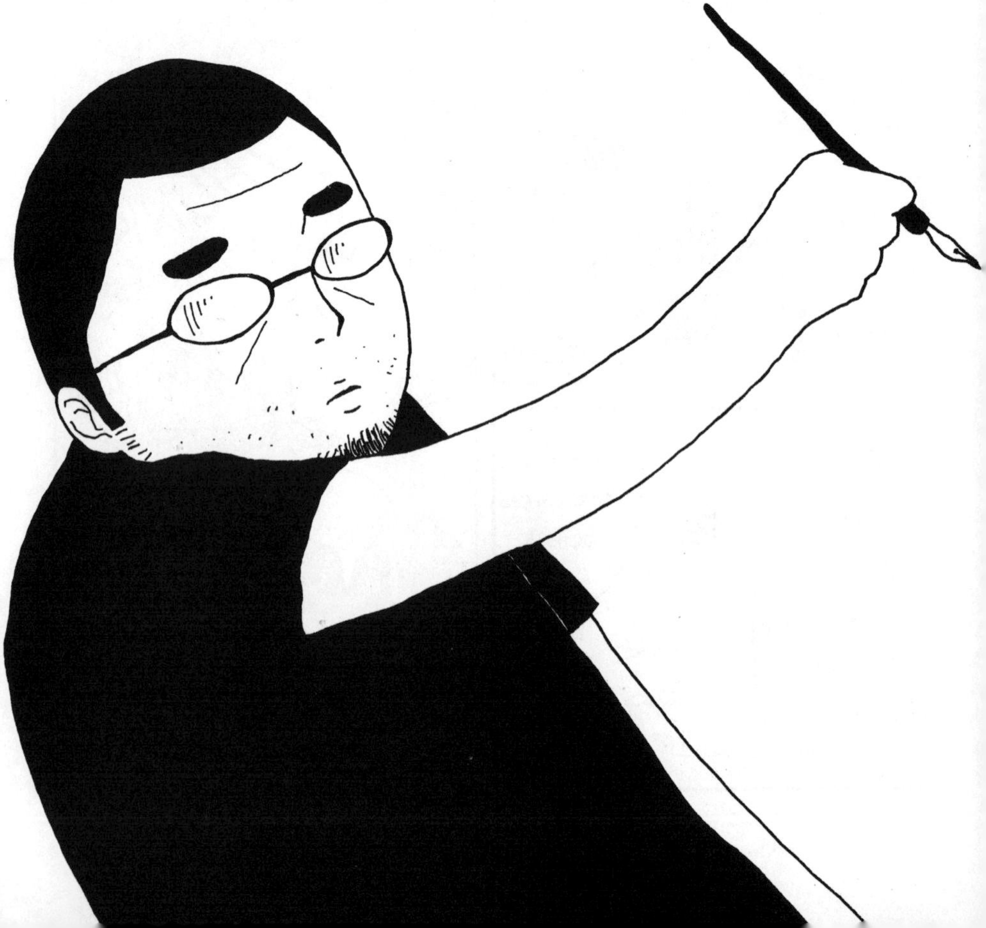

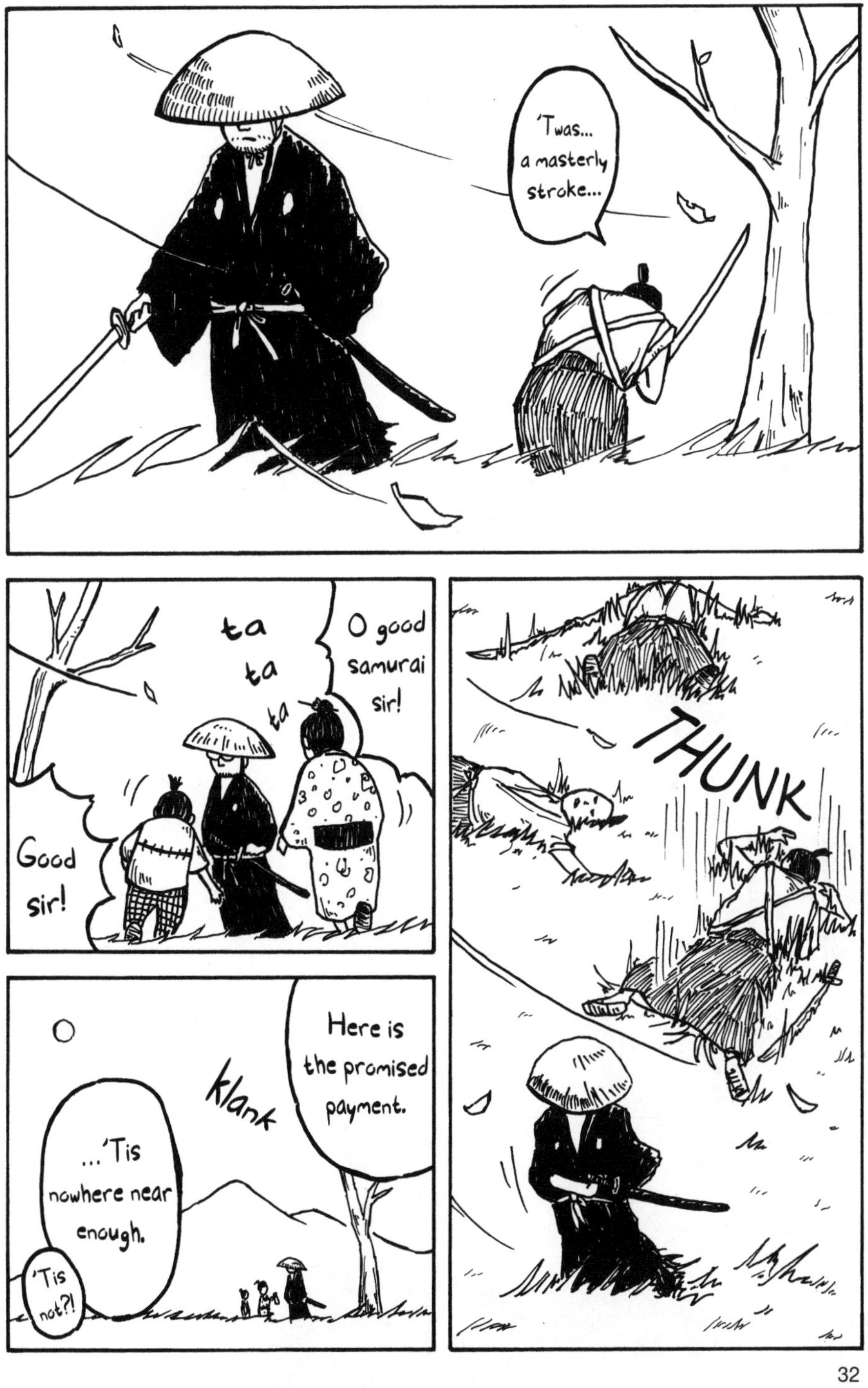
'Twas... a masterly stroke...
THUNK
O good samurai sir!
ta ta ta
Good sir!
Here is the promised payment.
klank
O
...'Tis nowhere near enough.
'Tis not?!

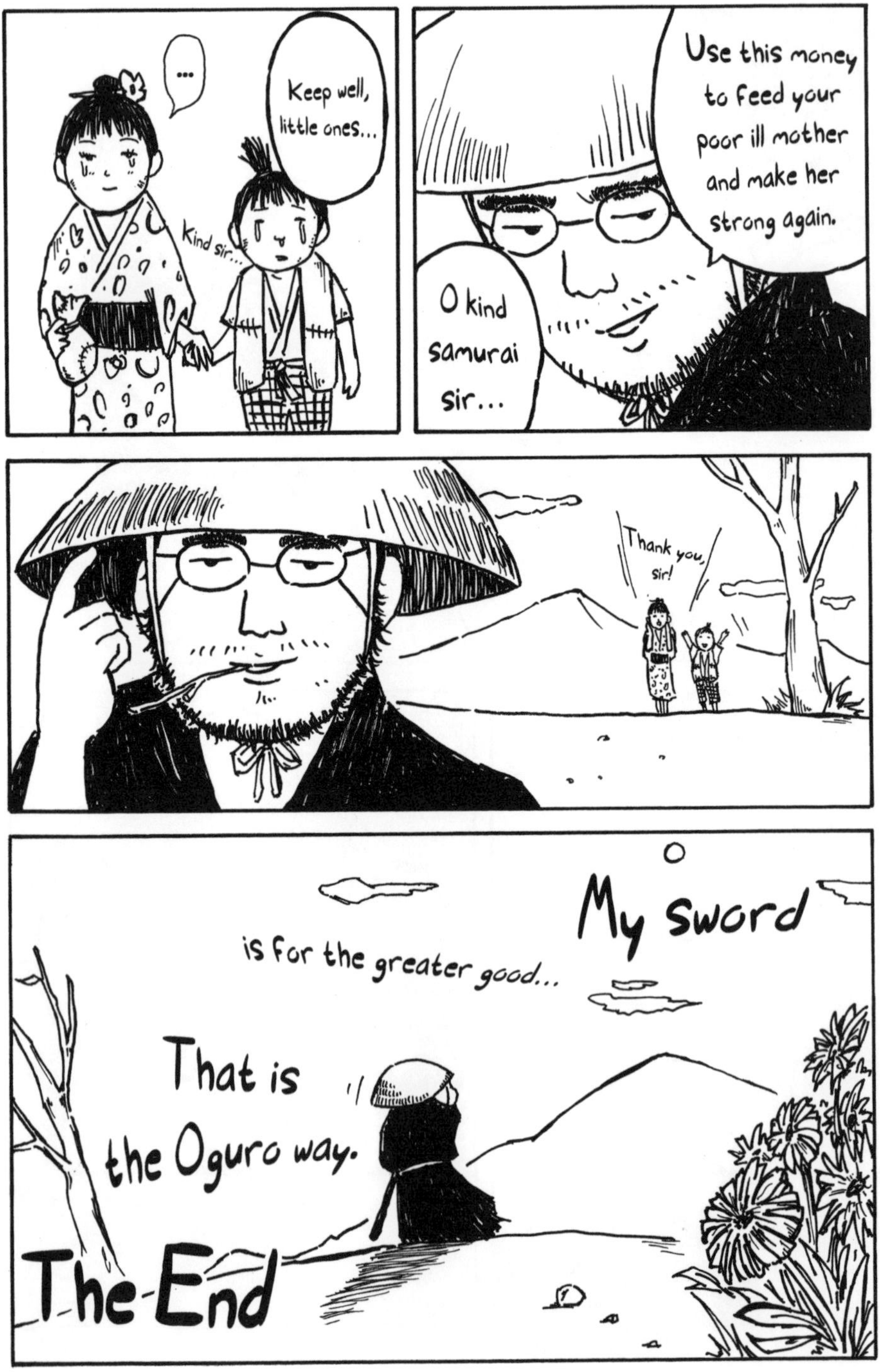
...
Keep well, little ones...
Kind sir...
Use this money to feed your poor ill mother and make her strong again.
O kind samurai sir...
Thank you, sir!
My sword is for the greater good...
That is the Oguro way.
The End

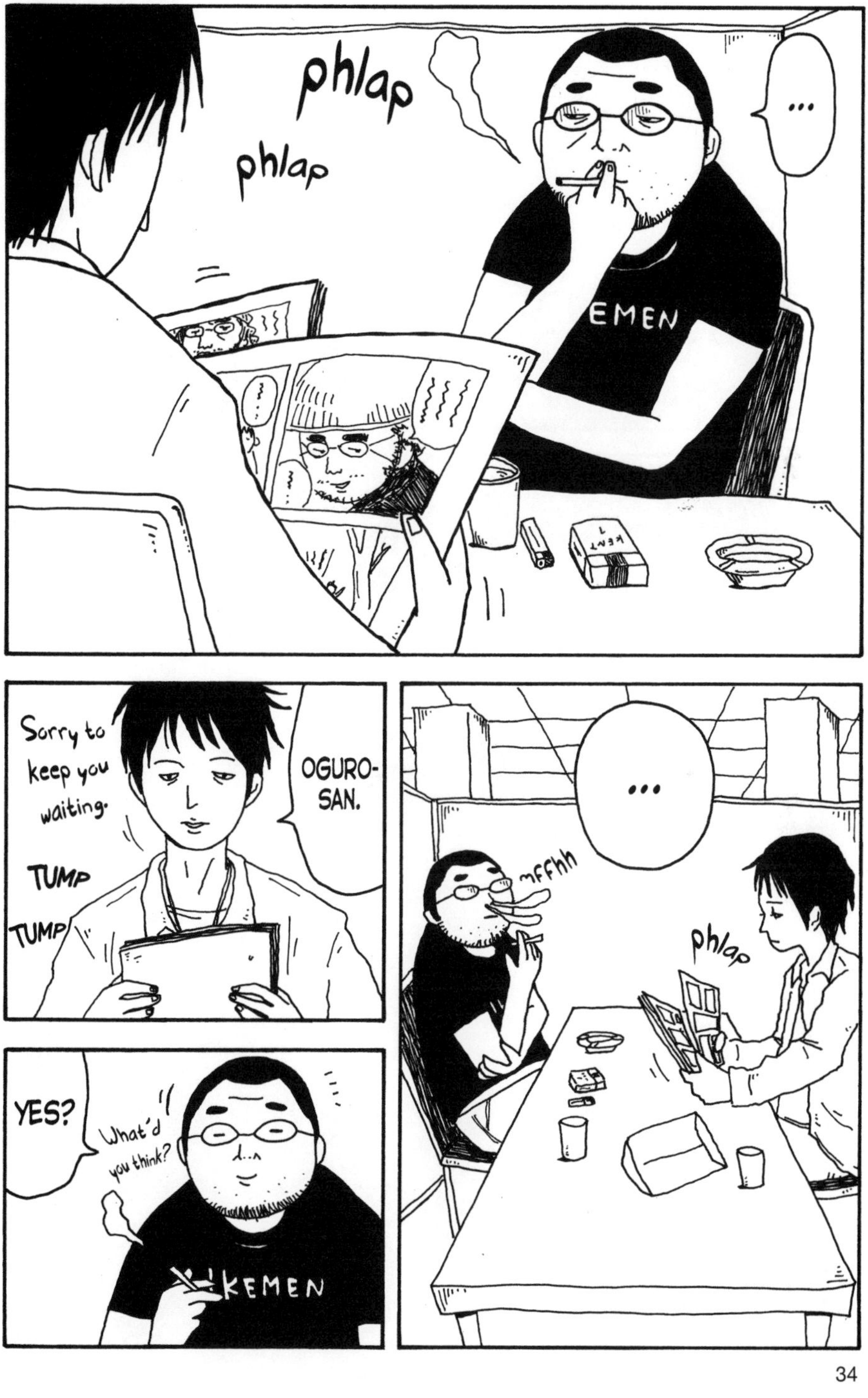
…
phlap
phlap
…
mffhh
phlap
OGURO-SAN.
Sorry to keep you waiting.
TUMP
TUMP
YES?
What'd you think?

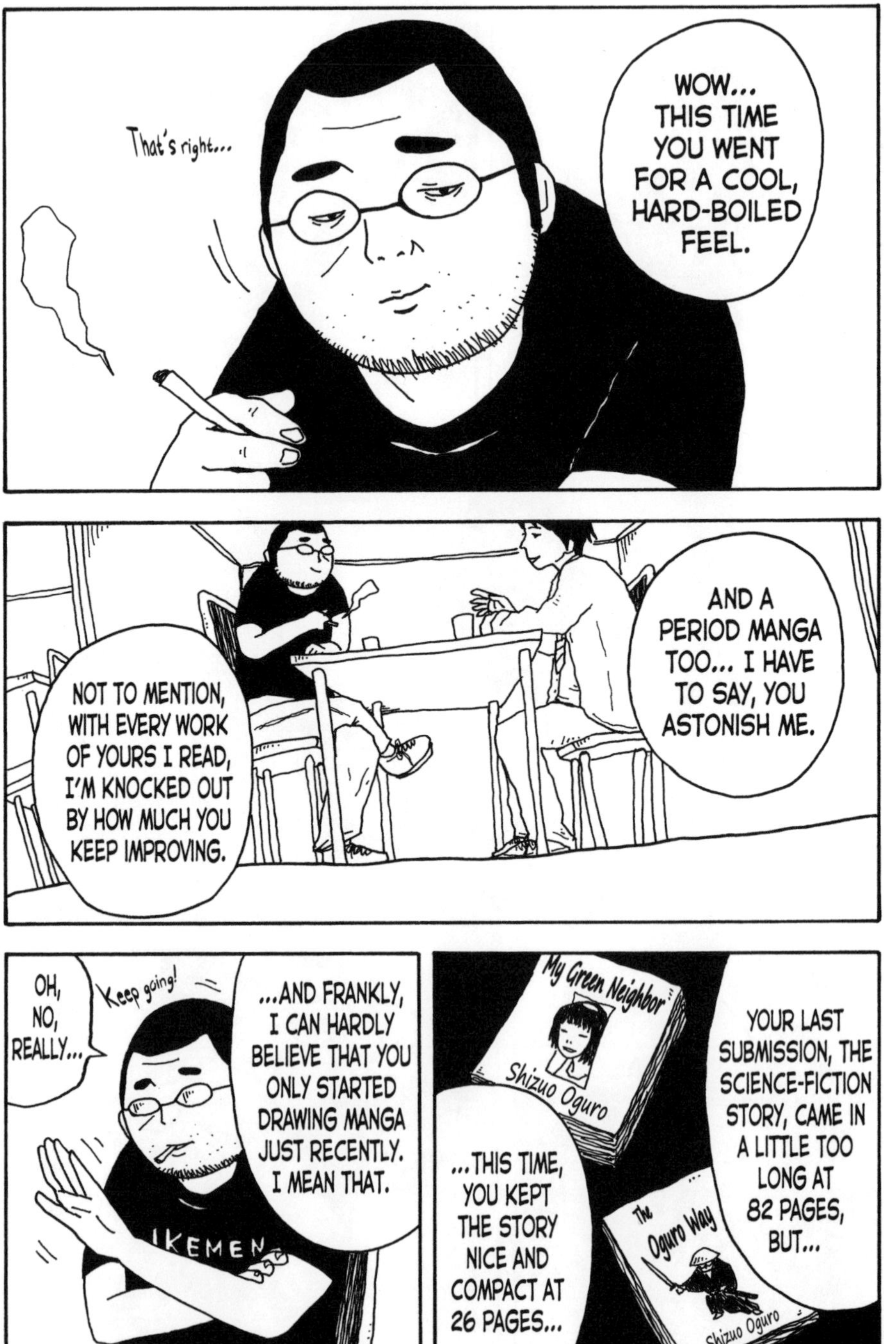

WOW... THIS TIME YOU WENT FOR A COOL, HARD-BOILED FEEL.
That's right...
AND A PERIOD MANGA TOO... I HAVE TO SAY, YOU ASTONISH ME.
NOT TO MENTION, WITH EVERY WORK OF YOURS I READ, I'M KNOCKED OUT BY HOW MUCH YOU KEEP IMPROVING.
My Green Neighbor
Shizuo Oguro
YOUR LAST SUBMISSION, THE SCIENCE-FICTION STORY, CAME IN A LITTLE TOO LONG AT 82 PAGES, BUT...
The Oguro Way
Shizuo Oguro
...THIS TIME, YOU KEPT THE STORY NICE AND COMPACT AT 26 PAGES...
...AND FRANKLY, I CAN HARDLY BELIEVE THAT YOU ONLY STARTED DRAWING MANGA JUST RECENTLY. I MEAN THAT.
Keep going!
OH, NO, REALLY...
IKEMEN

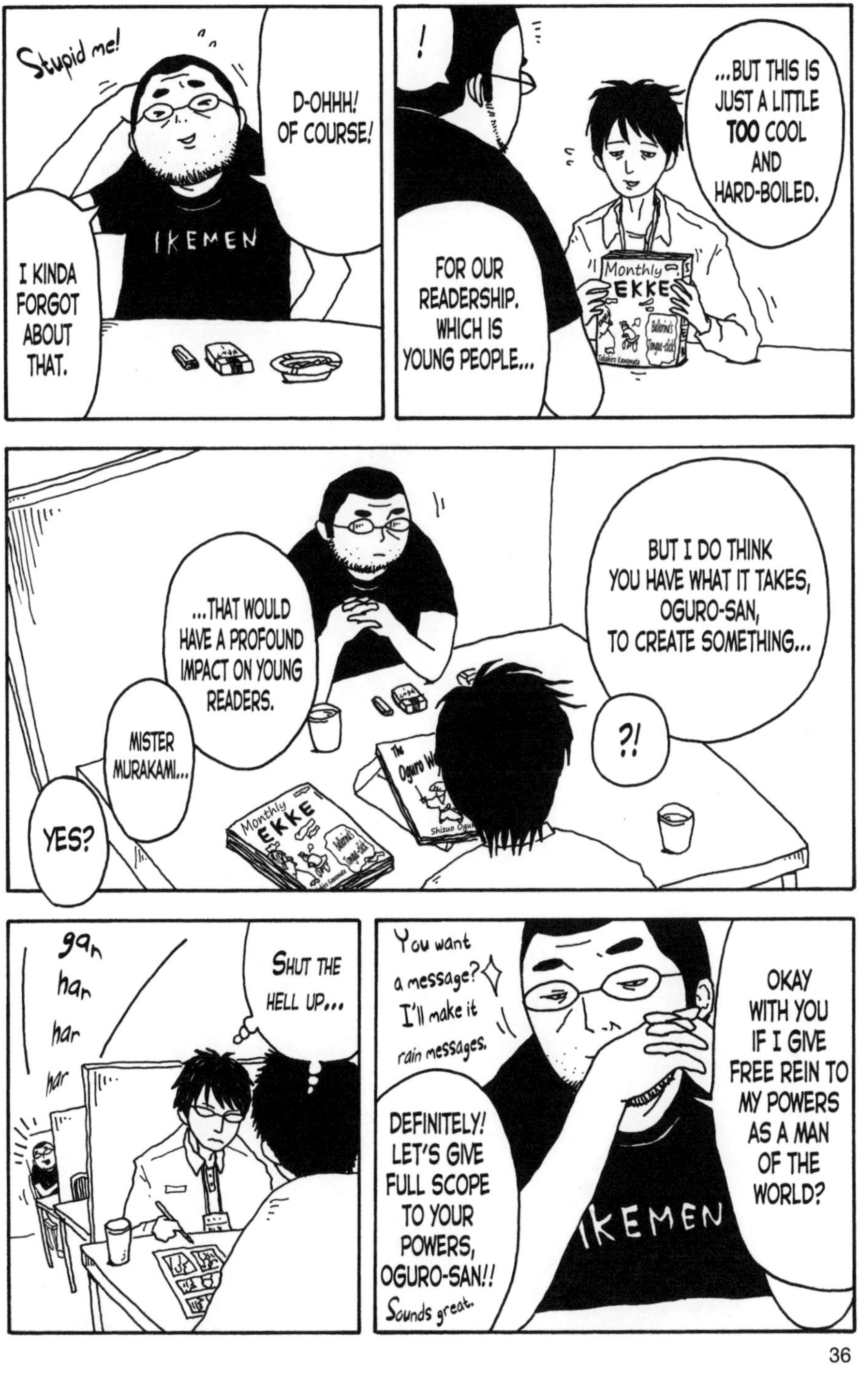

...BUT THIS IS JUST A LITTLE TOO COOL AND HARD-BOILED.
!
FOR OUR READERSHIP. WHICH IS YOUNG PEOPLE...
Monthly EKKE
D-OHHH! OF COURSE!
Stupid me!
IKEMEN
I KINDA FORGOT ABOUT THAT.
BUT I DO THINK YOU HAVE WHAT IT TAKES, OGURO-SAN, TO CREATE SOMETHING...
...THAT WOULD HAVE A PROFOUND IMPACT ON YOUNG READERS.
?!
MISTER MURAKAMI...
YES?
Monthly EKKE
OKAY WITH YOU IF I GIVE FREE REIN TO MY POWERS AS A MAN OF THE WORLD?
You want a message? I'll make it rain messages.
IKEMEN
DEFINITELY! LET'S GIVE FULL SCOPE TO YOUR POWERS, OGURO-SAN!!
Sounds great.
SHUT THE HELL UP...
gan har har har

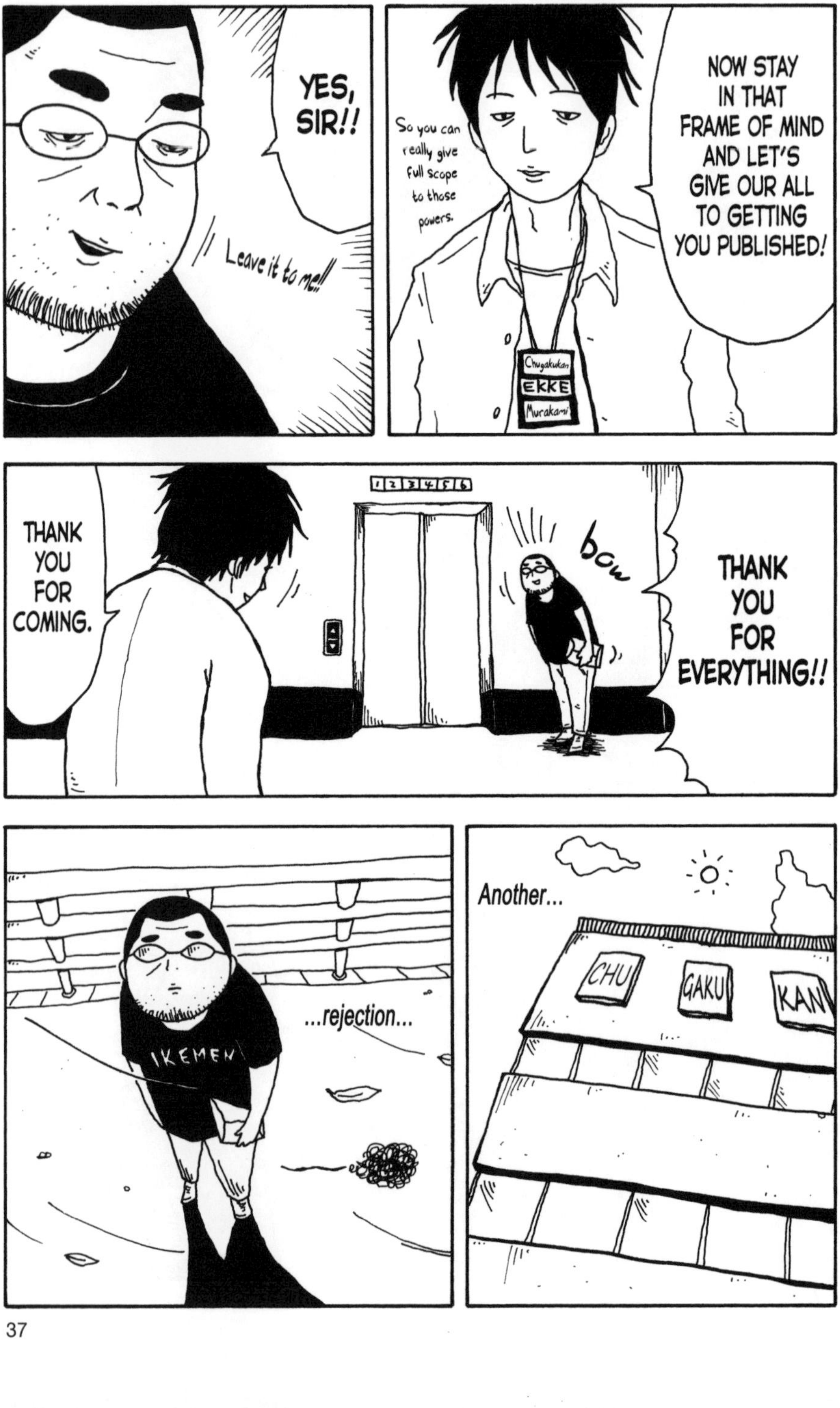
NOW STAY IN THAT FRAME OF MIND AND LET'S GIVE OUR ALL TO GETTING YOU PUBLISHED!
So you can really give full scope to those powers.
Chugakukan
EKKE
Murakami
YES, SIR!!
Leave it to me!!
THANK YOU FOR EVERYTHING!!
bow
1 2 3 4 5 6
THANK YOU FOR COMING.
Another...
CHU GAKU KAN
...rejection...
IKEMEN

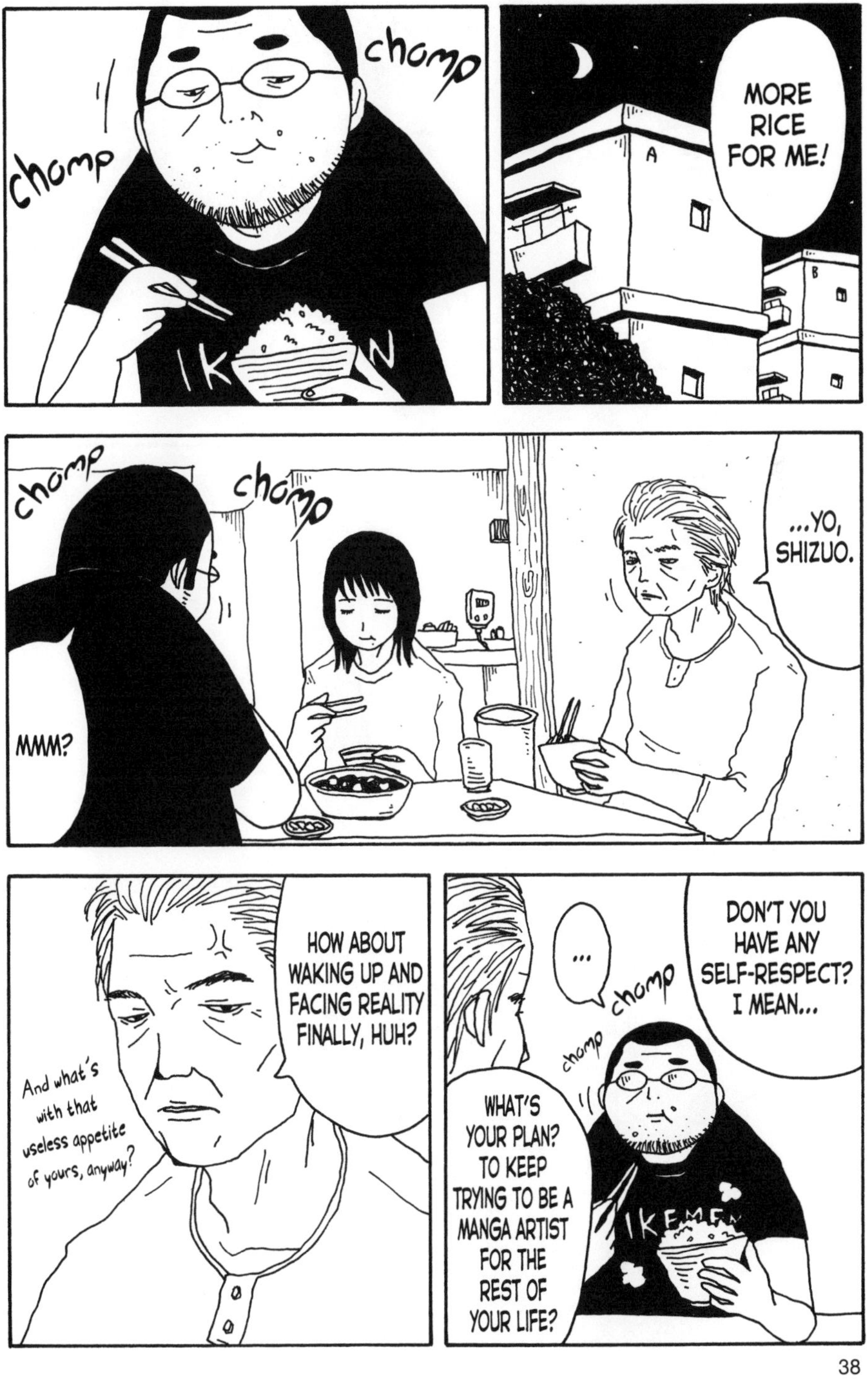
MORE RICE FOR ME!
chomp
chomp
...YO, SHIZUO.
chomp
chomp
MMM?
DON'T YOU HAVE ANY SELF-RESPECT? I MEAN...
...
chomp
chomp
WHAT'S YOUR PLAN? TO KEEP TRYING TO BE A MANGA ARTIST FOR THE REST OF YOUR LIFE?
HOW ABOUT WAKING UP AND FACING REALITY FINALLY, HUH?
And what's with that useless appetite of yours, anyway?

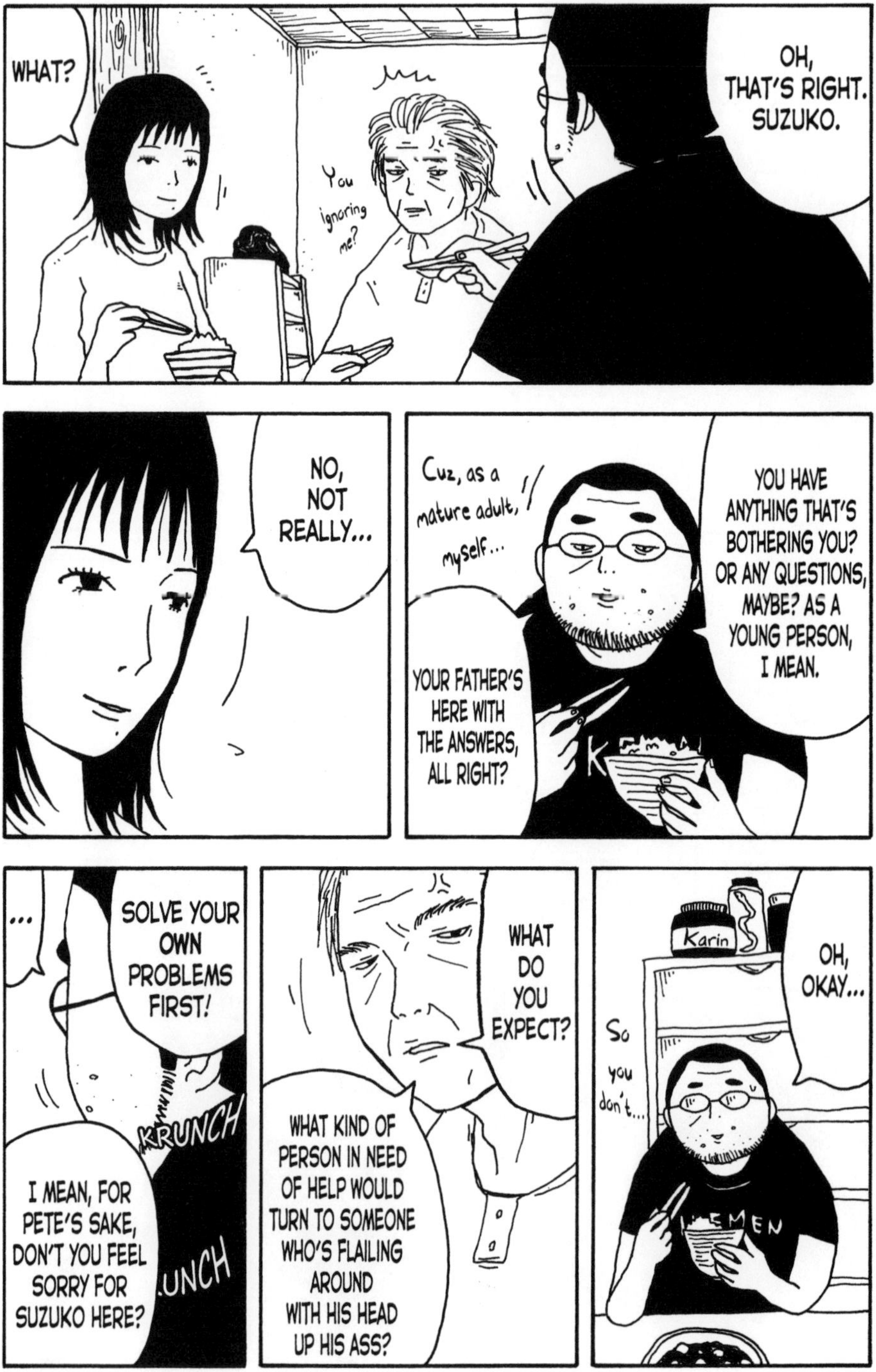
OH, THAT'S RIGHT. SUZUKO.
You ignoring me?
WHAT?
YOU HAVE ANYTHING THAT'S BOTHERING YOU? OR ANY QUESTIONS, MAYBE? AS A YOUNG PERSON, I MEAN.
Cuz, as a mature adult, myself...
YOUR FATHER'S HERE WITH THE ANSWERS, ALL RIGHT?
NO, NOT REALLY...
OH, OKAY...
So you don't...
Karin
WHAT DO YOU EXPECT?
WHAT KIND OF PERSON IN NEED OF HELP WOULD TURN TO SOMEONE WHO'S FLAILING AROUND WITH HIS HEAD UP HIS ASS?
SOLVE YOUR OWN PROBLEMS FIRST!
...
KRUNCH
I MEAN, FOR PETE'S SAKE, DON'T YOU FEEL SORRY FOR SUZUKO HERE?
.UNCH

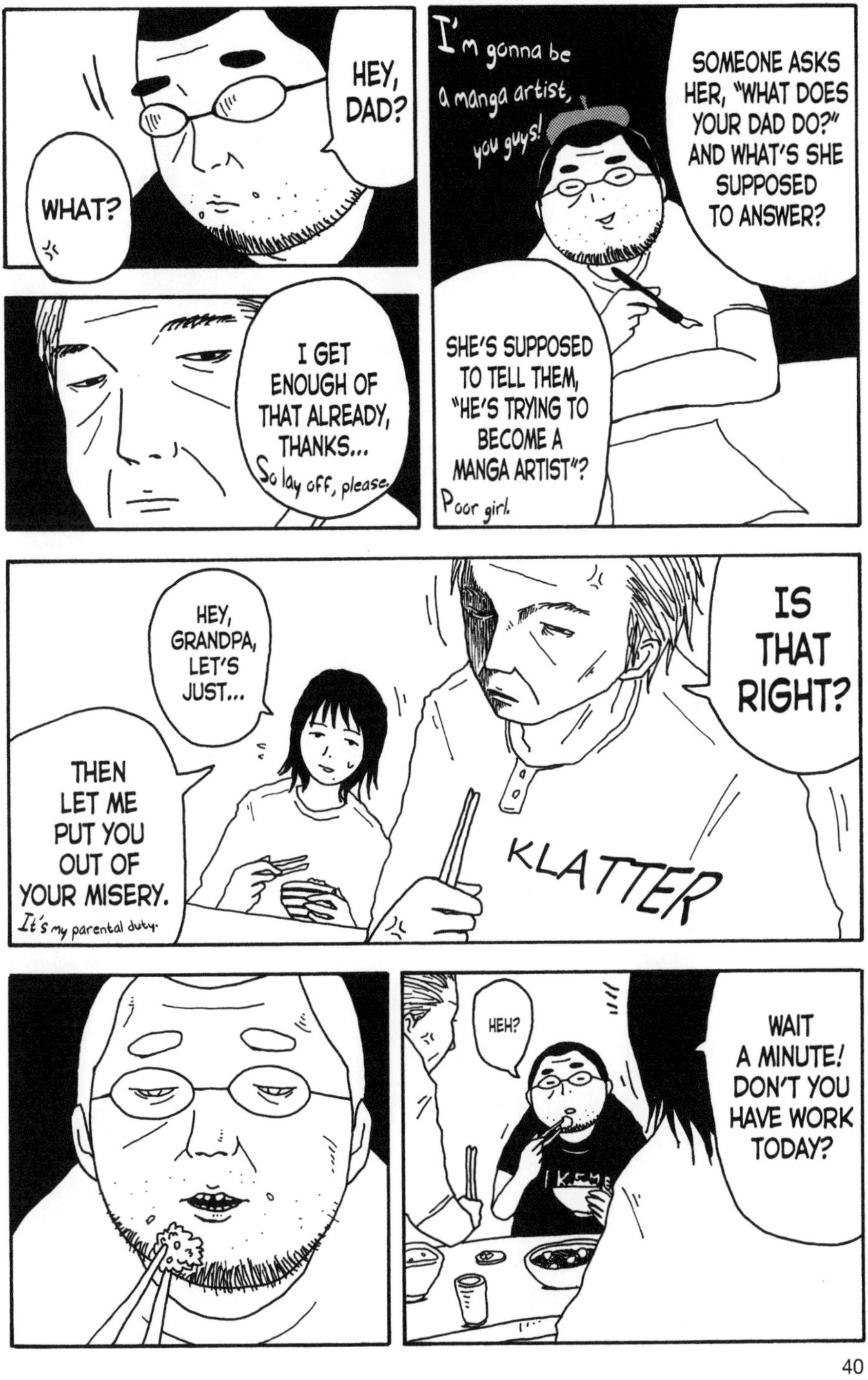
SOMEONE ASKS HER, "WHAT DOES YOUR DAD DO?" AND WHAT'S SHE SUPPOSED TO ANSWER?
I'm gonna be a manga artist, you guys!
SHE'S SUPPOSED TO TELL THEM, "HE'S TRYING TO BECOME A MANGA ARTIST"?
Poor girl.
HEY, DAD?
WHAT?
I GET ENOUGH OF THAT ALREADY, THANKS...
So lay off, please.
IS THAT RIGHT?
HEY, GRANDPA, LET'S JUST...
KLATTER
THEN LET ME PUT YOU OUT OF YOUR MISERY.
It's my parental duty.
WAIT A MINUTE! DON'T YOU HAVE WORK TODAY?
HEH?

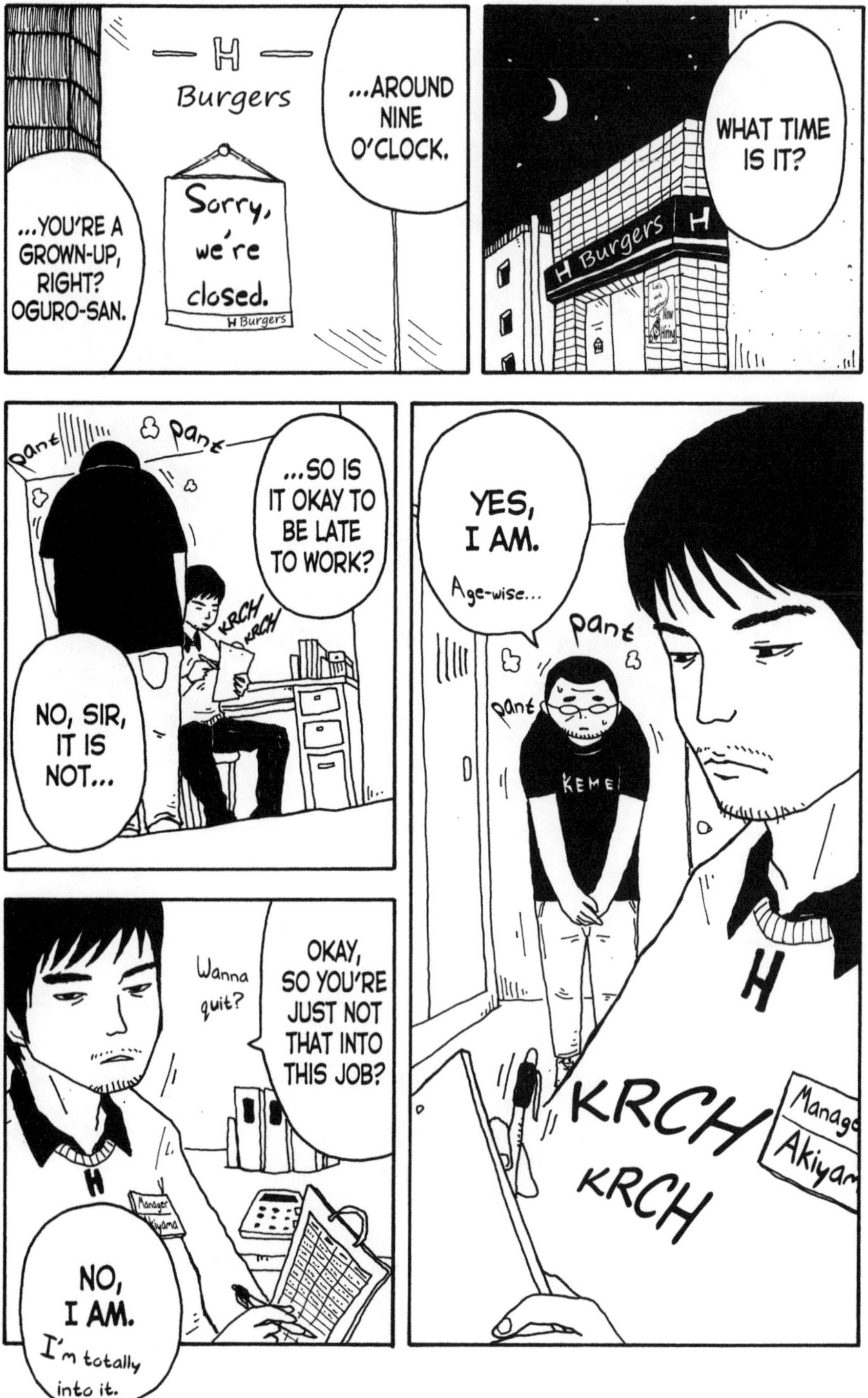
H Burgers
Now Hiring
WHAT TIME IS IT?
H
Burgers
Sorry, we're closed.
H Burgers
...AROUND NINE O'CLOCK.
...YOU'RE A GROWN-UP, RIGHT? OGURO-SAN.
YES, I AM.
Age-wise...
pant
pant
KEME
KRCH
KRCH
pant
pant
...SO IS IT OKAY TO BE LATE TO WORK?
KRCH KRCH
NO, SIR, IT IS NOT...
OKAY, SO YOU'RE JUST NOT THAT INTO THIS JOB?
Wanna quit?
Manager Akiyama
NO, I AM.
I'm totally into it.

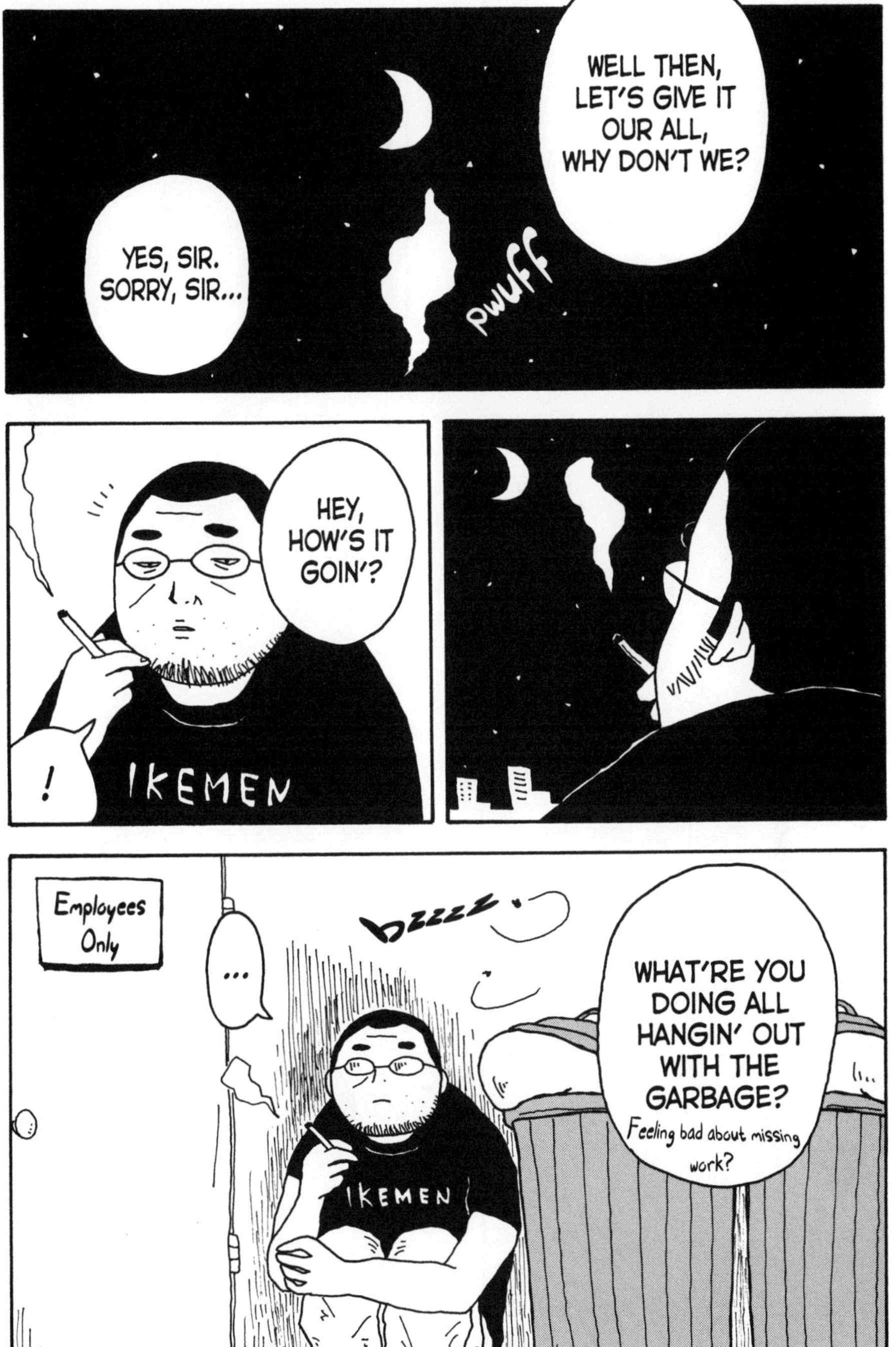
WELL THEN, LET'S GIVE IT OUR ALL, WHY DON'T WE?
pwuff
YES, SIR. SORRY, SIR...
HEY, HOW'S IT GOIN'?
!
IKEMEN
WHAT'RE YOU DOING ALL HANGIN' OUT WITH THE GARBAGE?
Feeling bad about missing work?
bzzzz
IKEMEN
...
Employees Only

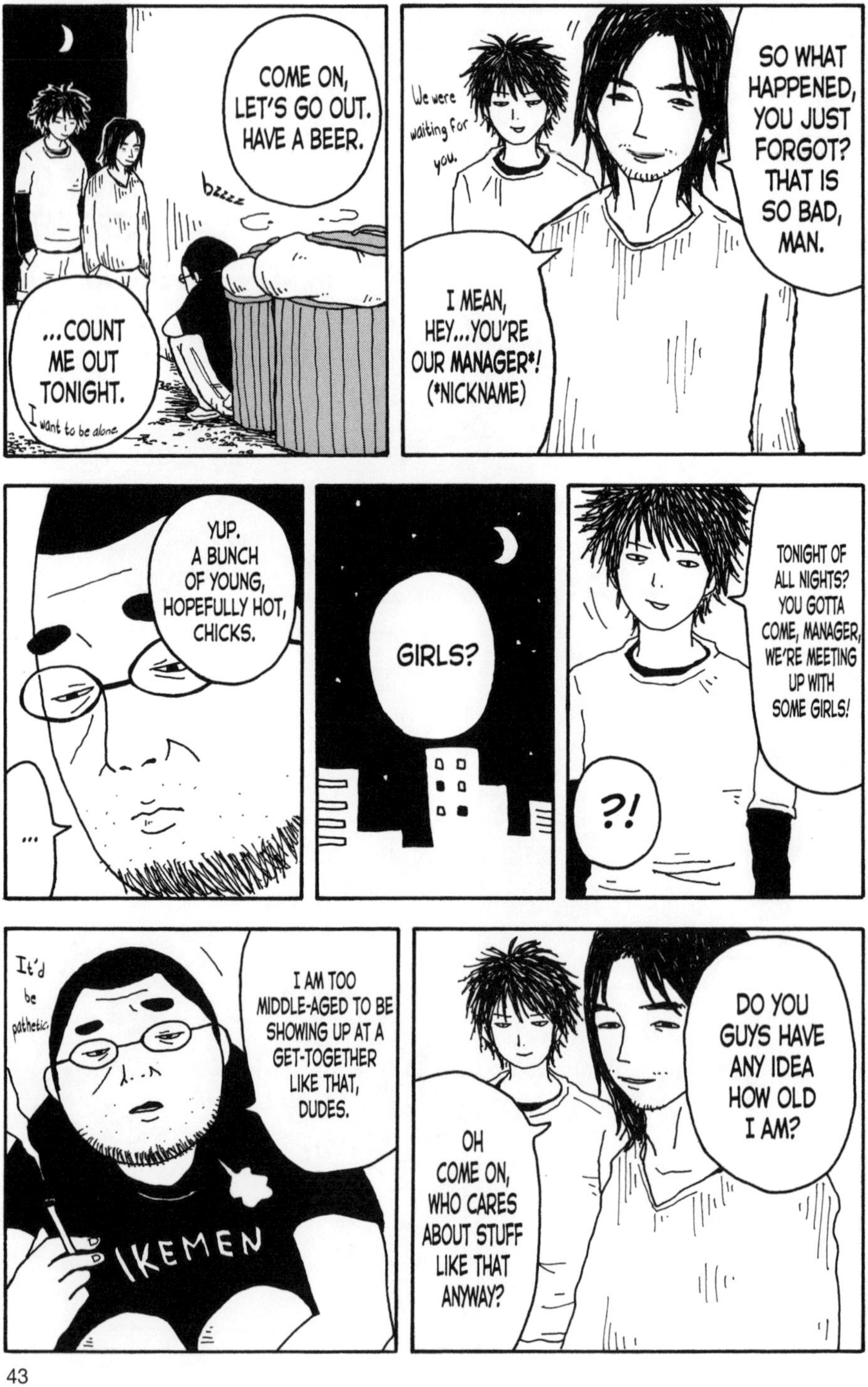
SO WHAT HAPPENED, YOU JUST FORGOT? THAT IS SO BAD, MAN.
We were waiting for you.
I MEAN, HEY...YOU'RE OUR MANAGER*! (*NICKNAME)
COME ON, LET'S GO OUT. HAVE A BEER.
bzzzz
...COUNT ME OUT TONIGHT.
I want to be alone.
TONIGHT OF ALL NIGHTS? YOU GOTTA COME, MANAGER, WE'RE MEETING UP WITH SOME GIRLS!
?!
GIRLS?
YUP. A BUNCH OF YOUNG, HOPEFULLY HOT, CHICKS.
...
DO YOU GUYS HAVE ANY IDEA HOW OLD I AM?
OH COME ON, WHO CARES ABOUT STUFF LIKE THAT ANYWAY?
I AM TOO MIDDLE-AGED TO BE SHOWING UP AT A GET-TOGETHER LIKE THAT, DUDES.
It'd be pathetic.
IKEMEN

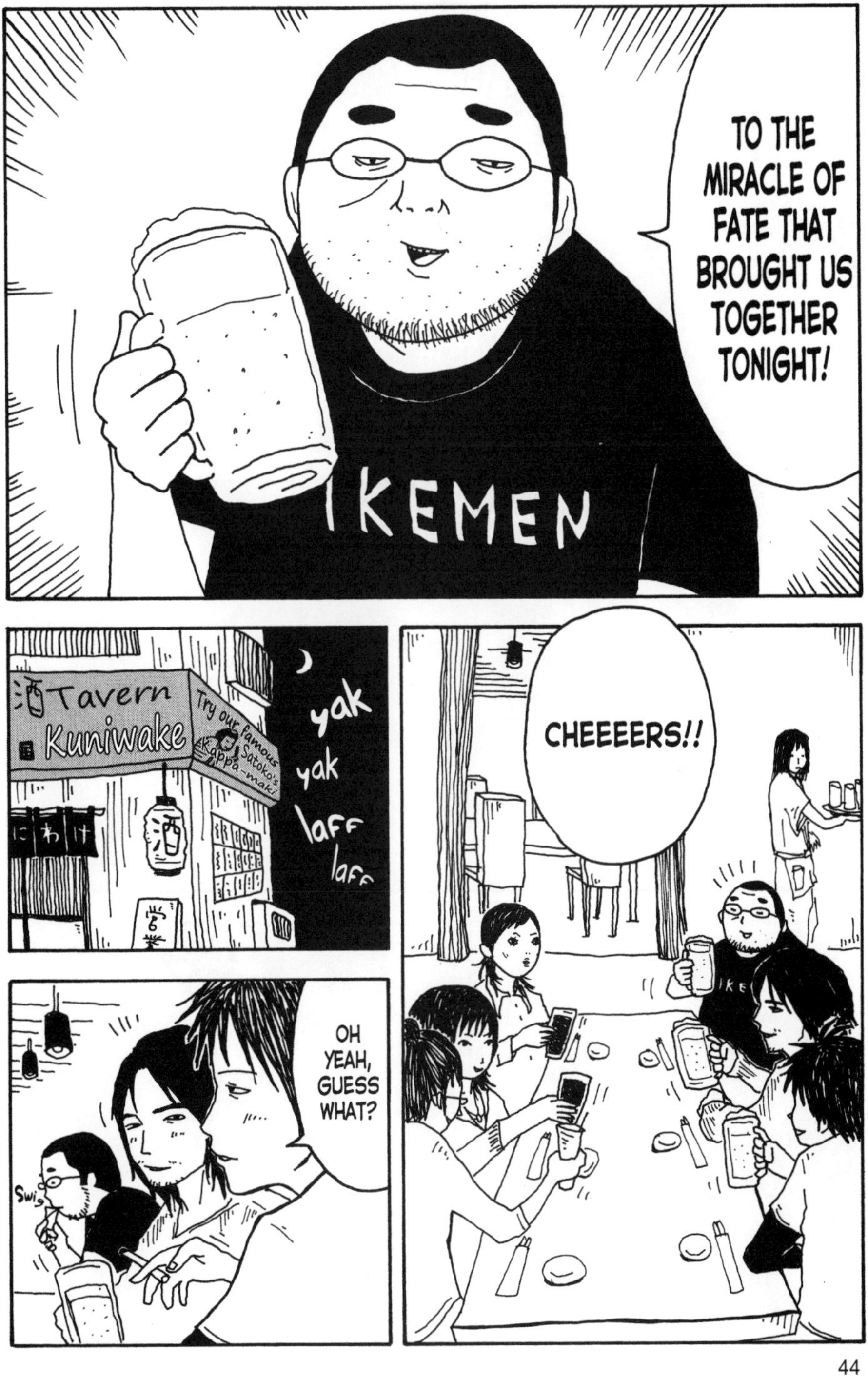
TO THE MIRACLE OF FATE THAT BROUGHT US TOGETHER TONIGHT!
IKEMEN
CHEEEERS!!
Tavern Kuniwake
Try our famous Satoko's Kappa-maki
にわけ
yak yak laff laff
OH YEAH, GUESS WHAT?
Swig

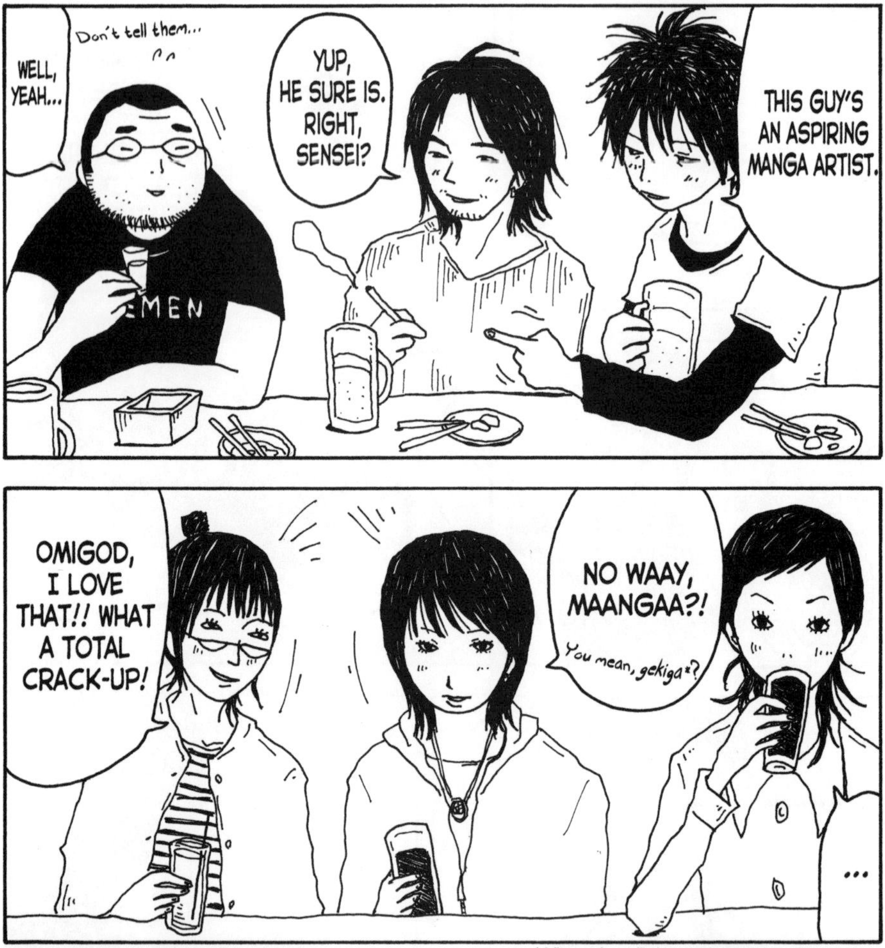
THIS GUY'S AN ASPIRING MANGA ARTIST.
YUP, HE SURE IS. RIGHT, SENSEI?
Don't tell them...
WELL, YEAH...
NO WAAY, MAANGAA?!
You mean, gekiga*?
OMIGOD, I LOVE THAT!! WHAT A TOTAL CRACK-UP!
...

* Visceral, realistic manga popular with adults.

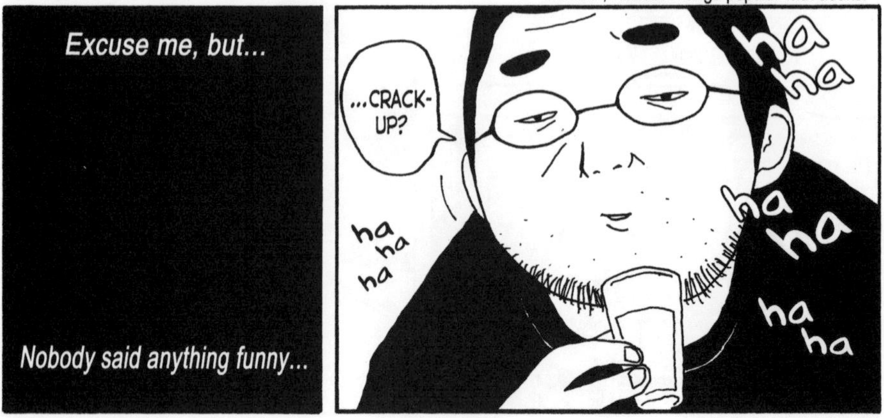
ha ha
...CRACK-UP?
ha ha
ha ha
ha ha ha
Excuse me, but...
Nobody said anything funny...

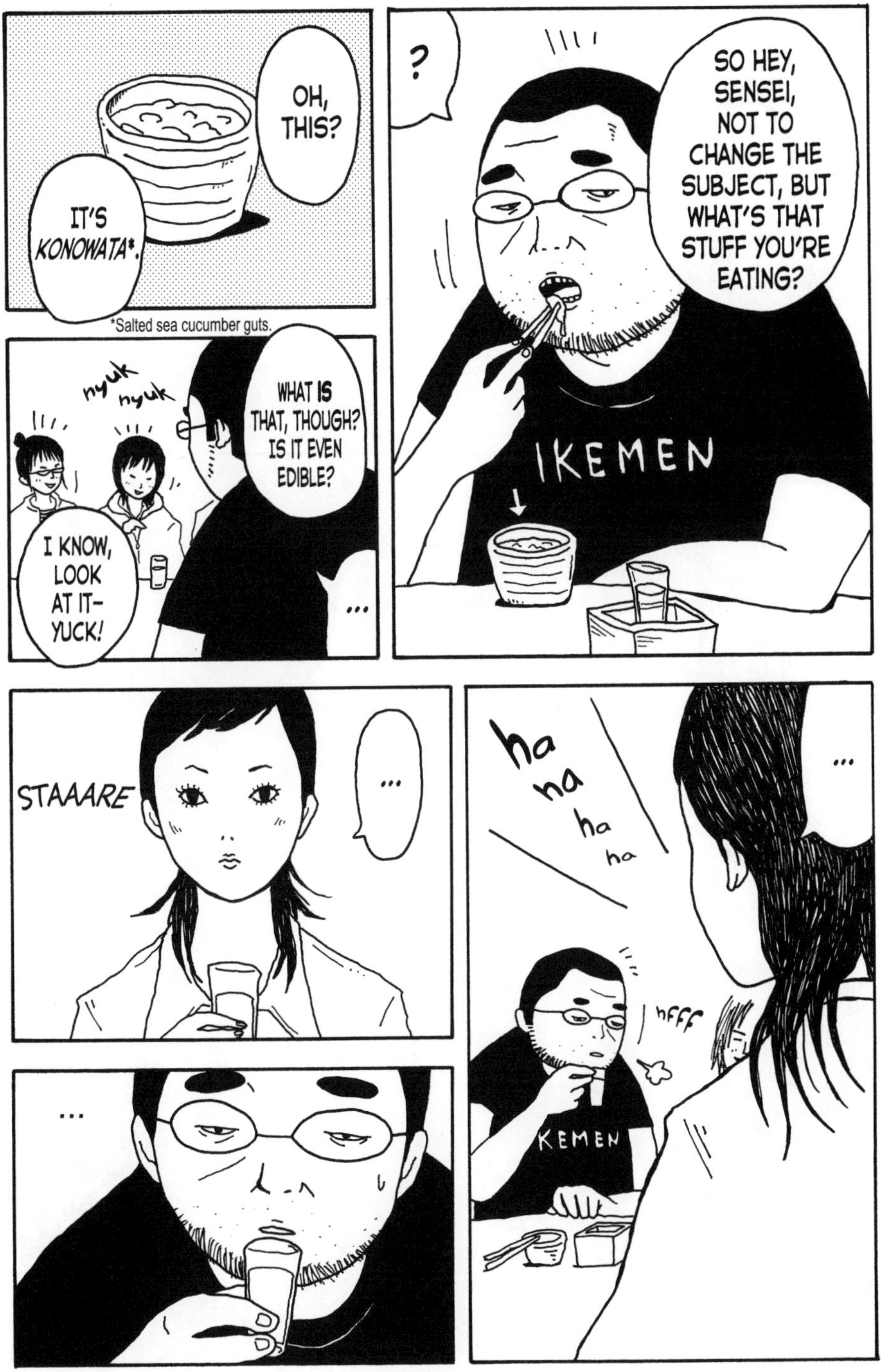
SO HEY, SENSEI, NOT TO CHANGE THE SUBJECT, BUT WHAT'S THAT STUFF YOU'RE EATING?
?
IKEMEN
OH, THIS?
IT'S *KONOWATA**.
WHAT **IS** THAT, THOUGH? IS IT EVEN EDIBLE?
nyuk nyuk
I KNOW, LOOK AT IT-YUCK!
...
...
ha ha ha ha
hfff
KEMEN
...
STAAARE
...
*Salted sea cucumber guts.

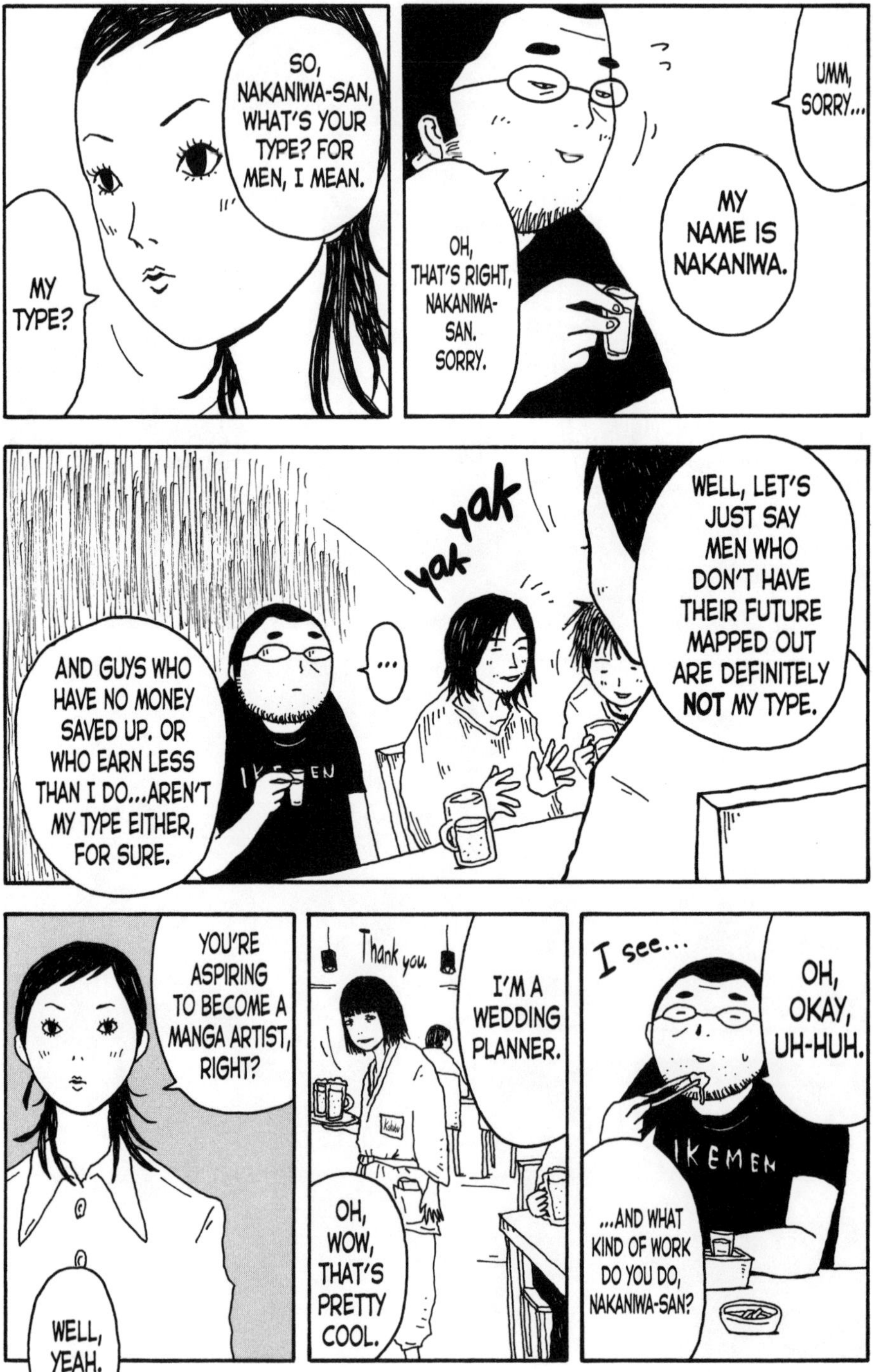
UMM, SORRY...
MY NAME IS NAKANIWA.
OH, THAT'S RIGHT, NAKANIWA-SAN. SORRY.
SO, NAKANIWA-SAN, WHAT'S YOUR TYPE? FOR MEN, I MEAN.
MY TYPE?
WELL, LET'S JUST SAY MEN WHO DON'T HAVE THEIR FUTURE MAPPED OUT ARE DEFINITELY **NOT** MY TYPE.
yak yak
...
IKEMEN
AND GUYS WHO HAVE NO MONEY SAVED UP. OR WHO EARN LESS THAN I DO...AREN'T MY TYPE EITHER, FOR SURE.
I see...
OH, OKAY, UH-HUH.
IKEMEN
...AND WHAT KIND OF WORK DO YOU DO, NAKANIWA-SAN?
Thank you.
I'M A WEDDING PLANNER.
OH, WOW, THAT'S PRETTY COOL.
YOU'RE ASPIRING TO BECOME A MANGA ARTIST, RIGHT?
WELL, YEAH.

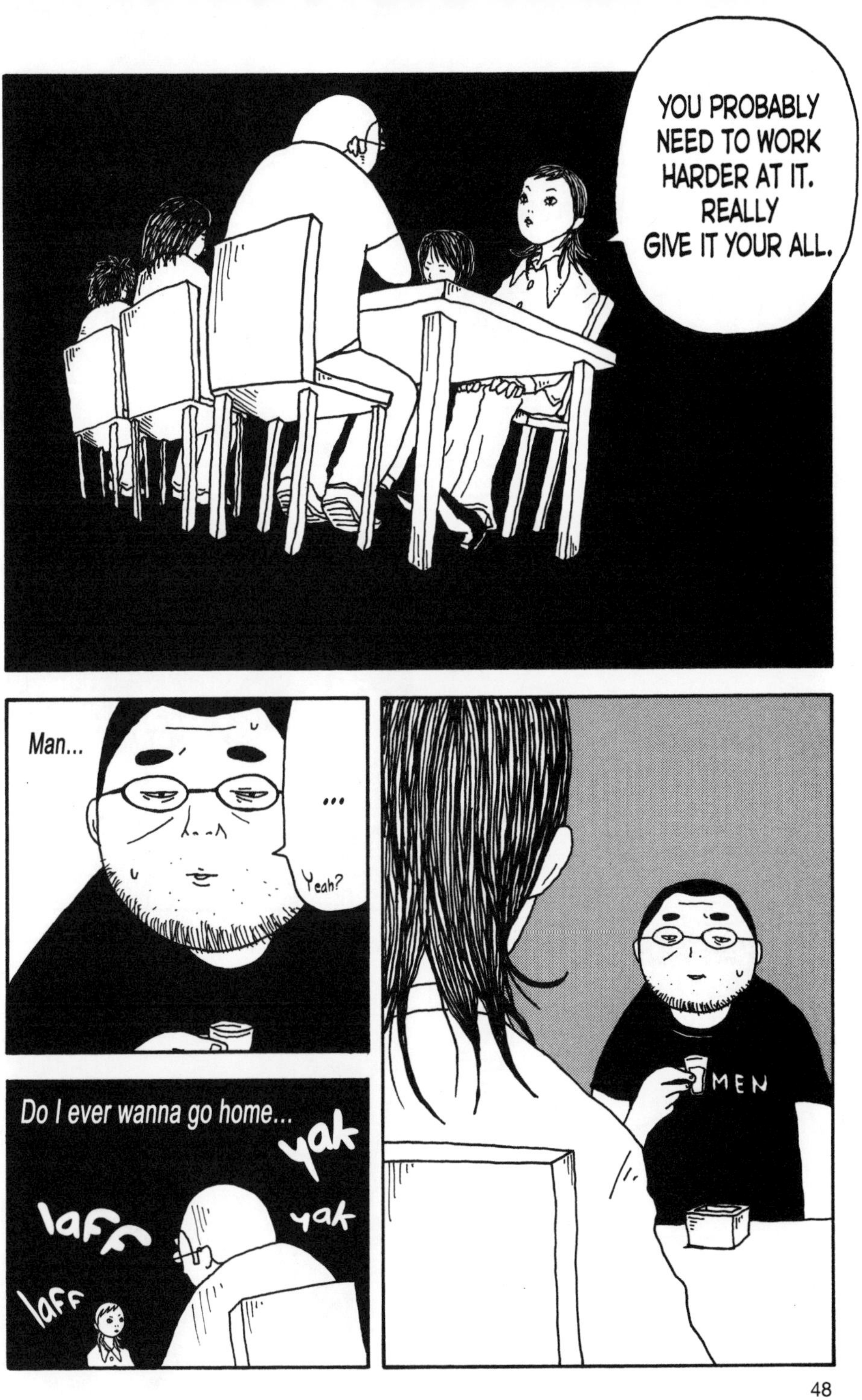
YOU PROBABLY NEED TO WORK HARDER AT IT. REALLY GIVE IT YOUR ALL.
MEN
Man...
...
Yeah?
Do I ever wanna go home...
yak
laff
yak
laff

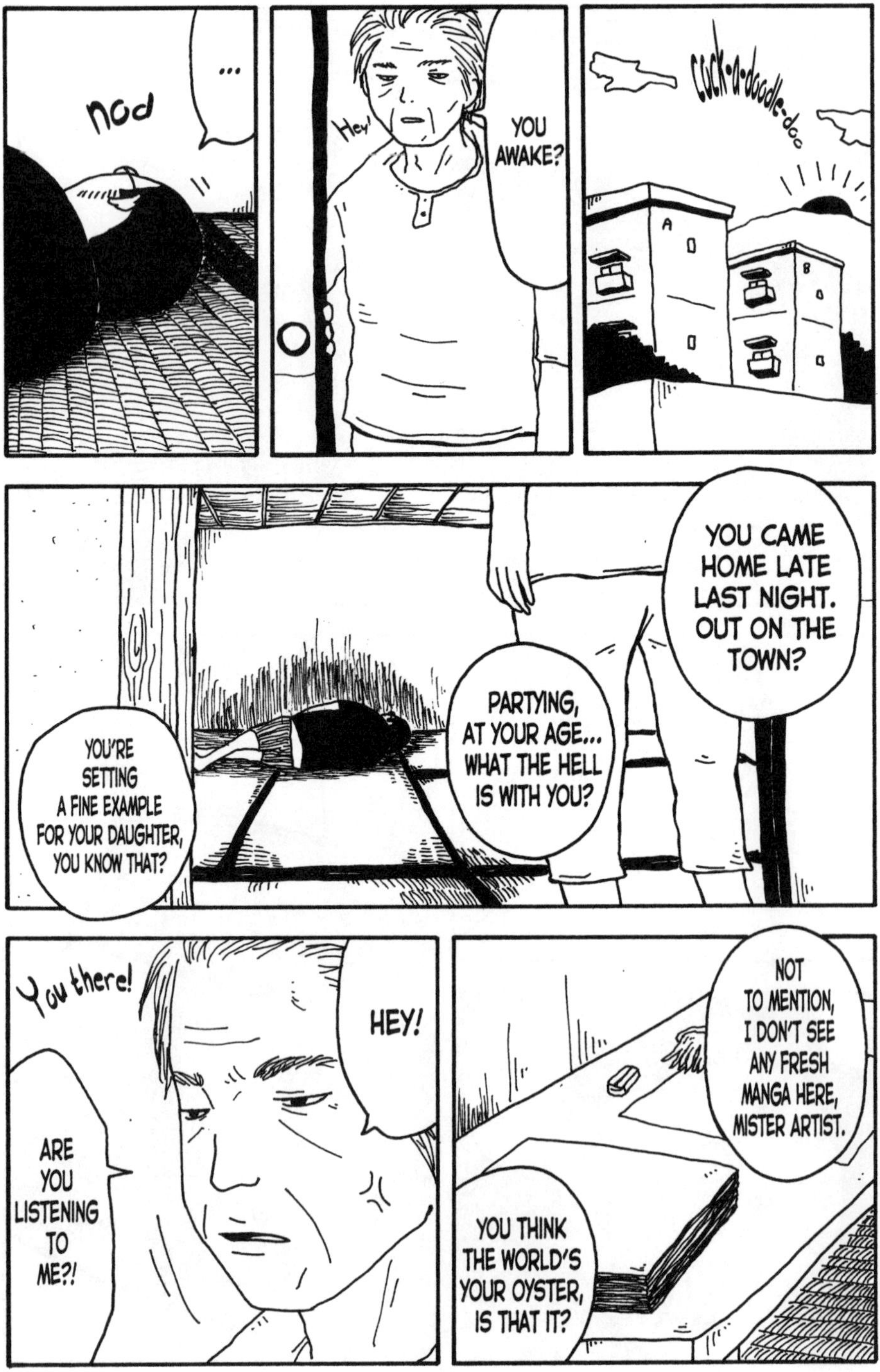
Cock-a-doodle-doo
Hey!
YOU AWAKE?
...
nod
YOU CAME HOME LATE LAST NIGHT. OUT ON THE TOWN?
PARTYING, AT YOUR AGE... WHAT THE HELL IS WITH YOU?
YOU'RE SETTING A FINE EXAMPLE FOR YOUR DAUGHTER, YOU KNOW THAT?
NOT TO MENTION, I DON'T SEE ANY FRESH MANGA HERE, MISTER ARTIST.
YOU THINK THE WORLD'S YOUR OYSTER, IS THAT IT?
HEY!
You there!
ARE YOU LISTENING TO ME?!

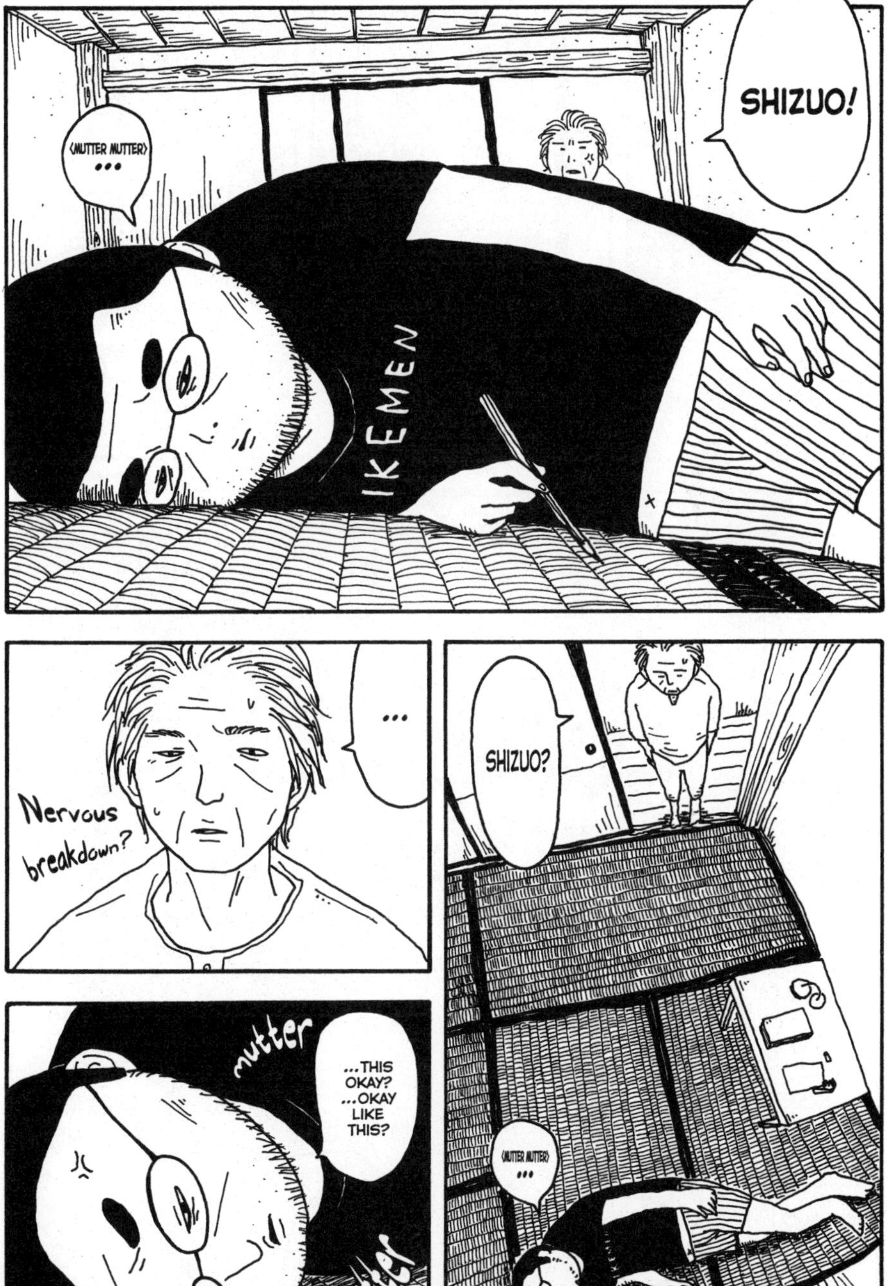
SHIZUO!
<MUTTER MUTTER> ...
IKEMEN
SHIZUO?
<MUTTER MUTTER> ...
...
Nervous breakdown?
...THIS OKAY? ...OKAY LIKE THIS?
mutter
mutter
mutter

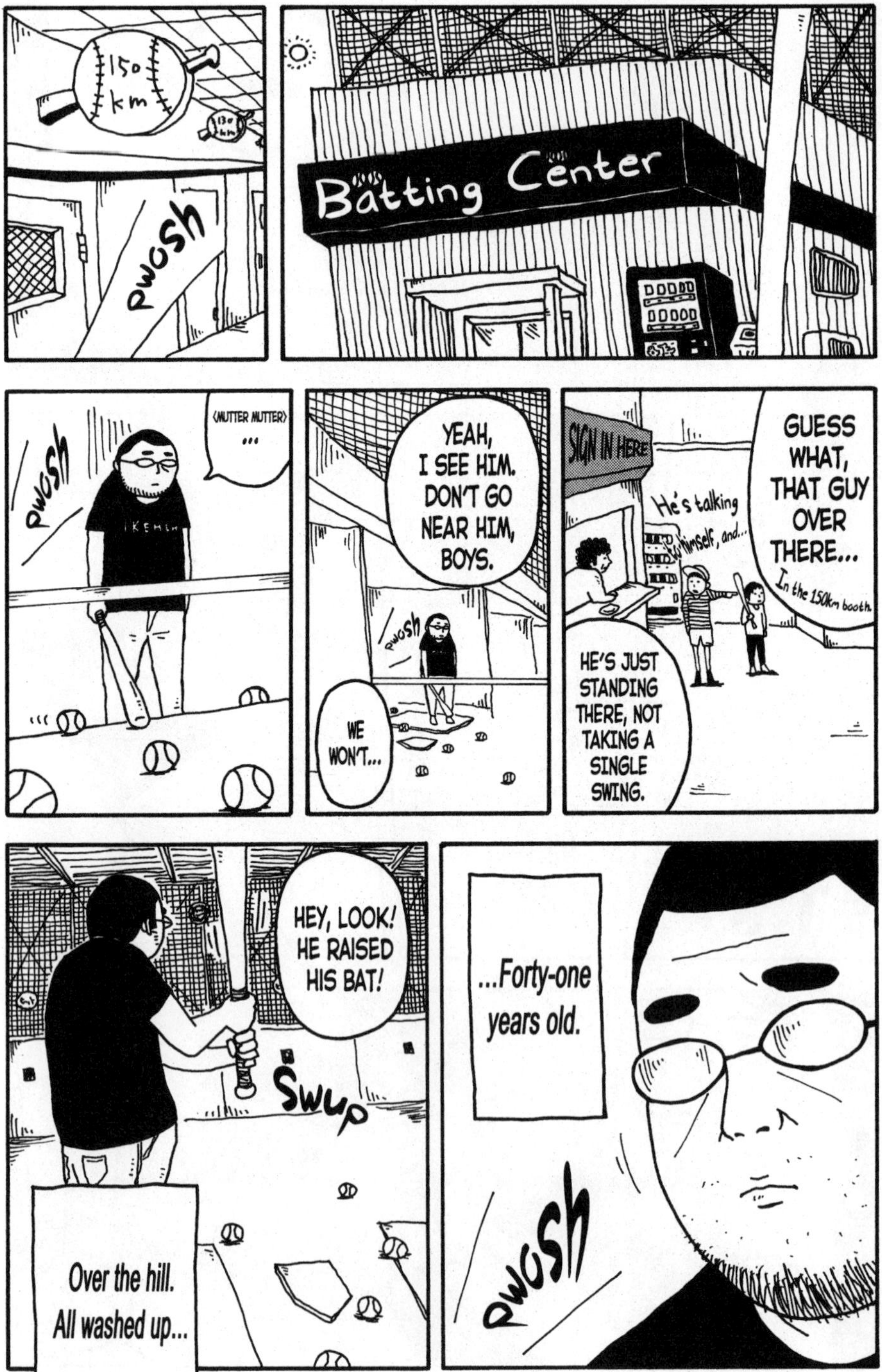
Batting Center
150 km
130 km
PWOSH
SIGN IN HERE
GUESS WHAT, THAT GUY OVER THERE...
In the 150km booth.
He's talking to himself, and...
HE'S JUST STANDING THERE, NOT TAKING A SINGLE SWING.
YEAH, I SEE HIM. DON'T GO NEAR HIM, BOYS.
PWOSH
WE WON'T...
PWOSH
<MUTTER MUTTER> ...
...Forty-one years old.
PWOSH
HEY, LOOK! HE RAISED HIS BAT!
SWUP
Over the hill. All washed up...

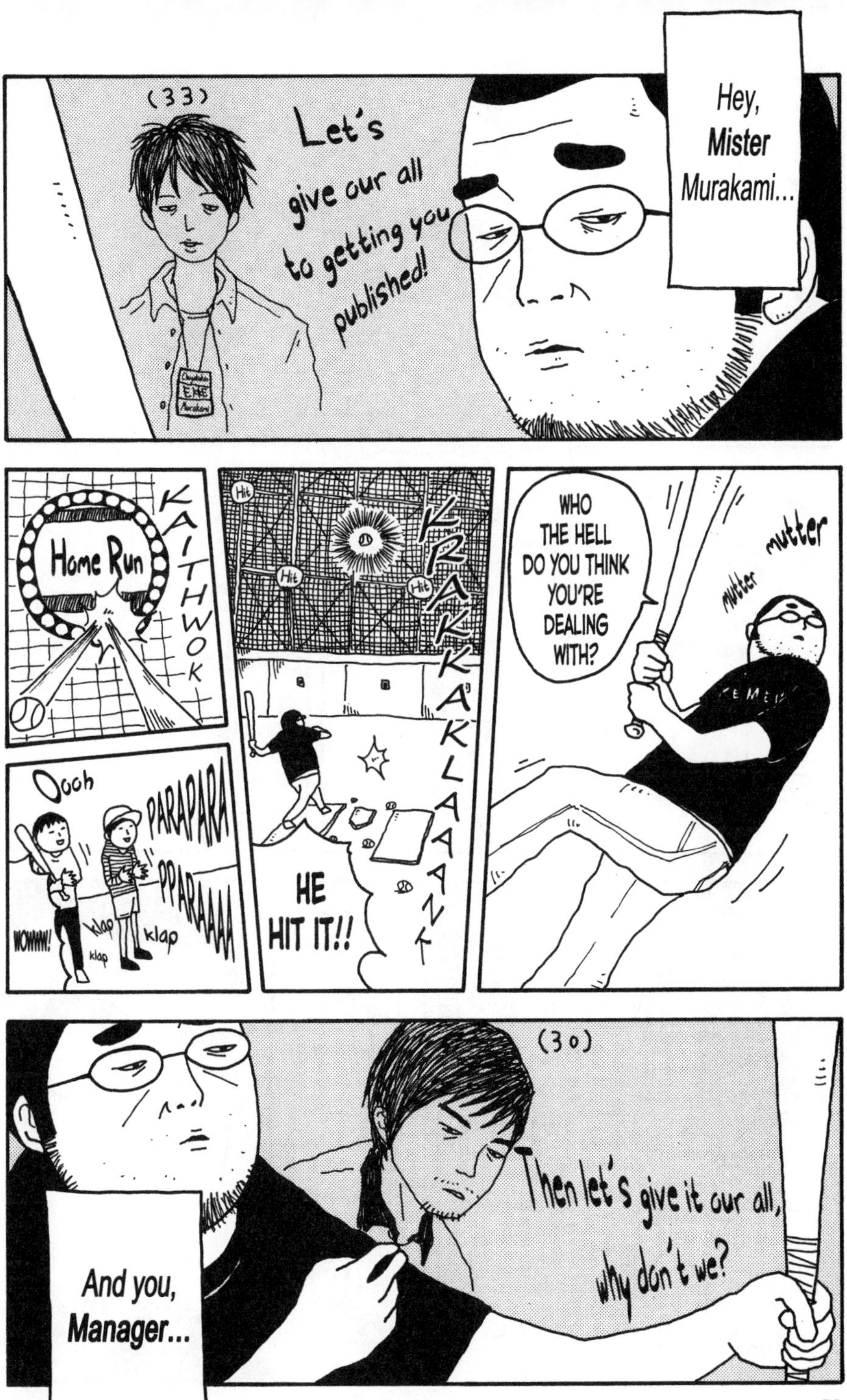

Hey, Mister Murakami...
(33)
Let's give our all to getting you published!
KAITHWOK
Home Run
Hit
Hit
Hit
KRAKKAKLAAAANK
WHO THE HELL DO YOU THINK YOU'RE DEALING WITH?
mutter mutter
Oooh
PARAPARA PPARAAAAA
WOWWW!
klap klap klap
HE HIT IT!!
(30)
Then let's give it our all, why don't we?
And you, Manager...

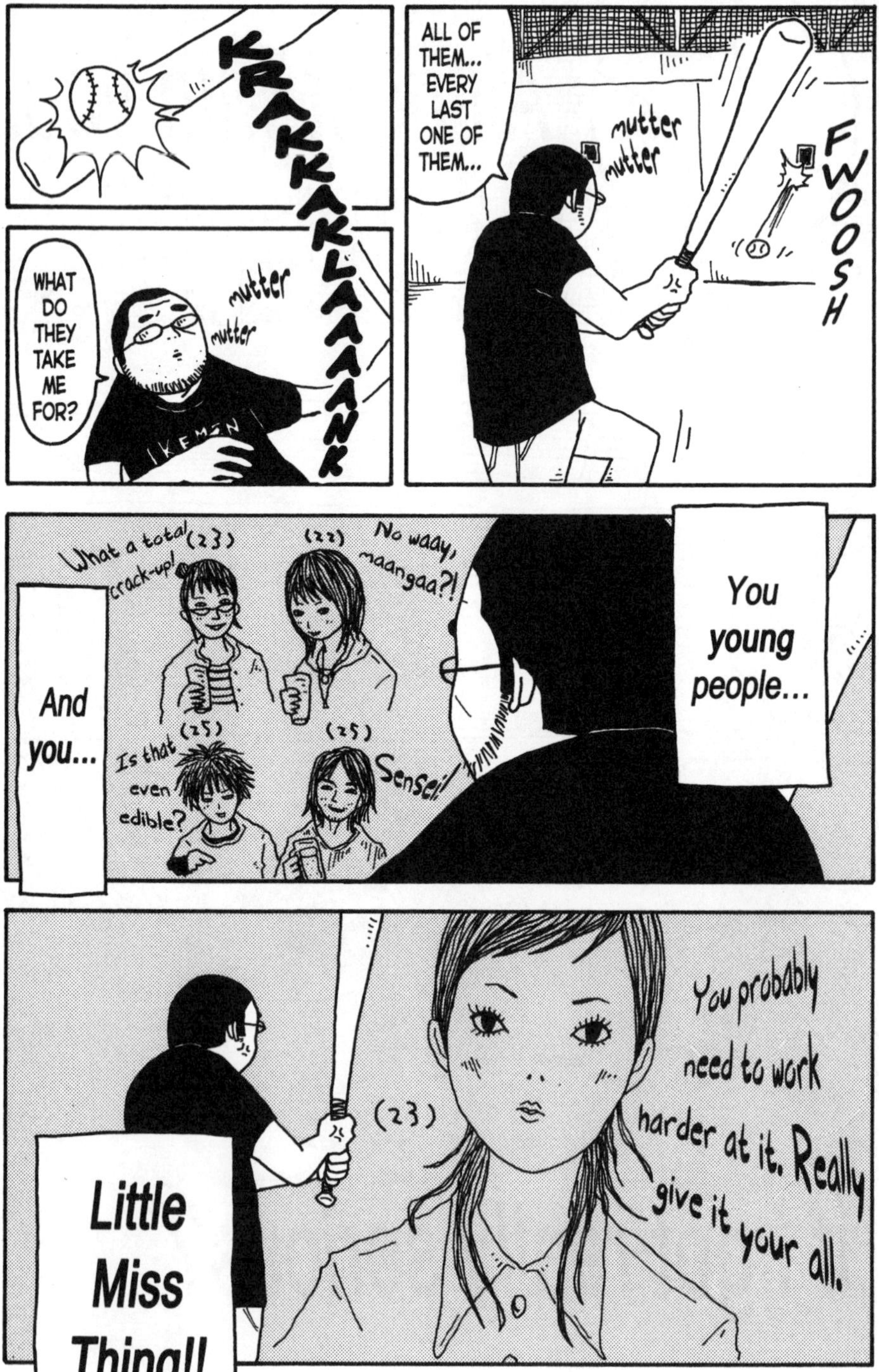
ALL OF THEM... EVERY LAST ONE OF THEM...
mutter mutter
FWOOSH
KRAKKAKLAAAAANK
WHAT DO THEY TAKE ME FOR?
mutter mutter
IKEMEN
You young people...
(22)
No waay, maangaa?!
(23)
What a total crack-up!
(25)
Sensei!
(25)
Is that even edible?
And you...
You probably need to work harder at it. Really give it your all.
(23)
Little Miss Thing!!

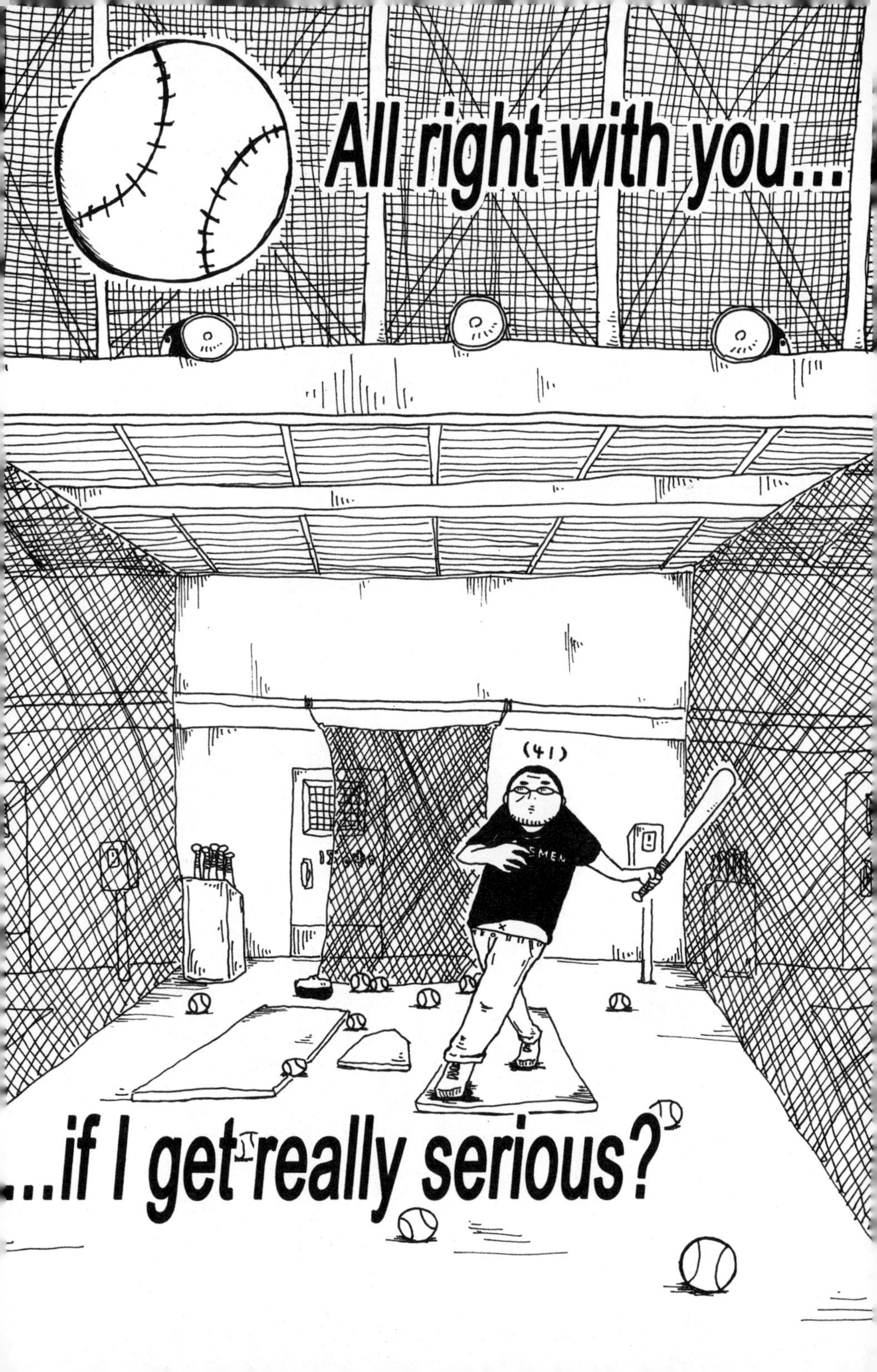
All right with you...
(41)
...if I get really serious?

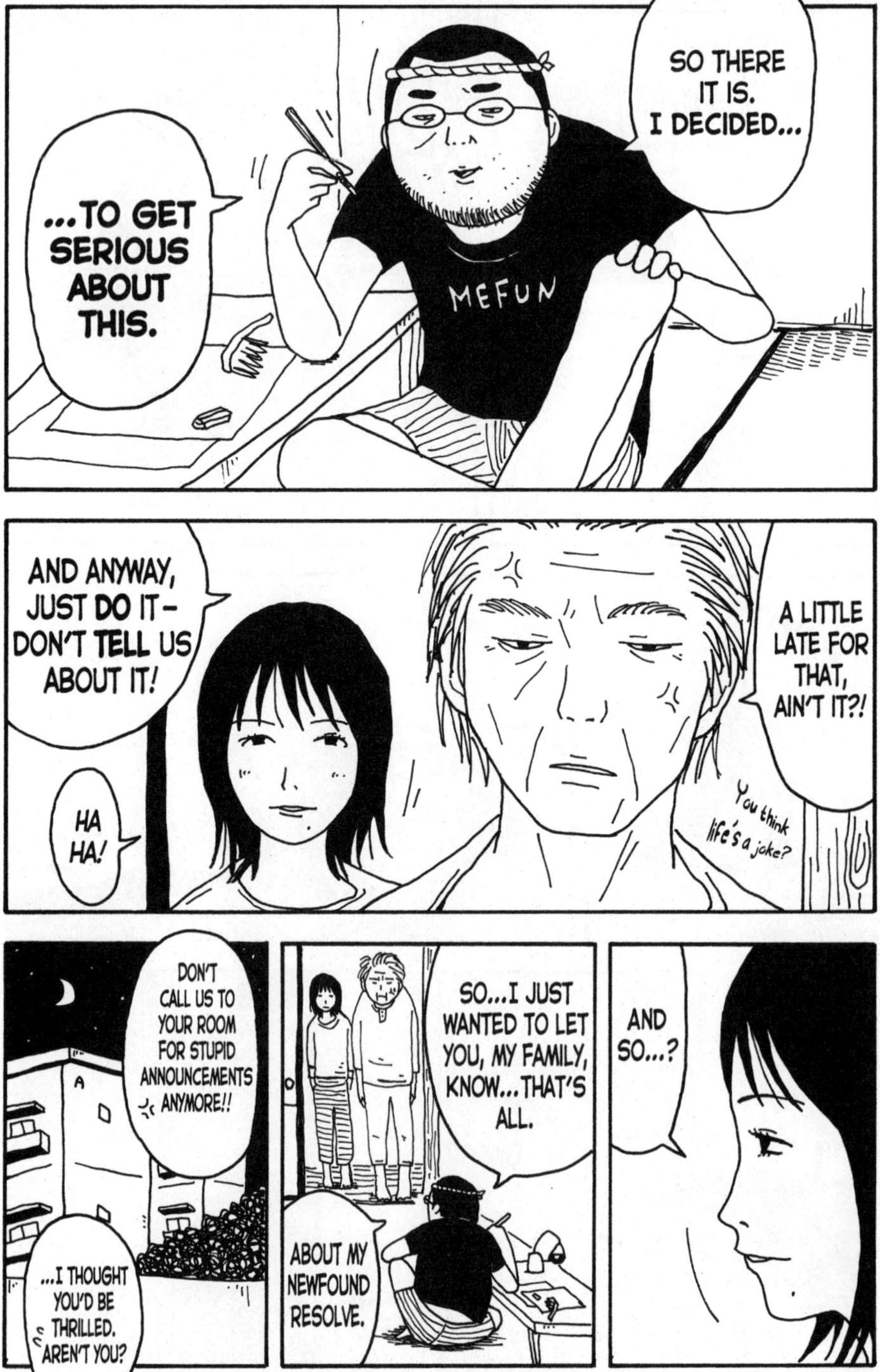
SO THERE IT IS. I DECIDED...
MEFUN
...TO GET SERIOUS ABOUT THIS.
A LITTLE LATE FOR THAT, AIN'T IT?!
You think life's a joke?
AND ANYWAY, JUST DO IT– DON'T TELL US ABOUT IT!
HA HA!
AND SO...?
SO...I JUST WANTED TO LET YOU, MY FAMILY, KNOW...THAT'S ALL.
ABOUT MY NEWFOUND RESOLVE.
DON'T CALL US TO YOUR ROOM FOR STUPID ANNOUNCEMENTS ANYMORE!!
...I THOUGHT YOU'D BE THRILLED. AREN'T YOU?

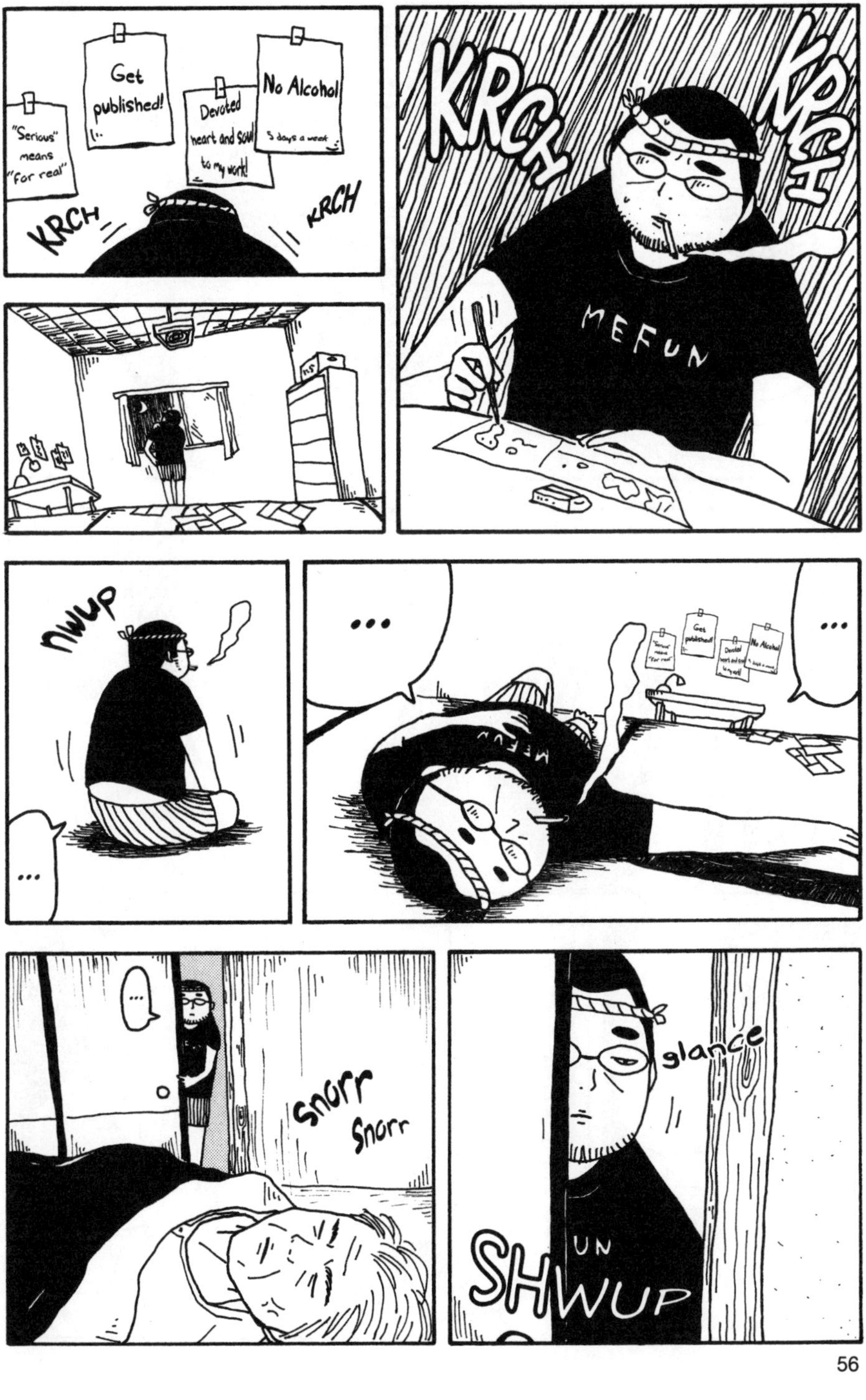
KRCH
KRCH
MEFUN
Get published!
"Serious" means "for real"
Devoted heart and soul to my work!
No Alcohol
5 days a week
KRCH
KRCH
...
...
nwup
...
glance
SHWUP
...
Snorr
Snorr

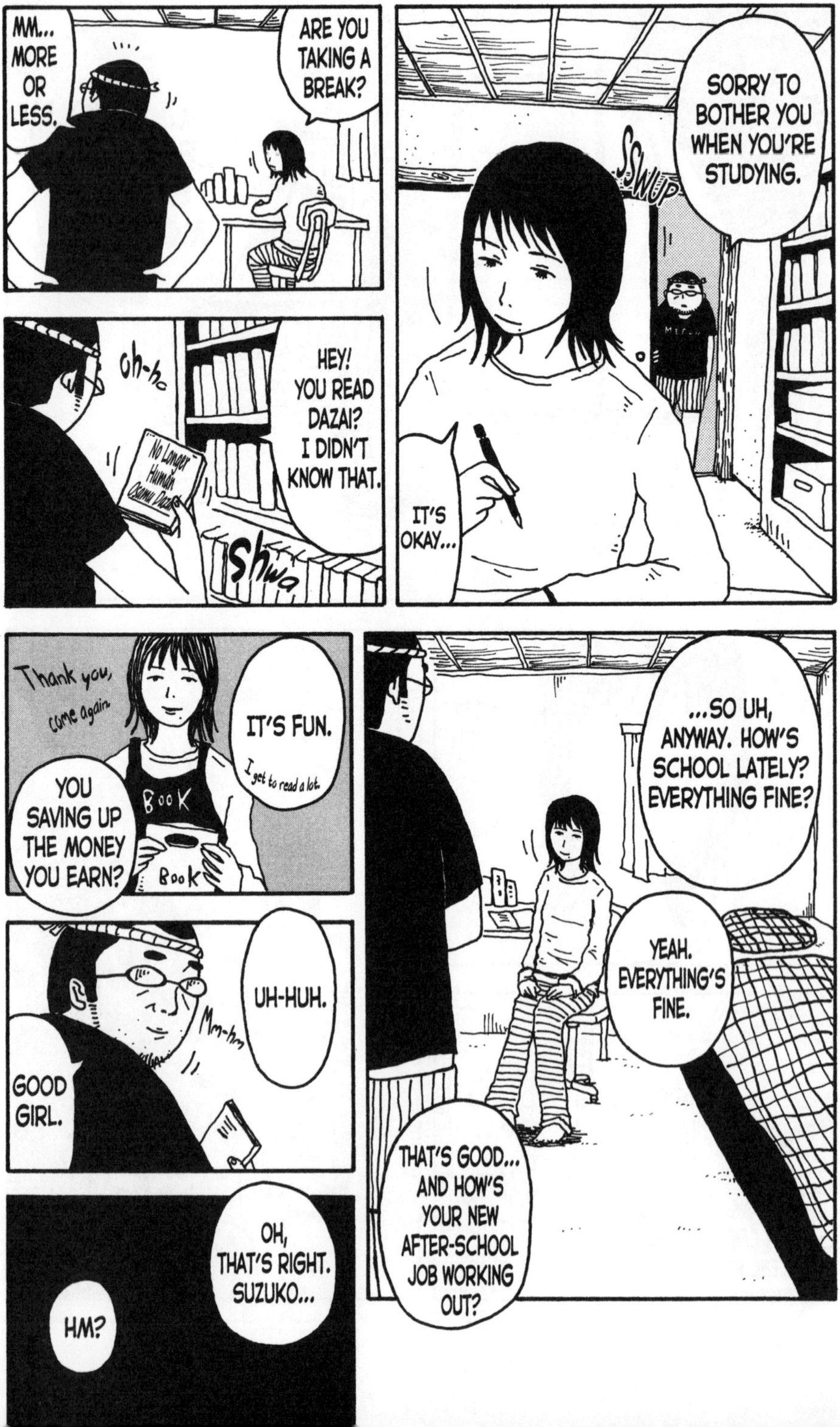
SORRY TO BOTHER YOU WHEN YOU'RE STUDYING.
SSWUP
IT'S OKAY...
ARE YOU TAKING A BREAK?
MM... MORE OR LESS.
HEY! YOU READ DAZAI? I DIDN'T KNOW THAT.
Oh-ho
No Longer Human Osamu Dazai
Shwa
...SO UH, ANYWAY. HOW'S SCHOOL LATELY? EVERYTHING FINE?
YEAH. EVERYTHING'S FINE.
THAT'S GOOD... AND HOW'S YOUR NEW AFTER-SCHOOL JOB WORKING OUT?
IT'S FUN.
I get to read a lot.
Thank you, come again.
BOOK
Book
YOU SAVING UP THE MONEY YOU EARN?
UH-HUH.
Mm-hm
GOOD GIRL.
OH, THAT'S RIGHT. SUZUKO...
HM?

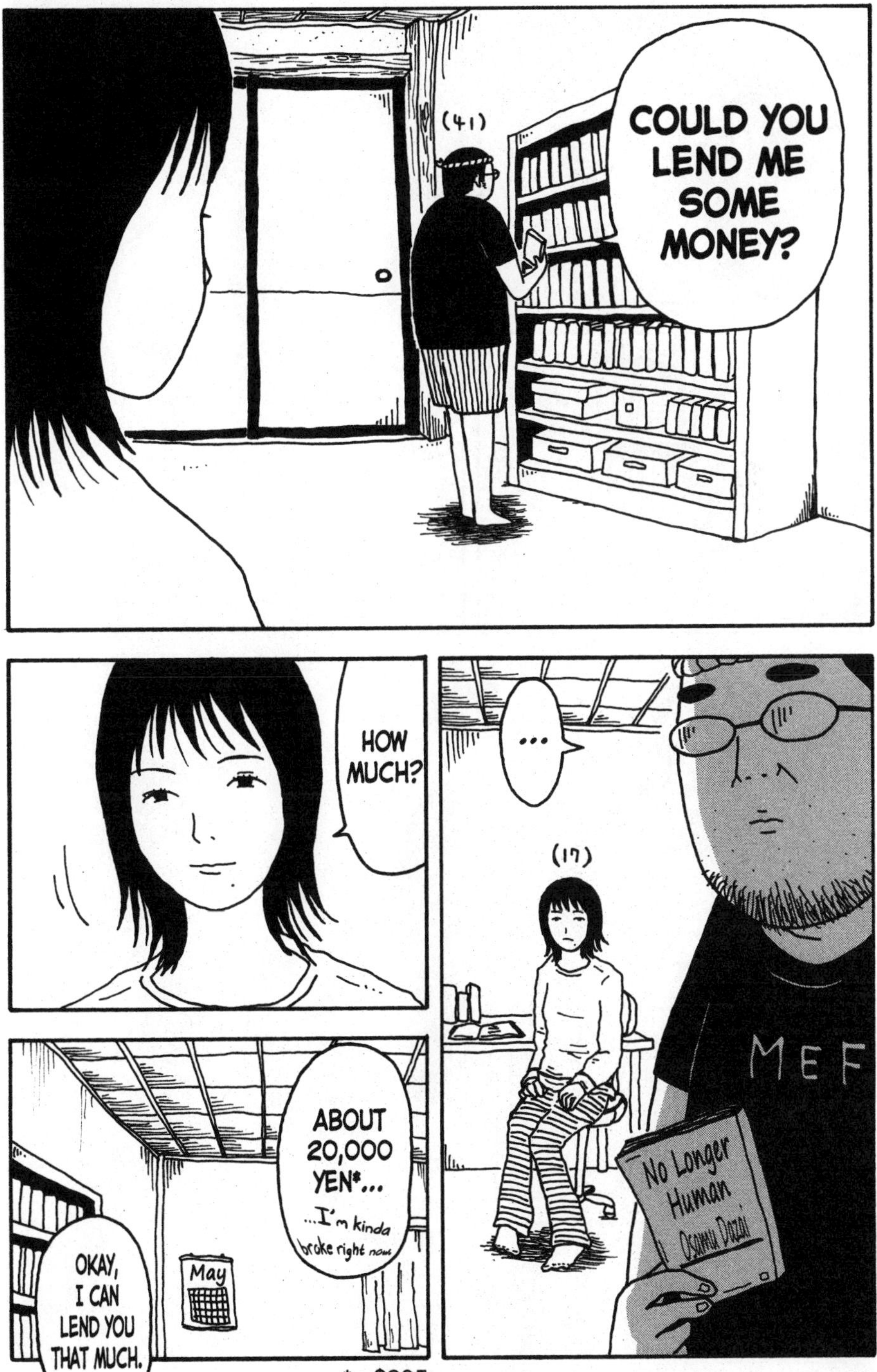
(41)
COULD YOU LEND ME SOME MONEY?
...
...
(17)
MEF
No Longer Human
Osamu Dazai
HOW MUCH?
ABOUT 20,000 YEN*...
...I'm kinda broke right now
May
OKAY, I CAN LEND YOU THAT MUCH.

* ~$205

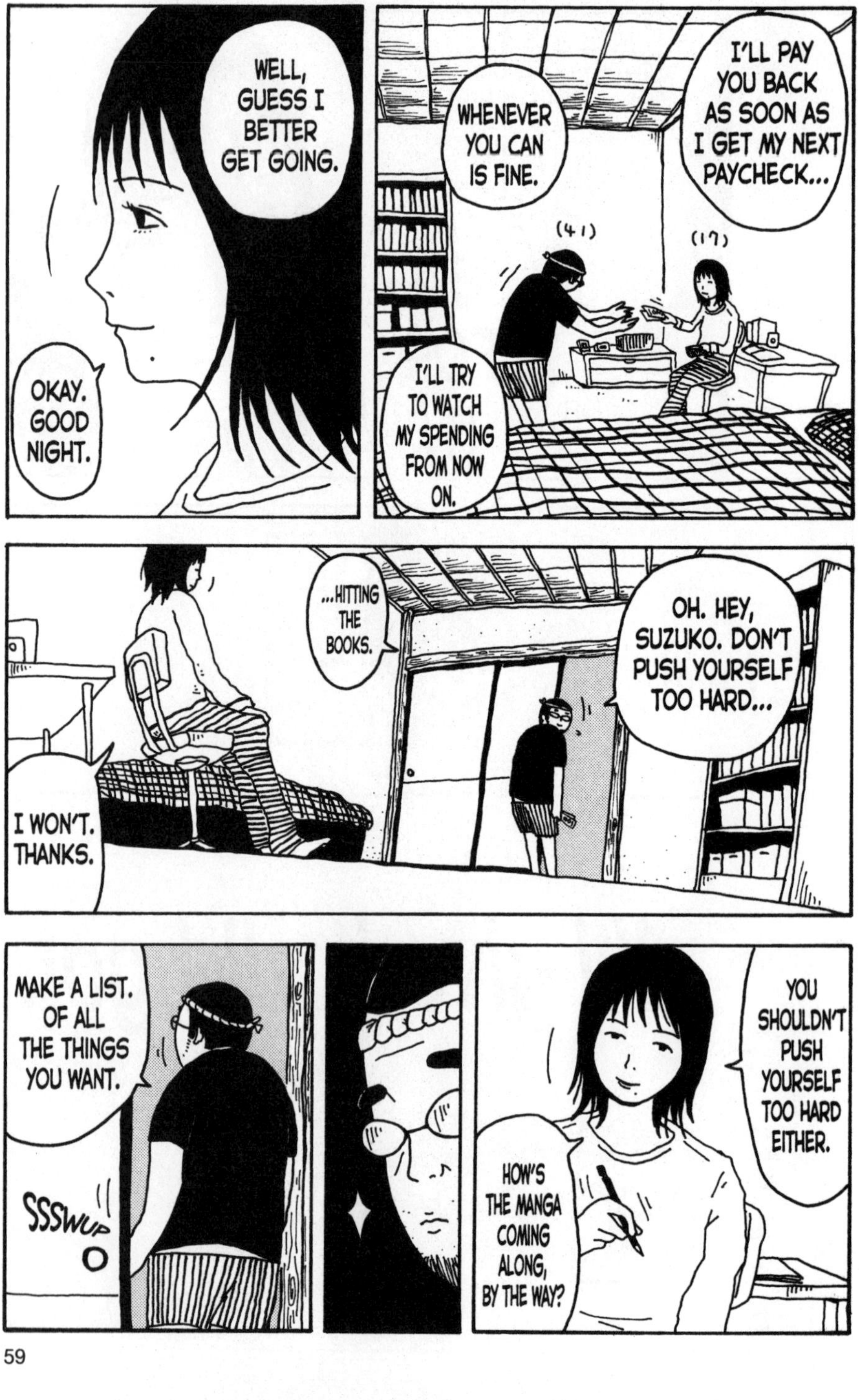
I'LL PAY YOU BACK AS SOON AS I GET MY NEXT PAYCHECK...
WHENEVER YOU CAN IS FINE.
(17)
(41)
I'LL TRY TO WATCH MY SPENDING FROM NOW ON.
WELL, GUESS I BETTER GET GOING.
OKAY. GOOD NIGHT.
OH. HEY, SUZUKO. DON'T PUSH YOURSELF TOO HARD...
...HITTING THE BOOKS.
I WON'T. THANKS.
YOU SHOULDN'T PUSH YOURSELF TOO HARD EITHER.
HOW'S THE MANGA COMING ALONG, BY THE WAY?
MAKE A LIST. OF ALL THE THINGS YOU WANT.
SSSWUP

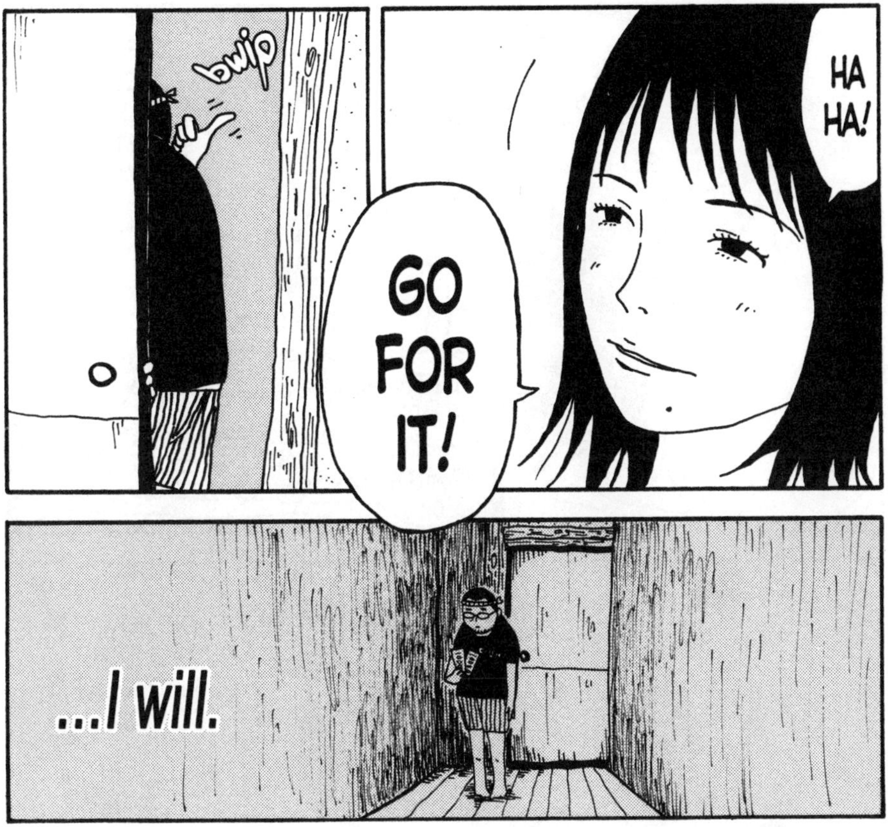
HA HA!
GO FOR IT!
bwip
...I will.

I'll give it all I got.

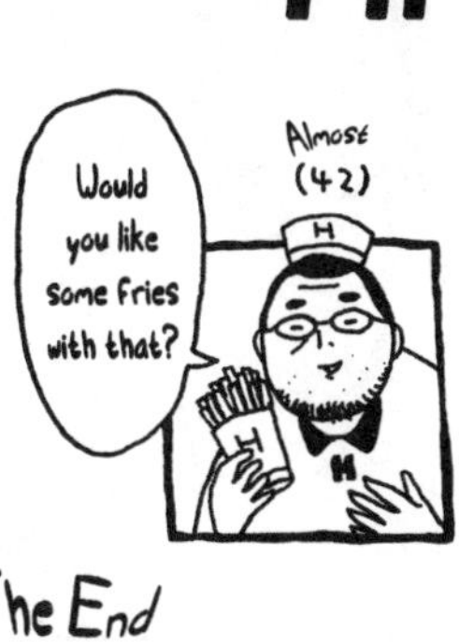
Almost (42)
Would you like some fries with that?

The End

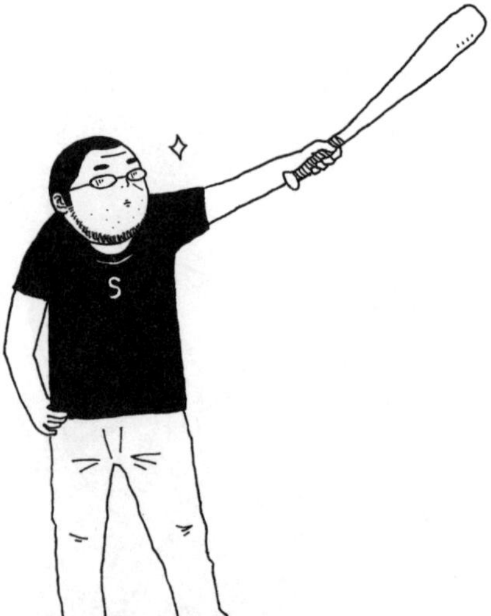
S

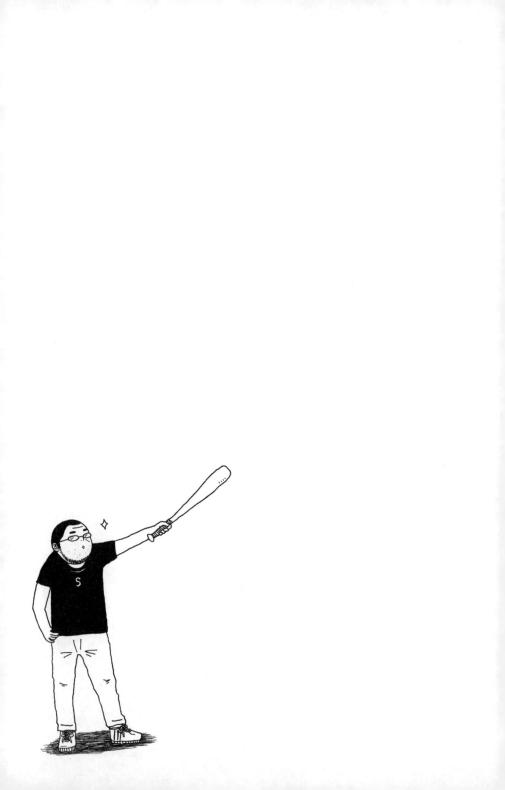

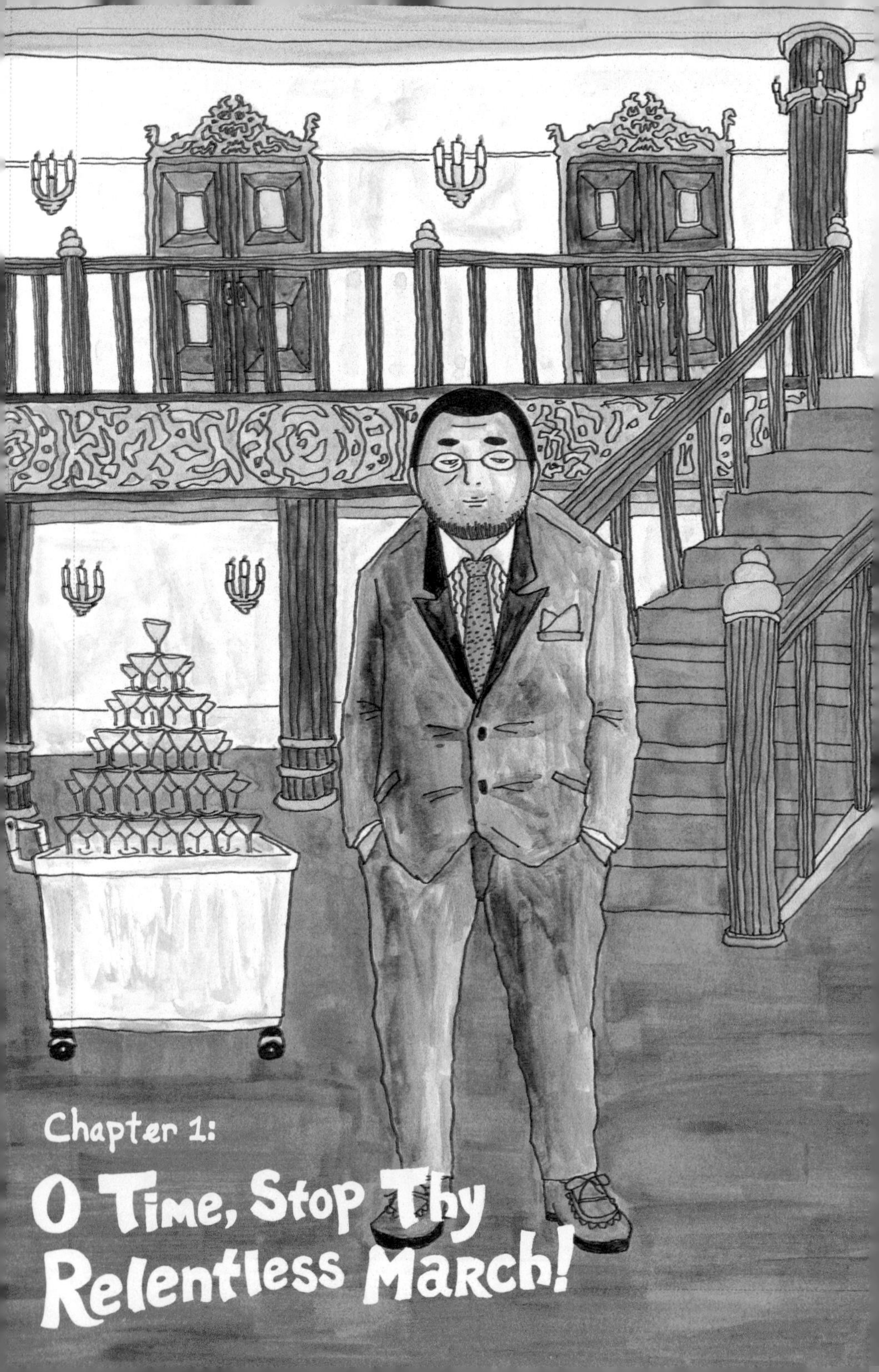
Chapter 1:
O Time, Stop Thy Relentless March!

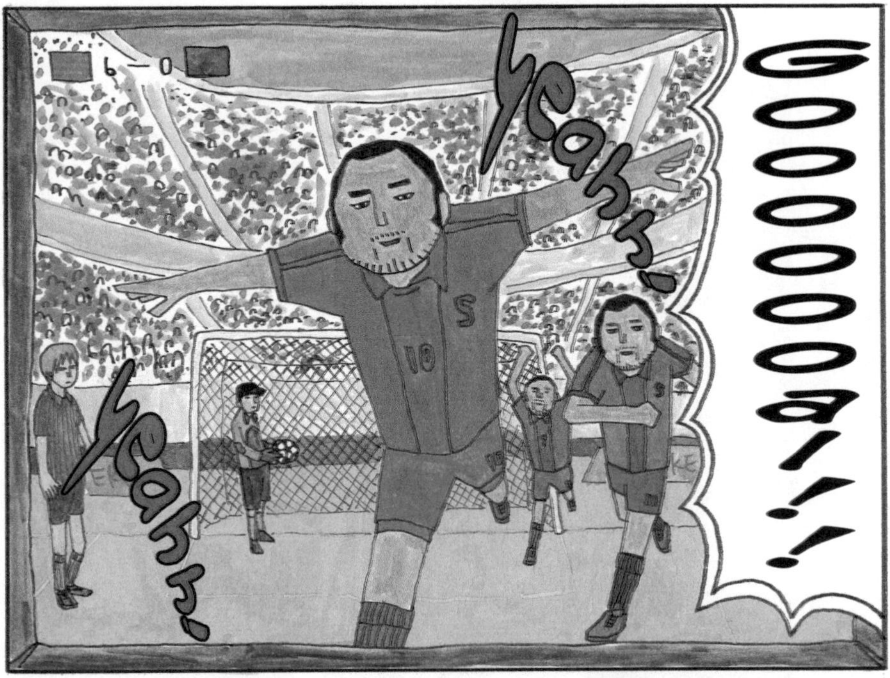
6-0
Gooooooal!!!
Yeahh!
Yeahh!

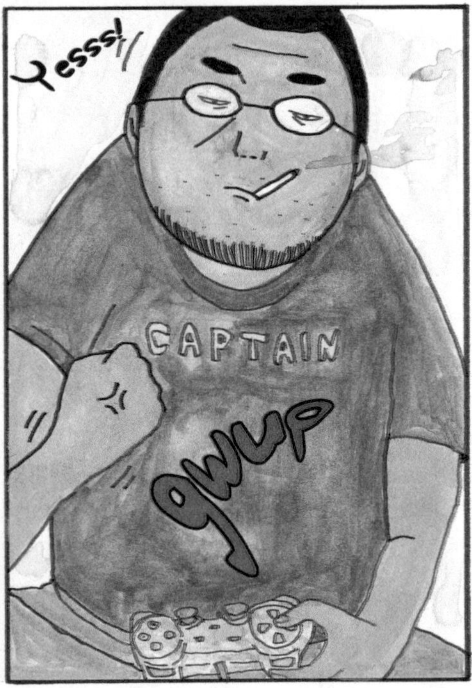
Yesss!
CAPTAIN
gwup

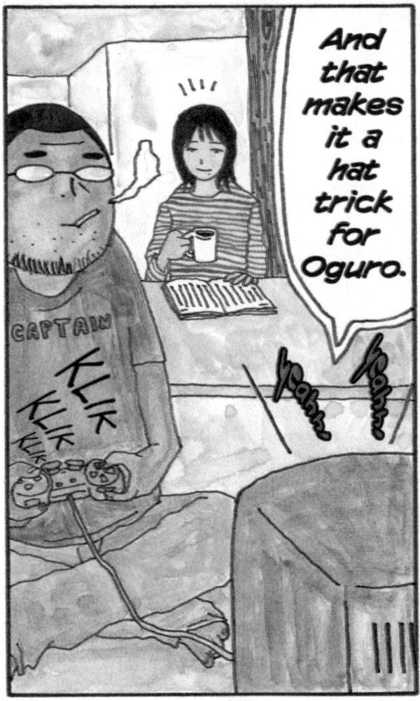
And that makes it a hat trick for Oguro.
Yeahh!
Yeahh!
CAPTAIN
KLIK
KLIK
KLIK

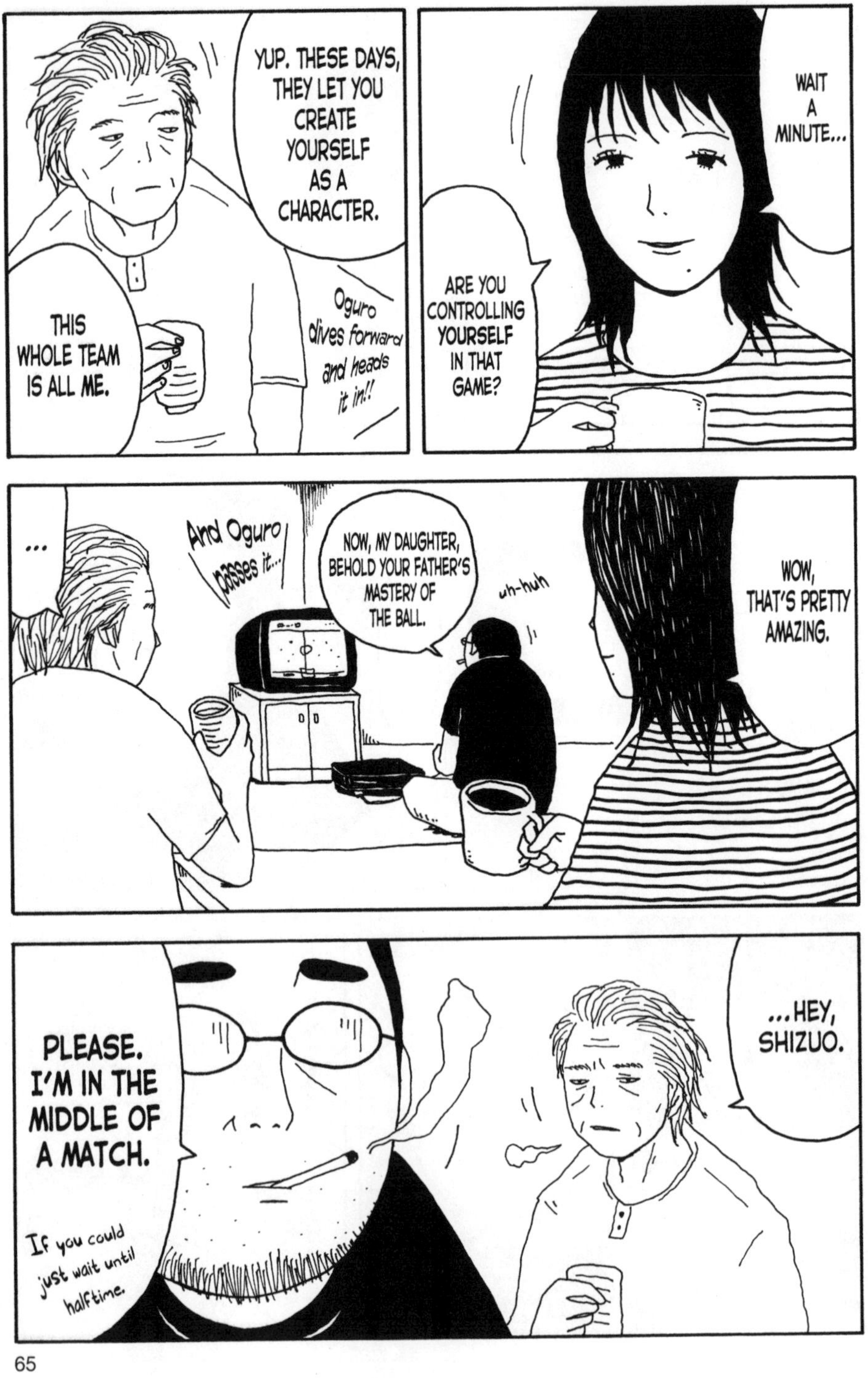
WAIT A MINUTE...
ARE YOU CONTROLLING YOURSELF IN THAT GAME?
YUP. THESE DAYS, THEY LET YOU CREATE YOURSELF AS A CHARACTER.
Oguro dives forward and heads it in!!
THIS WHOLE TEAM IS ALL ME.
WOW, THAT'S PRETTY AMAZING.
uh-huh
NOW, MY DAUGHTER, BEHOLD YOUR FATHER'S MASTERY OF THE BALL.
And Oguro passes it...
...
...HEY, SHIZUO.
PLEASE. I'M IN THE MIDDLE OF A MATCH.
If you could just wait until halftime.

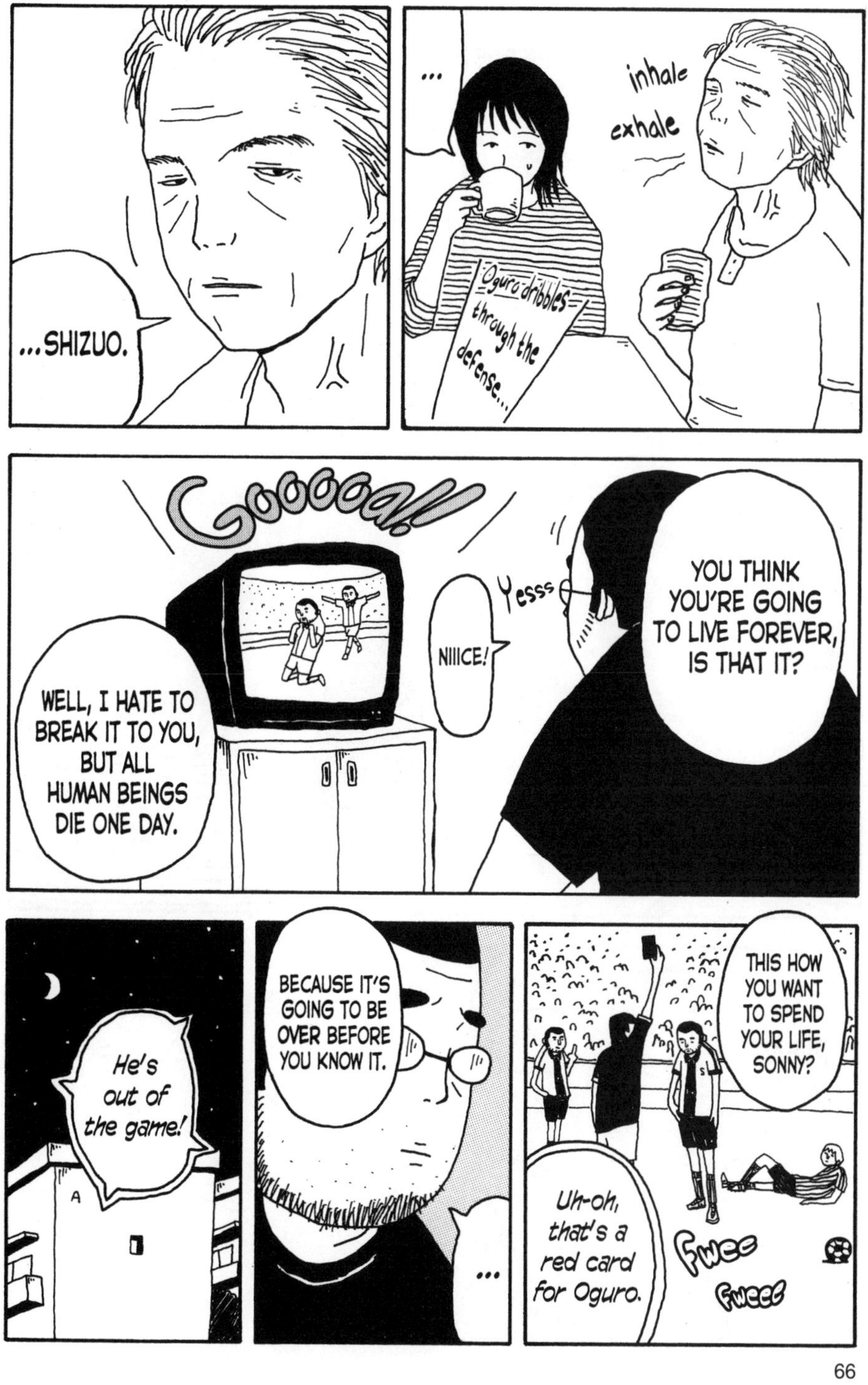
...
inhale
exhale
Oguro dribbles through the defense...
...SHIZUO.
YOU THINK YOU'RE GOING TO LIVE FOREVER, IS THAT IT?
Yesss
NIIICE!
Gooooal!!
WELL, I HATE TO BREAK IT TO YOU, BUT ALL HUMAN BEINGS DIE ONE DAY.
THIS HOW YOU WANT TO SPEND YOUR LIFE, SONNY?
Uh-oh, that's a red card for Oguro.
Fwee
Fweee
BECAUSE IT'S GOING TO BE OVER BEFORE YOU KNOW IT.
...
He's out of the game!

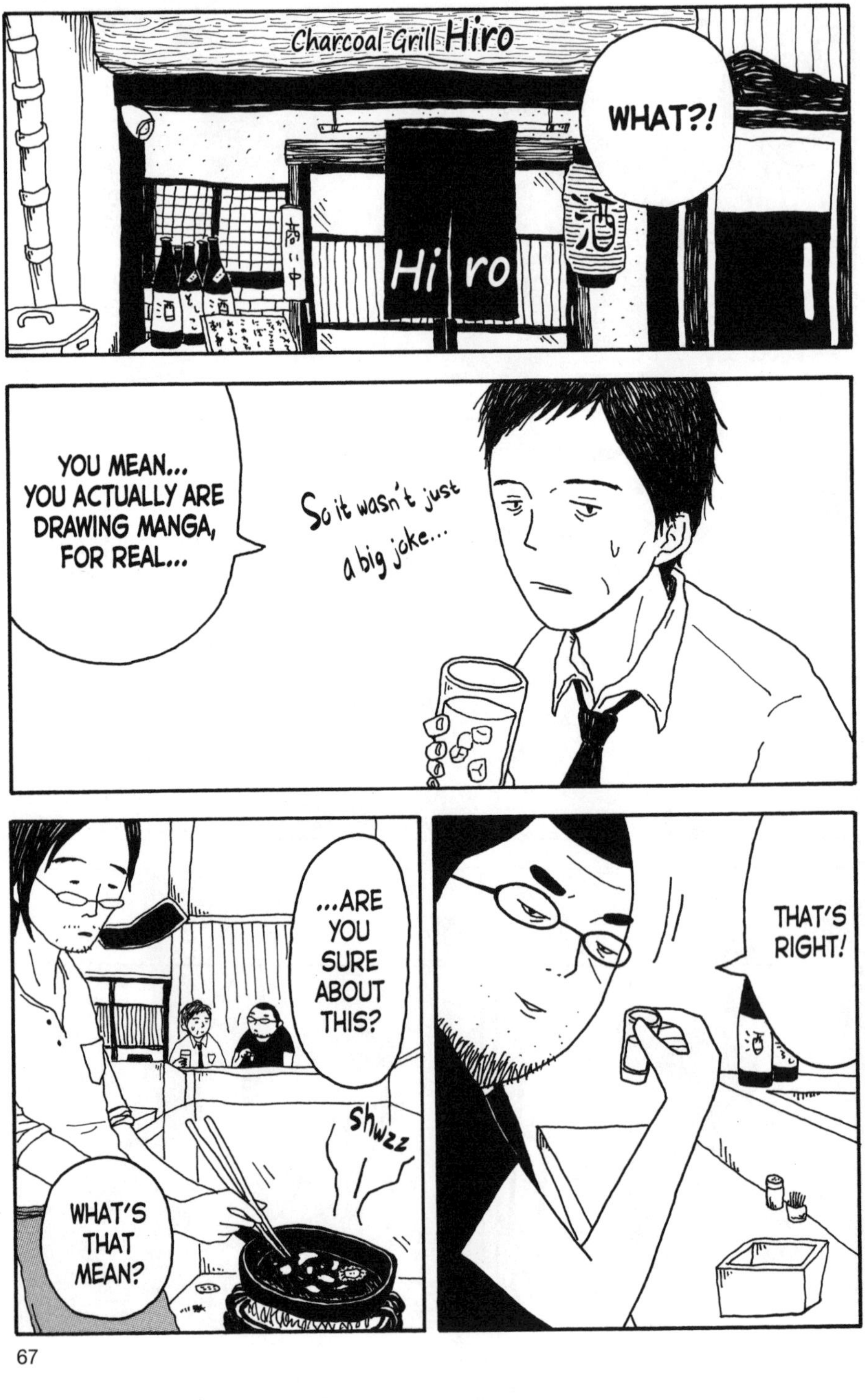
Charcoal Grill Hiro
WHAT?!
商い中
Hi ro
酒
YOU MEAN... YOU ACTUALLY ARE DRAWING MANGA, FOR REAL...
So it wasn't just a big joke...
THAT'S RIGHT!
...ARE YOU SURE ABOUT THIS?
Shwzz
WHAT'S THAT MEAN?

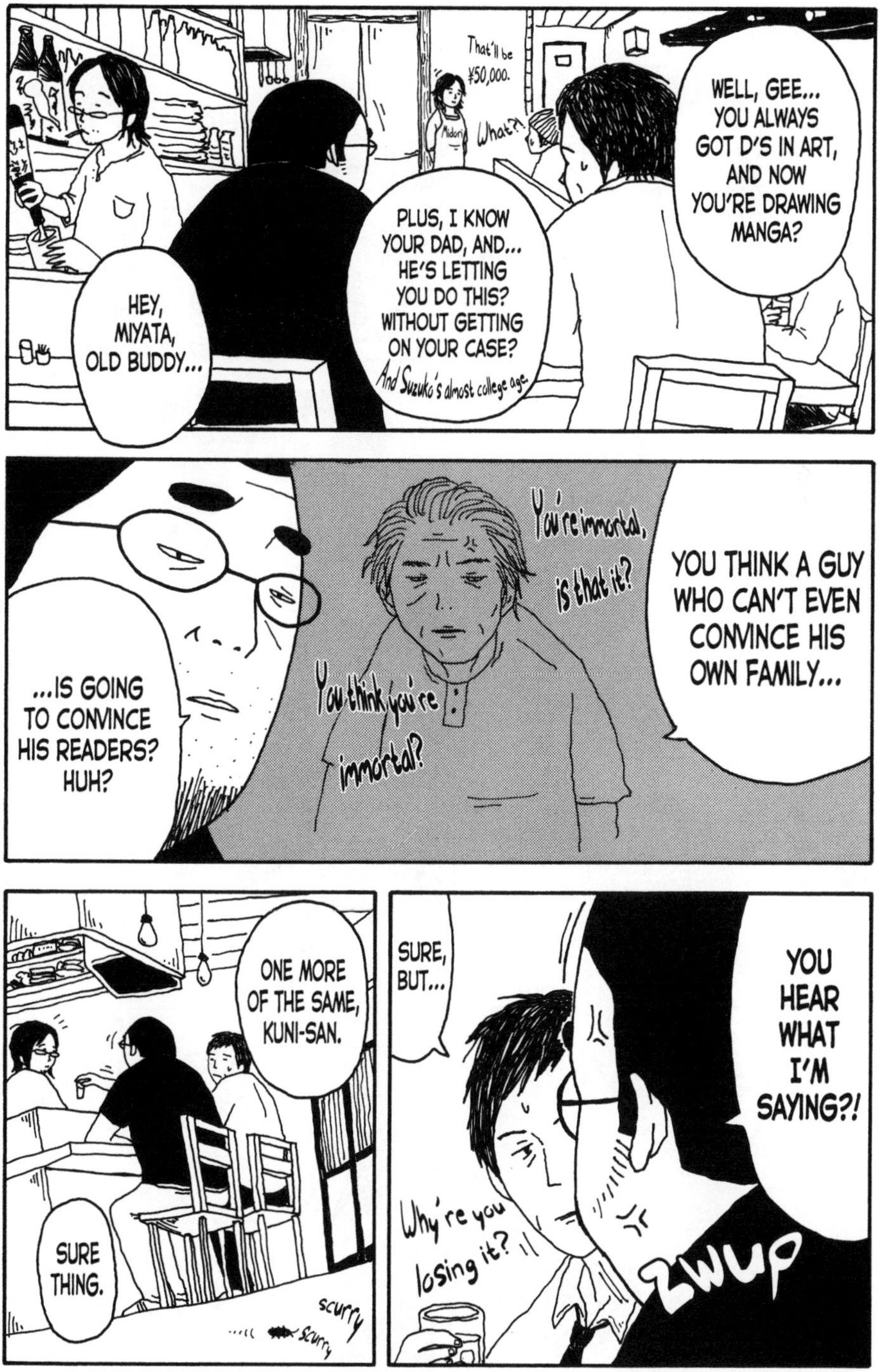
WELL, GEE... YOU ALWAYS GOT D'S IN ART, AND NOW YOU'RE DRAWING MANGA?
That'll be ¥50,000.
What?!
PLUS, I KNOW YOUR DAD, AND... HE'S LETTING YOU DO THIS? WITHOUT GETTING ON YOUR CASE?
And Suzuko's almost college age.
HEY, MIYATA, OLD BUDDY...
YOU THINK A GUY WHO CAN'T EVEN CONVINCE HIS OWN FAMILY...
You're immortal, is that it?
You think you're immortal?
...IS GOING TO CONVINCE HIS READERS? HUH?
YOU HEAR WHAT I'M SAYING?!
SURE, BUT...
ZWUP
Why're you losing it?
ONE MORE OF THE SAME, KUNI-SAN.
SURE THING.
scurry
scurry

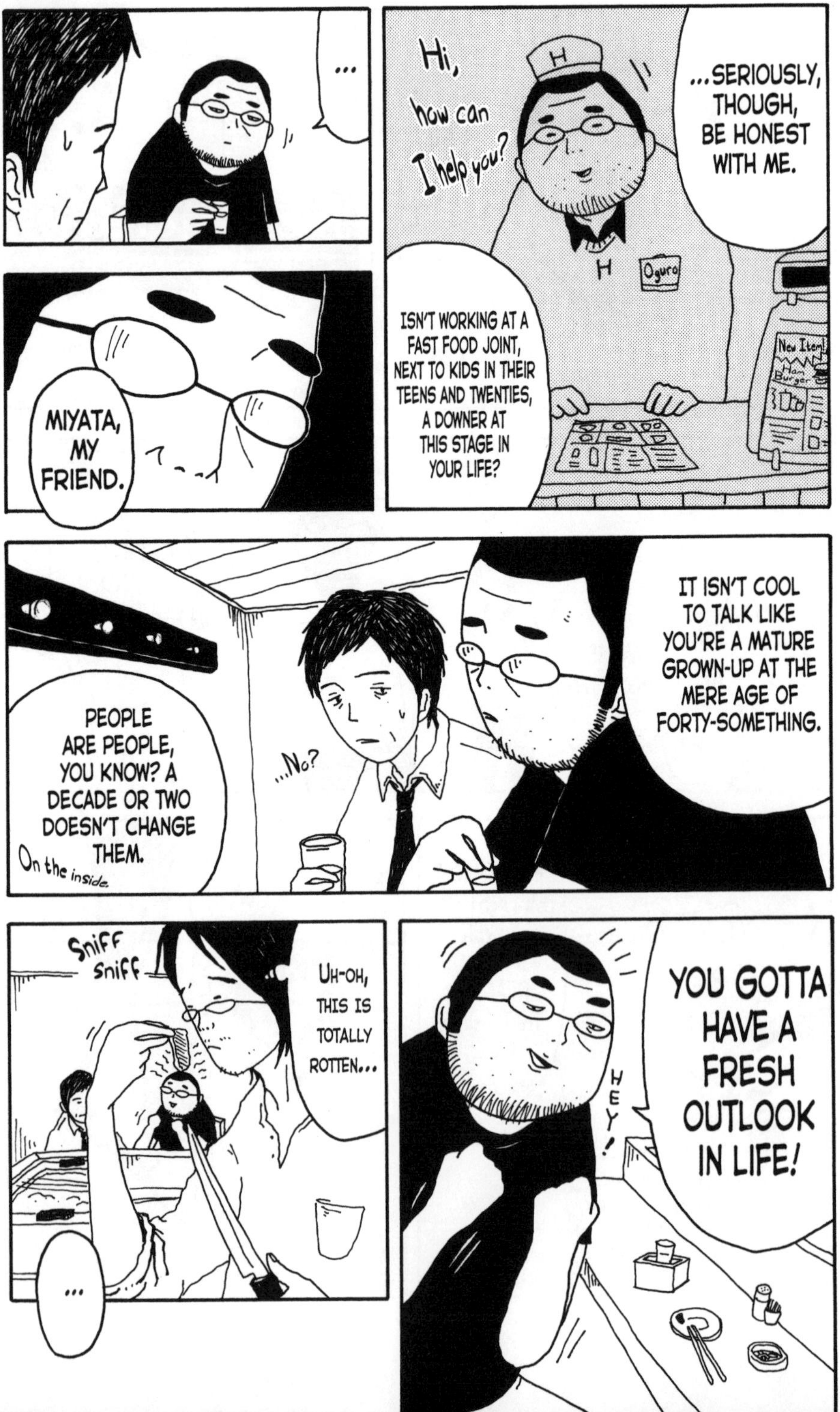
...SERIOUSLY, THOUGH, BE HONEST WITH ME.
Hi, how can I help you?
H
Oguro
New Item! Ham Burger
ISN'T WORKING AT A FAST FOOD JOINT, NEXT TO KIDS IN THEIR TEENS AND TWENTIES, A DOWNER AT THIS STAGE IN YOUR LIFE?
...
MIYATA, MY FRIEND.
IT ISN'T COOL TO TALK LIKE YOU'RE A MATURE GROWN-UP AT THE MERE AGE OF FORTY-SOMETHING.
...No?
PEOPLE ARE PEOPLE, YOU KNOW? A DECADE OR TWO DOESN'T CHANGE THEM.
On the inside.
YOU GOTTA HAVE A FRESH OUTLOOK IN LIFE!
HEY!
UH-OH, THIS IS TOTALLY ROTTEN...
Sniff sniff
...

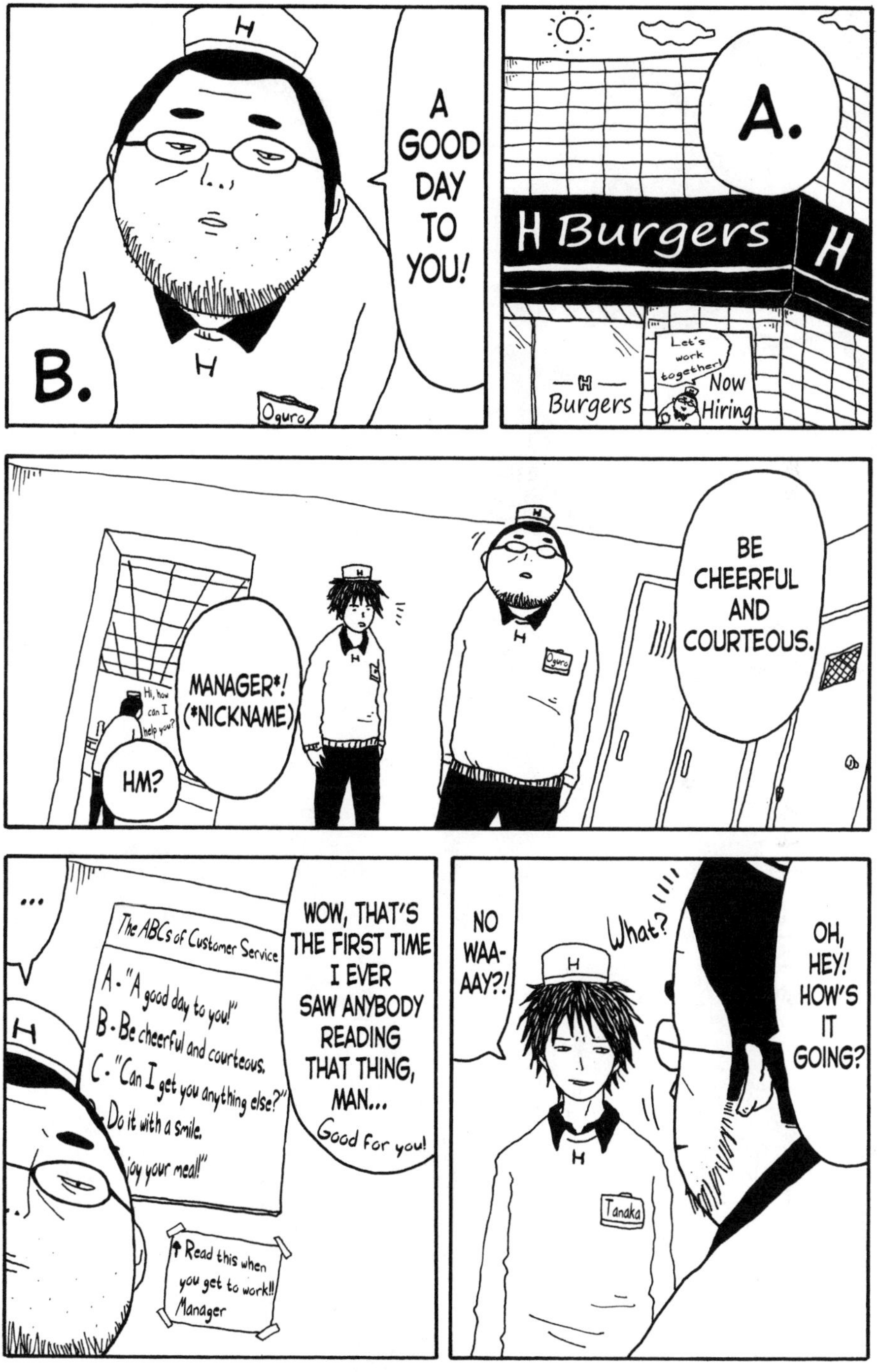
A.
H Burgers
H
Let's work together!
Now Hiring
— H — Burgers
A GOOD DAY TO YOU!
B.
H
Oguro
BE CHEERFUL AND COURTEOUS.
Oguro
MANAGER*! (*NICKNAME)
Hi, how can I help you?
HM?
OH, HEY! HOW'S IT GOING?
What?
NO WAA-AAY?!
Tanaka
WOW, THAT'S THE FIRST TIME I EVER SAW ANYBODY READING THAT THING, MAN...
Good for you!
...
The ABCs of Customer Service
A - "A good day to you!"
B - Be cheerful and courteous.
C - "Can I get you anything else?"
Do it with a smile.
joy your meal!"
↑ Read this when you get to work!! Manager

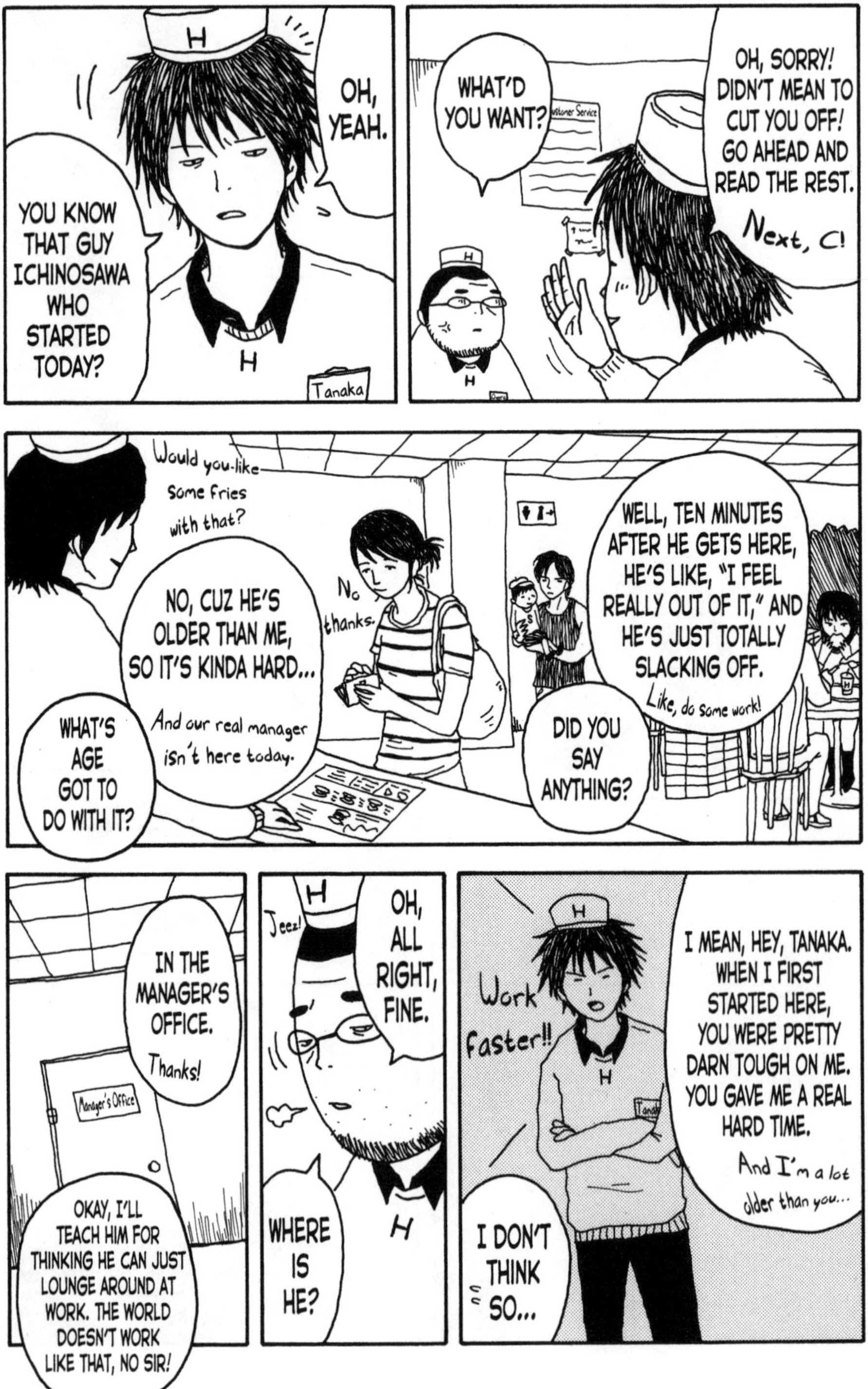
OH, SORRY! DIDN'T MEAN TO CUT YOU OFF! GO AHEAD AND READ THE REST.
Next, C!
WHAT'D YOU WANT?
ustomer Service
YOU KNOW THAT GUY ICHINOSAWA WHO STARTED TODAY?
OH, YEAH.
Tanaka
WELL, TEN MINUTES AFTER HE GETS HERE, HE'S LIKE, "I FEEL REALLY OUT OF IT," AND HE'S JUST TOTALLY SLACKING OFF.
Like, do some work!
DID YOU SAY ANYTHING?
Would you like some fries with that?
No thanks.
NO, CUZ HE'S OLDER THAN ME, SO IT'S KINDA HARD...
And our real manager isn't here today.
WHAT'S AGE GOT TO DO WITH IT?
I MEAN, HEY, TANAKA. WHEN I FIRST STARTED HERE, YOU WERE PRETTY DARN TOUGH ON ME. YOU GAVE ME A REAL HARD TIME.
And I'm a lot older than you...
Work faster!!
I DON'T THINK SO...
OH, ALL RIGHT, FINE.
Jeez!
WHERE IS HE?
IN THE MANAGER'S OFFICE.
Thanks!
Manager's Office
OKAY, I'LL TEACH HIM FOR THINKING HE CAN JUST LOUNGE AROUND AT WORK. THE WORLD DOESN'T WORK LIKE THAT, NO SIR!

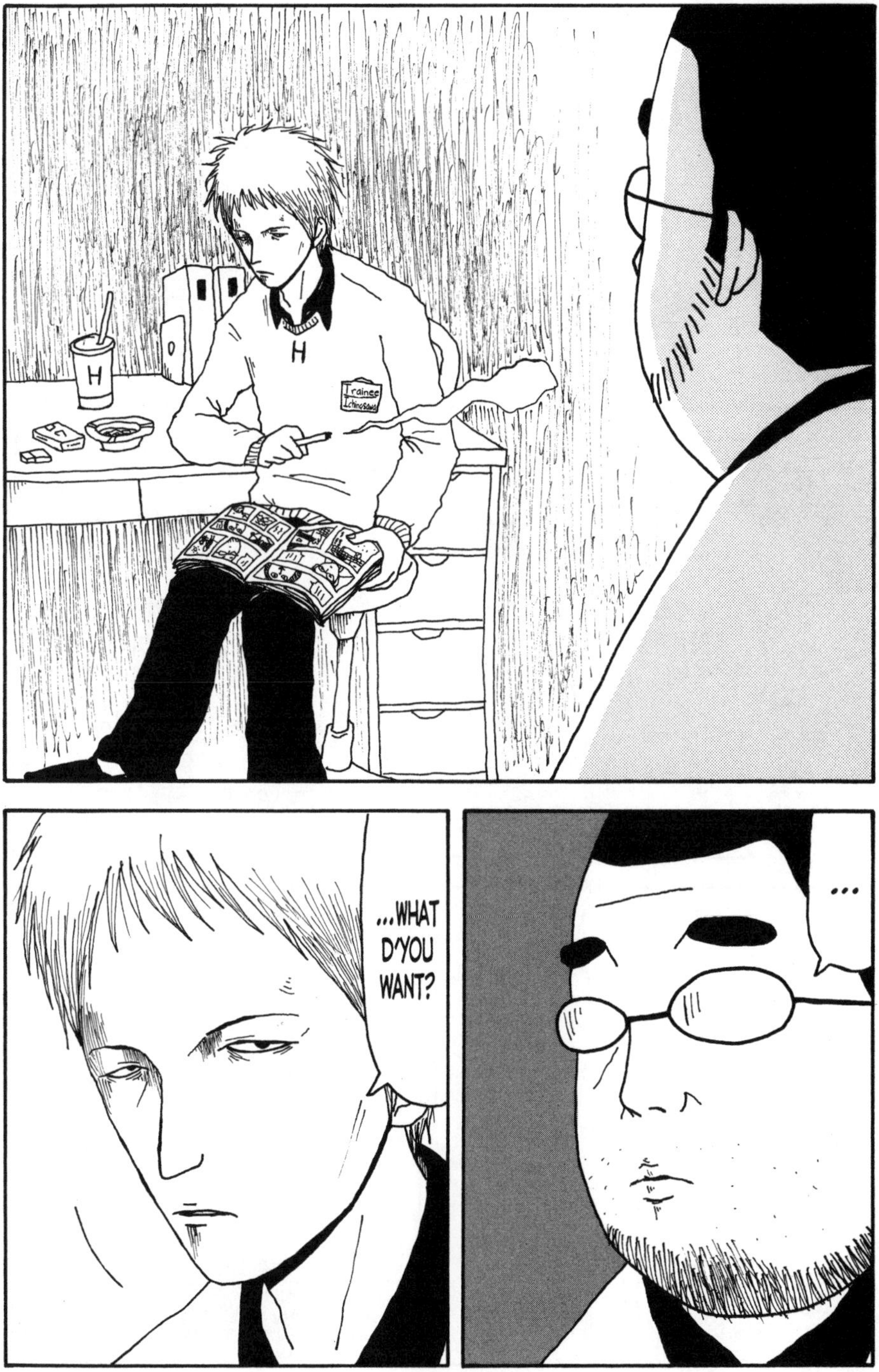
Trainee Ichinosawa
...
...WHAT D'YOU WANT?

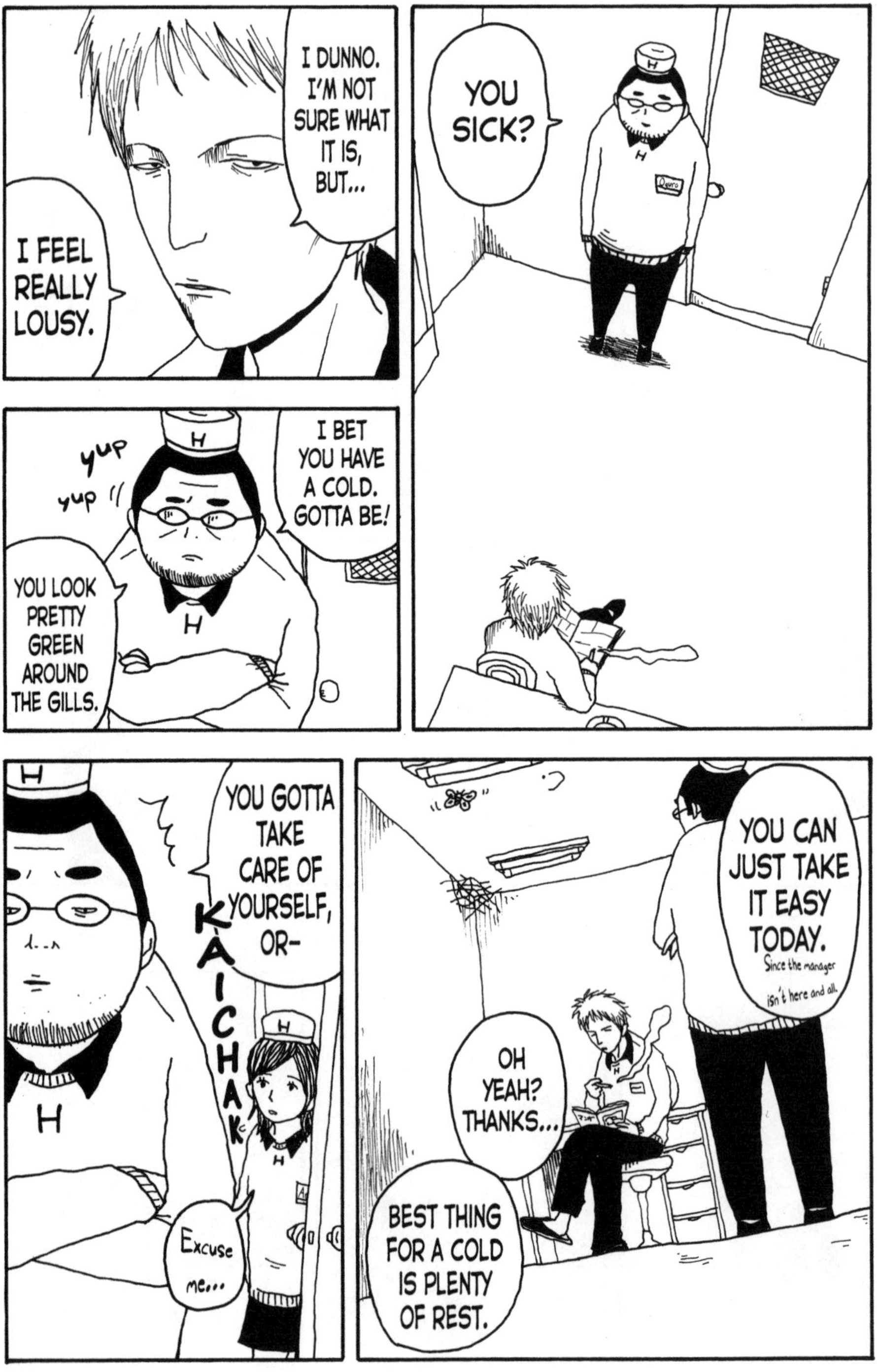
YOU SICK?
I DUNNO. I'M NOT SURE WHAT IT IS, BUT...
I FEEL REALLY LOUSY.
I BET YOU HAVE A COLD. GOTTA BE!
yup yup
YOU LOOK PRETTY GREEN AROUND THE GILLS.
YOU CAN JUST TAKE IT EASY TODAY.
Since the manager isn't here and all.
OH YEAH? THANKS...
BEST THING FOR A COLD IS PLENTY OF REST.
YOU GOTTA TAKE CARE OF YOURSELF, OR-
KAICHAK
Excuse me...

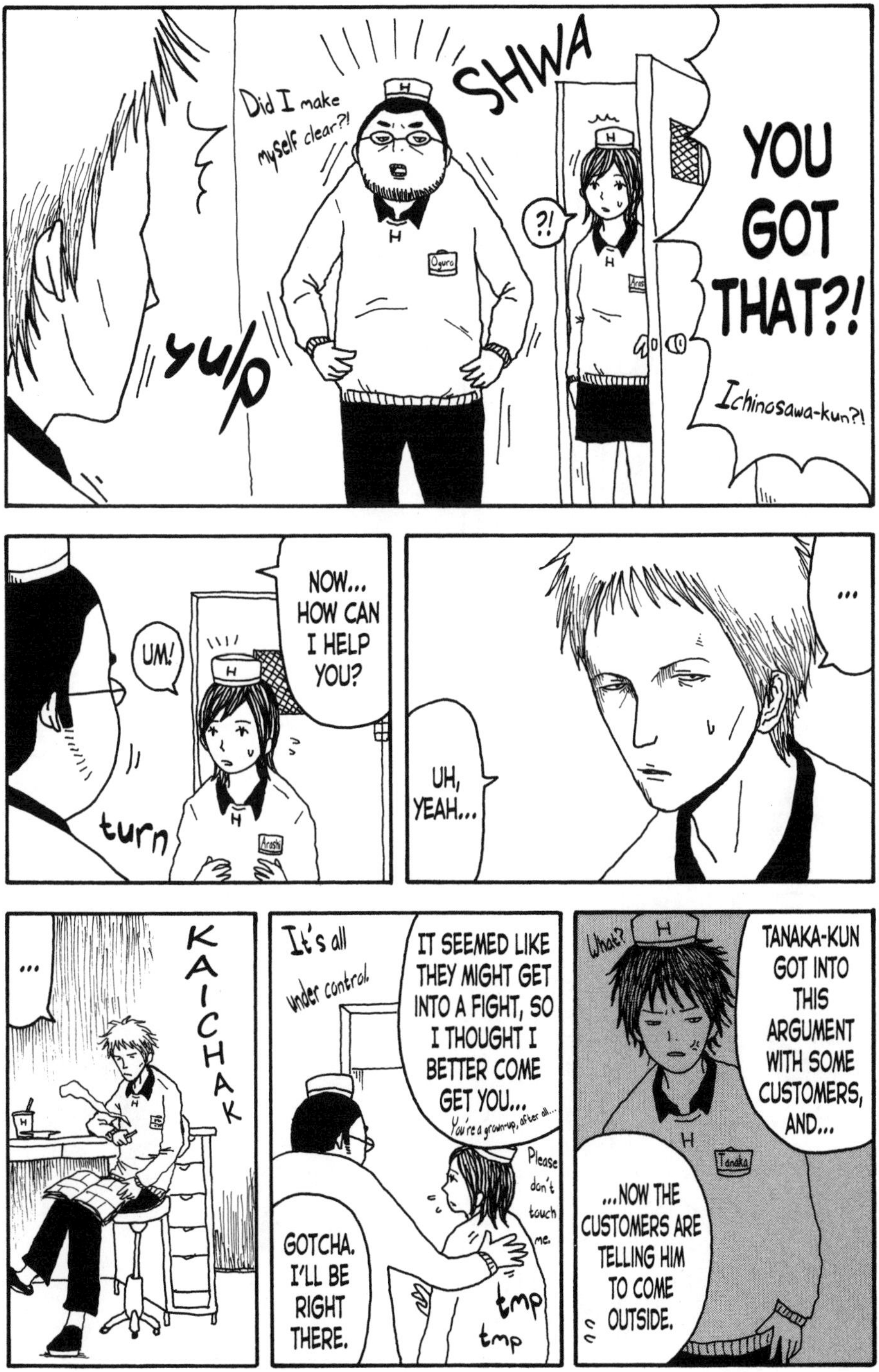
YOU GOT THAT?!
Ichinosawa-kun?!
SHWA
?!
Did I make myself clear?!
yulp
...
UH, YEAH...
NOW... HOW CAN I HELP YOU?
UM!
turn
TANAKA-KUN GOT INTO THIS ARGUMENT WITH SOME CUSTOMERS, AND...
What?
...NOW THE CUSTOMERS ARE TELLING HIM TO COME OUTSIDE.
IT SEEMED LIKE THEY MIGHT GET INTO A FIGHT, SO I THOUGHT I BETTER COME GET YOU...
You're a grown-up, after all...
It's all under control.
Please don't touch me.
GOTCHA. I'LL BE RIGHT THERE.
tmp
tmp
KAICHAK
...

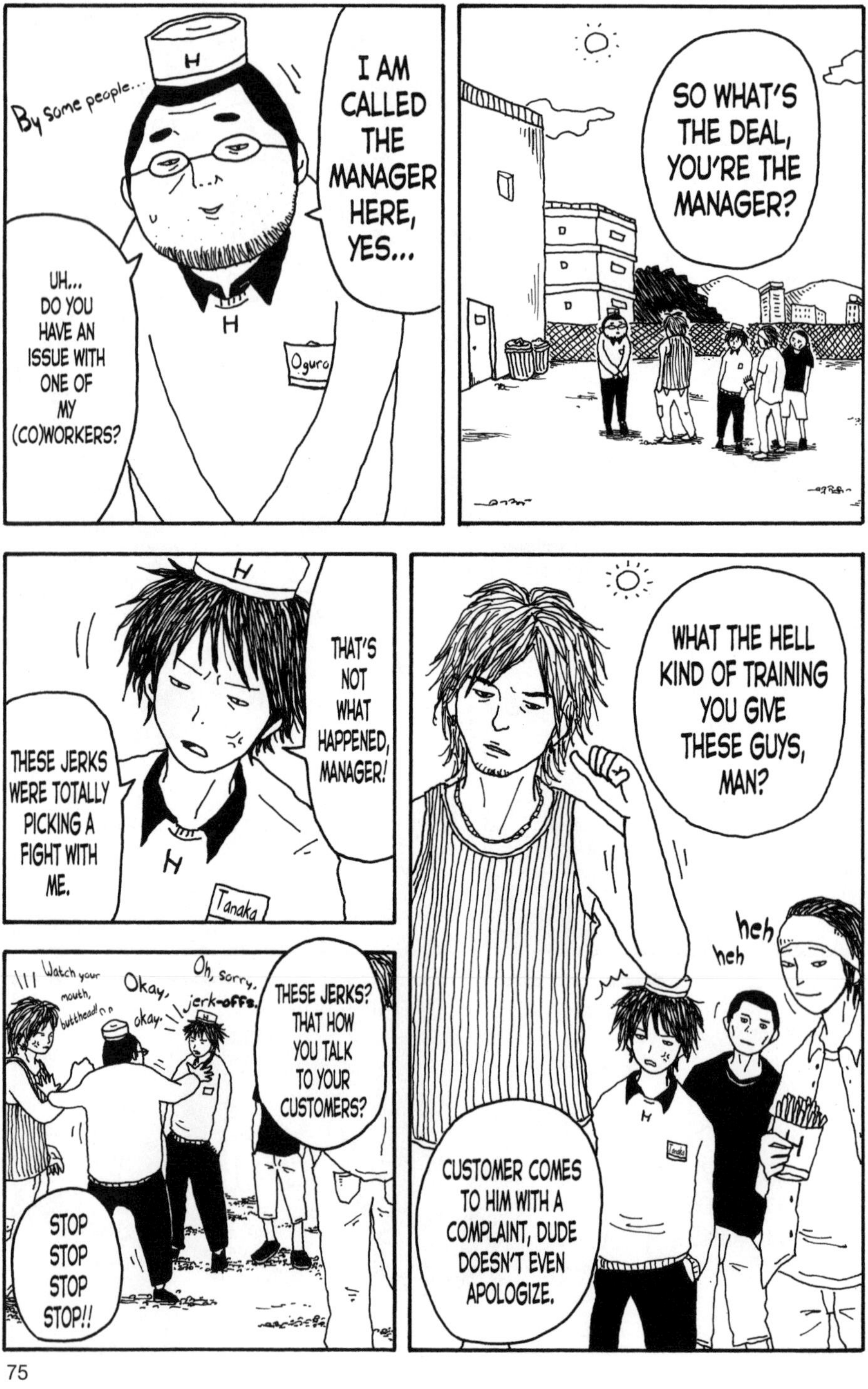
SO WHAT'S THE DEAL, YOU'RE THE MANAGER?
I AM CALLED THE MANAGER HERE, YES...
By some people...
Oguro
UH... DO YOU HAVE AN ISSUE WITH ONE OF MY (CO)WORKERS?
WHAT THE HELL KIND OF TRAINING YOU GIVE THESE GUYS, MAN?
heh
heh
Tanaka
CUSTOMER COMES TO HIM WITH A COMPLAINT, DUDE DOESN'T EVEN APOLOGIZE.
THAT'S NOT WHAT HAPPENED, MANAGER!
THESE JERKS WERE TOTALLY PICKING A FIGHT WITH ME.
Tanaka
THESE JERKS? THAT HOW YOU TALK TO YOUR CUSTOMERS?
Oh, sorry, jerk-offs.
Okay, okay.
Watch your mouth, butthead!
STOP STOP STOP STOP!!

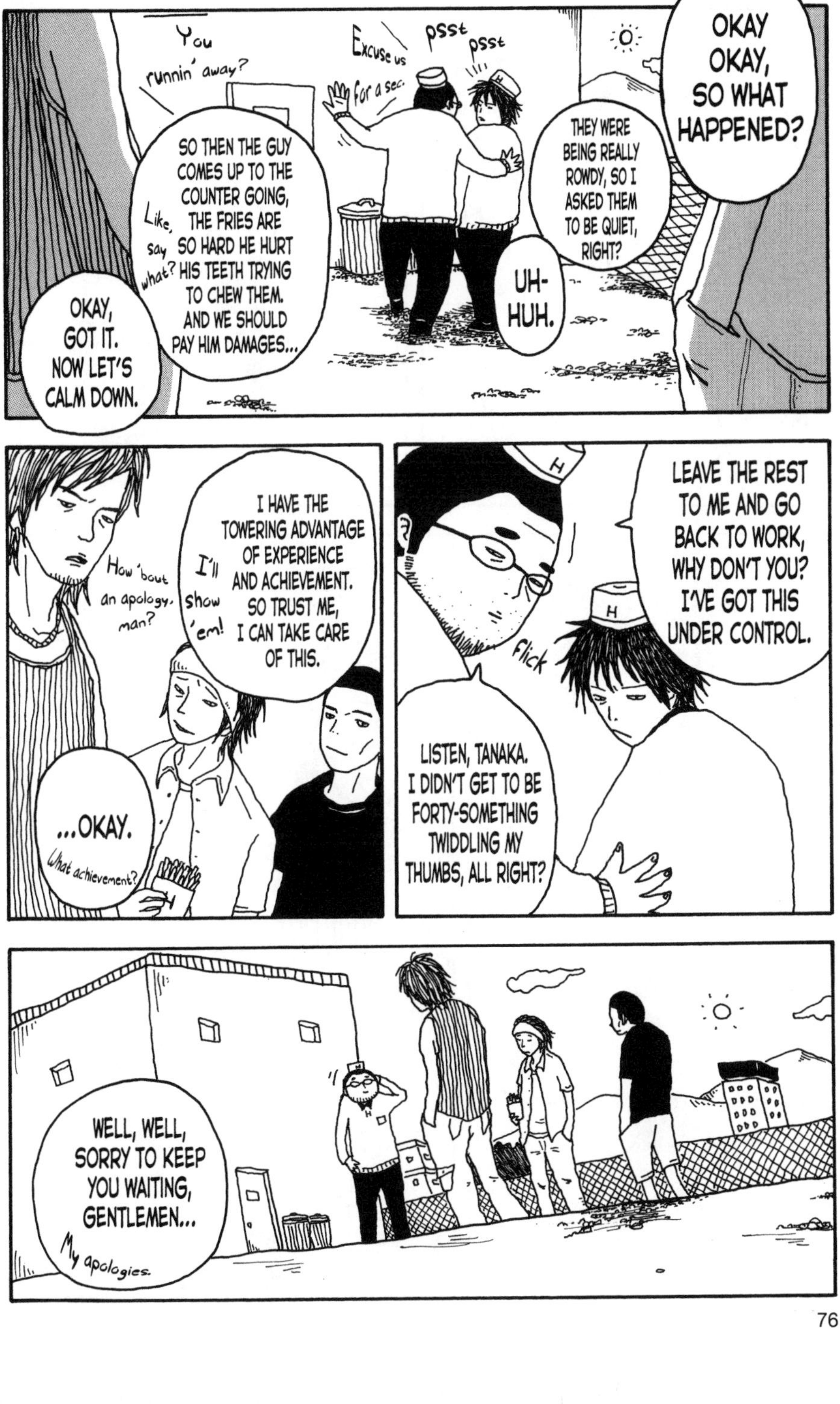

OKAY OKAY, SO WHAT HAPPENED?
THEY WERE BEING REALLY ROWDY, SO I ASKED THEM TO BE QUIET, RIGHT?
psst psst
Excuse us
For a sec.
UH-HUH.
You runnin' away?
SO THEN THE GUY COMES UP TO THE COUNTER GOING, THE FRIES ARE SO HARD HE HURT HIS TEETH TRYING TO CHEW THEM. AND WE SHOULD PAY HIM DAMAGES...
Like, say what?
OKAY, GOT IT. NOW LET'S CALM DOWN.
LEAVE THE REST TO ME AND GO BACK TO WORK, WHY DON'T YOU? I'VE GOT THIS UNDER CONTROL.
Flick
LISTEN, TANAKA. I DIDN'T GET TO BE FORTY-SOMETHING TWIDDLING MY THUMBS, ALL RIGHT?
I HAVE THE TOWERING ADVANTAGE OF EXPERIENCE AND ACHIEVEMENT. SO TRUST ME, I CAN TAKE CARE OF THIS.
I'll show 'em!
How 'bout an apology, man?
...OKAY.
What achievement?
WELL, WELL, SORRY TO KEEP YOU WAITING, GENTLEMEN...
My apologies.

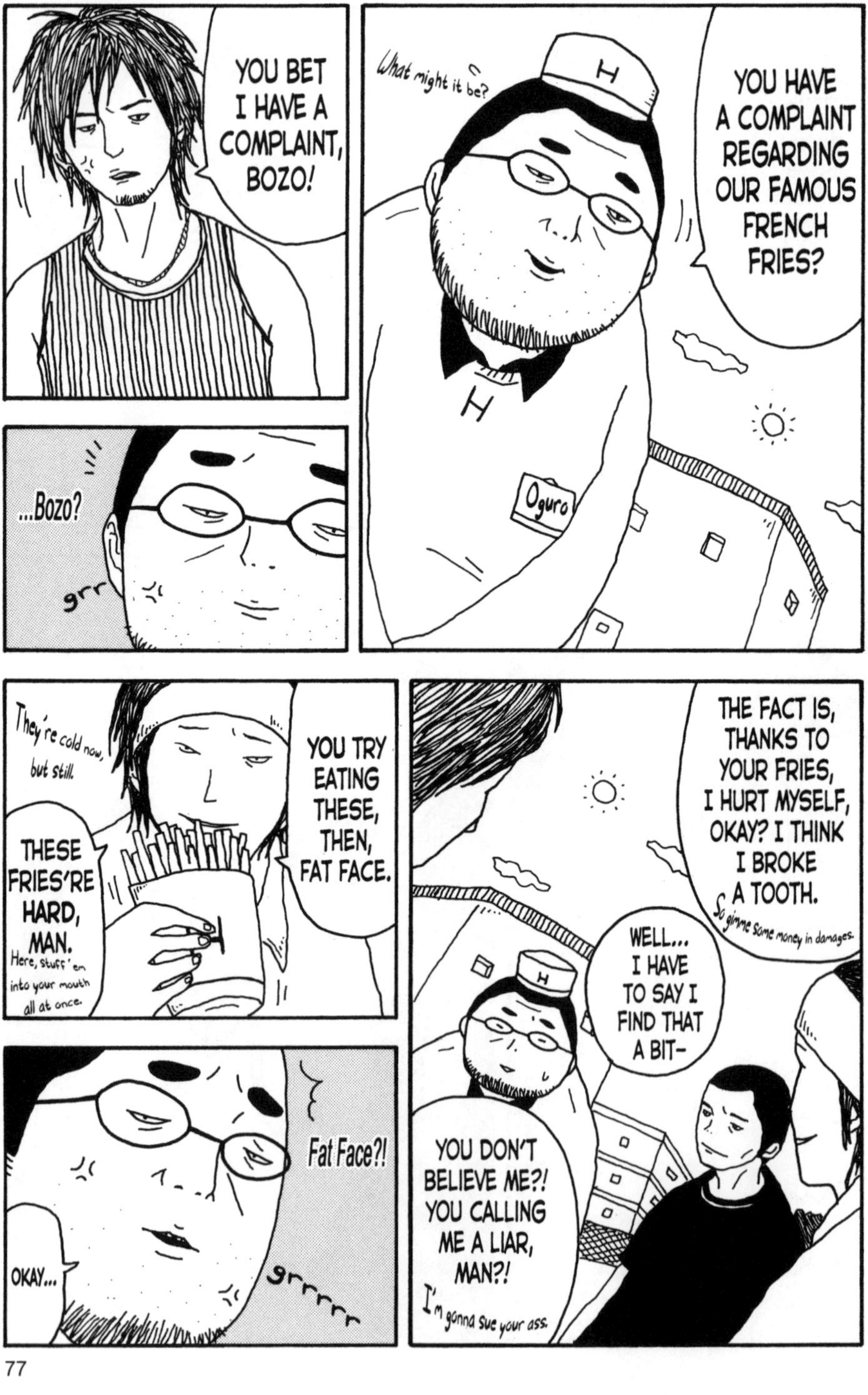
What might it be?
YOU HAVE A COMPLAINT REGARDING OUR FAMOUS FRENCH FRIES?
Oguro
YOU BET I HAVE A COMPLAINT, BOZO!
...Bozo?
grr
THE FACT IS, THANKS TO YOUR FRIES, I HURT MYSELF, OKAY? I THINK I BROKE A TOOTH.
So gimme some money in damages.
WELL... I HAVE TO SAY I FIND THAT A BIT-
YOU DON'T BELIEVE ME?! YOU CALLING ME A LIAR, MAN?!
I'm gonna sue your ass.
YOU TRY EATING THESE, THEN, FAT FACE.
They're cold now, but still.
THESE FRIES'RE HARD, MAN.
Here, stuff 'em into your mouth all at once.
Fat Face?!
OKAY...
grrrrr

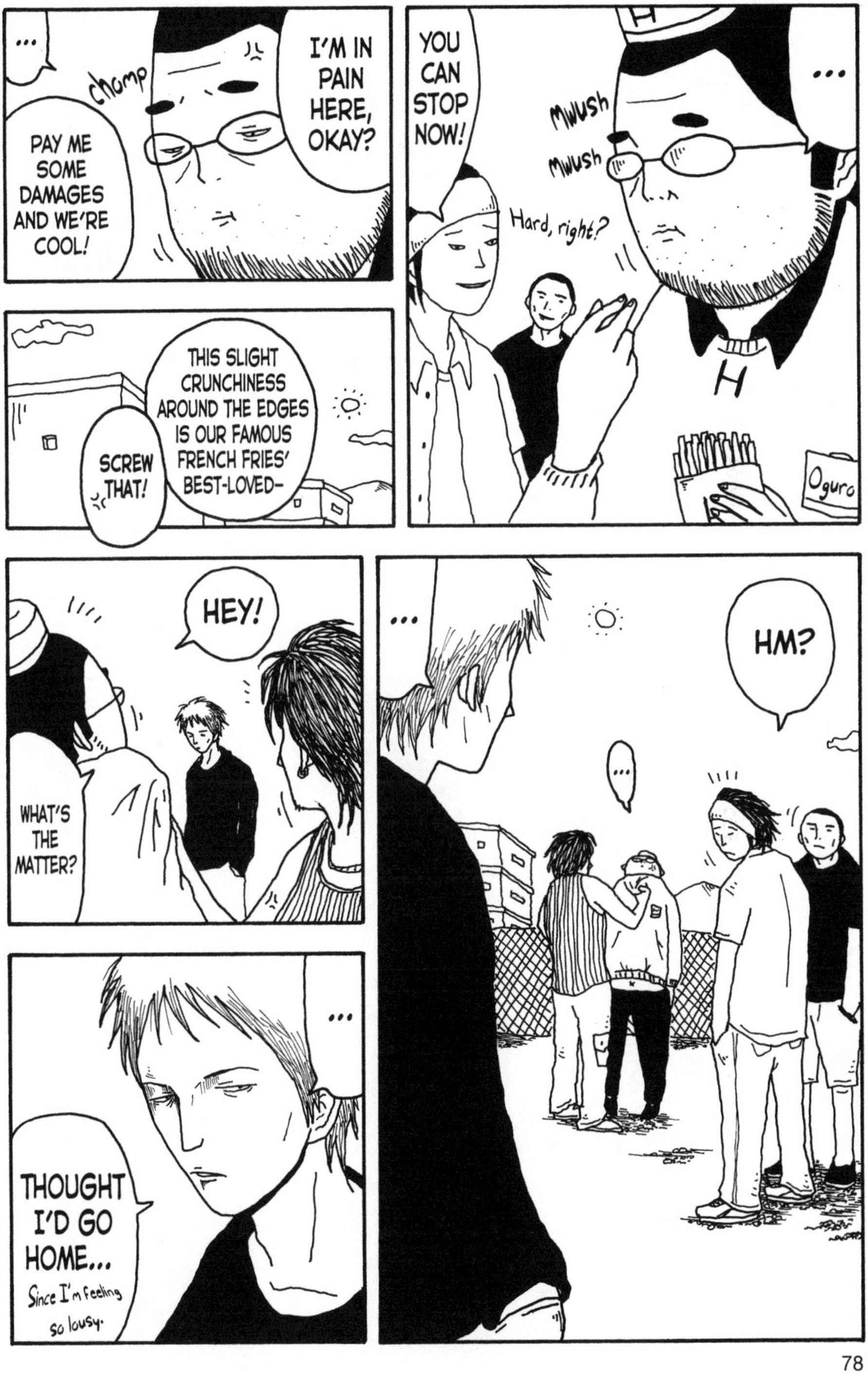
YOU CAN STOP NOW!
...
Mwush
Mwush
Hard, right?
Oguro
I'M IN PAIN HERE, OKAY?
chomp
...
PAY ME SOME DAMAGES AND WE'RE COOL!
THIS SLIGHT CRUNCHINESS AROUND THE EDGES IS OUR FAMOUS FRENCH FRIES' BEST-LOVED–
SCREW THAT!
...
HM?
...
HEY!
WHAT'S THE MATTER?
...
THOUGHT I'D GO HOME...
Since I'm feeling so lousy.

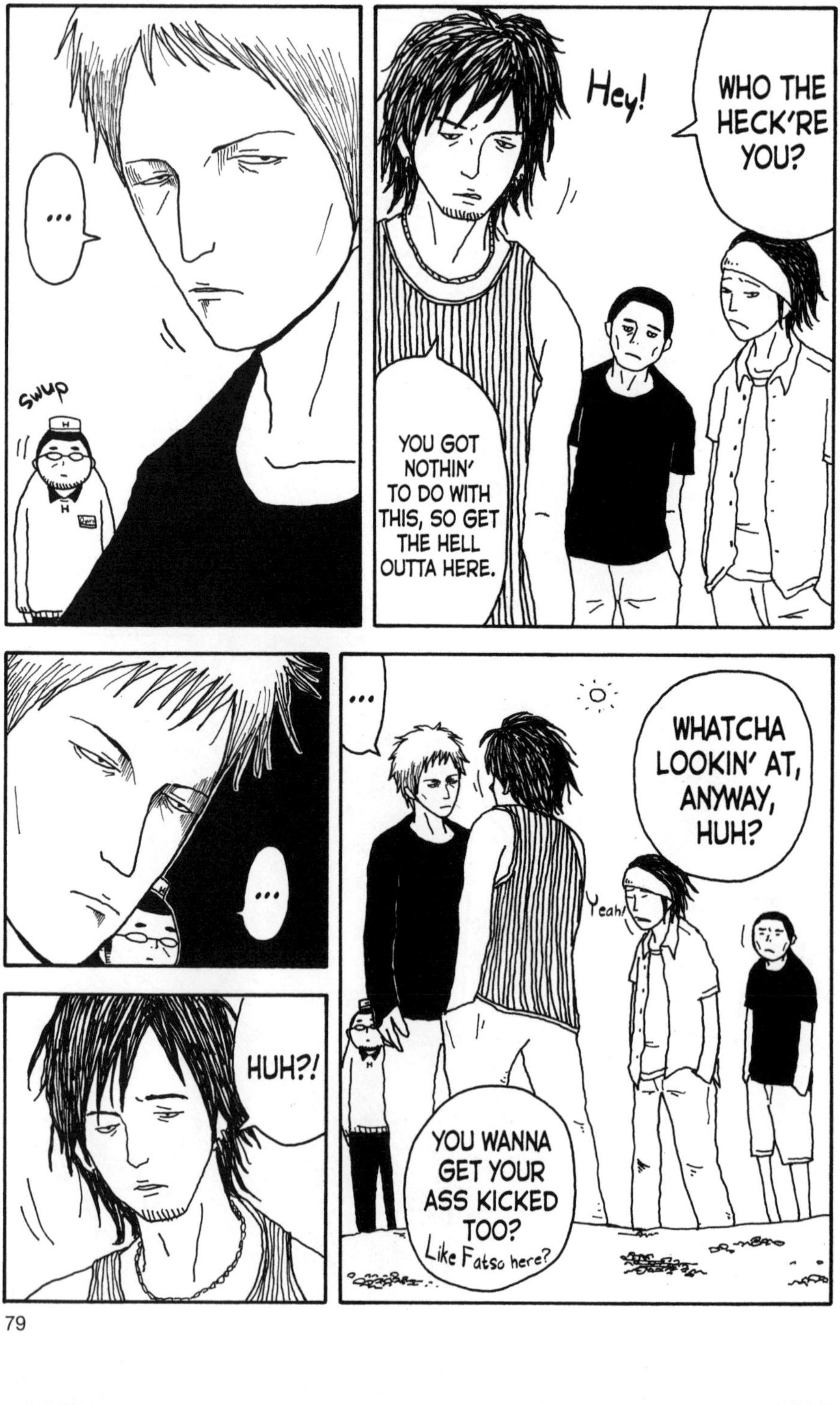
Hey!
WHO THE HECK'RE YOU?
YOU GOT NOTHIN' TO DO WITH THIS, SO GET THE HELL OUTTA HERE.
...
swup
WHATCHA LOOKIN' AT, ANYWAY, HUH?
...
Yeah!
YOU WANNA GET YOUR ASS KICKED TOO?
Like Fatso here?
...
HUH?!

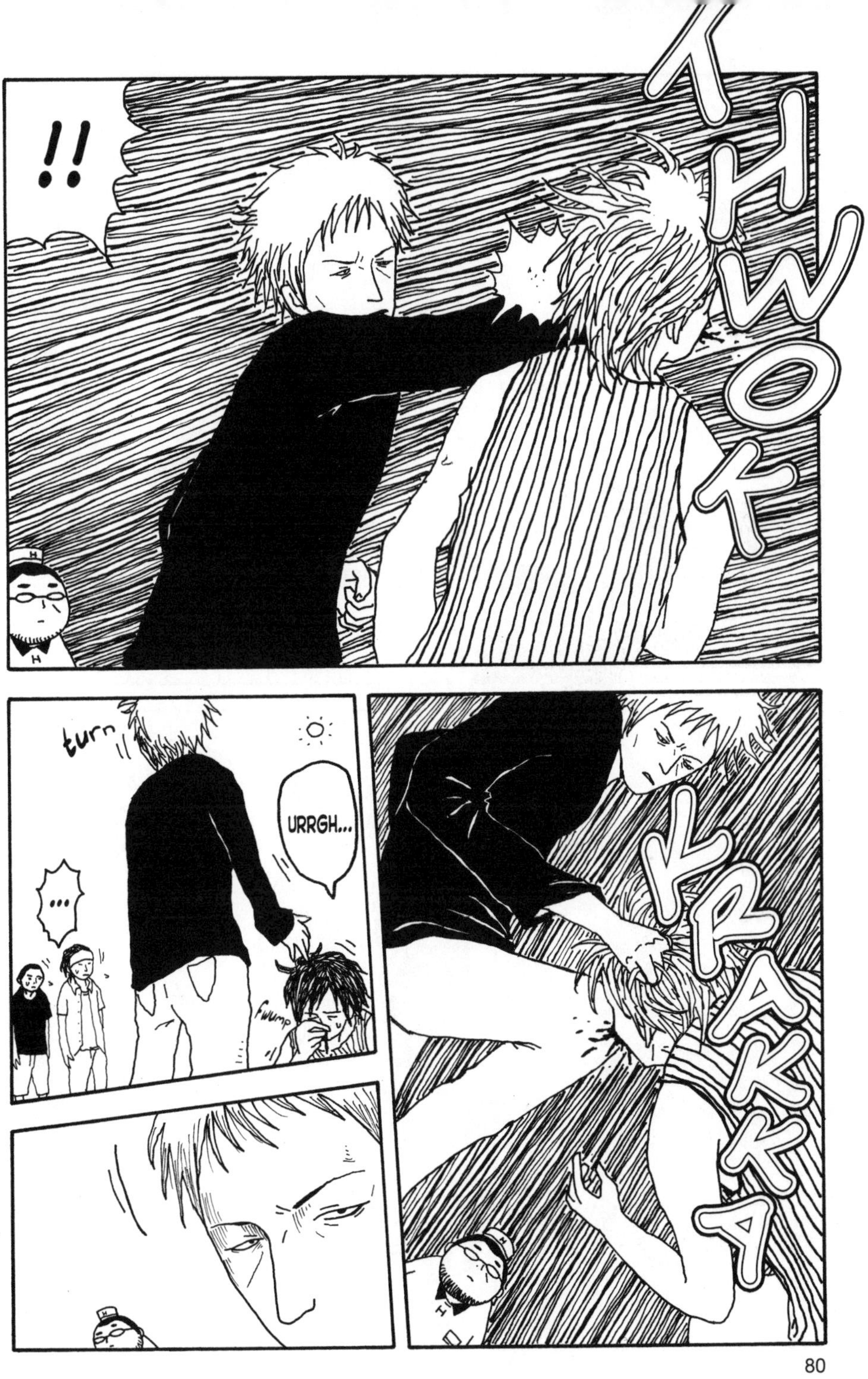
THWOK
!!
KRAKKA
turn
URRGH...
...
fwump

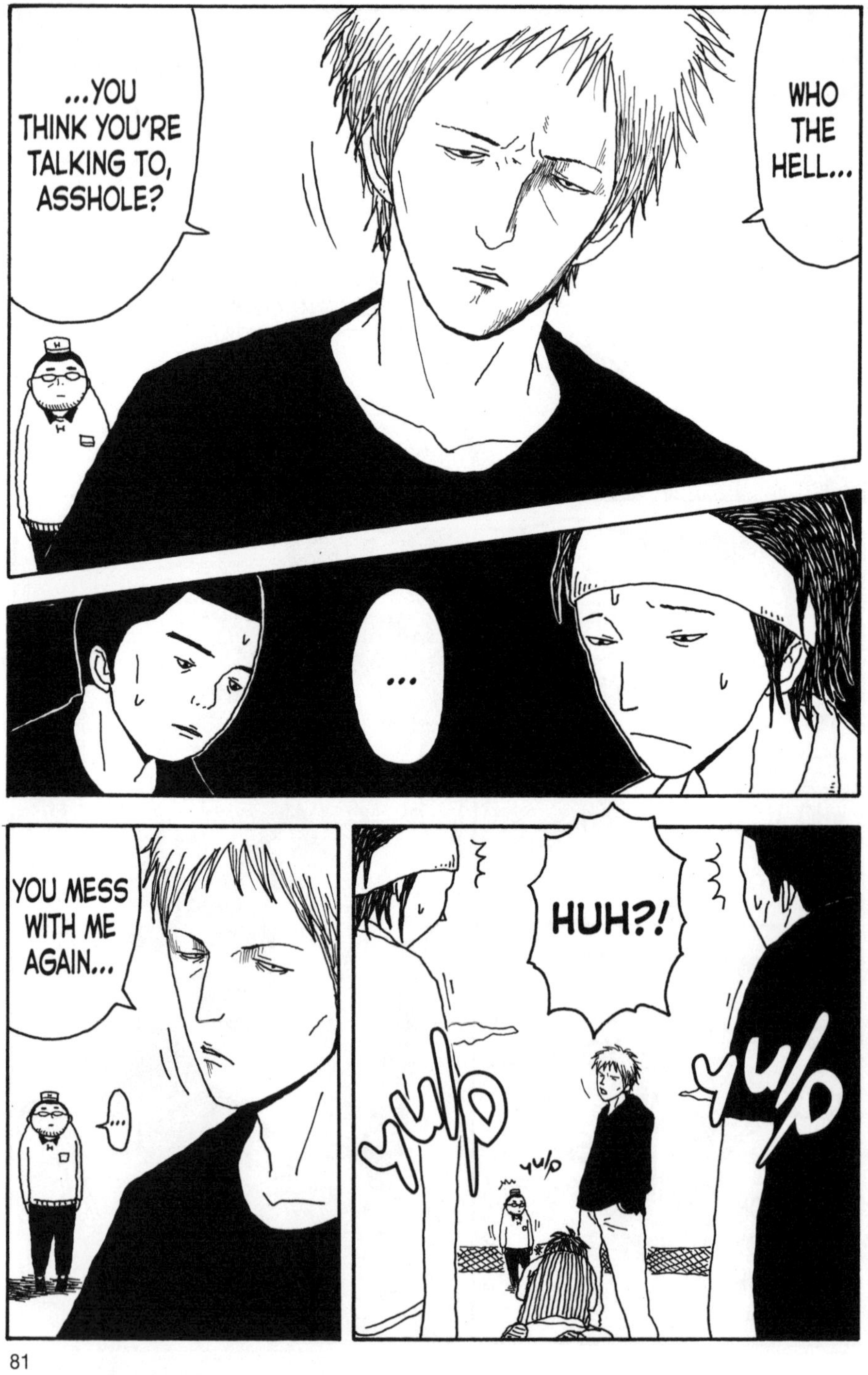
WHO THE HELL...
...YOU THINK YOU'RE TALKING TO, ASSHOLE?
...
HUH?!
gulp
gulp
gulp
YOU MESS WITH ME AGAIN...
...

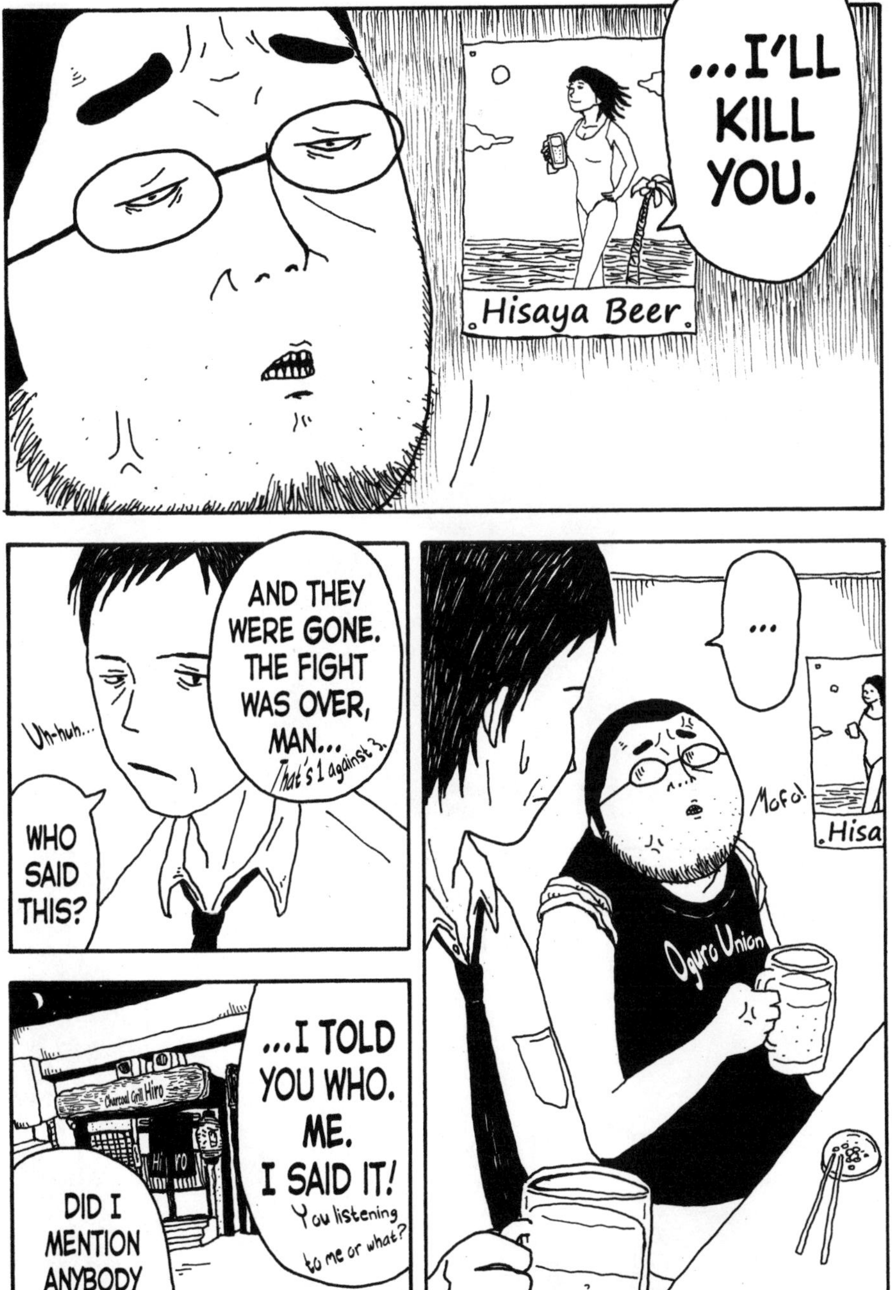
...I'LL KILL YOU.
Hisaya Beer
...
Mofo!
Hisa
Oguro Union
AND THEY WERE GONE. THE FIGHT WAS OVER, MAN...
That's 1 against 3.
Uh-huh...
WHO SAID THIS?
...I TOLD YOU WHO. ME. I SAID IT!
You listening to me or what?
Charcoal Grill Hiro
DID I MENTION ANYBODY ELSE? HUH?
No, I did not!

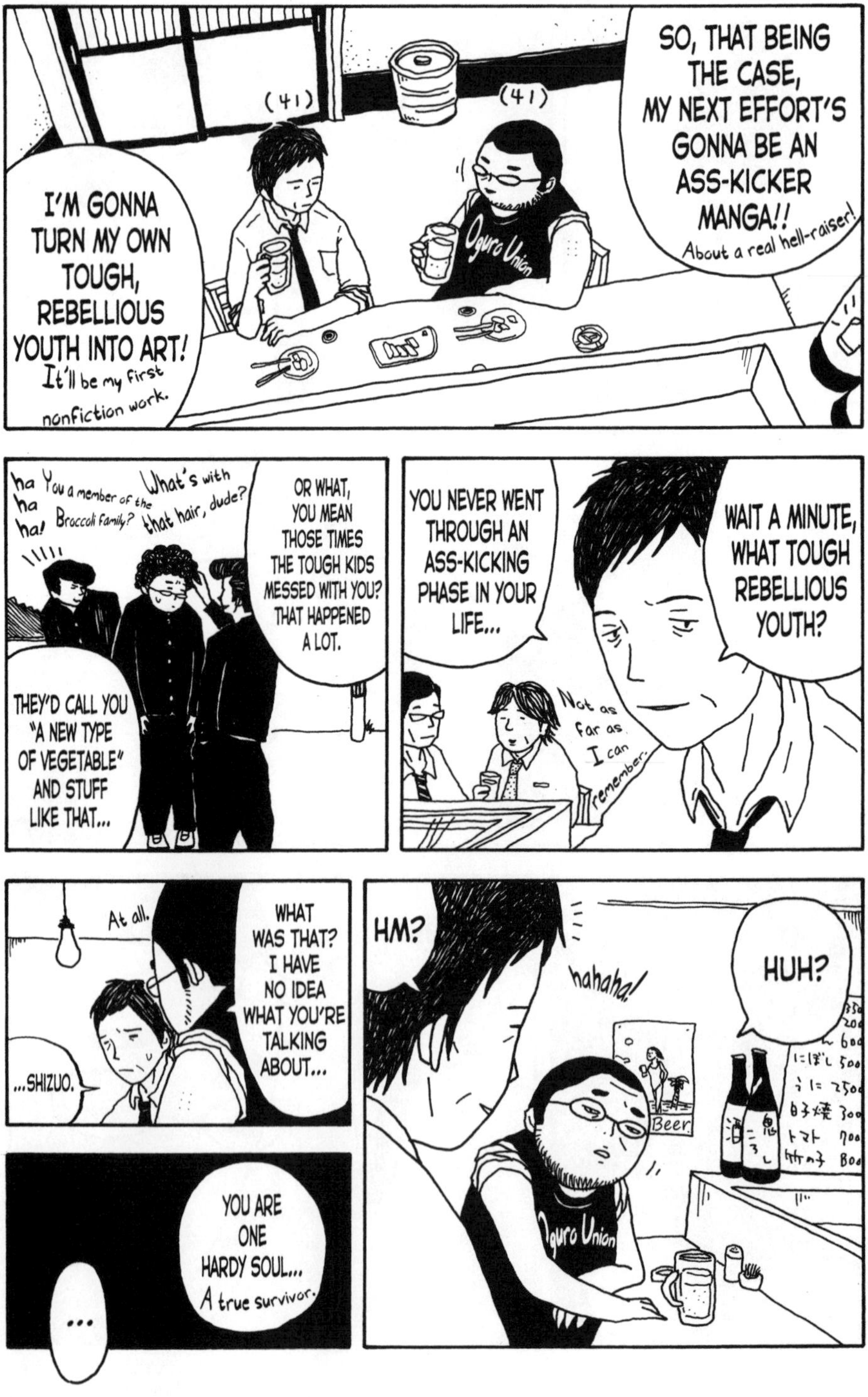
SO, THAT BEING THE CASE, MY NEXT EFFORT'S GONNA BE AN ASS-KICKER MANGA!!
About a real hell-raiser!
(41)
(41)
Oguro Union
I'M GONNA TURN MY OWN TOUGH, REBELLIOUS YOUTH INTO ART!
It'll be my first nonfiction work.
WAIT A MINUTE, WHAT TOUGH REBELLIOUS YOUTH?
YOU NEVER WENT THROUGH AN ASS-KICKING PHASE IN YOUR LIFE...
Not as far as I can remember.
OR WHAT, YOU MEAN THOSE TIMES THE TOUGH KIDS MESSED WITH YOU? THAT HAPPENED A LOT.
What's with that hair, dude?
You a member of the Broccoli Family?
ha ha ha!
THEY'D CALL YOU "A NEW TYPE OF VEGETABLE" AND STUFF LIKE THAT...
HUH?
hahaha!
HM?
Beer
Oguro Union
WHAT WAS THAT? I HAVE NO IDEA WHAT YOU'RE TALKING ABOUT...
At all.
...SHIZUO.
YOU ARE ONE HARDY SOUL...
A true survivor.
...

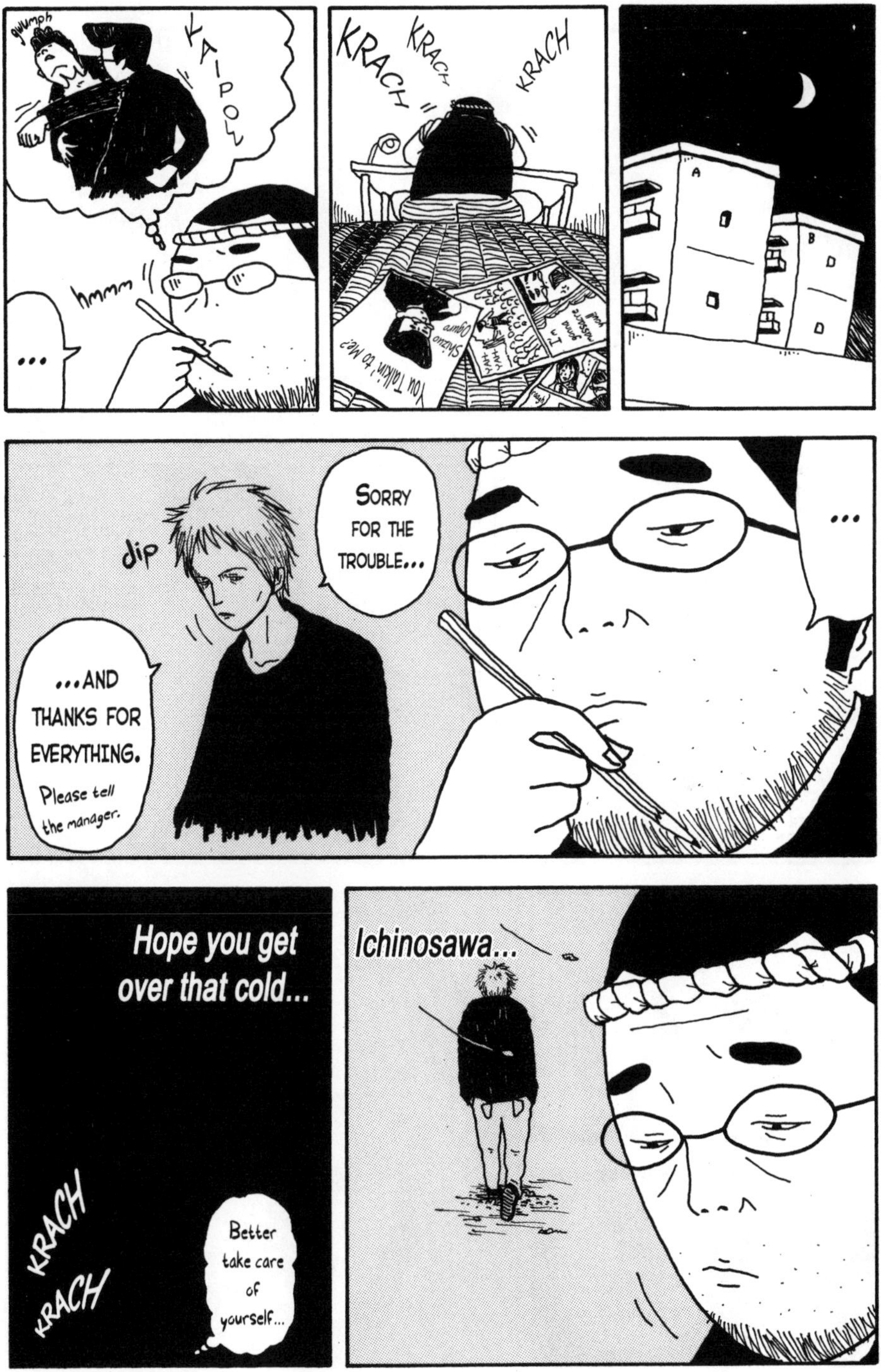
KRACH
KRACH
KRACH
You Talkin' to Me?
Shizuo Ogura
gwumph
KAIPOW
hmmm
...
...
SORRY FOR THE TROUBLE...
dip
...AND THANKS FOR EVERYTHING.
Please tell the manager.
Ichinosawa...
Hope you get over that cold...
KRACH
KRACH
Better take care of yourself...

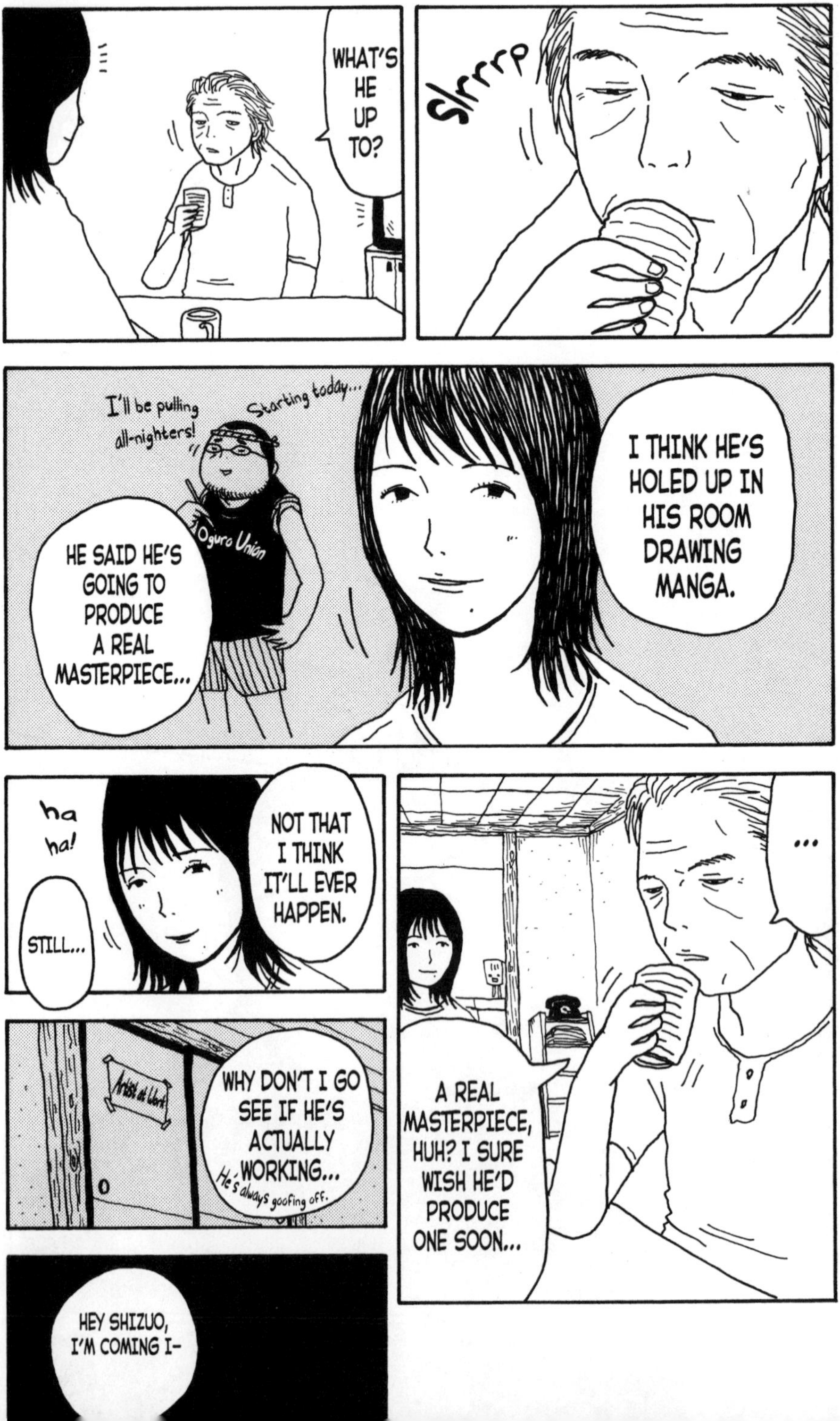

slrrrp
WHAT'S HE UP TO?
I THINK HE'S HOLED UP IN HIS ROOM DRAWING MANGA.
Starting today...
I'll be pulling all-nighters!
Oguro Union
HE SAID HE'S GOING TO PRODUCE A REAL MASTERPIECE...
...
A REAL MASTERPIECE, HUH? I SURE WISH HE'D PRODUCE ONE SOON...
NOT THAT I THINK IT'LL EVER HAPPEN.
ha ha!
STILL...
WHY DON'T I GO SEE IF HE'S ACTUALLY WORKING...
He's always goofing off.
HEY SHIZUO, I'M COMING I-

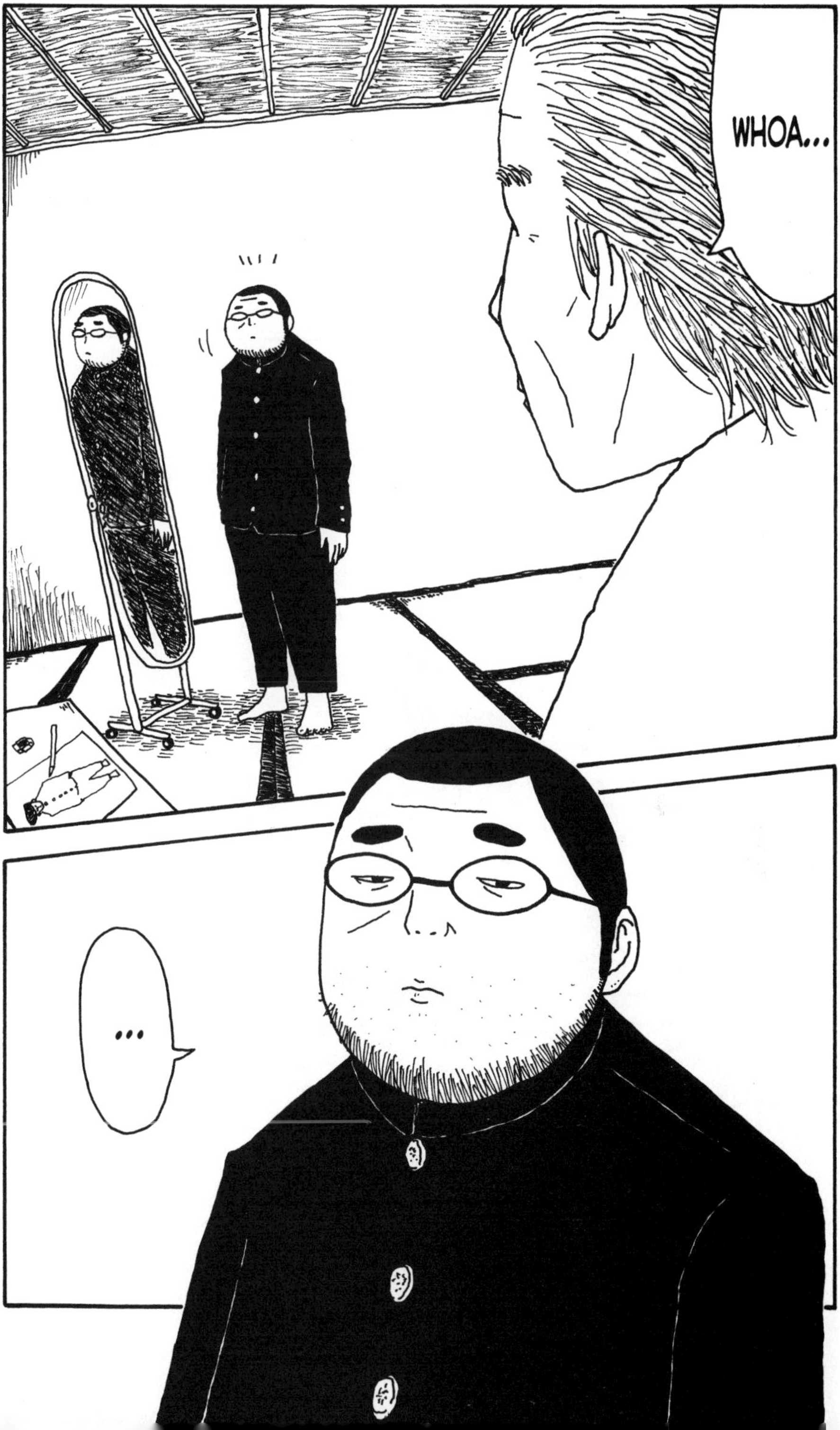
WHOA...
...

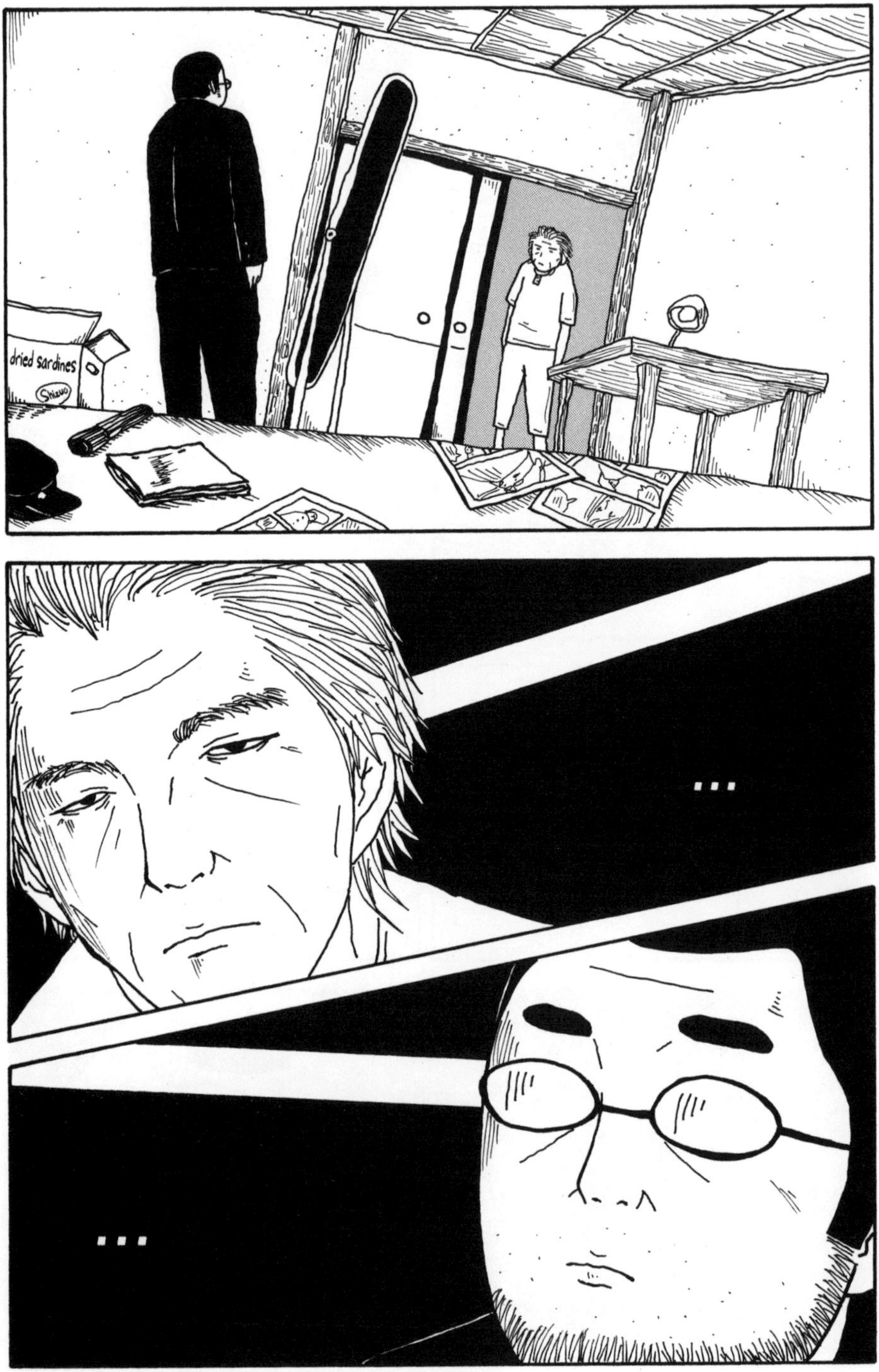
dried sardines
Shizuo
...
...

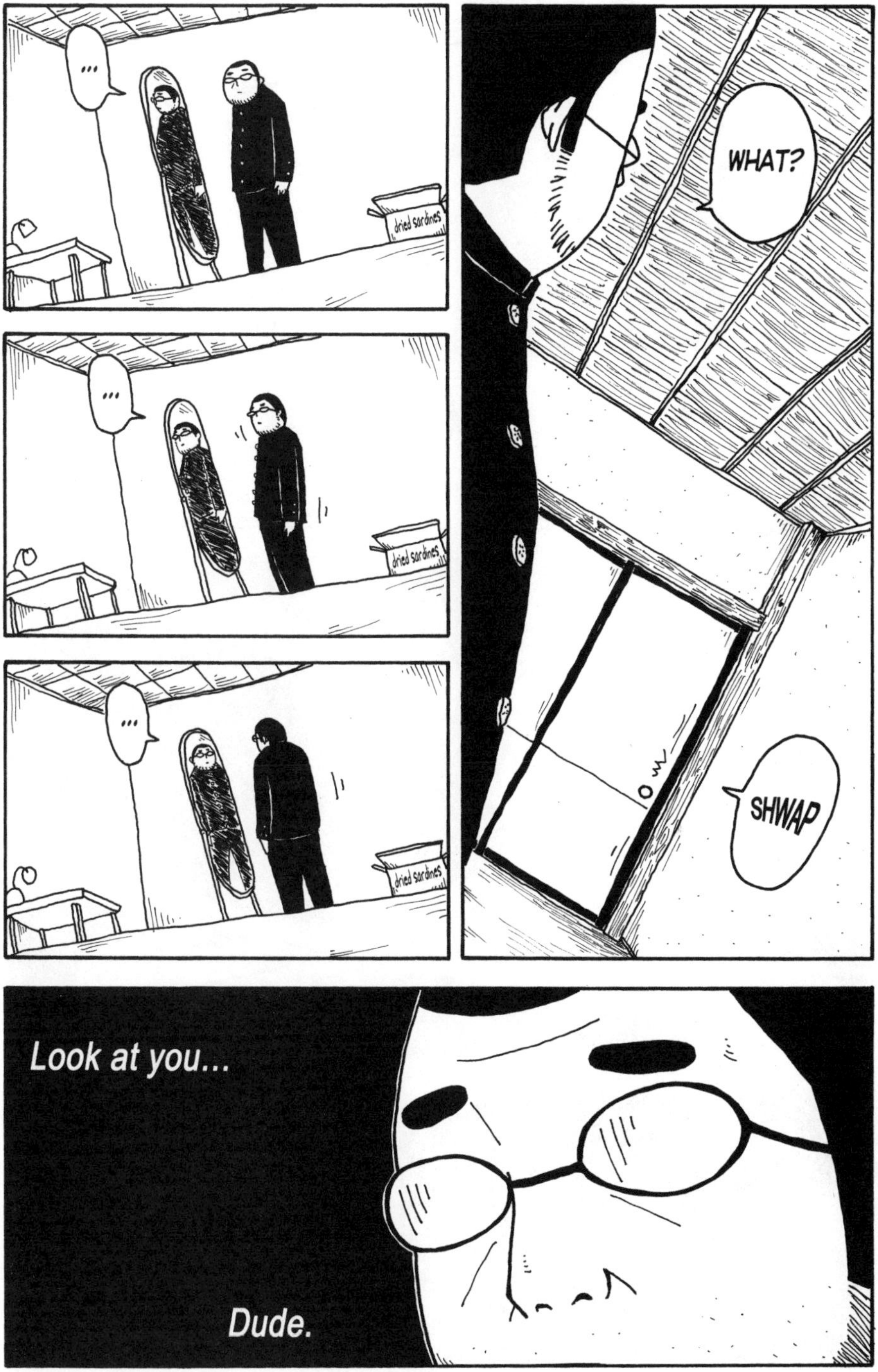
WHAT?
SHWAP
...
dried sardines
...
dried sardines
...
dried sardines
Look at you...
Dude.

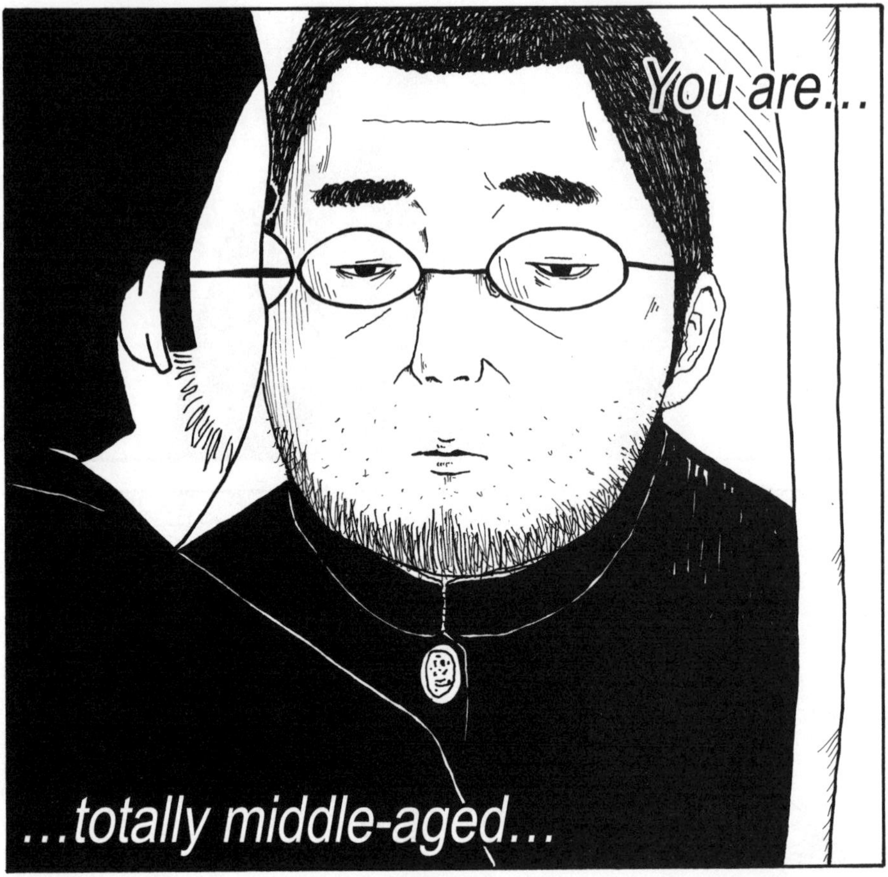
You are...
...totally middle-aged...
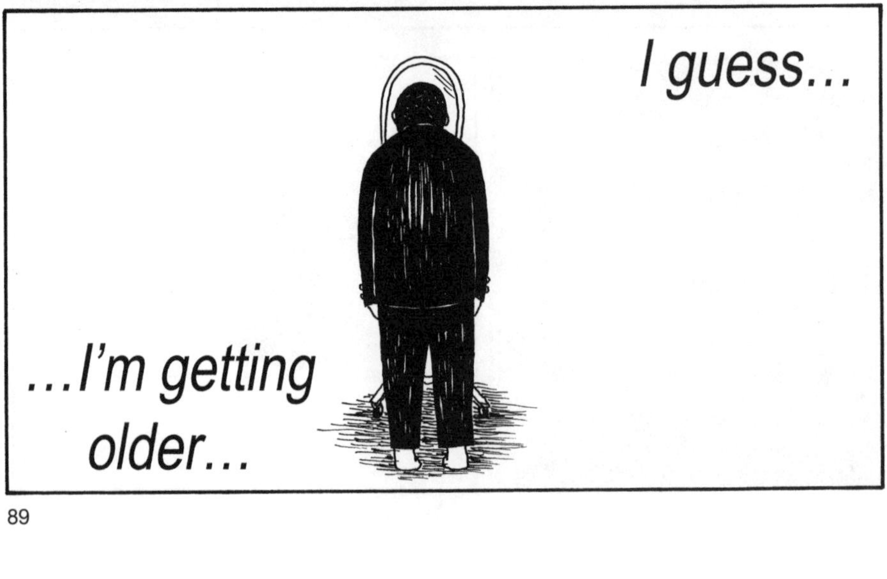
I guess...
...I'm getting older...

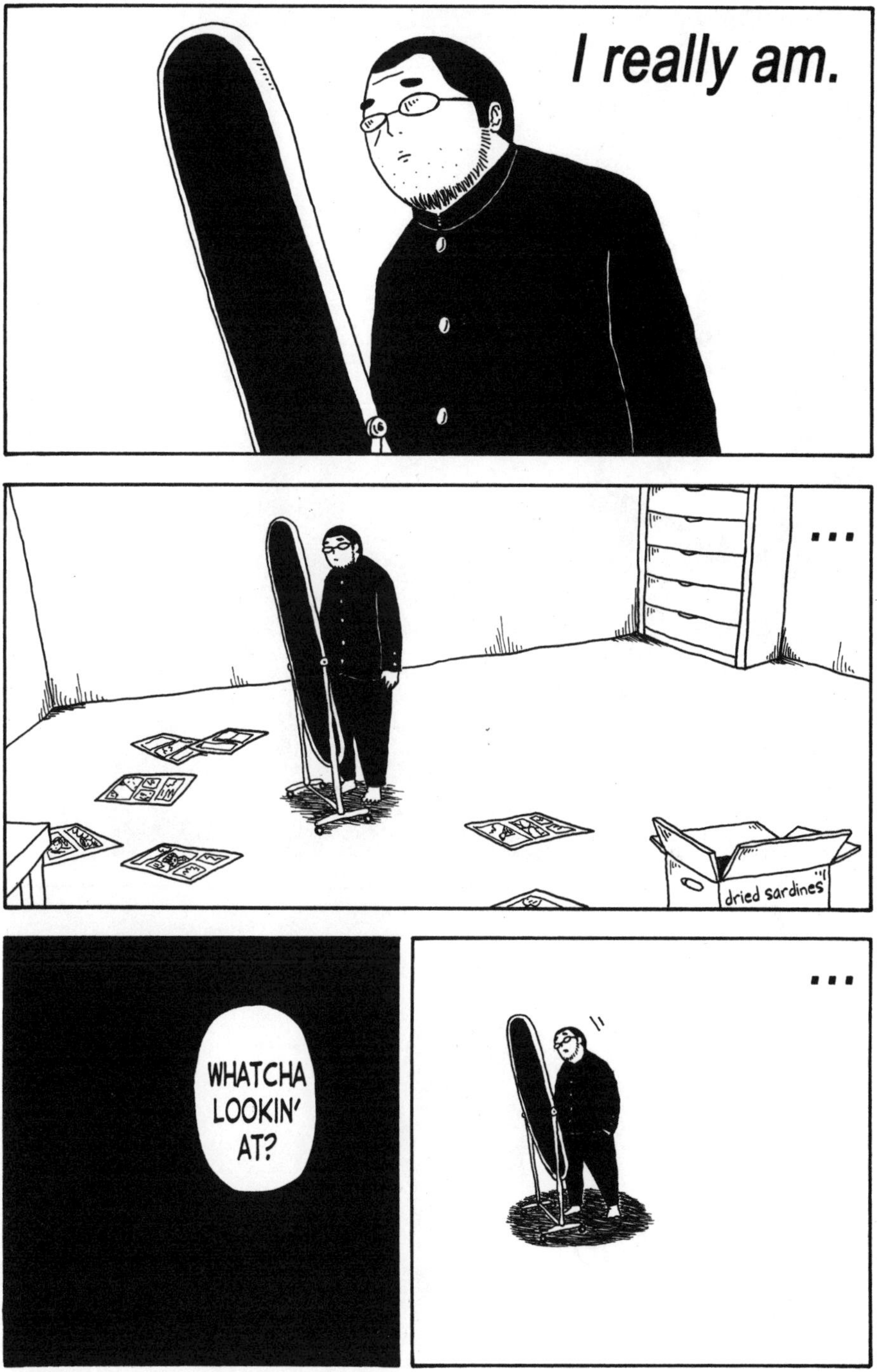
I really am.
...
dried sardines
...
WHATCHA LOOKIN' AT?

Chapter 2:

It Tastes Best When It's Starting to Go Bad

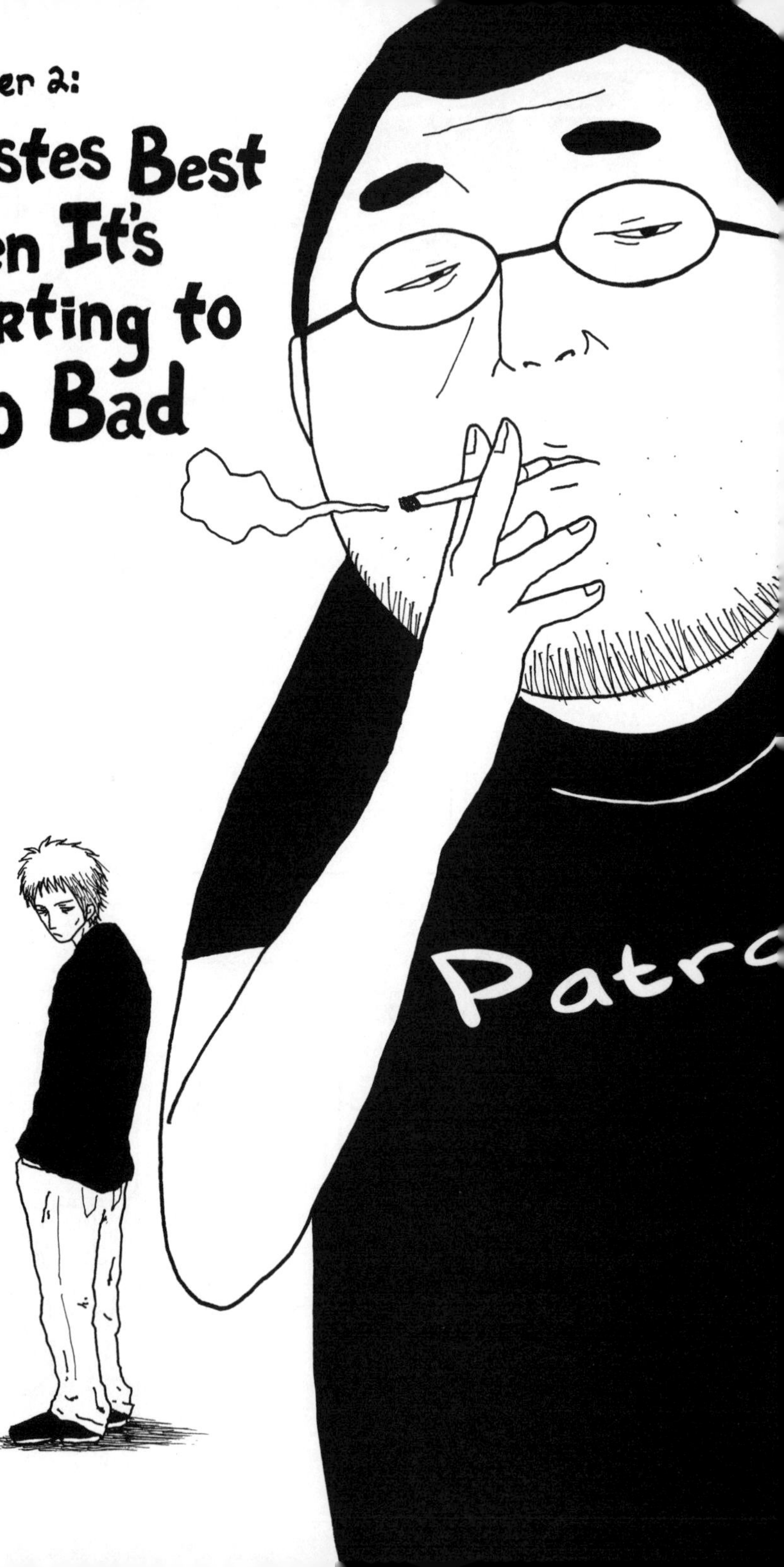

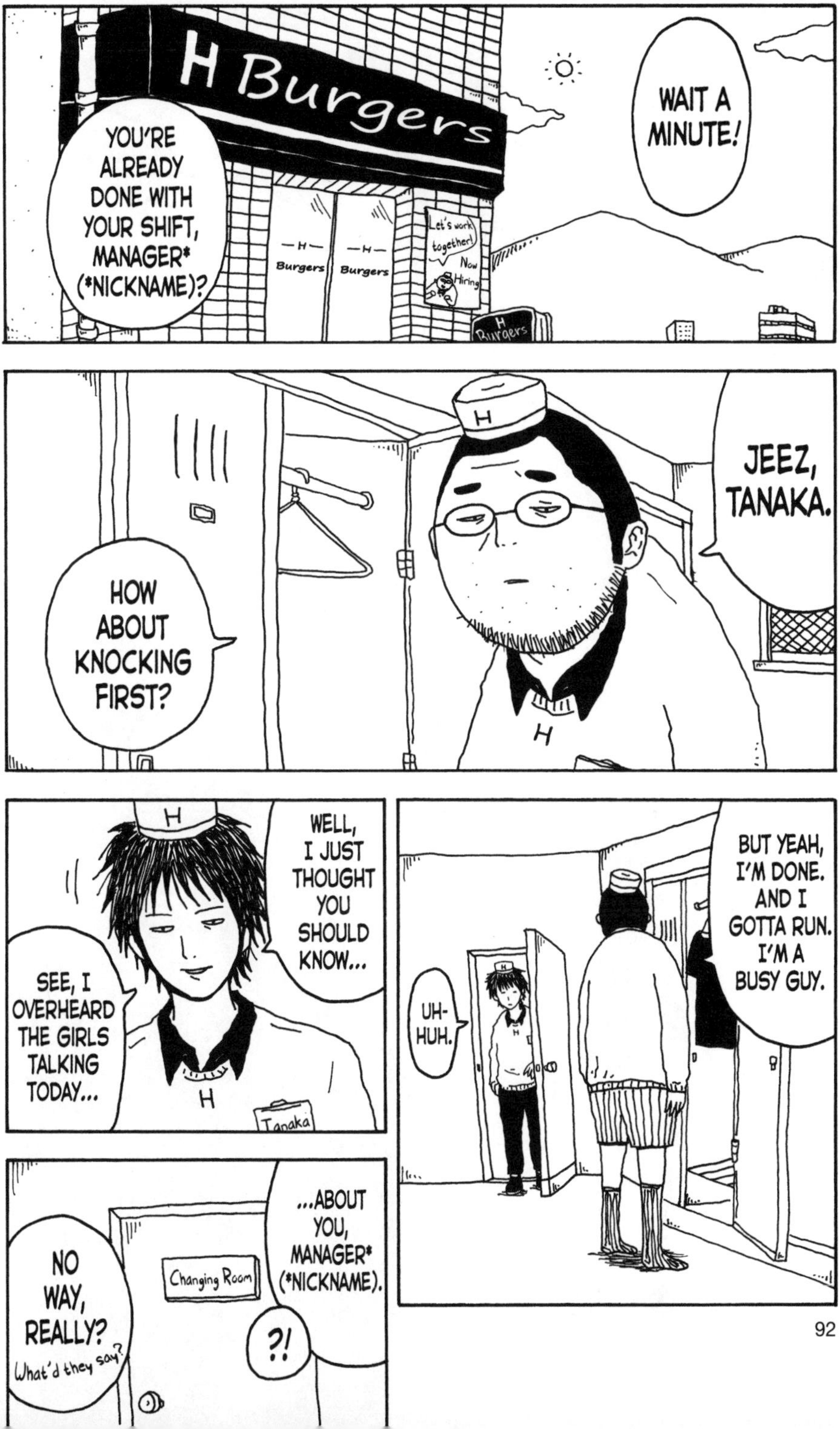
H Burgers
WAIT A MINUTE!
YOU'RE ALREADY DONE WITH YOUR SHIFT, MANAGER* (*NICKNAME)?
Let's work together! Now Hiring
JEEZ, TANAKA.
HOW ABOUT KNOCKING FIRST?
BUT YEAH, I'M DONE. AND I GOTTA RUN. I'M A BUSY GUY.
UH-HUH.
WELL, I JUST THOUGHT YOU SHOULD KNOW...
SEE, I OVERHEARD THE GIRLS TALKING TODAY...
Tanaka
...ABOUT YOU, MANAGER* (*NICKNAME).
?!
Changing Room
NO WAY, REALLY?
What'd they say?

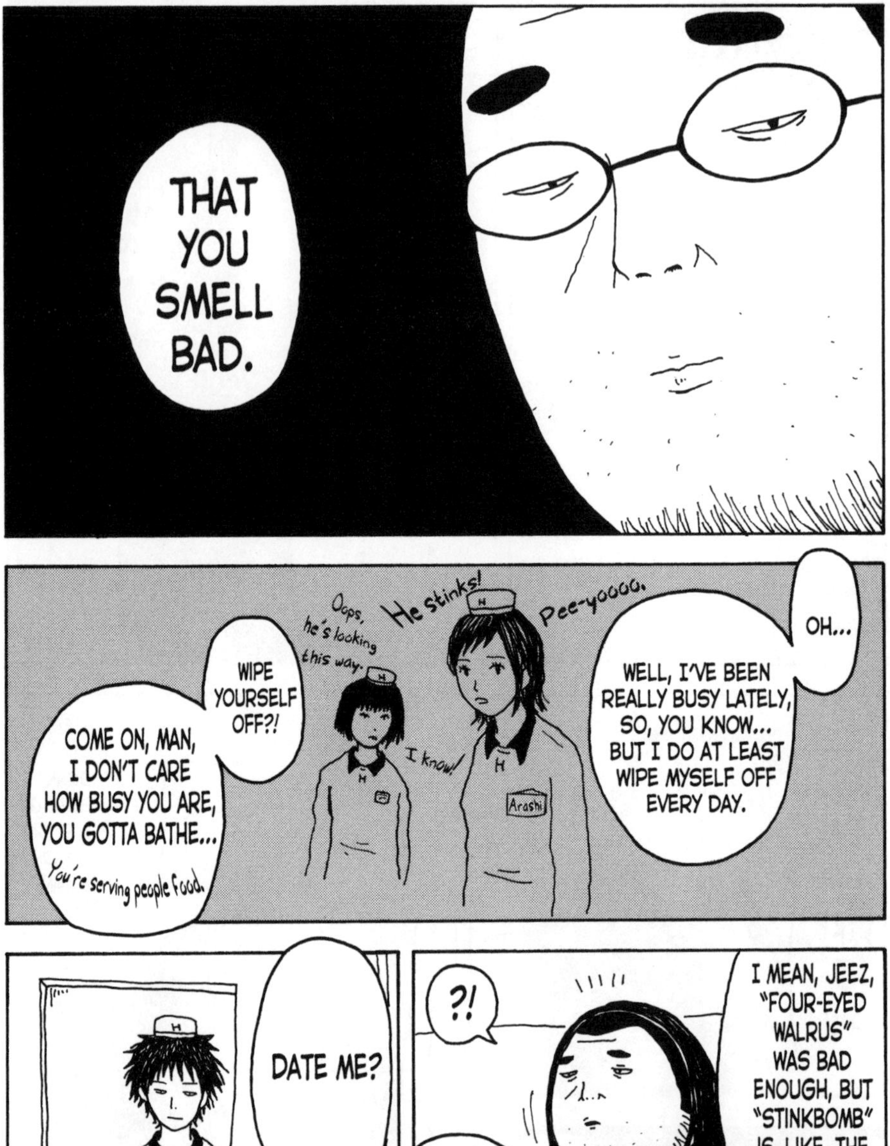
THAT YOU SMELL BAD.
OH...
WELL, I'VE BEEN REALLY BUSY LATELY, SO, YOU KNOW... BUT I DO AT LEAST WIPE MYSELF OFF EVERY DAY.
Pee-yoooo.
He stinks!
Oops, he's looking this way.
Arashi
I know!
WIPE YOURSELF OFF?!
COME ON, MAN, I DON'T CARE HOW BUSY YOU ARE, YOU GOTTA BATHE...
You're serving people food.
I MEAN, JEEZ, "FOUR-EYED WALRUS" WAS BAD ENOUGH, BUT "STINKBOMB" IS, LIKE, THE KISS OF DEATH, MAN.
?!
GIRLS WILL NEVER, EVER DATE YOU IF YOU SMELL BAD.
DATE ME?
Tanaka
LISTEN, TANAKA, KIDDO...

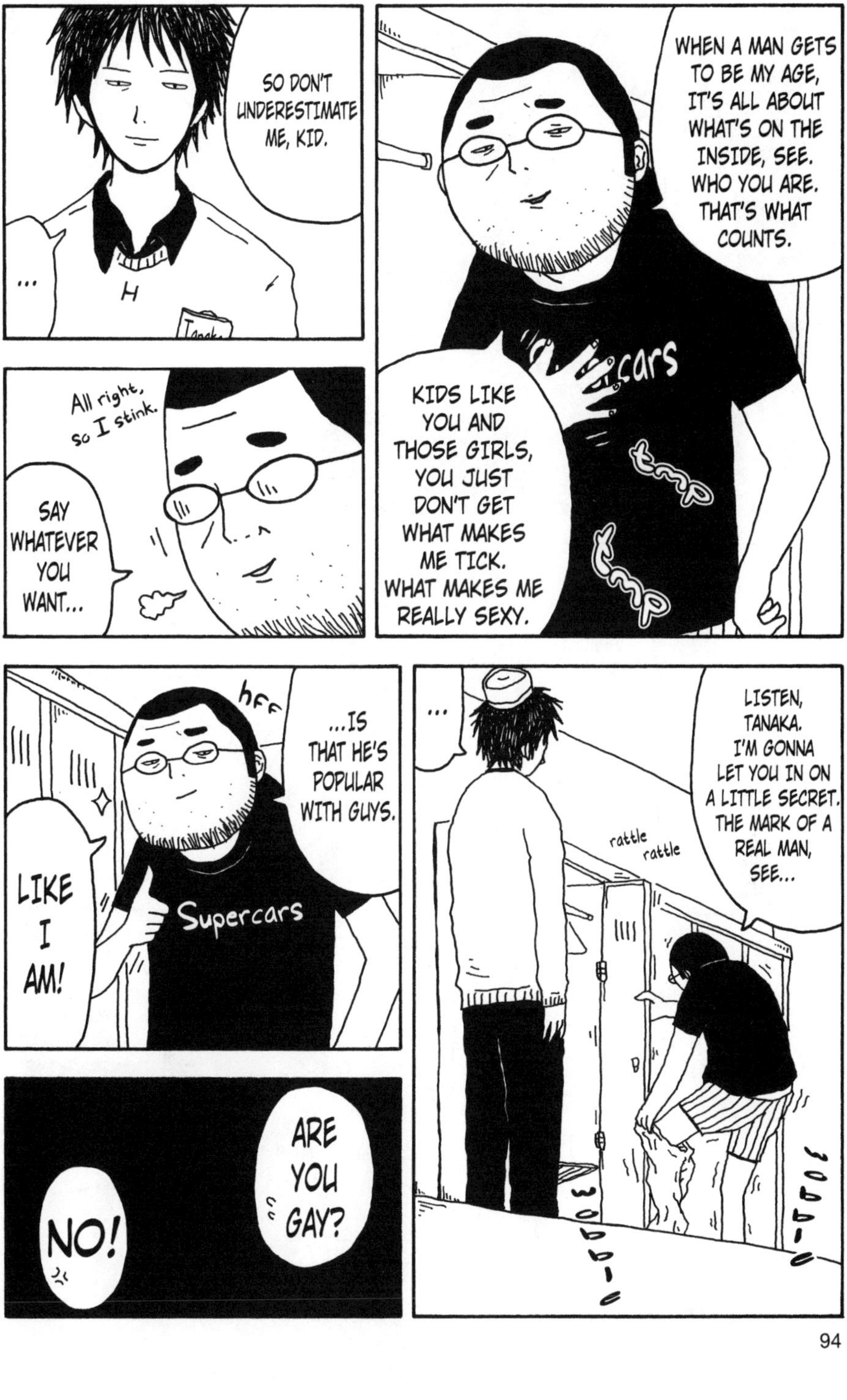
WHEN A MAN GETS TO BE MY AGE, IT'S ALL ABOUT WHAT'S ON THE INSIDE, SEE. WHO YOU ARE. THAT'S WHAT COUNTS.
KIDS LIKE YOU AND THOSE GIRLS, YOU JUST DON'T GET WHAT MAKES ME TICK. WHAT MAKES ME REALLY SEXY.
SO DON'T UNDERESTIMATE ME, KID.
...
All right, so I stink.
SAY WHATEVER YOU WANT...
LISTEN, TANAKA. I'M GONNA LET YOU IN ON A LITTLE SECRET. THE MARK OF A REAL MAN, SEE...
...
rattle rattle
wobble
wobble
hff
...IS THAT HE'S POPULAR WITH GUYS.
LIKE I AM!
Supercars
ARE YOU GAY?
NO!

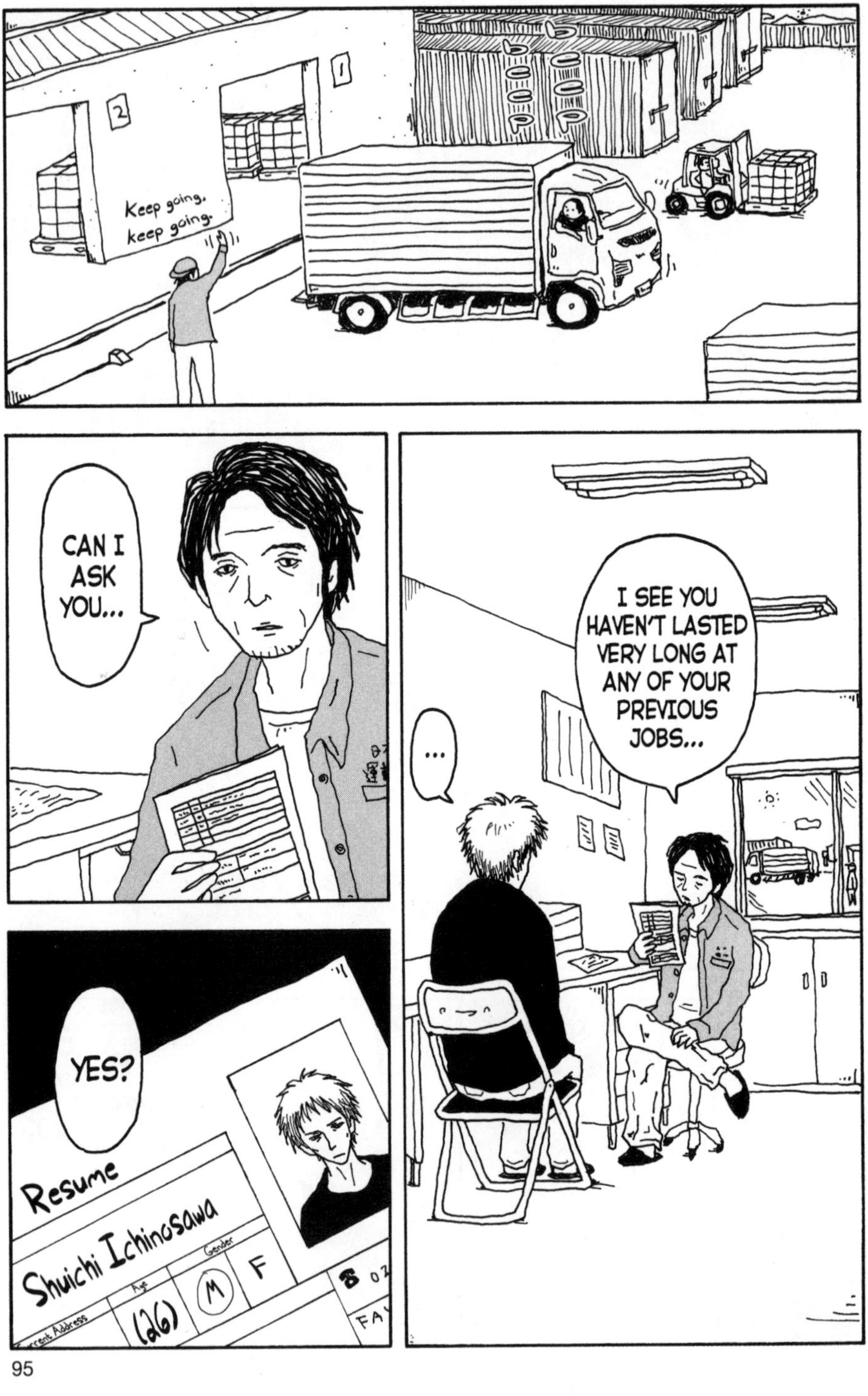
beep beep
Keep going, keep going.
I SEE YOU HAVEN'T LASTED VERY LONG AT ANY OF YOUR PREVIOUS JOBS...
...
CAN I ASK YOU...
YES?
Resume
Shuichi Ichinosawa
Gender
Age
(26)
M
F

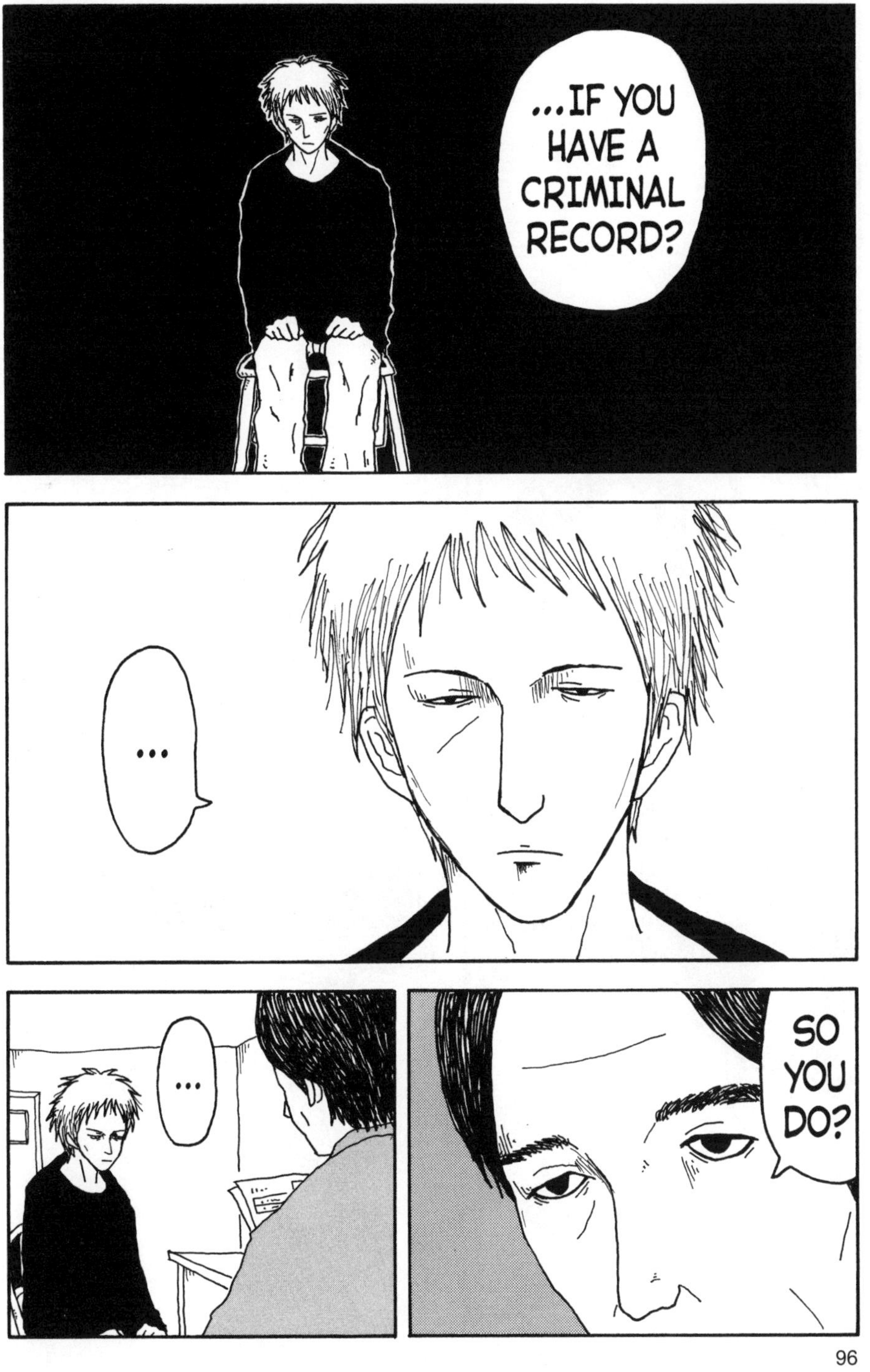
...IF YOU HAVE A CRIMINAL RECORD?
...
SO YOU DO?
...

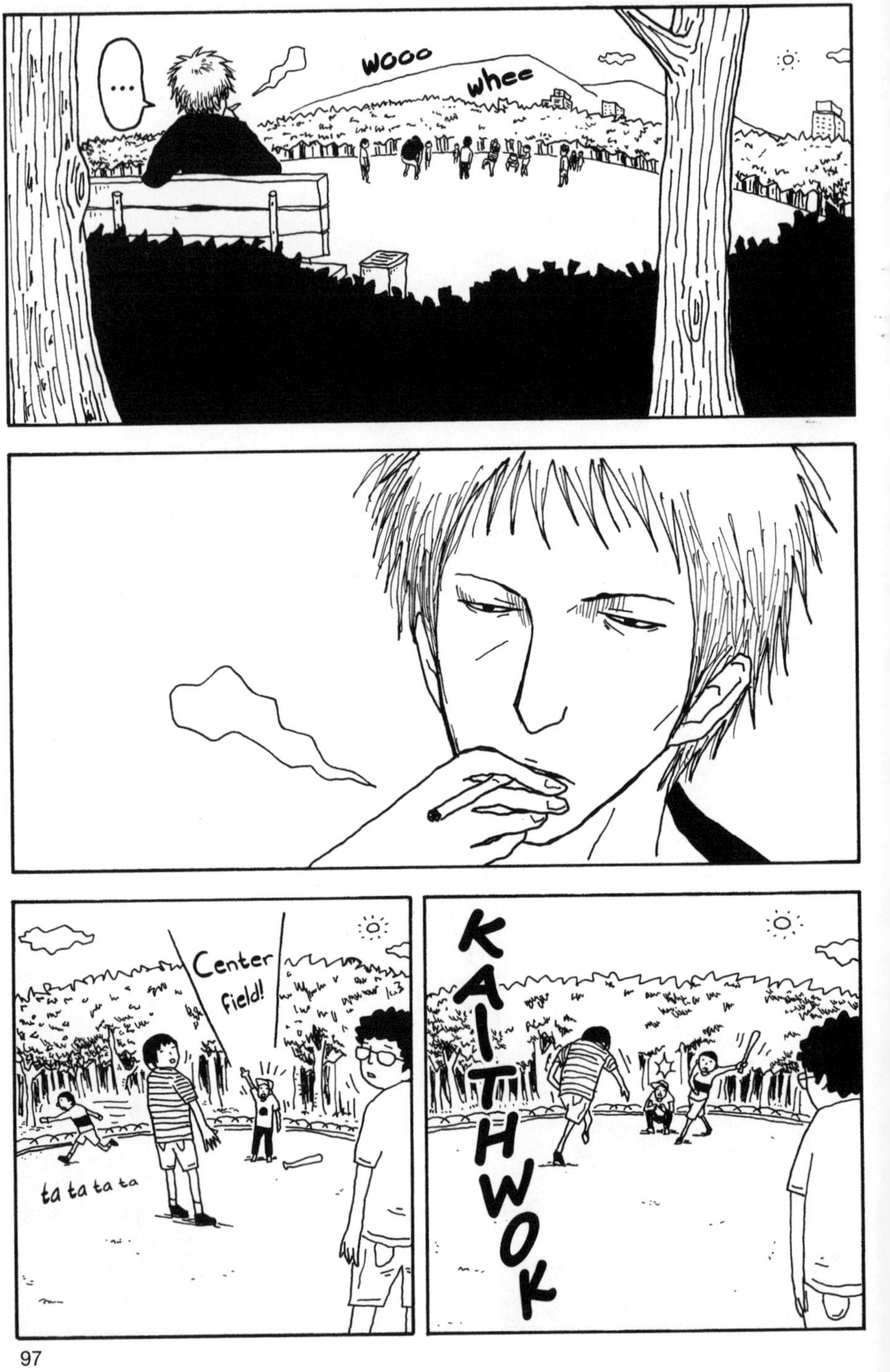
...
wooo
whee
KAITHWOK
Center field!
ta ta ta ta

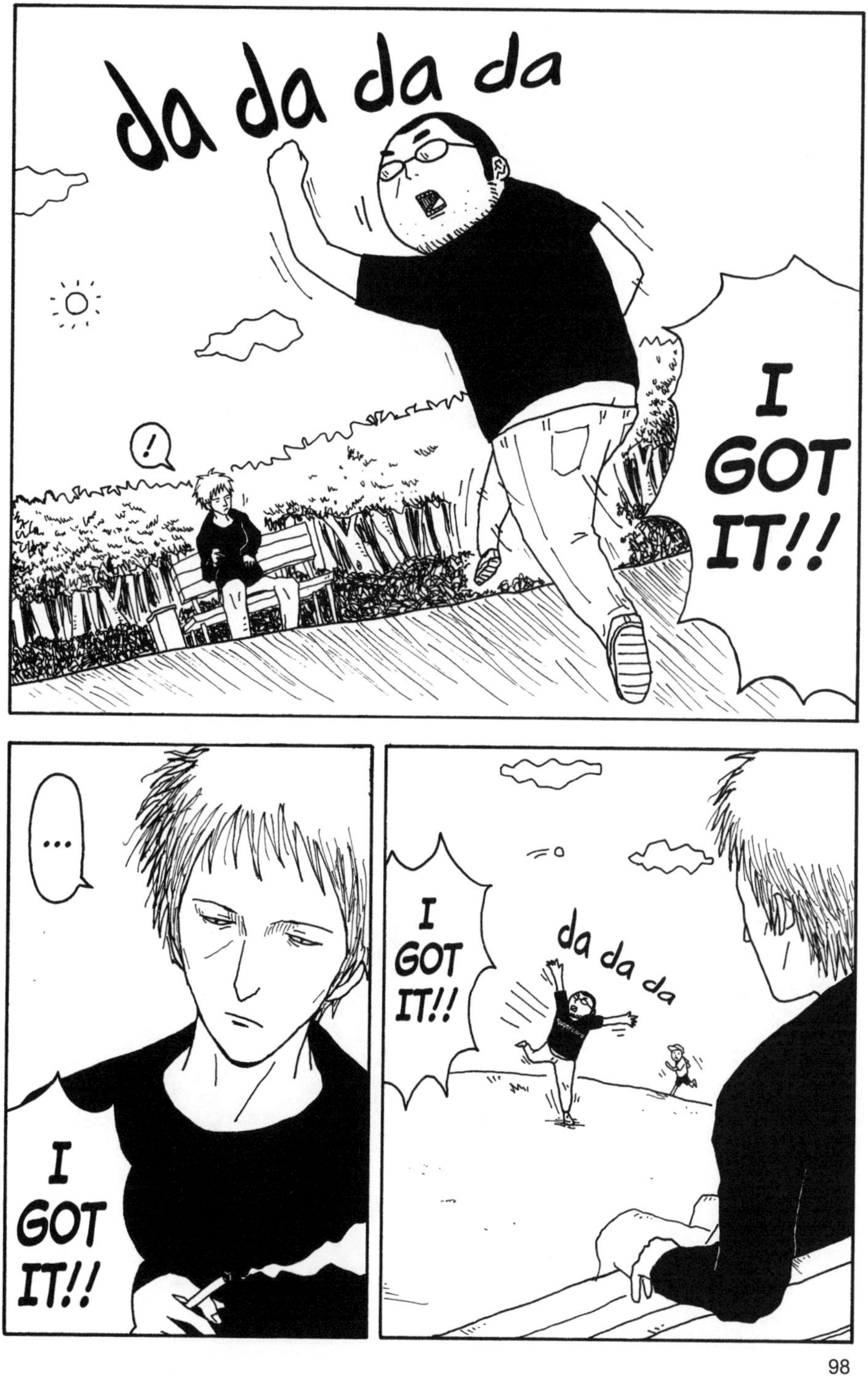
da da da da
!
I GOT IT!!
I GOT IT!!
da da da
...
I GOT IT!!

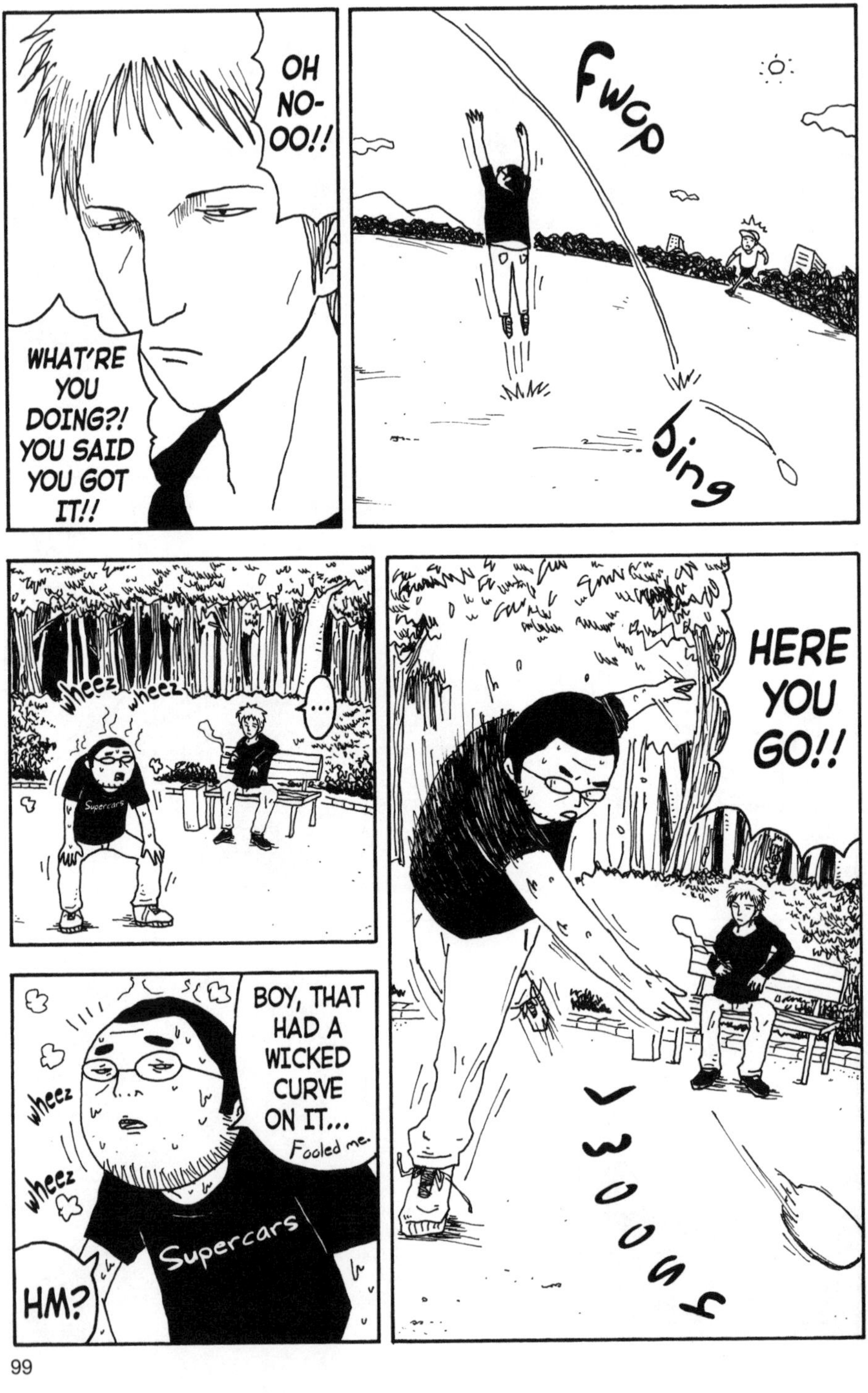
fwop
bing
OH NO-OO!!
WHAT'RE YOU DOING?! YOU SAID YOU GOT IT!!
HERE YOU GO!!
vwoosh
wheez
wheez
...
BOY, THAT HAD A WICKED CURVE ON IT...
Fooled me.
wheez
wheez
Supercars
HM?

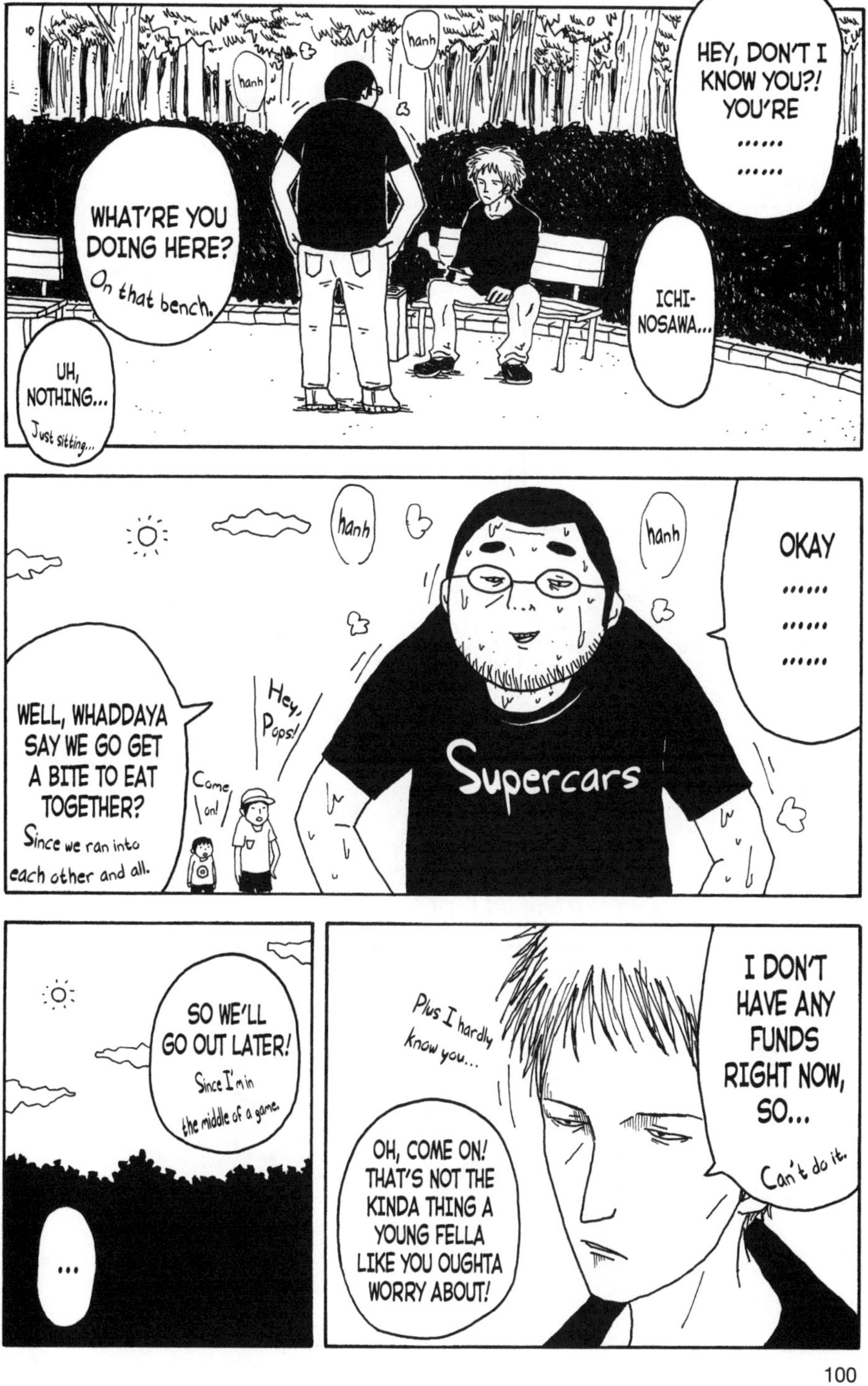
HEY, DON'T I KNOW YOU?! YOU'RE ....
ICHI-NOSAWA...
hanh
hanh
WHAT'RE YOU DOING HERE? On that bench.
UH, NOTHING... Just sitting...
OKAY ....
hanh
hanh
Hey, Pops!
Come on!
WELL, WHADDAYA SAY WE GO GET A BITE TO EAT TOGETHER? Since we ran into each other and all.
I DON'T HAVE ANY FUNDS RIGHT NOW, SO... Can't do it.
Plus I hardly know you...
OH, COME ON! THAT'S NOT THE KINDA THING A YOUNG FELLA LIKE YOU OUGHTA WORRY ABOUT!
SO WE'LL GO OUT LATER! Since I'm in the middle of a game.
...

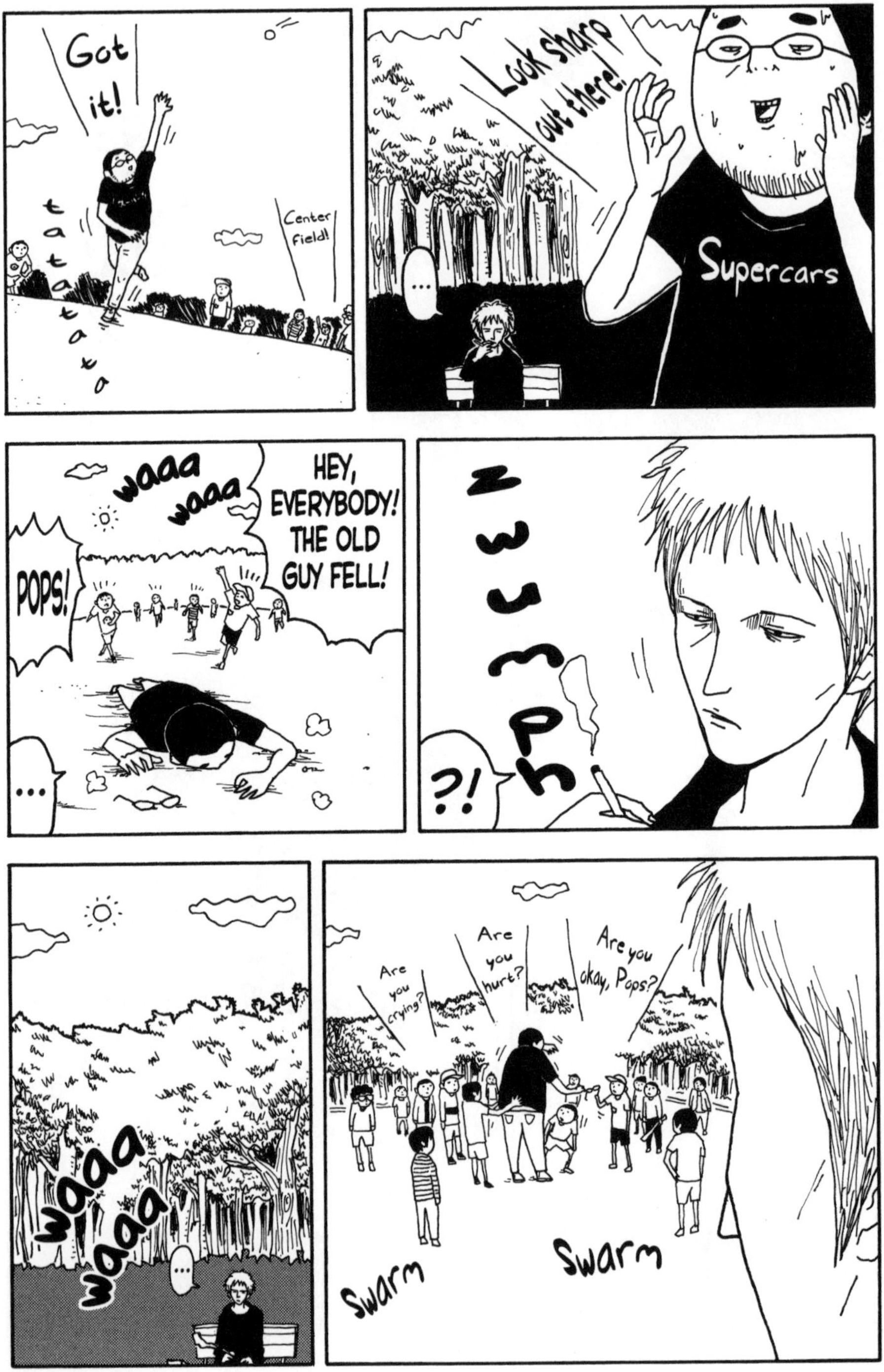
Look sharp out there!
Supercars
...
Got it!
Center field!
tatatatata
HEY, EVERYBODY! THE OLD GUY FELL!
waaa waaa
POPS!
...
zwumph
?!
Are you okay, Pops?
Are you hurt?
Are you crying?
Swarm
Swarm
waaa waaa
...

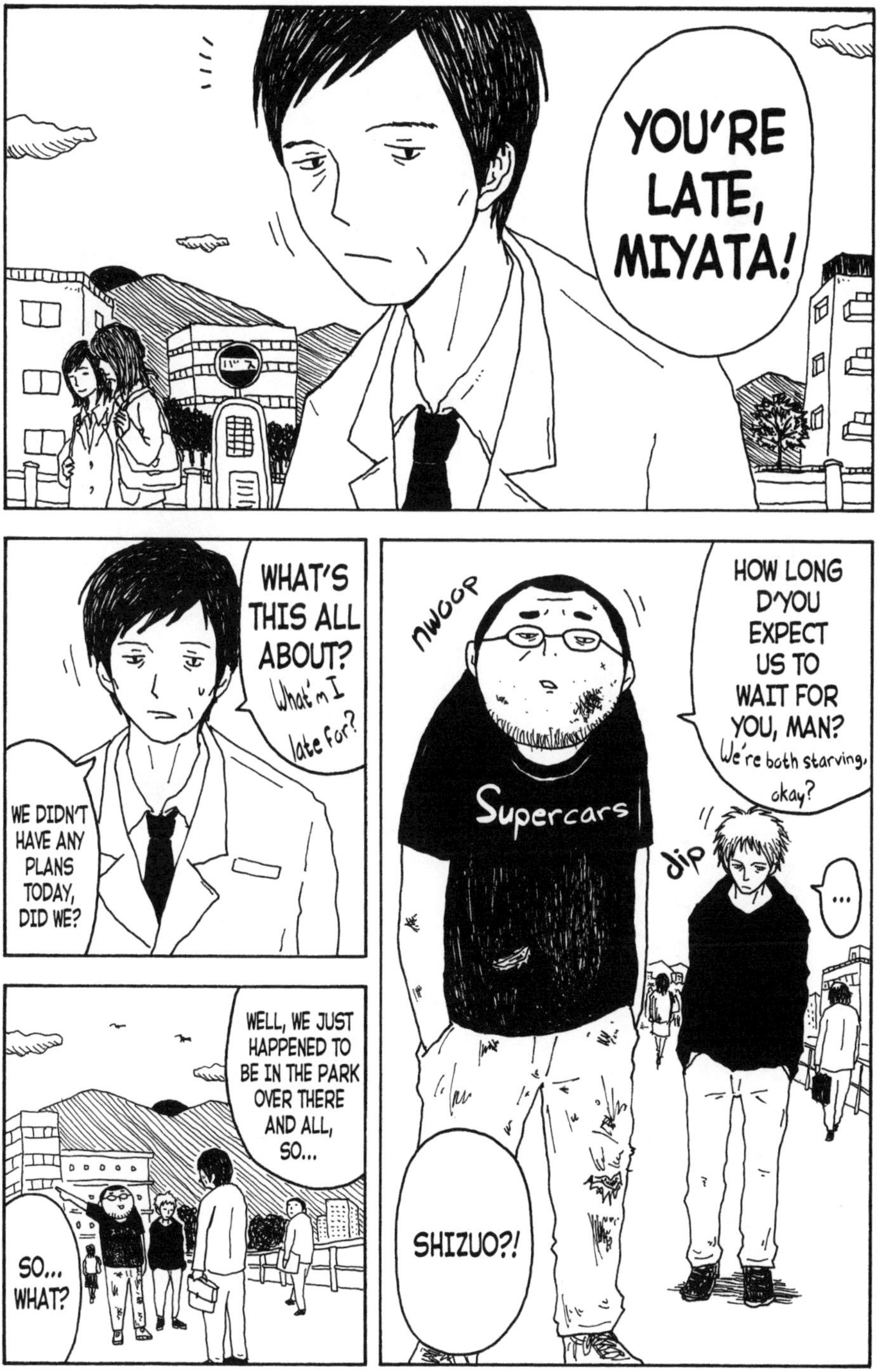
YOU'RE LATE, MIYATA!
HOW LONG D'YOU EXPECT US TO WAIT FOR YOU, MAN? We're both starving, okay?
nwoop
...
dip
SHIZUO?!
WHAT'S THIS ALL ABOUT? What'm I late for?
WE DIDN'T HAVE ANY PLANS TODAY, DID WE?
WELL, WE JUST HAPPENED TO BE IN THE PARK OVER THERE AND ALL, SO...
SO... WHAT?

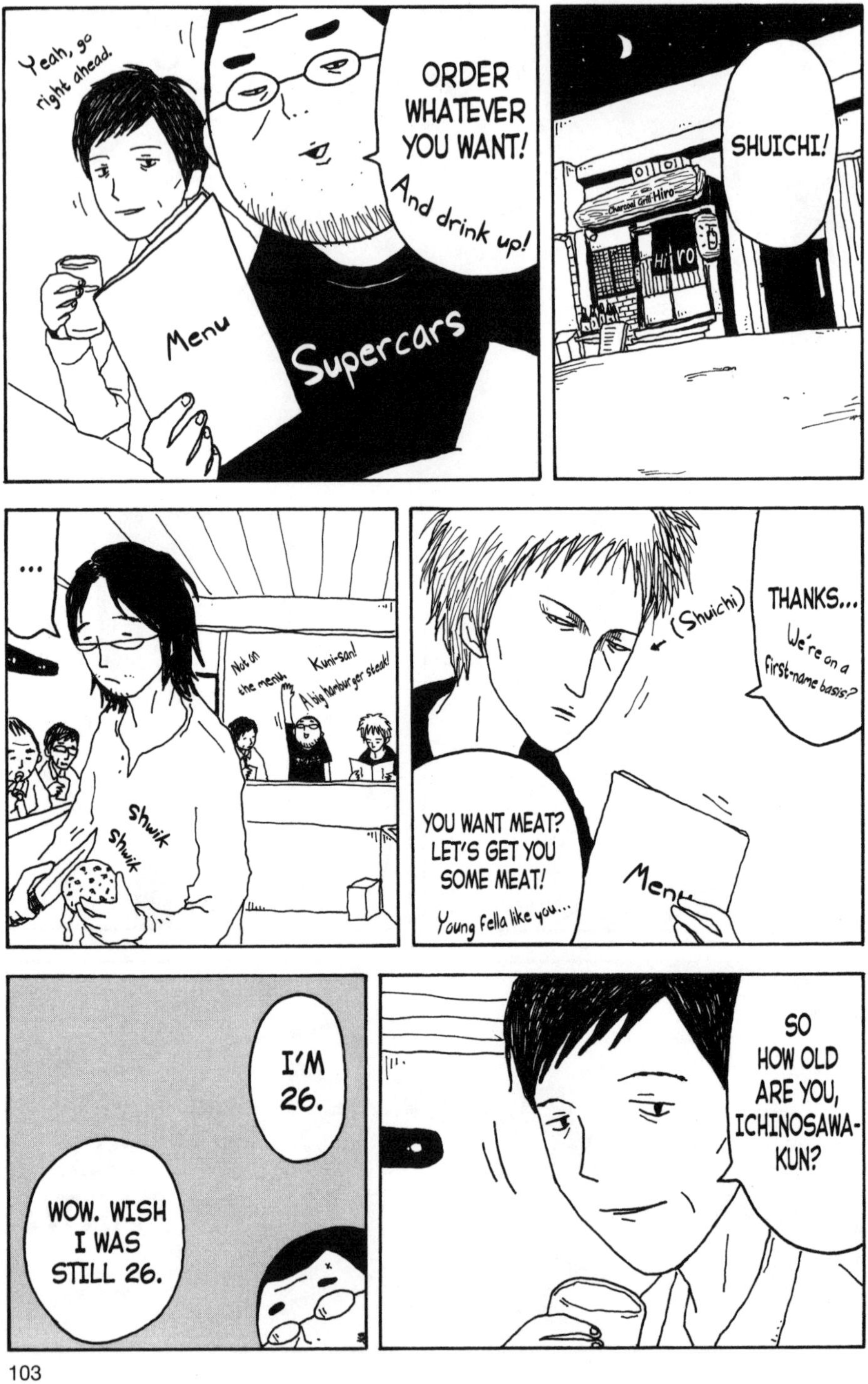
SHUICHI!
Charcoal Grill Hiro
Hiro
ORDER WHATEVER YOU WANT!
And drink up!
Yeah, go right ahead.
Supercars
Menu
THANKS...
We're on a first-name basis?
(Shuichi)
YOU WANT MEAT? LET'S GET YOU SOME MEAT!
Young fella like you...
Menu
...
Kuni-san!
A big hamburger steak!
Not on the menu.
Shwik
Shwik
SO HOW OLD ARE YOU, ICHINOSAWA-KUN?
I'M 26.
WOW. WISH I WAS STILL 26.

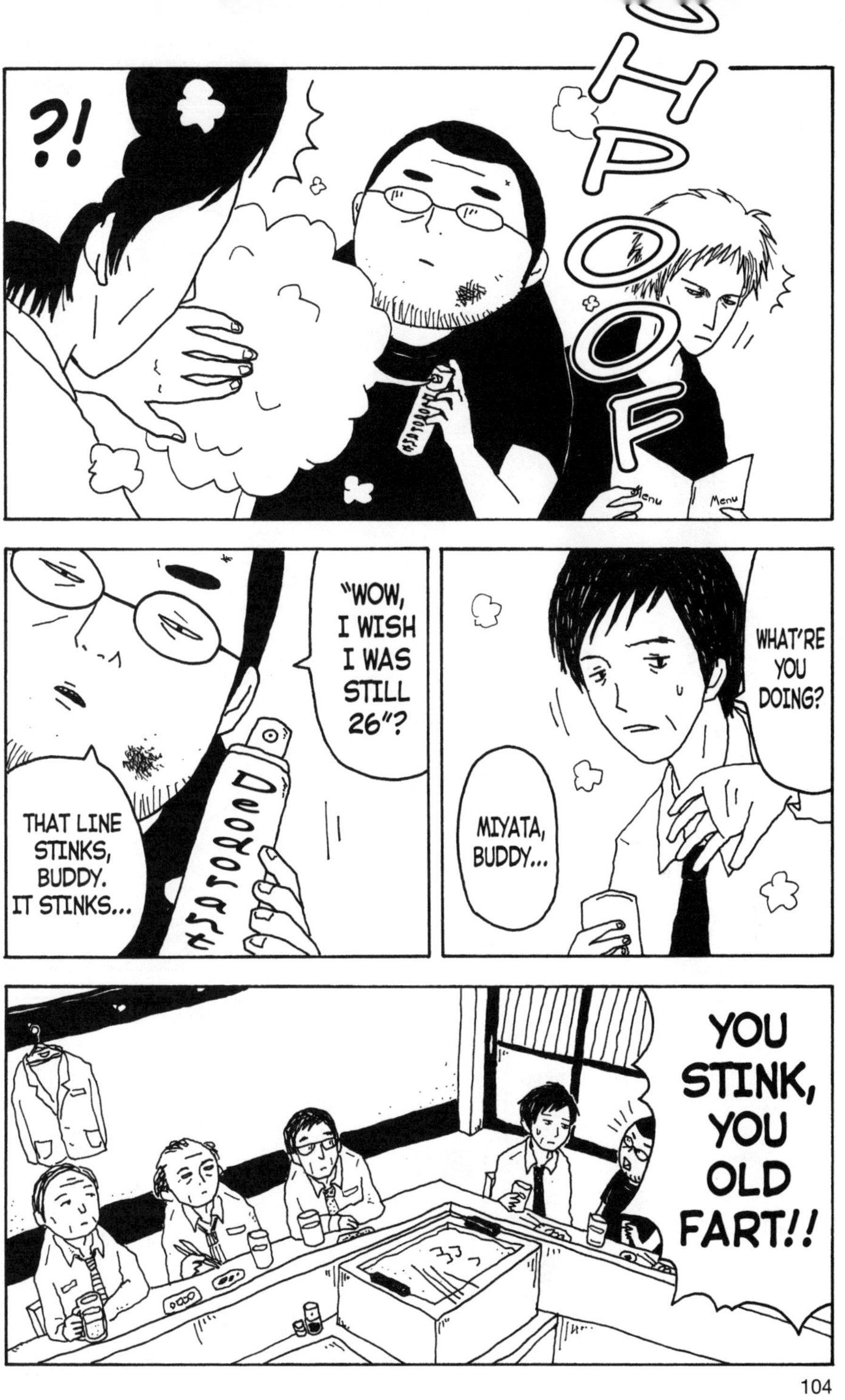
SHPOOF
?!
Menu
Menu
WHAT'RE YOU DOING?
MIYATA, BUDDY...
"WOW, I WISH I WAS STILL 26"?
Deodorant
THAT LINE STINKS, BUDDY. IT STINKS...
YOU STINK, YOU OLD FART!!

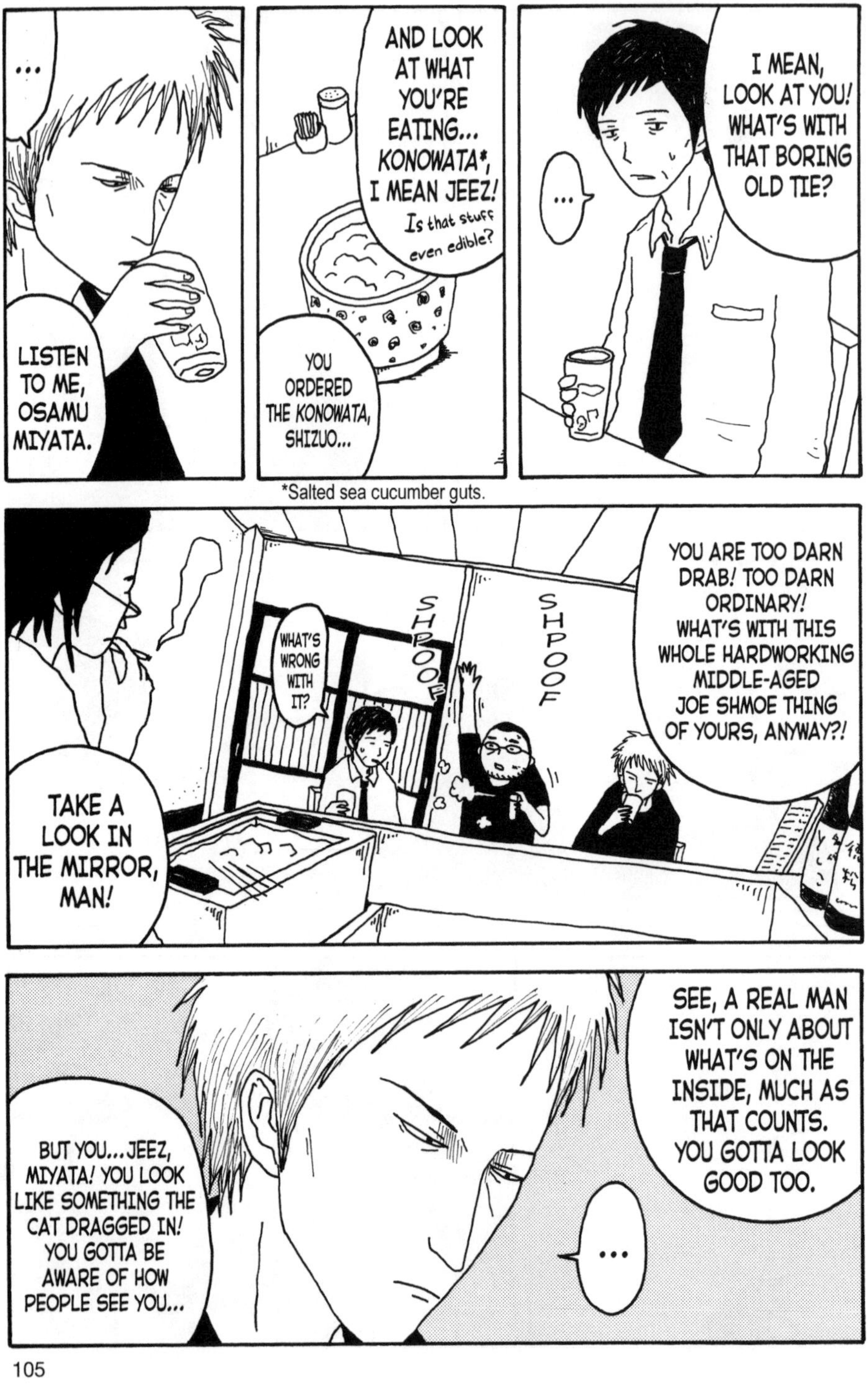
I MEAN, LOOK AT YOU! WHAT'S WITH THAT BORING OLD TIE?
...
AND LOOK AT WHAT YOU'RE EATING... KONOWATA*, I MEAN JEEZ!
Is that stuff even edible?
YOU ORDERED THE KONOWATA, SHIZUO...
...
LISTEN TO ME, OSAMU MIYATA.
YOU ARE TOO DARN DRAB! TOO DARN ORDINARY! WHAT'S WITH THIS WHOLE HARDWORKING MIDDLE-AGED JOE SHMOE THING OF YOURS, ANYWAY?!
SHPOOF
SHPOOF
WHAT'S WRONG WITH IT?
TAKE A LOOK IN THE MIRROR, MAN!
SEE, A REAL MAN ISN'T ONLY ABOUT WHAT'S ON THE INSIDE, MUCH AS THAT COUNTS. YOU GOTTA LOOK GOOD TOO.
...
BUT YOU...JEEZ, MIYATA! YOU LOOK LIKE SOMETHING THE CAT DRAGGED IN! YOU GOTTA BE AWARE OF HOW PEOPLE SEE YOU...

*Salted sea cucumber guts.

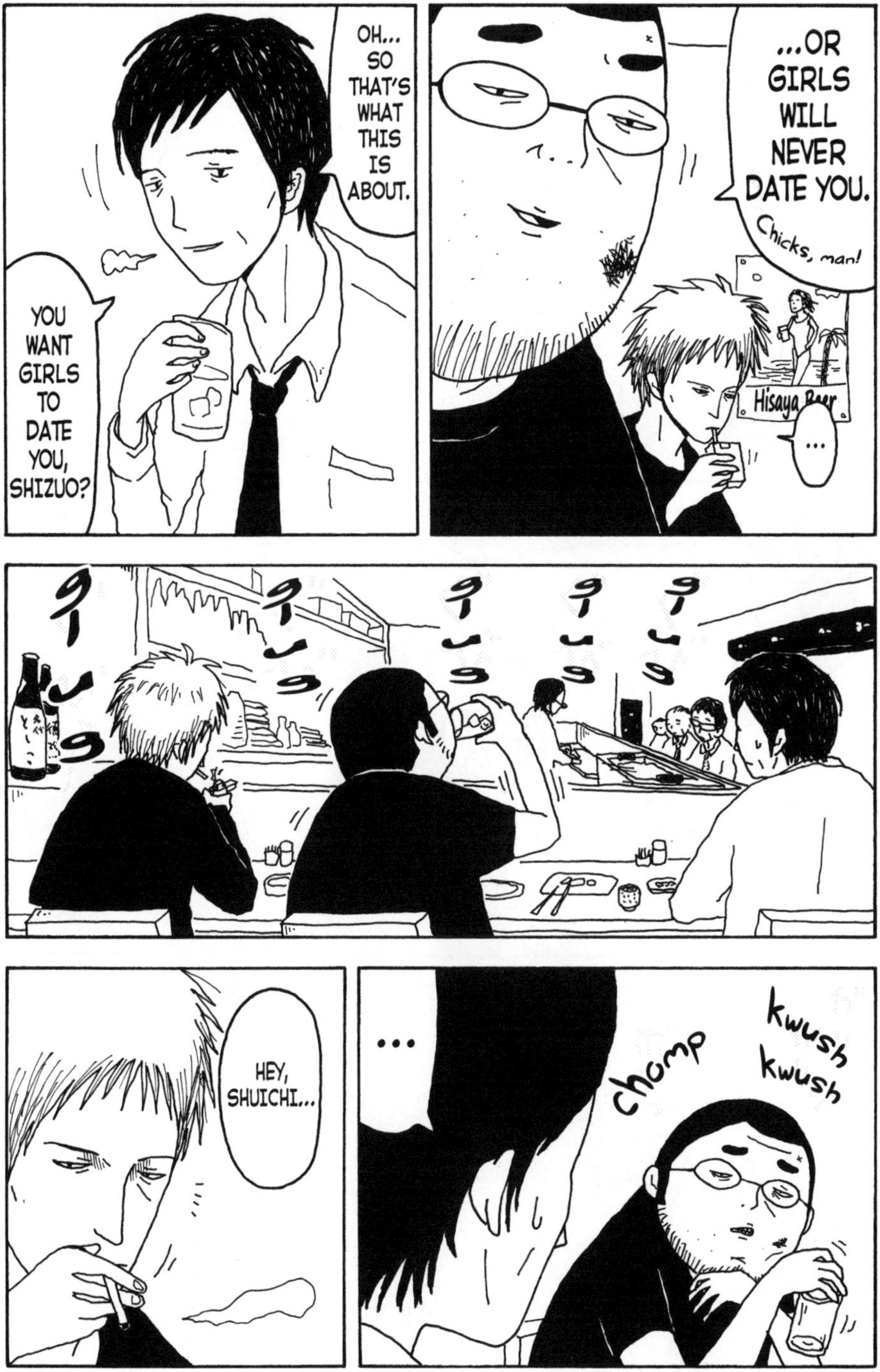
...OR GIRLS WILL NEVER DATE YOU.
Chicks, man!
Hisaya Beer
...
OH... SO THAT'S WHAT THIS IS ABOUT.
YOU WANT GIRLS TO DATE YOU, SHIZUO?
kwush kwush
chomp
...
HEY, SHUICHI...

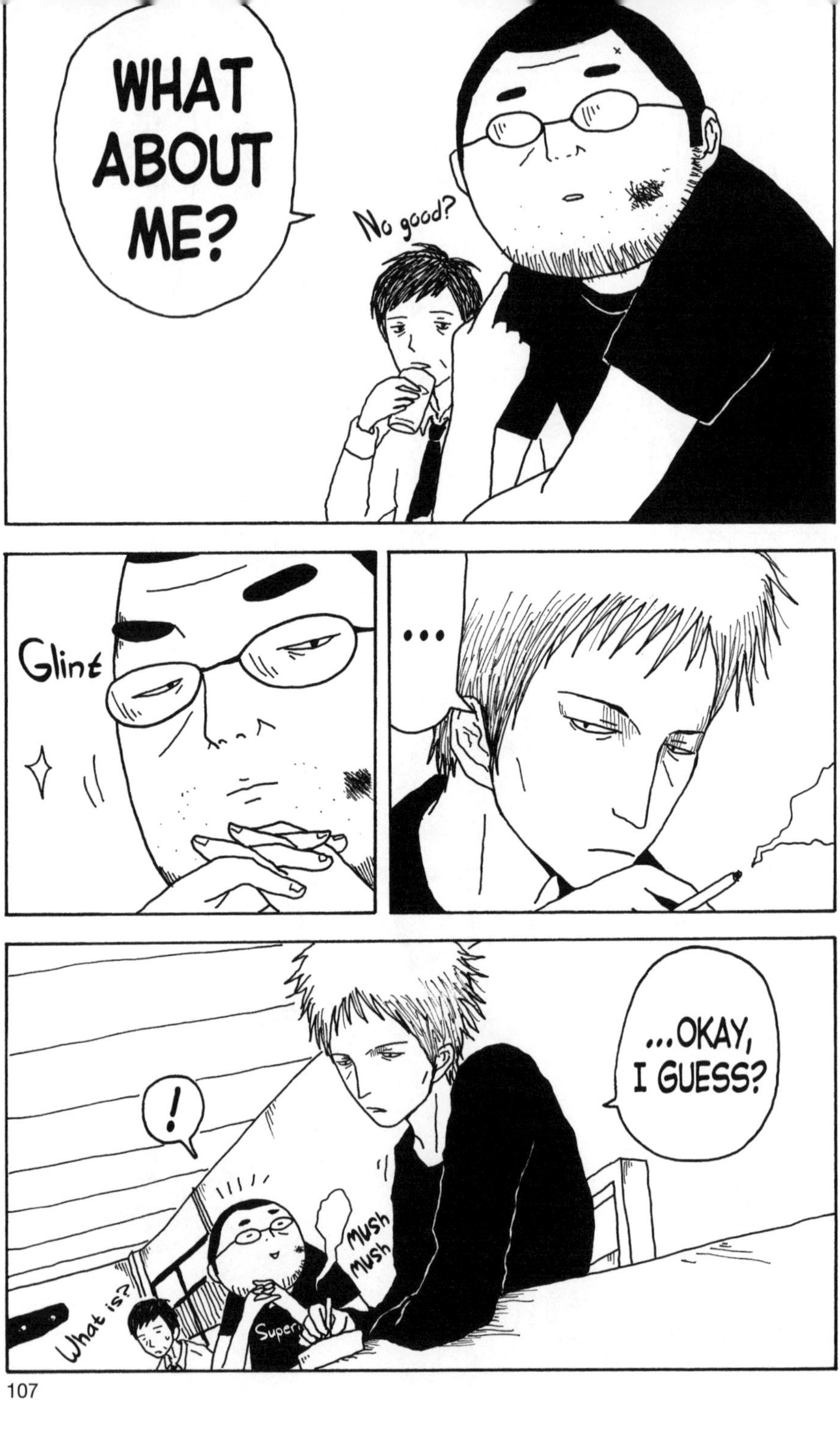
WHAT ABOUT ME?
No good?
...
Glint
...OKAY, I GUESS?
!
mush mush
What is?
Super

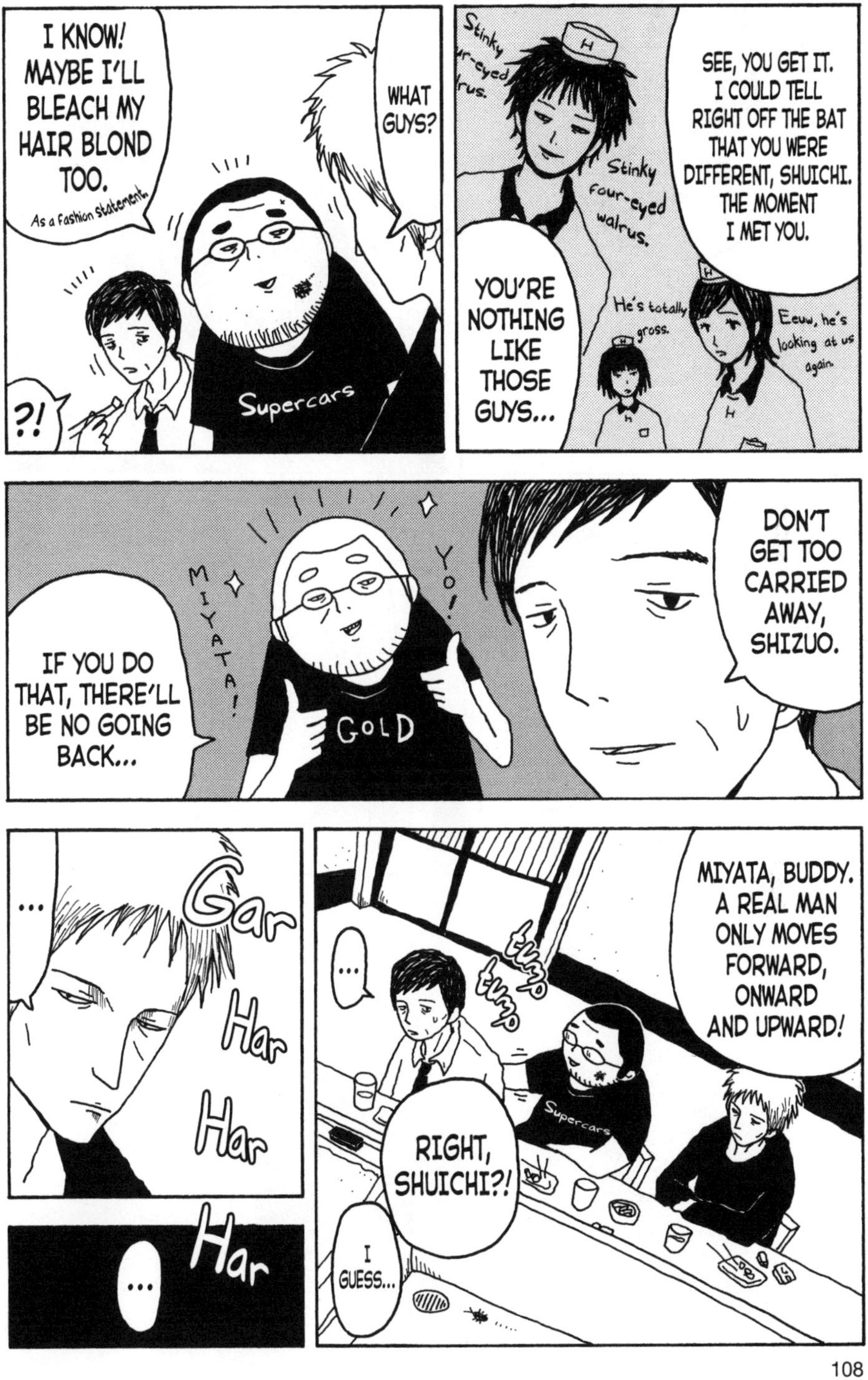
SEE, YOU GET IT. I COULD TELL RIGHT OFF THE BAT THAT YOU WERE DIFFERENT, SHUICHI. THE MOMENT I MET YOU.
Stinky four-eyed walrus.
YOU'RE NOTHING LIKE THOSE GUYS...
Eeuw, he's looking at us again.
He's totally gross.
WHAT GUYS?
I KNOW! MAYBE I'LL BLEACH MY HAIR BLOND TOO.
As a Fashion Statement.
Supercars
?!
DON'T GET TOO CARRIED AWAY, SHIZUO.
YO!
MIYATA!
GOLD
IF YOU DO THAT, THERE'LL BE NO GOING BACK...
MIYATA, BUDDY. A REAL MAN ONLY MOVES FORWARD, ONWARD AND UPWARD!
tump
tump
...
Supercars
RIGHT, SHUICHI?!
I GUESS...
...
Gar
Har
Har
Har
...

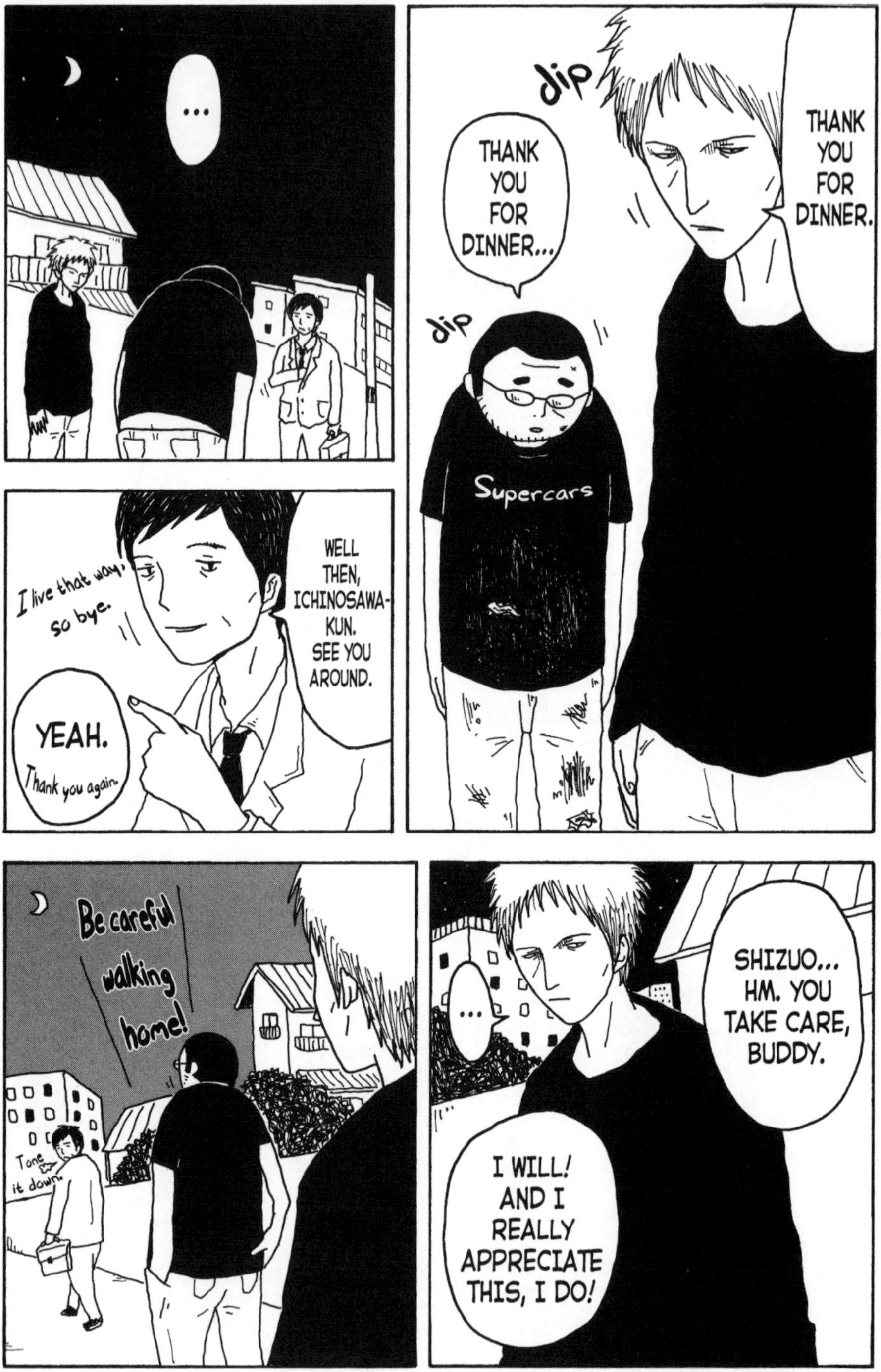
dip
THANK YOU FOR DINNER.
THANK YOU FOR DINNER...
dip
Supercars
...
WELL THEN, ICHINOSAWA-KUN. SEE YOU AROUND.
I live that way, so bye.
YEAH.
Thank you again.
SHIZUO... HM. YOU TAKE CARE, BUDDY.
...
I WILL! AND I REALLY APPRECIATE THIS, I DO!
Be careful walking home!
Tone it down.

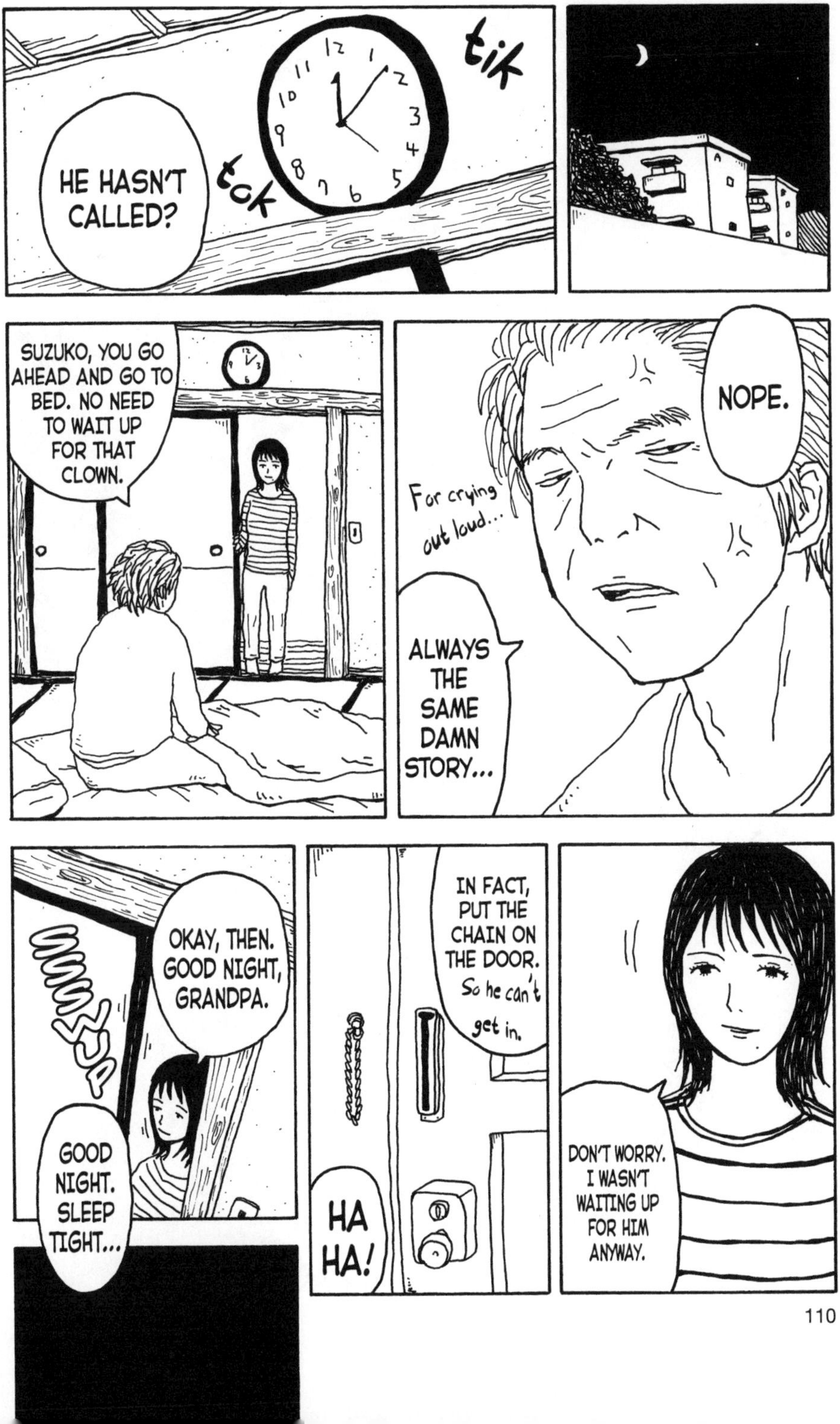
tik
HE HASN'T CALLED?
tok
NOPE.
For crying out loud...
ALWAYS THE SAME DAMN STORY...
SUZUKO, YOU GO AHEAD AND GO TO BED. NO NEED TO WAIT UP FOR THAT CLOWN.
DON'T WORRY. I WASN'T WAITING UP FOR HIM ANYWAY.
IN FACT, PUT THE CHAIN ON THE DOOR. So he can't get in.
HA HA!
OKAY, THEN. GOOD NIGHT, GRANDPA.
GOOD NIGHT. SLEEP TIGHT...

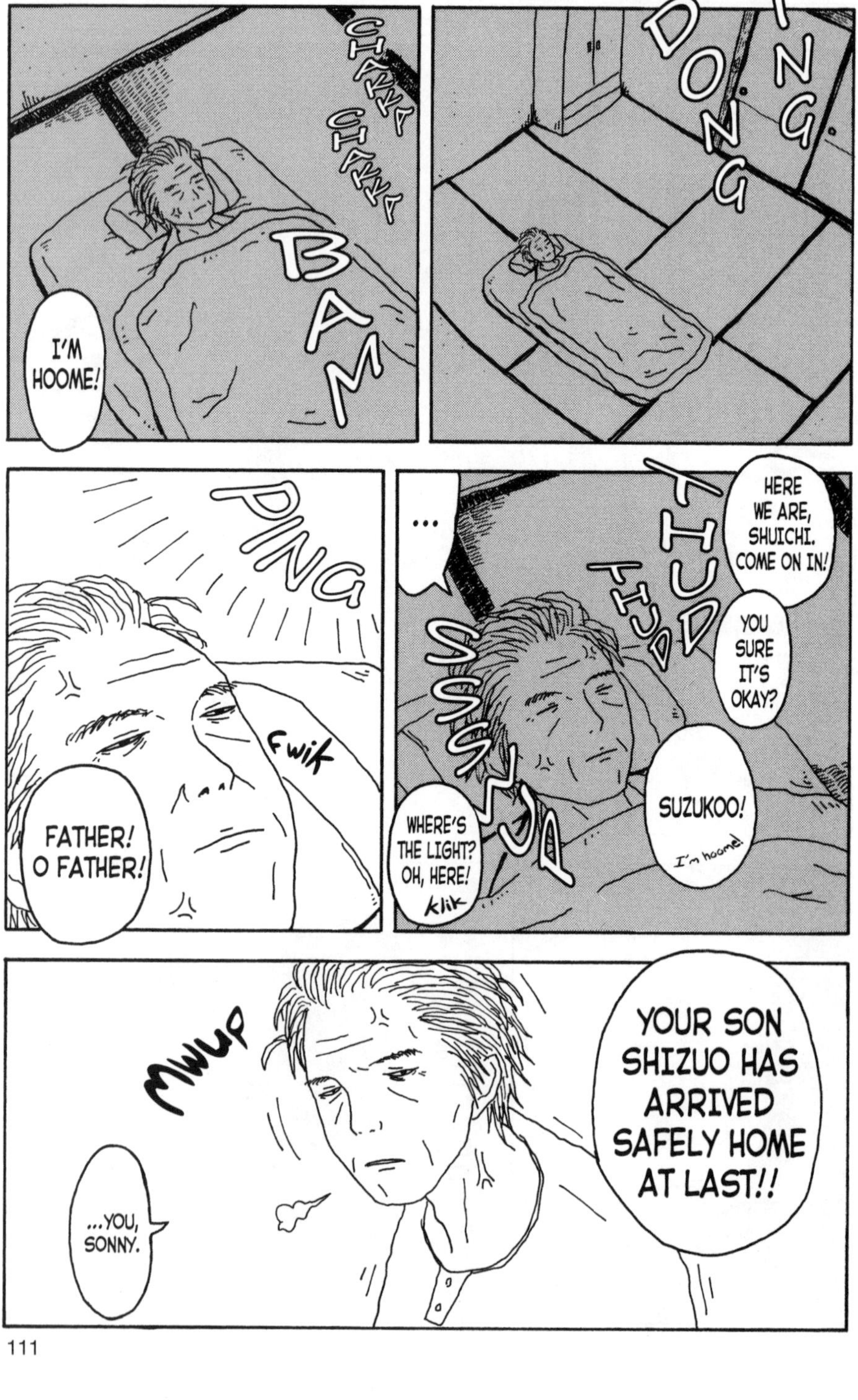
DING.
DONG.
CHAKKA CHAKKA CHAKKA
BAM
I'M HOOME!
HERE WE ARE, SHUICHI. COME ON IN!
THUD
THUD
YOU SURE IT'S OKAY?
SUZUKOO!
I'm hoome!
...
WHERE'S THE LIGHT? OH, HERE!
klik
PING
FATHER! O FATHER!
fwik
YOUR SON SHIZUO HAS ARRIVED SAFELY HOME AT LAST!!
MWUP
...YOU, SONNY.

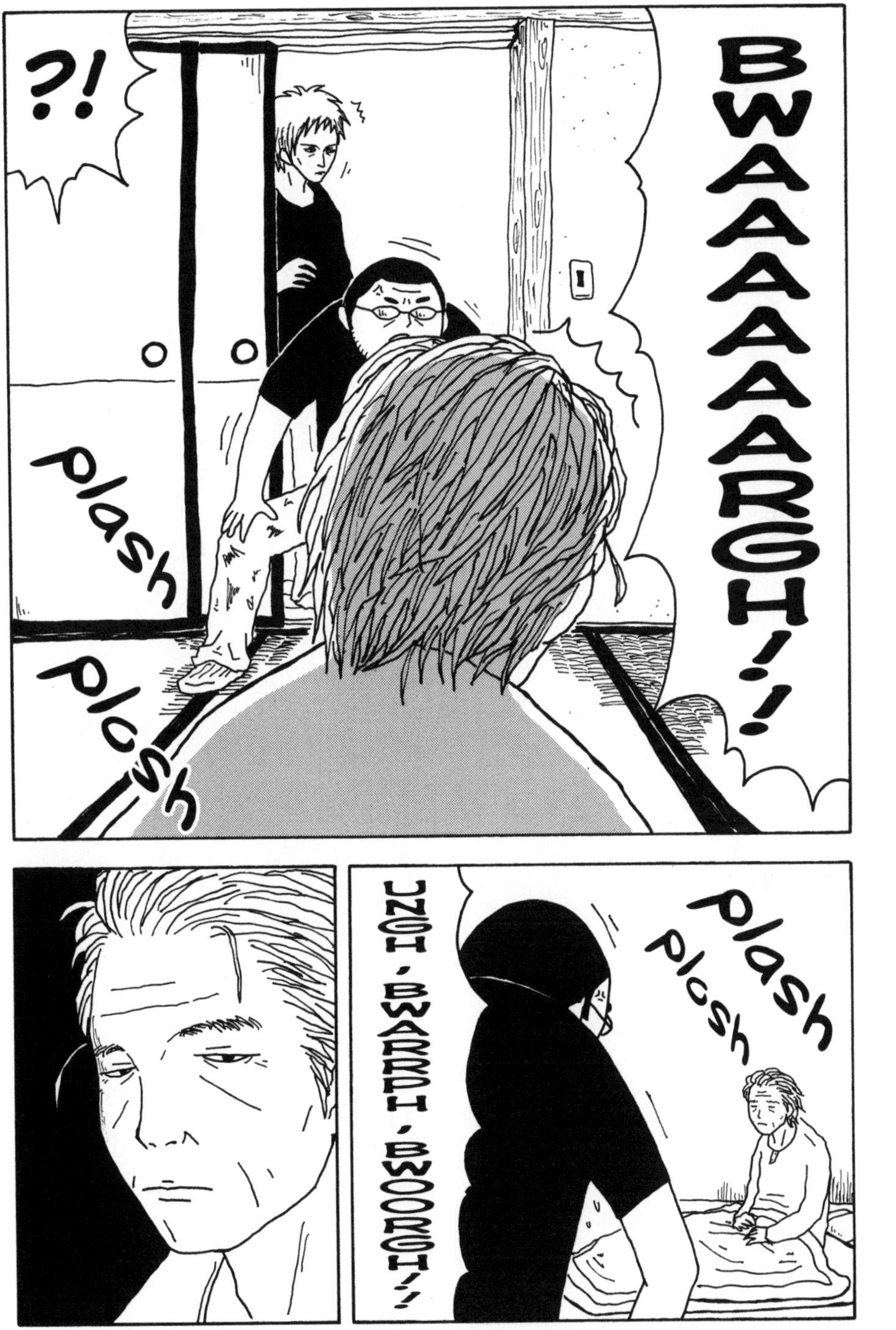
BWAAAAARGH!!
?!
plash
plosh
UNGH, BWARRPH, BWOORGH!!
plash
plosh

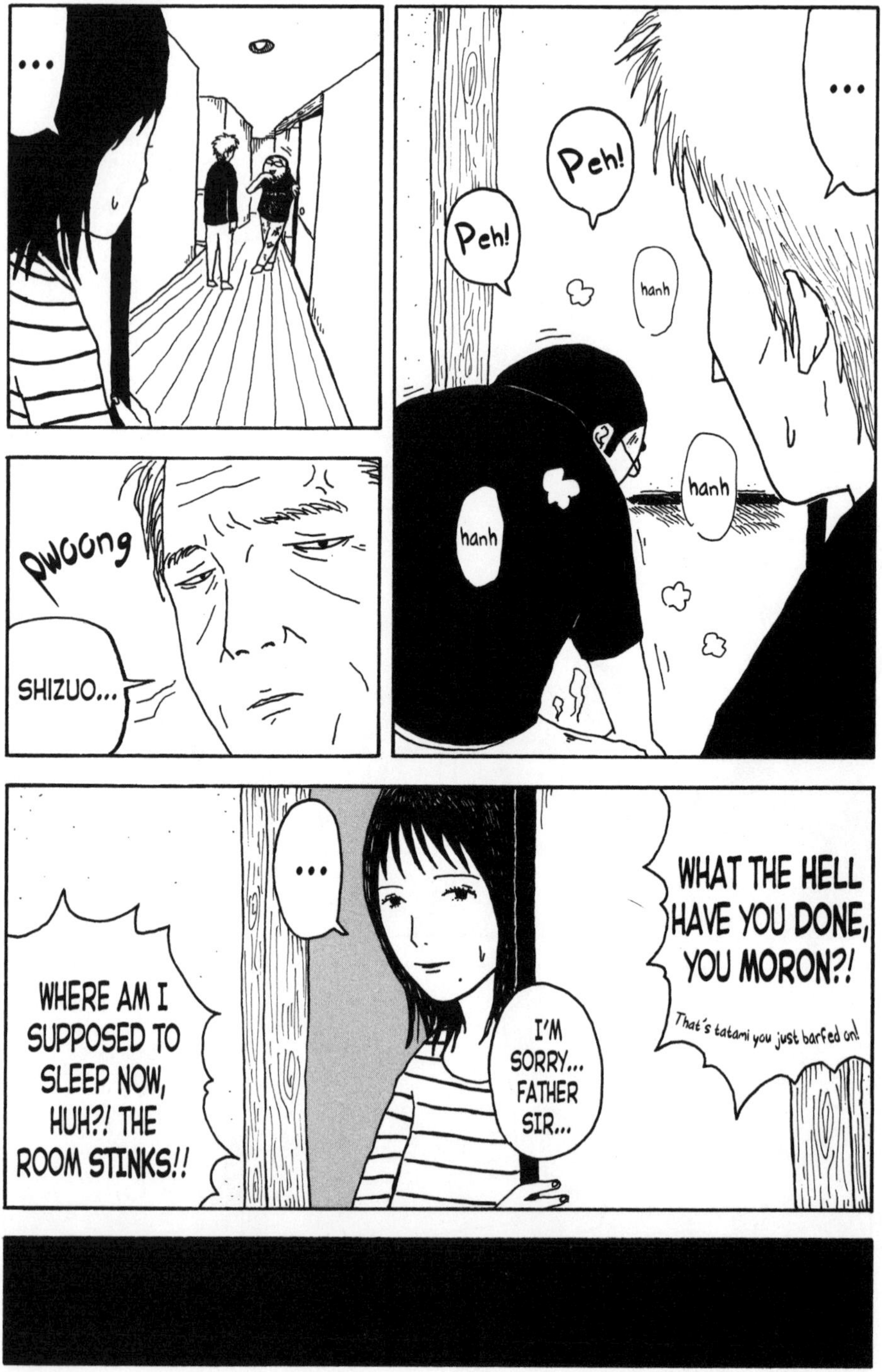
...
Peh!
Peh!
hanh
hanh
hanh
...
PWOONG
SHIZUO...
WHAT THE HELL HAVE YOU DONE, YOU MORON?!
That's tatami you just barfed on!
I'M SORRY... FATHER SIR...
...
WHERE AM I SUPPOSED TO SLEEP NOW, HUH?! THE ROOM STINKS!!

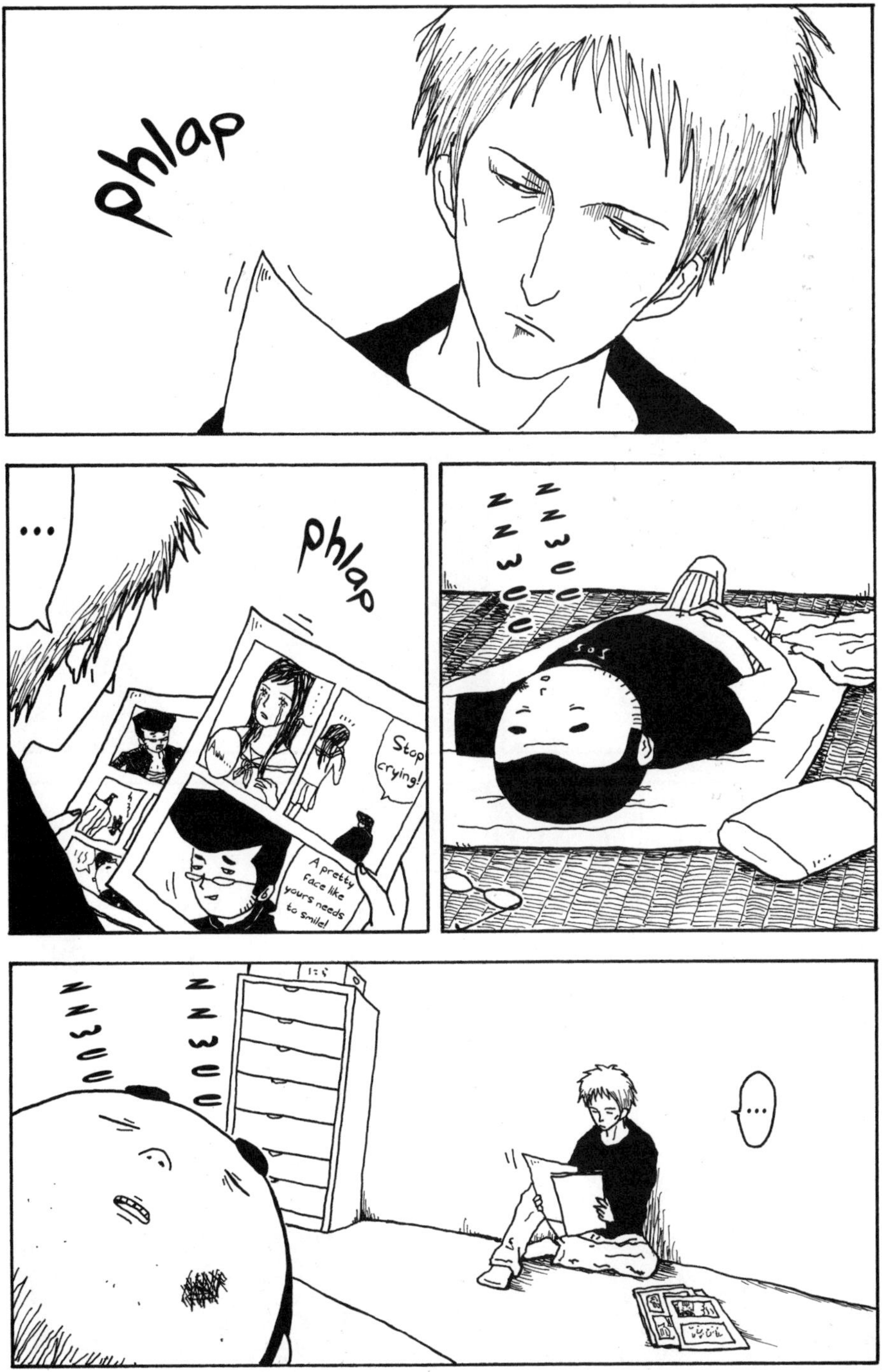
phlap
phlap
...
Stop crying!
Aww...
A pretty face like yours needs to smile!
...

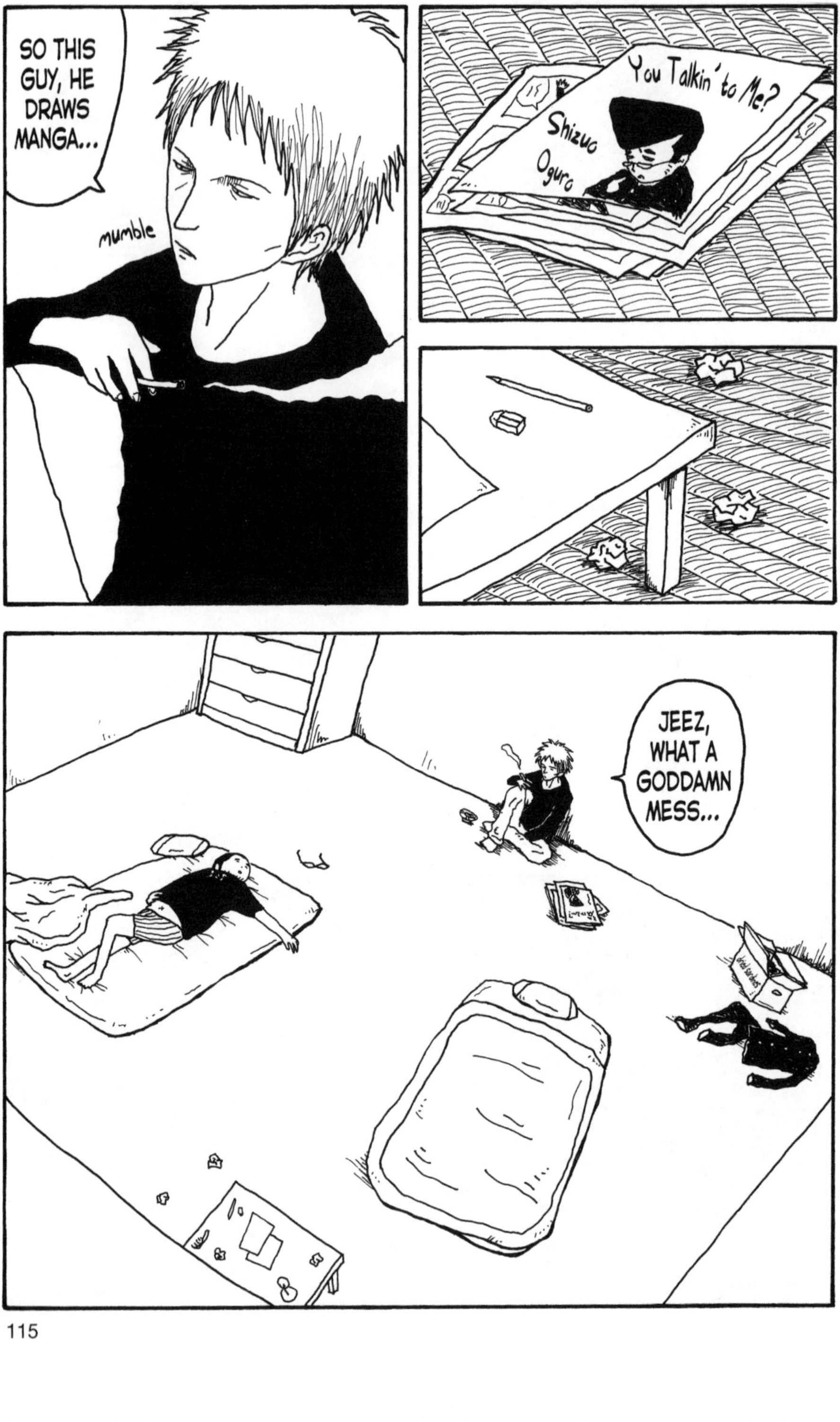
You Talkin' to Me?
Shizuo Oguro
SO THIS GUY, HE DRAWS MANGA...
mumble
JEEZ, WHAT A GODDAMN MESS...

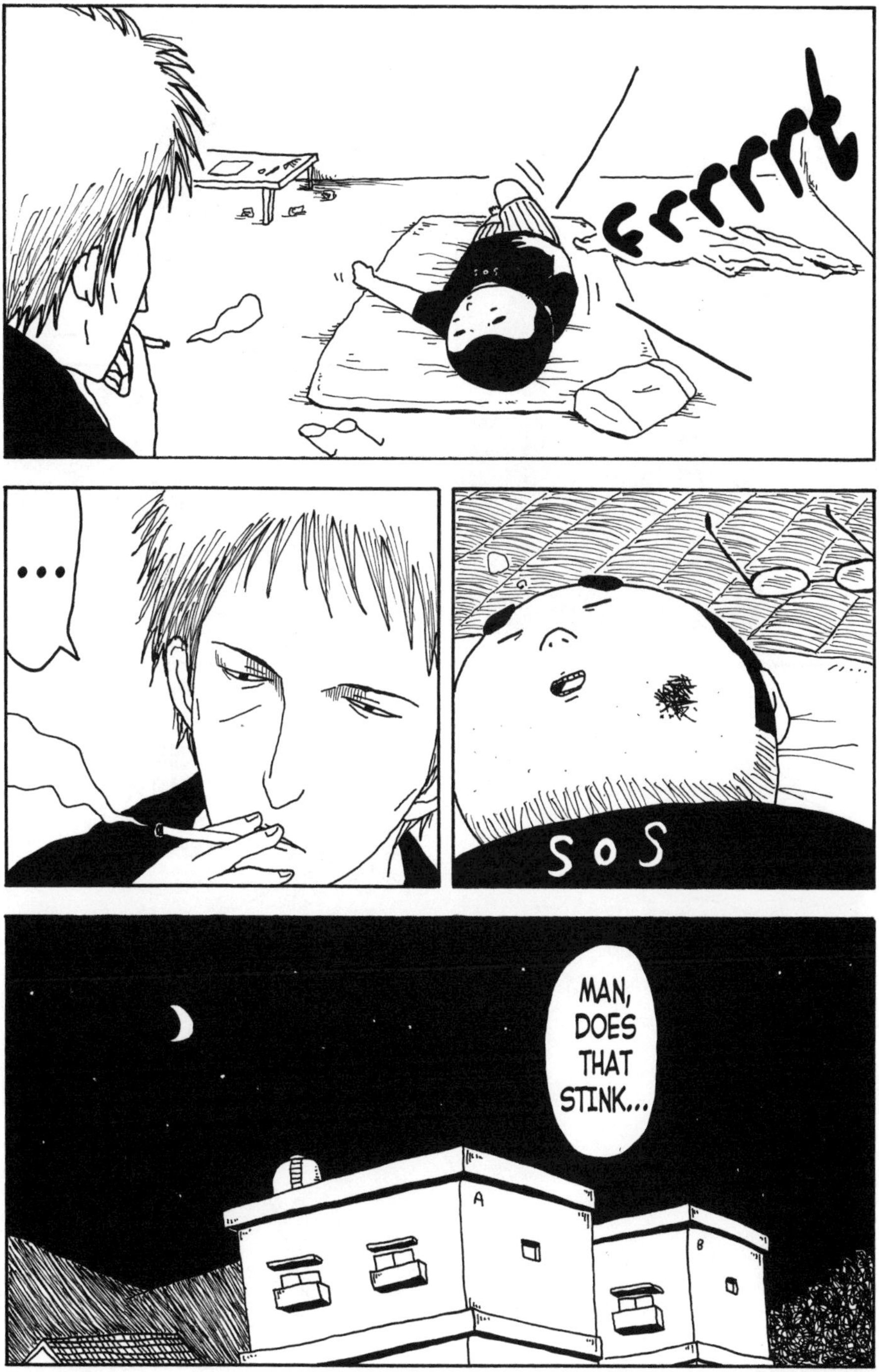
Frrrrt
SOS
...
MAN, DOES THAT STINK...
A
B

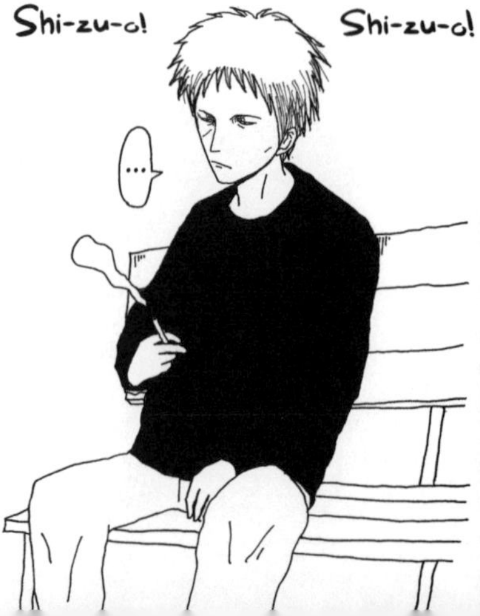
Shi-zu-o!
Shi-zu-o!
...

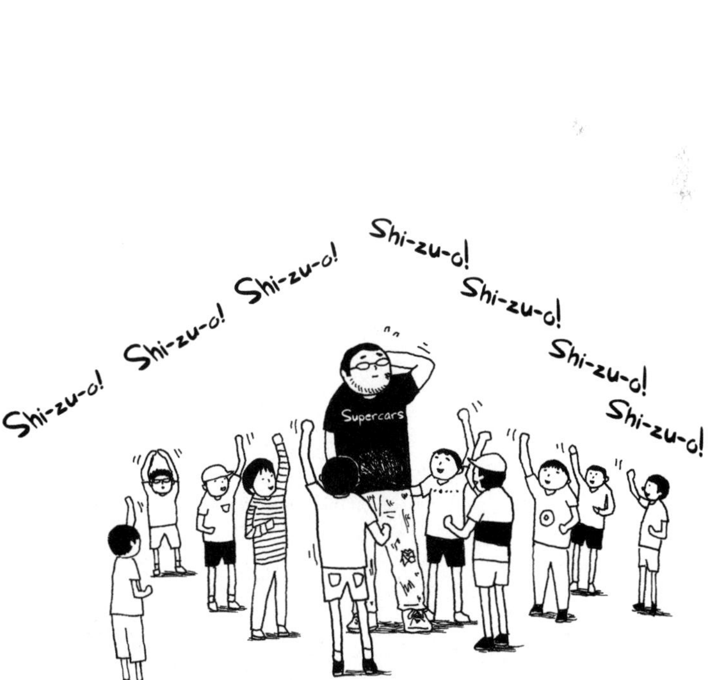
Shi-zu-o!
Shi-zu-o!
Shi-zu-o!
Shi-zu-o!
Shi-zu-o!
Shi-zu-o!
Shi-zu-o!
Supercars

Chapter 3:
Wrestling with Your Doubts... and Winning

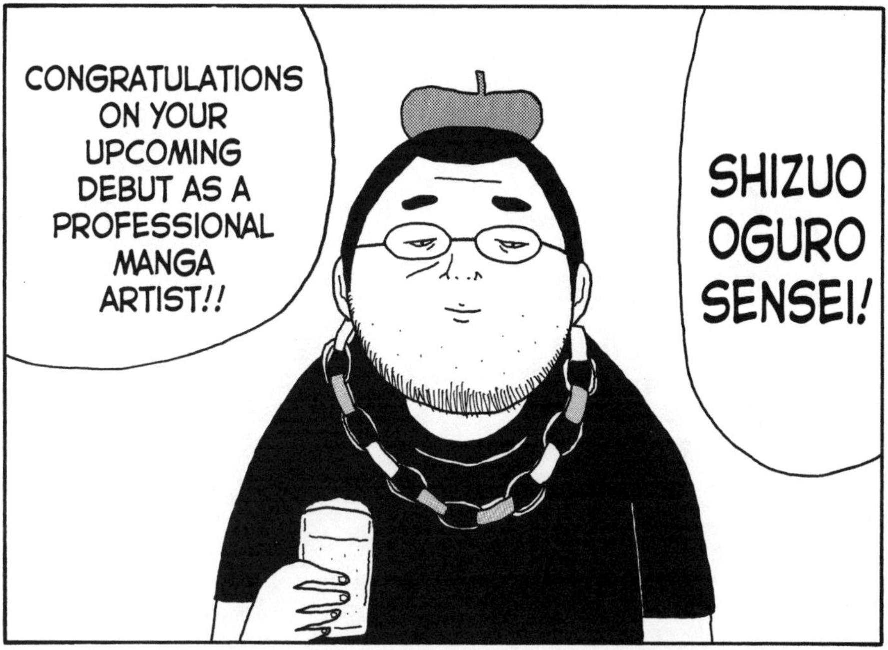
CONGRATULATIONS ON YOUR UPCOMING DEBUT AS A PROFESSIONAL MANGA ARTIST!!
SHIZUO OGURO SENSEI!

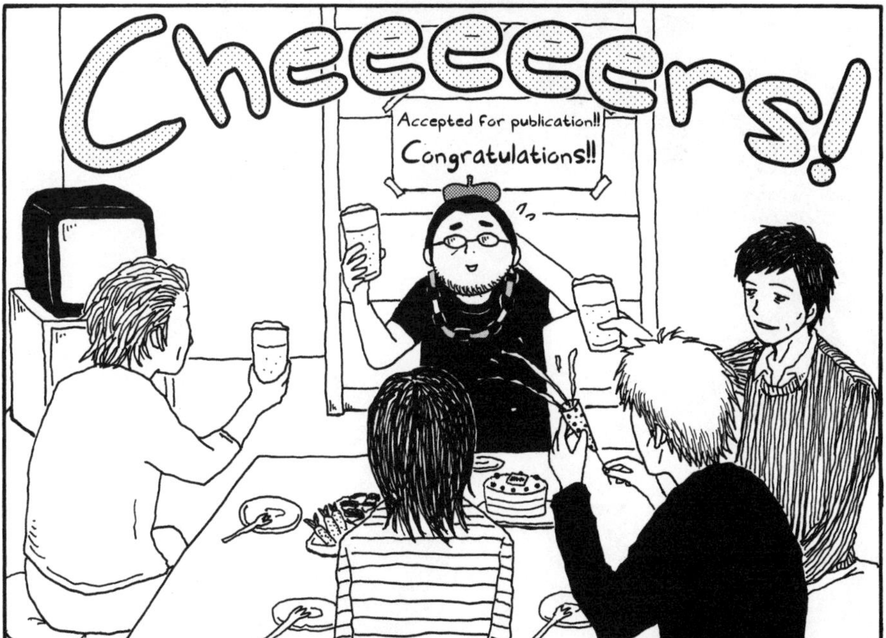
Cheeeers!
Accepted for publication!!
Congratulations!!

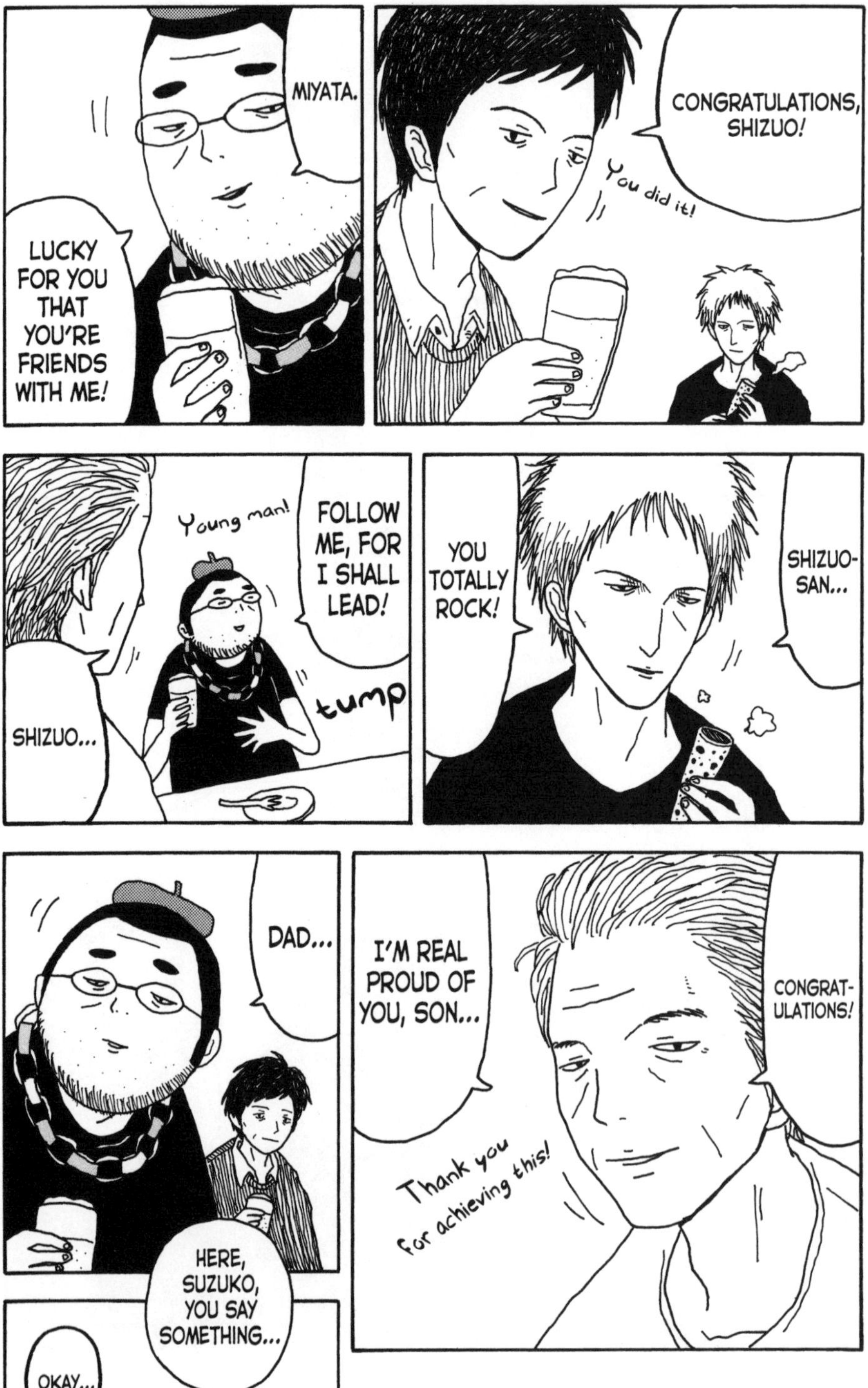
CONGRATULATIONS, SHIZUO!
You did it!
MIYATA.
LUCKY FOR YOU THAT YOU'RE FRIENDS WITH ME!
SHIZUO-SAN...
YOU TOTALLY ROCK!
FOLLOW ME, FOR I SHALL LEAD!
Young man!
tump
SHIZUO...
CONGRAT-ULATIONS!
I'M REAL PROUD OF YOU, SON...
Thank you for achieving this!
DAD...
HERE, SUZUKO, YOU SAY SOMETHING...
OKAY...

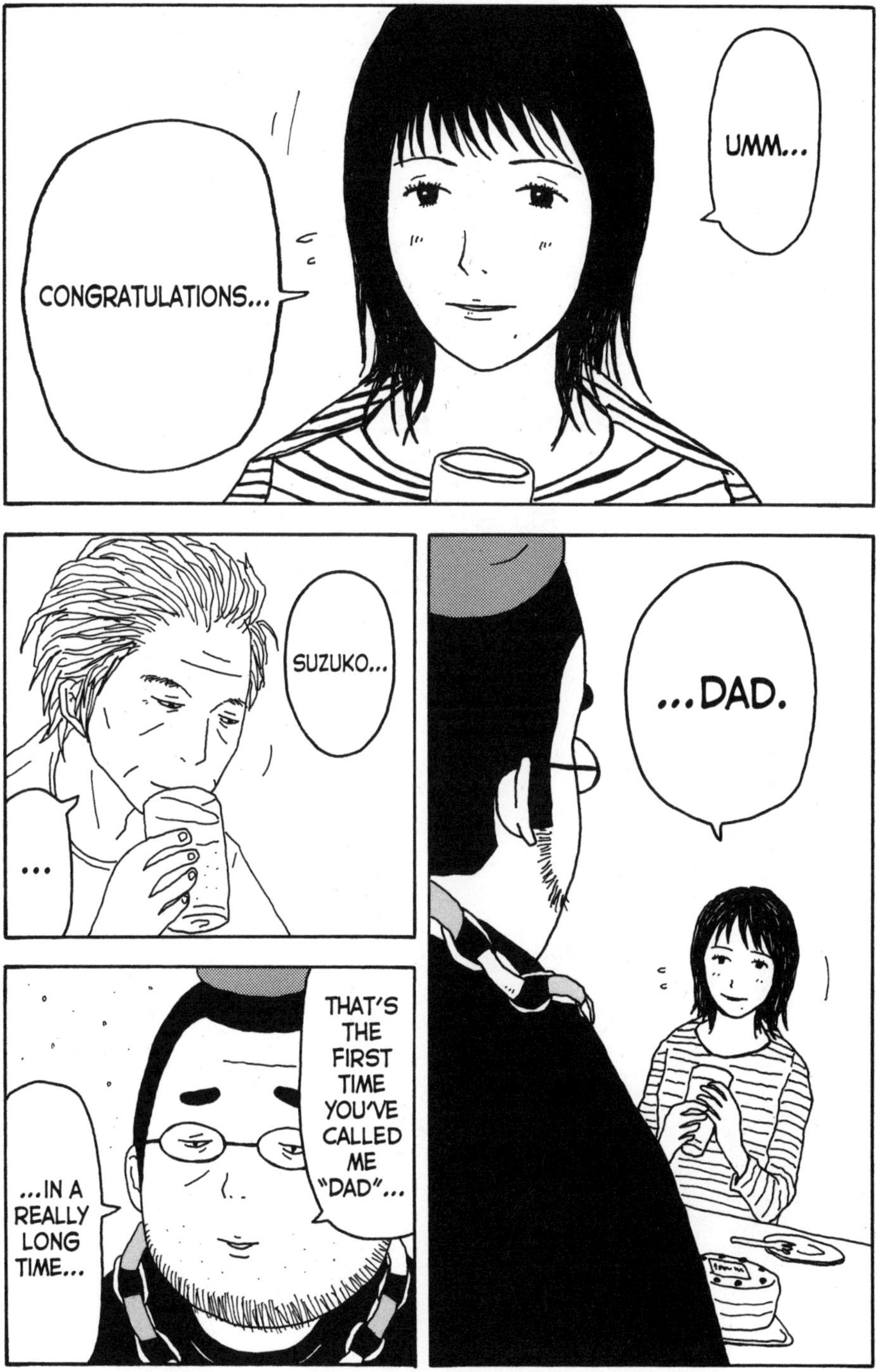
UMM...
CONGRATULATIONS...
...DAD.
SUZUKO...
...
THAT'S THE FIRST TIME YOU'VE CALLED ME "DAD"...
...IN A REALLY LONG TIME...

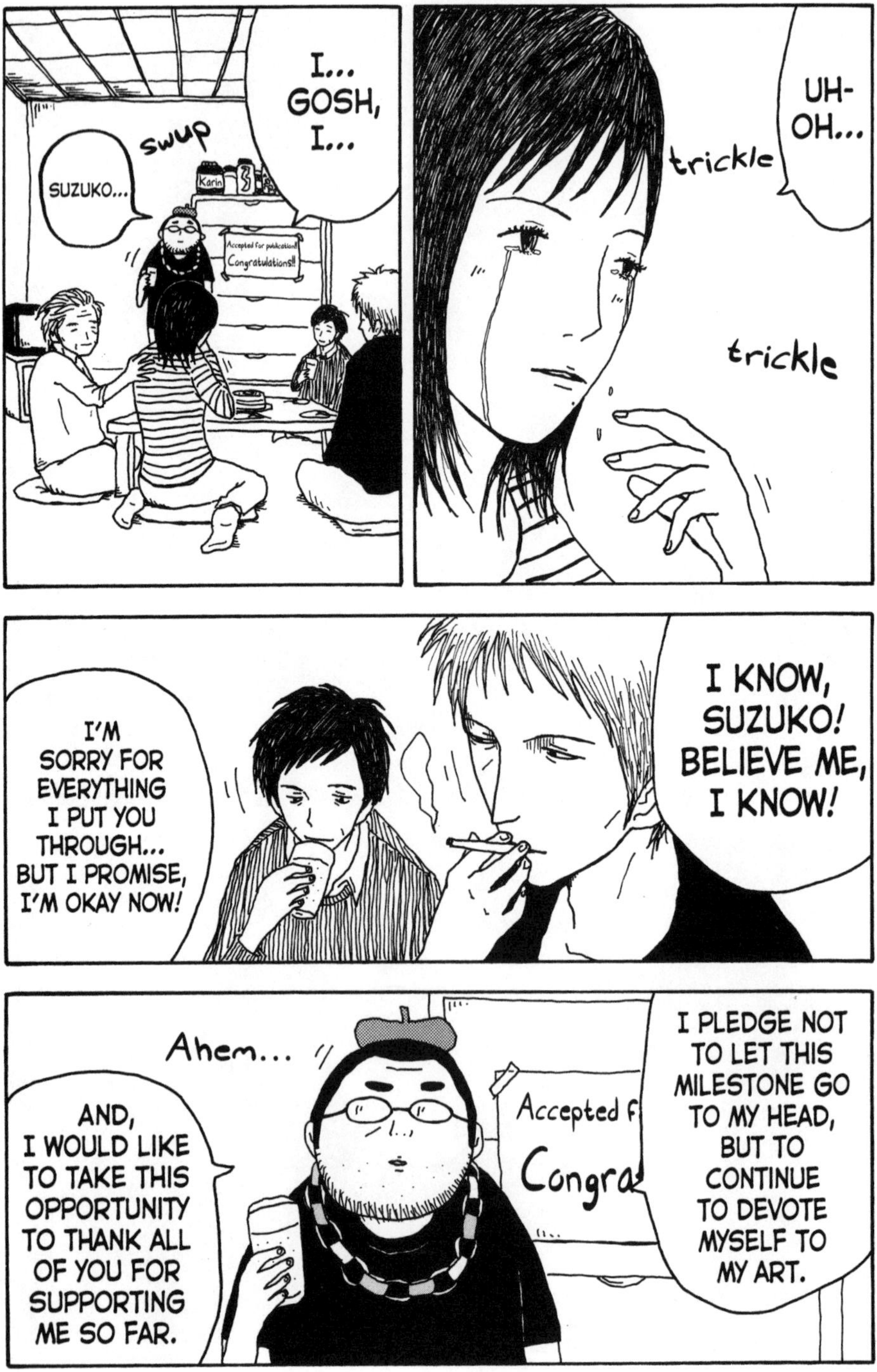
UH-OH...
trickle
trickle
I... GOSH, I...
swup
SUZUKO...
Karin
Accepted for publication!! Congratulations!!
I KNOW, SUZUKO! BELIEVE ME, I KNOW!
I'M SORRY FOR EVERYTHING I PUT YOU THROUGH... BUT I PROMISE, I'M OKAY NOW!
I PLEDGE NOT TO LET THIS MILESTONE GO TO MY HEAD, BUT TO CONTINUE TO DEVOTE MYSELF TO MY ART.
Ahem...
AND, I WOULD LIKE TO TAKE THIS OPPORTUNITY TO THANK ALL OF YOU FOR SUPPORTING ME SO FAR.

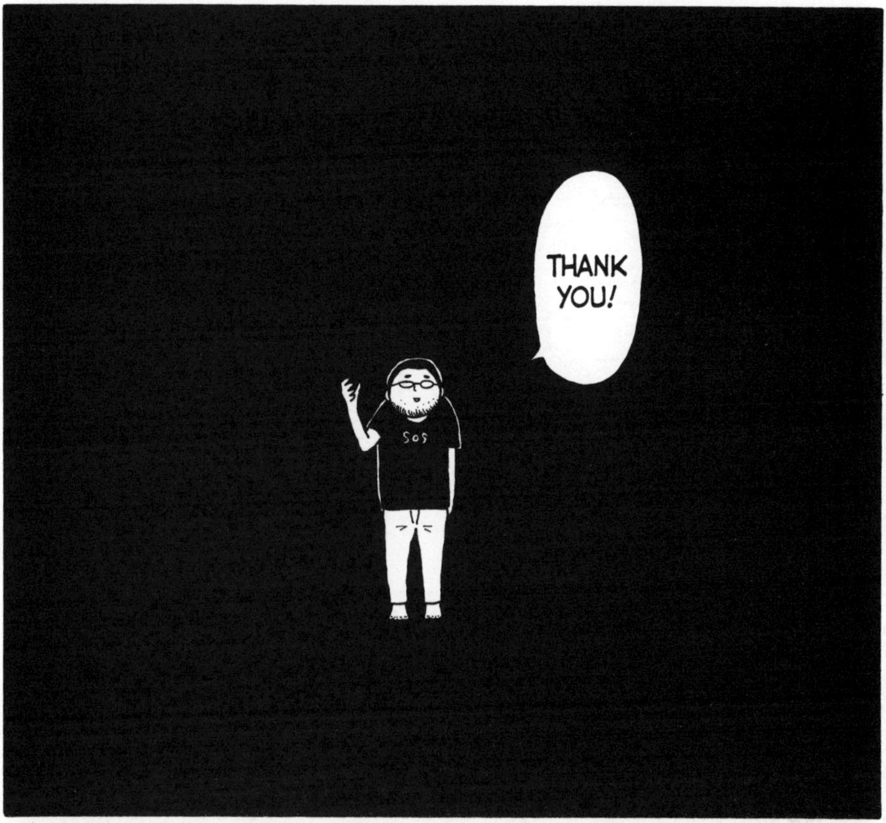
THANK YOU!
SOS

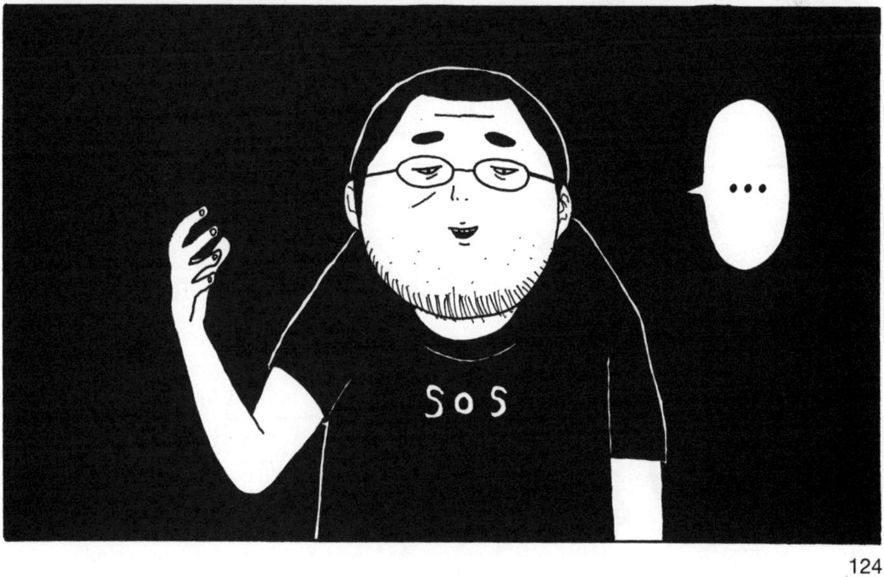
SOS
...

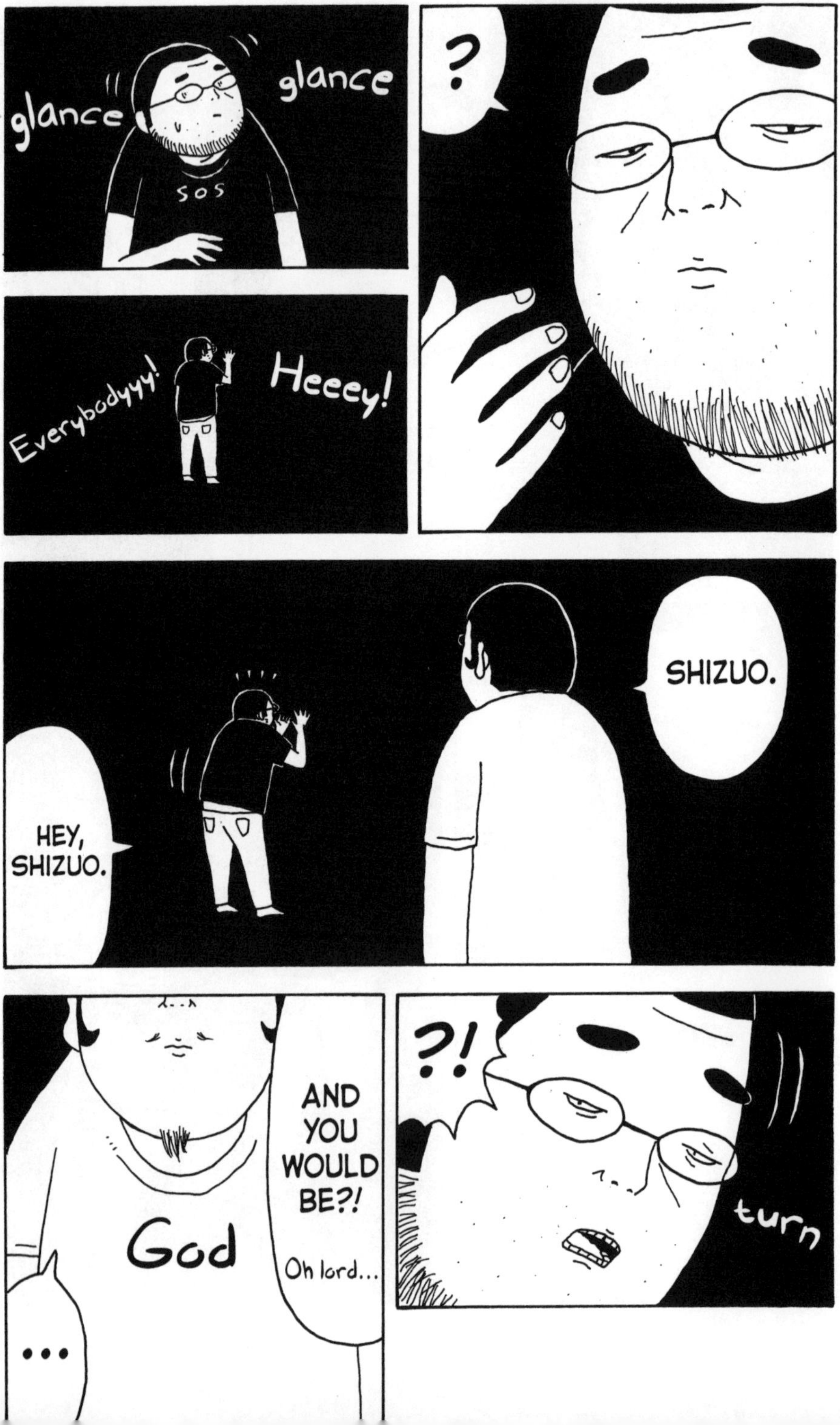
?
glance
glance
SOS
Heeeey!
Everybodyyy!
SHIZUO.
HEY, SHIZUO.
?!
turn
AND YOU WOULD BE?!
Oh lord...
God
...

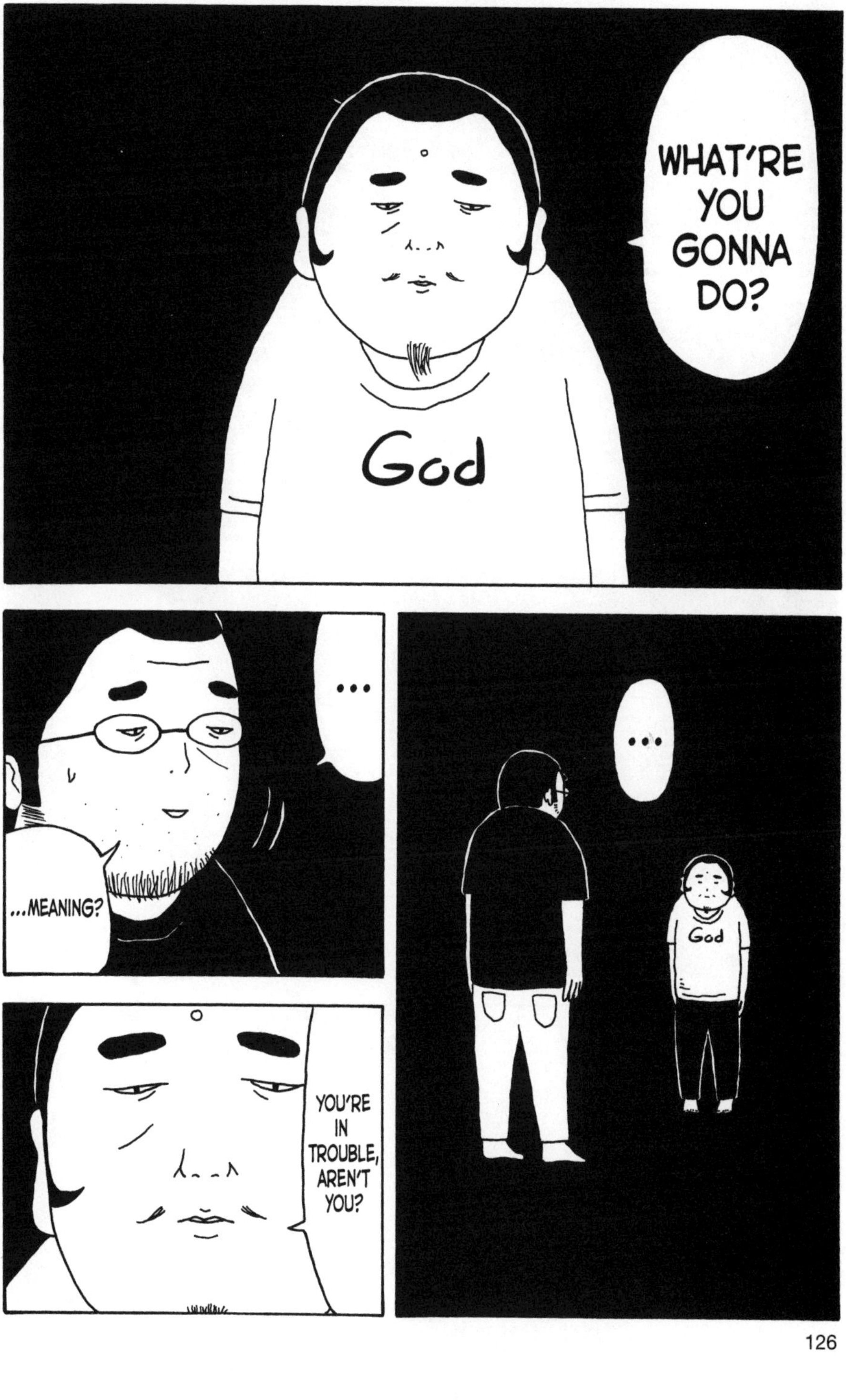
God
WHAT'RE YOU GONNA DO?
...
God
...
...MEANING?
YOU'RE IN TROUBLE, AREN'T YOU?

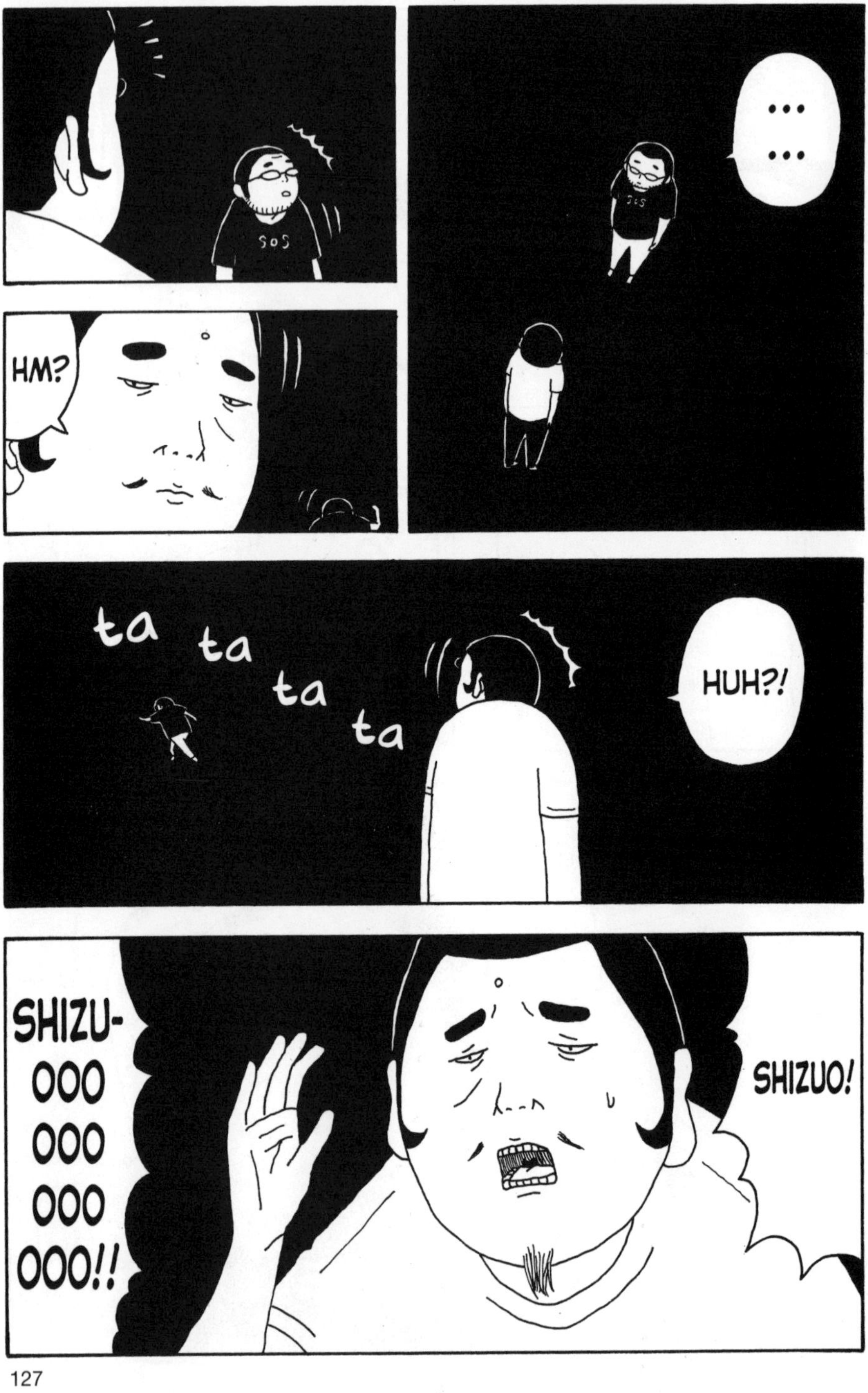
……
HM?
HUH?!
ta ta ta ta
SHIZUO!
SHIZU-OOOOOOOOOOOO!!

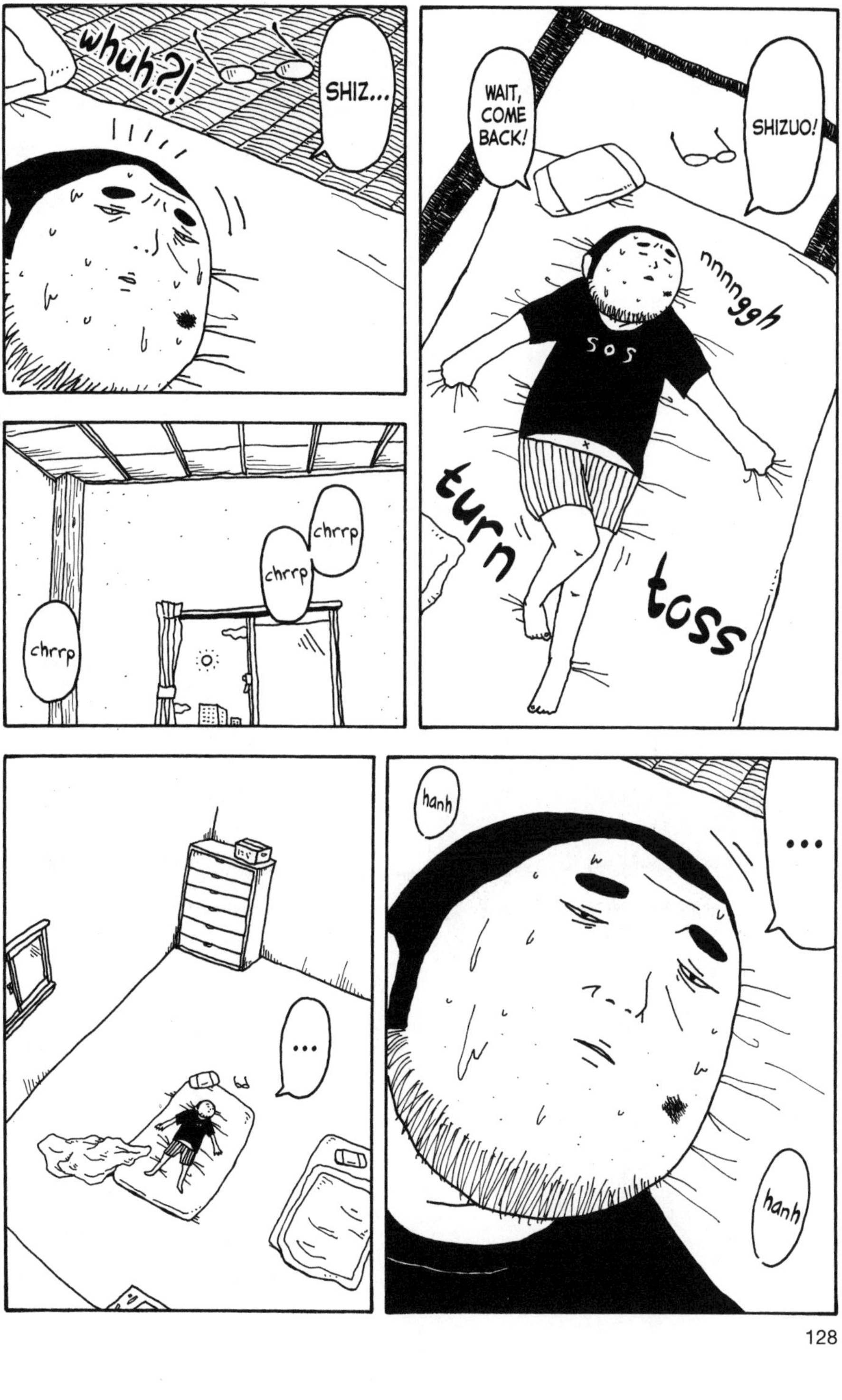
SHIZUO!
WAIT, COME BACK!
nnnnggh
turn
toss
SHIZ...
whuh?!
chrrp
chrrp
chrrp
hanh
...
hanh
...

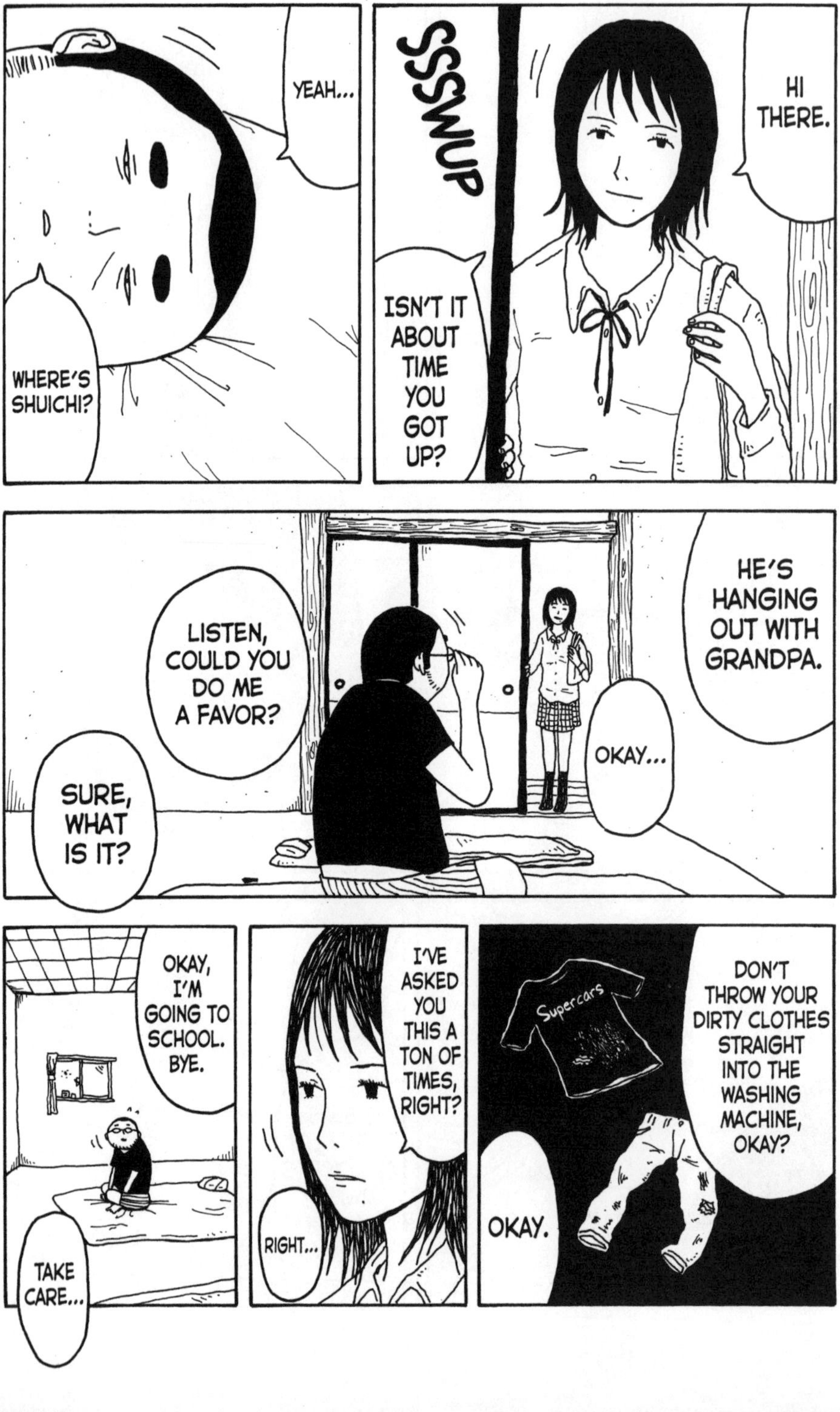
HI THERE.
SSSWUP
ISN'T IT ABOUT TIME YOU GOT UP?
YEAH...
WHERE'S SHUICHI?
HE'S HANGING OUT WITH GRANDPA.
OKAY...
LISTEN, COULD YOU DO ME A FAVOR?
SURE, WHAT IS IT?
DON'T THROW YOUR DIRTY CLOTHES STRAIGHT INTO THE WASHING MACHINE, OKAY?
Supercars
OKAY.
I'VE ASKED YOU THIS A TON OF TIMES, RIGHT?
RIGHT...
OKAY, I'M GOING TO SCHOOL. BYE.
TAKE CARE...

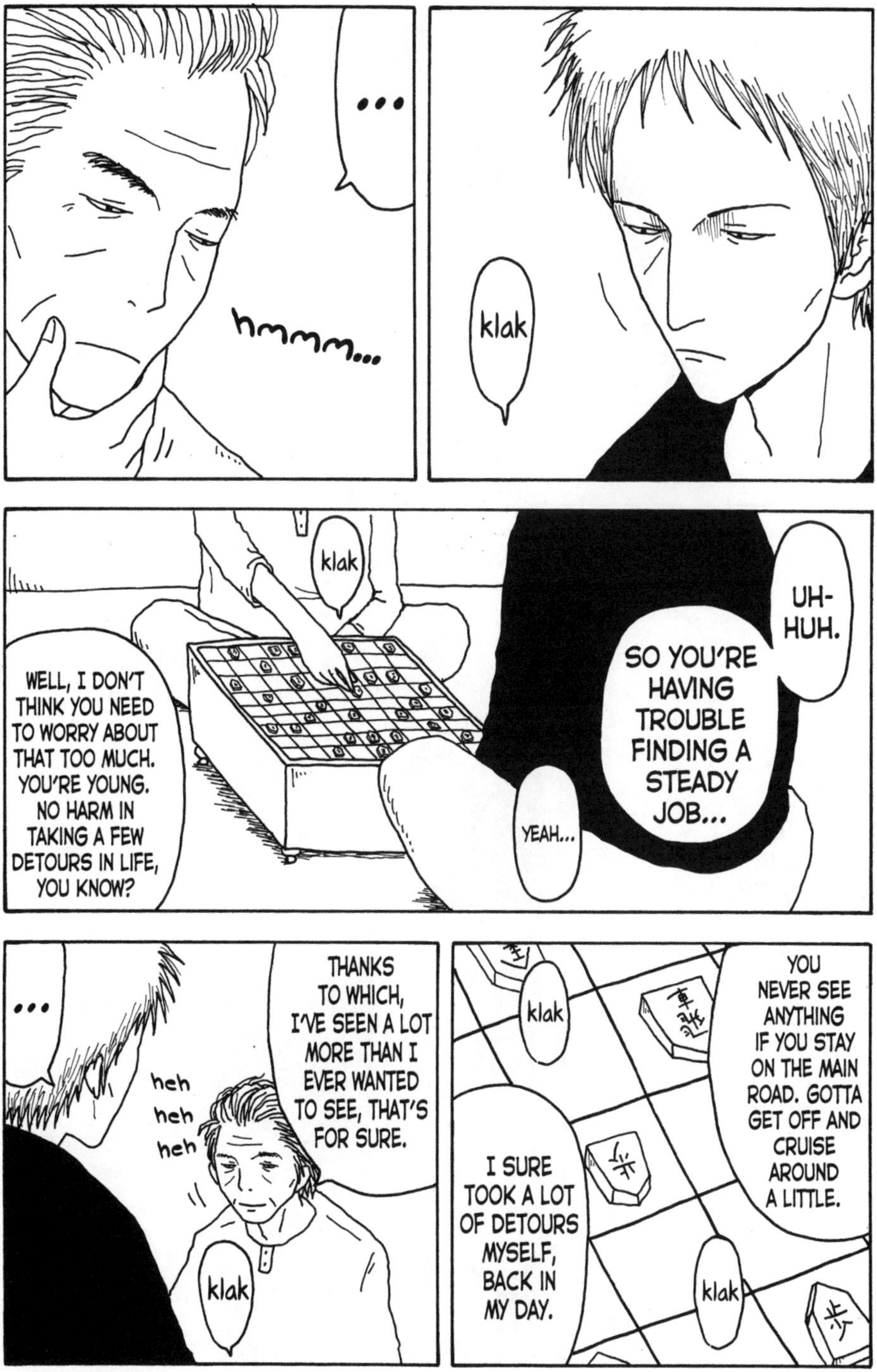
klak
...
hmmm...
UH-HUH.
SO YOU'RE HAVING TROUBLE FINDING A STEADY JOB...
klak
YEAH...
WELL, I DON'T THINK YOU NEED TO WORRY ABOUT THAT TOO MUCH. YOU'RE YOUNG. NO HARM IN TAKING A FEW DETOURS IN LIFE, YOU KNOW?
YOU NEVER SEE ANYTHING IF YOU STAY ON THE MAIN ROAD. GOTTA GET OFF AND CRUISE AROUND A LITTLE.
klak
I SURE TOOK A LOT OF DETOURS MYSELF, BACK IN MY DAY.
klak
THANKS TO WHICH, I'VE SEEN A LOT MORE THAN I EVER WANTED TO SEE, THAT'S FOR SURE.
...
heh heh heh
klak

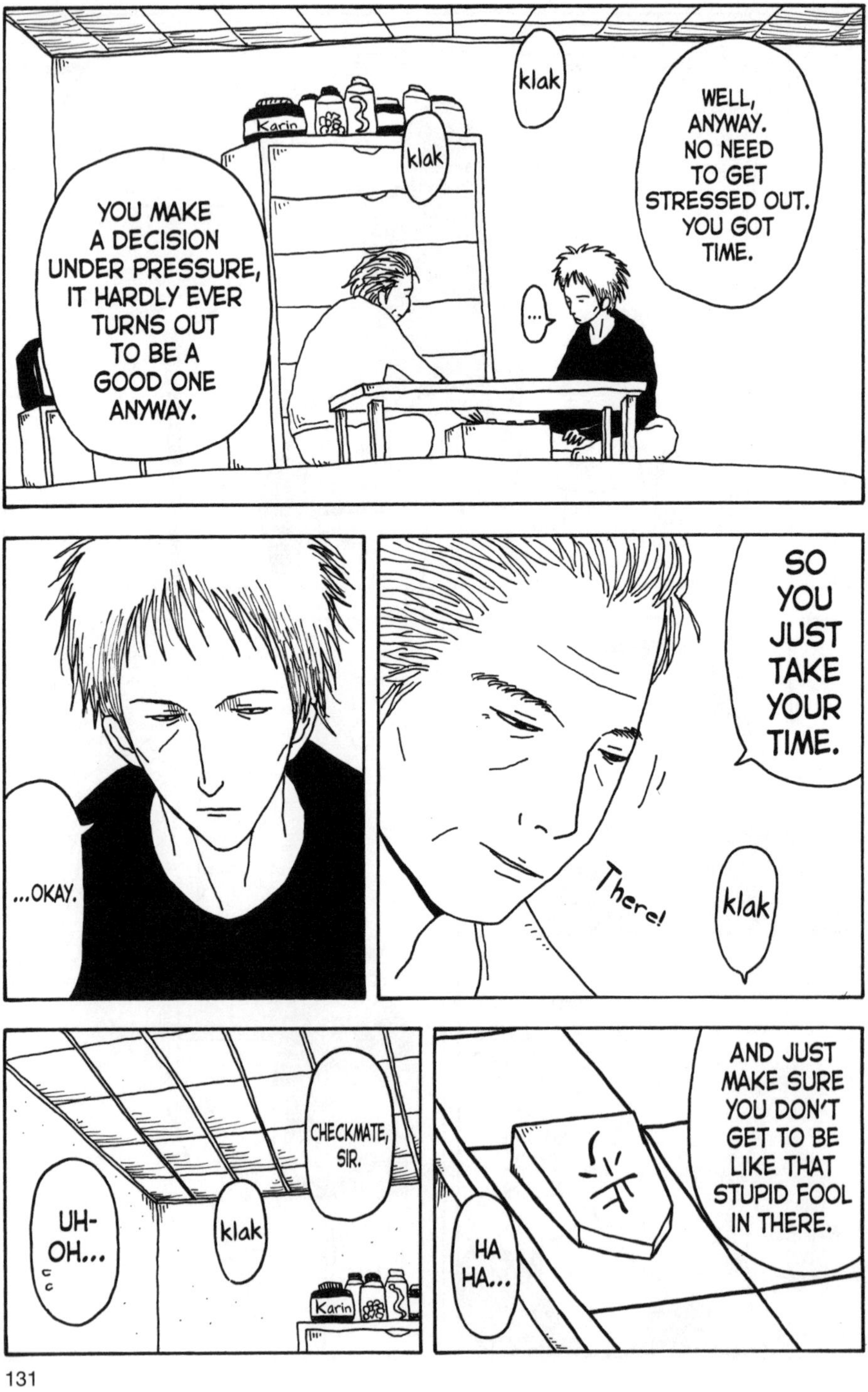
WELL, ANYWAY. NO NEED TO GET STRESSED OUT. YOU GOT TIME.
klak
klak
Karin
...
YOU MAKE A DECISION UNDER PRESSURE, IT HARDLY EVER TURNS OUT TO BE A GOOD ONE ANYWAY.
SO YOU JUST TAKE YOUR TIME.
klak
There!
...OKAY.
AND JUST MAKE SURE YOU DON'T GET TO BE LIKE THAT STUPID FOOL IN THERE.
HA HA...
CHECKMATE, SIR.
klak
UH-OH...
Karin

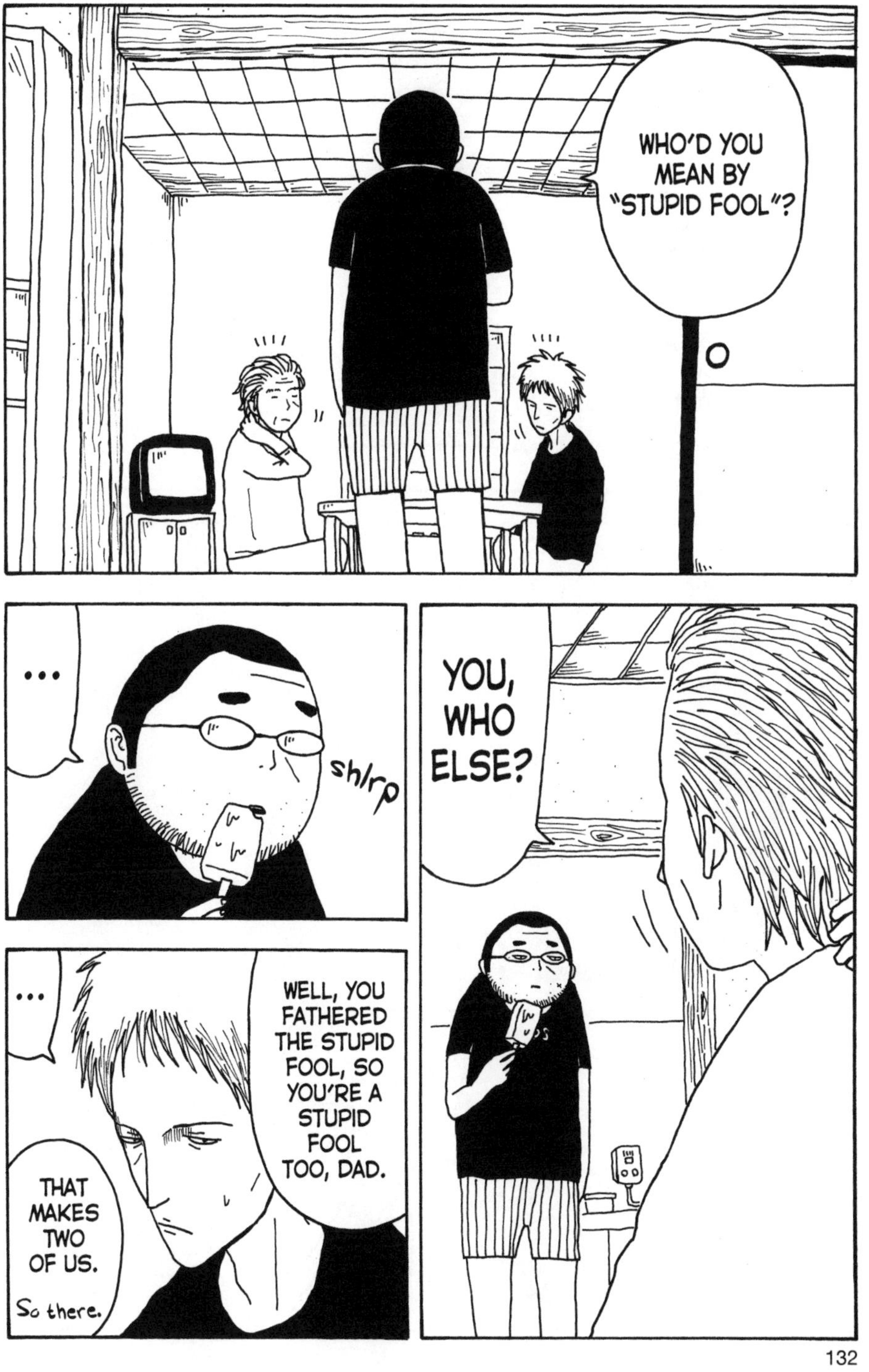
WHO'D YOU MEAN BY "STUPID FOOL"?
YOU, WHO ELSE?
...
shlrp
WELL, YOU FATHERED THE STUPID FOOL, SO YOU'RE A STUPID FOOL TOO, DAD.
...
THAT MAKES TWO OF US.
So there.

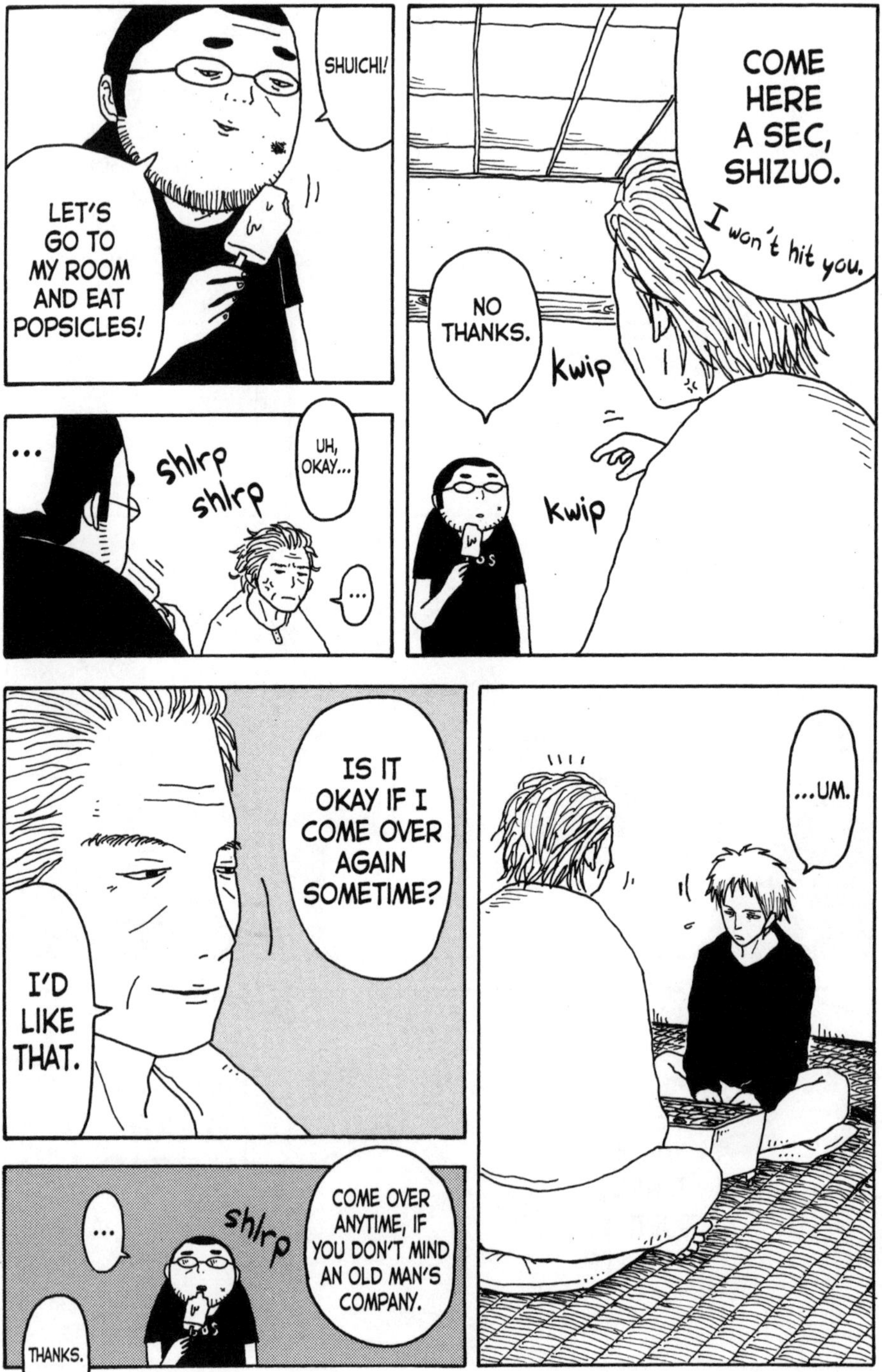
COME HERE A SEC, SHIZUO.
I won't hit you.
NO THANKS.
kwip
kwip
SHUICHI!
LET'S GO TO MY ROOM AND EAT POPSICLES!
UH, OKAY...
shlrp shlrp
...
...
...UM.
IS IT OKAY IF I COME OVER AGAIN SOMETIME?
I'D LIKE THAT.
COME OVER ANYTIME, IF YOU DON'T MIND AN OLD MAN'S COMPANY.
shlrp
...
THANKS.

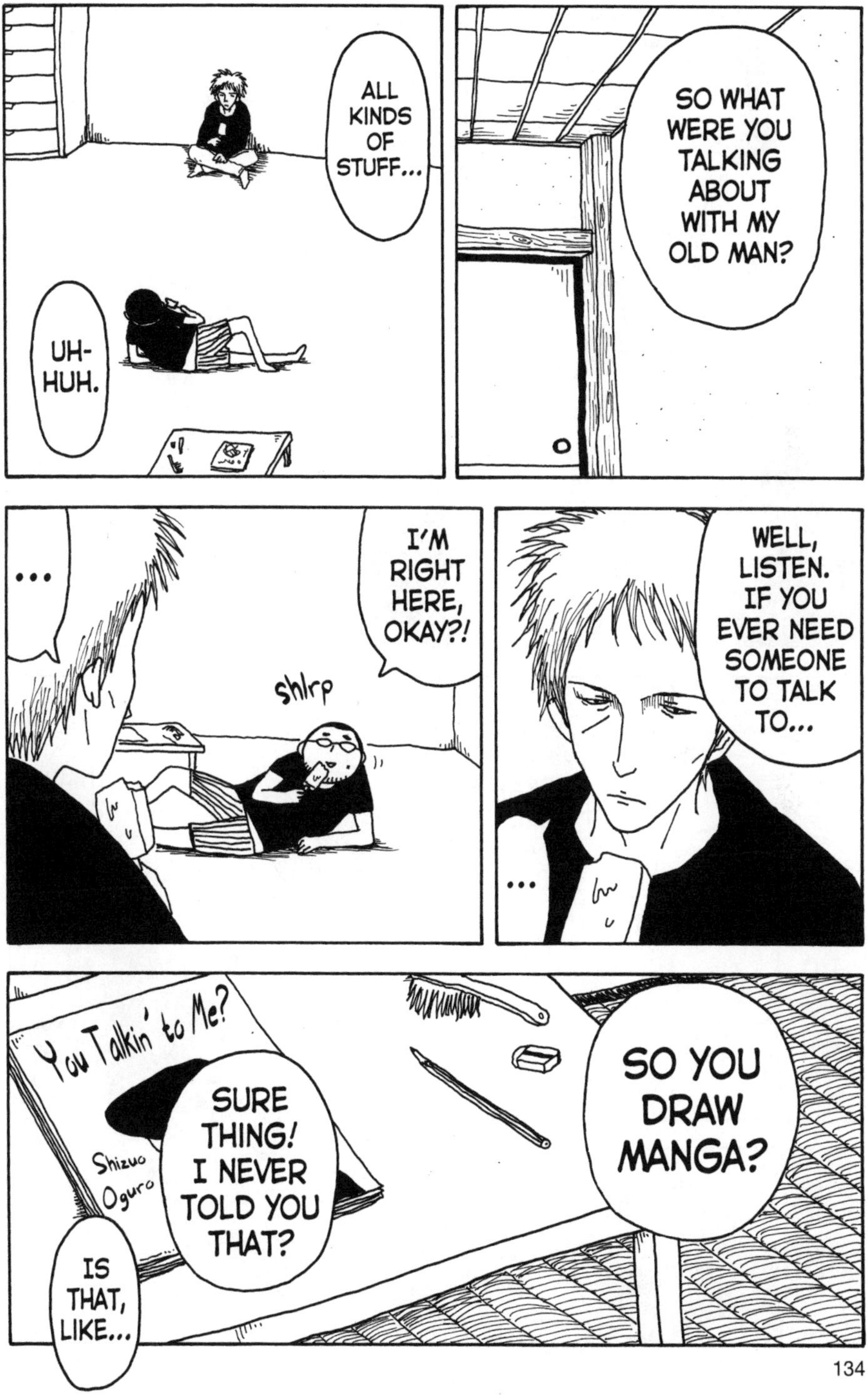
SO WHAT WERE YOU TALKING ABOUT WITH MY OLD MAN?
ALL KINDS OF STUFF...
UH-HUH.
WELL, LISTEN. IF YOU EVER NEED SOMEONE TO TALK TO...
...
I'M RIGHT HERE, OKAY?!
shlrp
...
SO YOU DRAW MANGA?
You Talkin' to Me?
SURE THING! I NEVER TOLD YOU THAT?
Shizuo Oguro
IS THAT, LIKE...

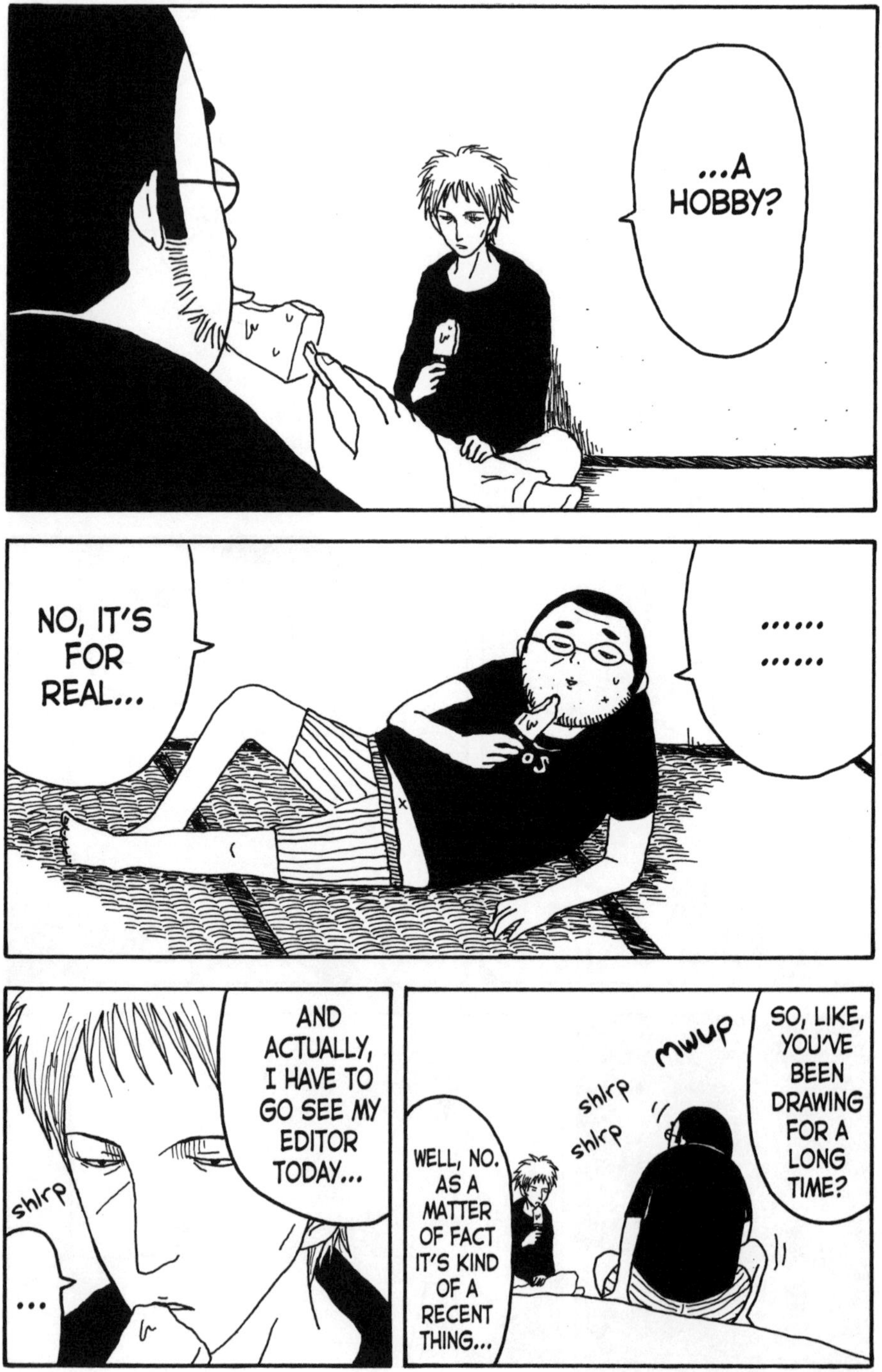
...A HOBBY?
....
NO, IT'S FOR REAL...
SO, LIKE, YOU'VE BEEN DRAWING FOR A LONG TIME?
mwup
shlrp
shlrp
WELL, NO. AS A MATTER OF FACT IT'S KIND OF A RECENT THING...
AND ACTUALLY, I HAVE TO GO SEE MY EDITOR TODAY...
shlrp
...

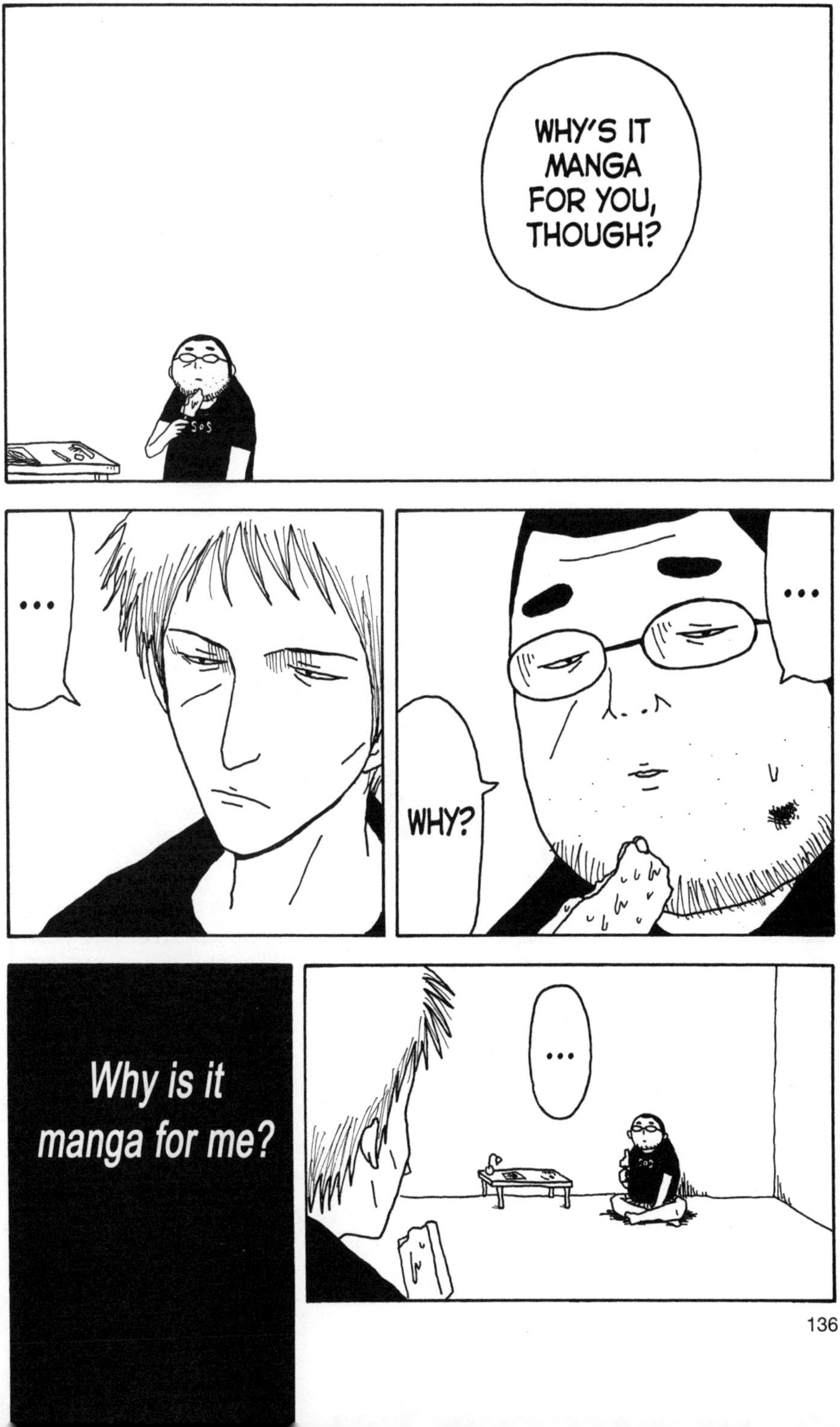
WHY'S IT MANGA FOR YOU, THOUGH?
...
WHY?
...
...
Why is it manga for me?

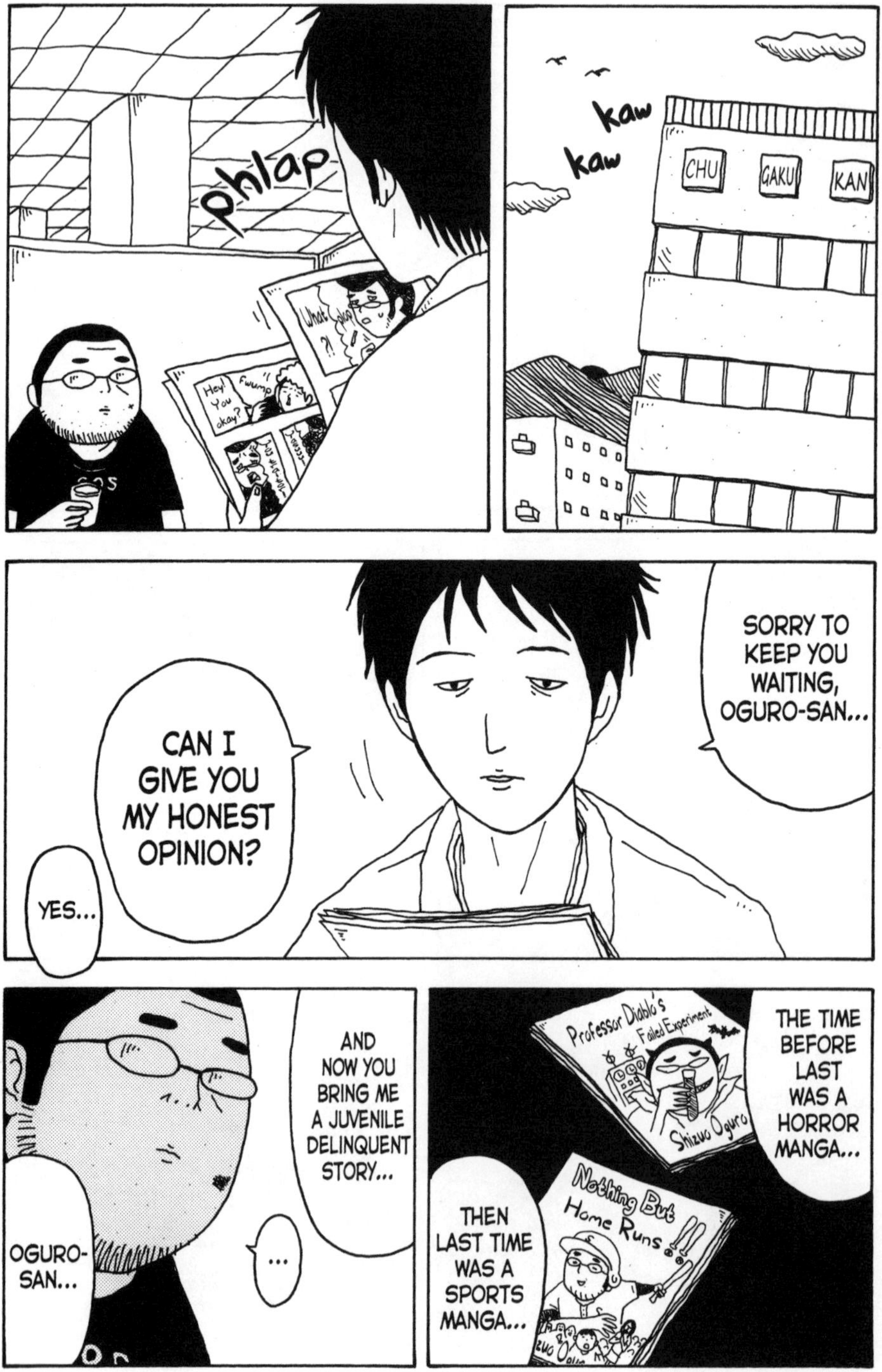
kaw
kaw
CHU
GAKU
KAN
phlap
What?!
Hey! You okay?
Fwump
SORRY TO KEEP YOU WAITING, OGURO-SAN...
CAN I GIVE YOU MY HONEST OPINION?
YES...
THE TIME BEFORE LAST WAS A HORROR MANGA...
Professor Diablo's Failed Experiment
Shizuo Oguro
Nothing But Home Runs!!
THEN LAST TIME WAS A SPORTS MANGA...
AND NOW YOU BRING ME A JUVENILE DELINQUENT STORY...
...
OGURO-SAN...

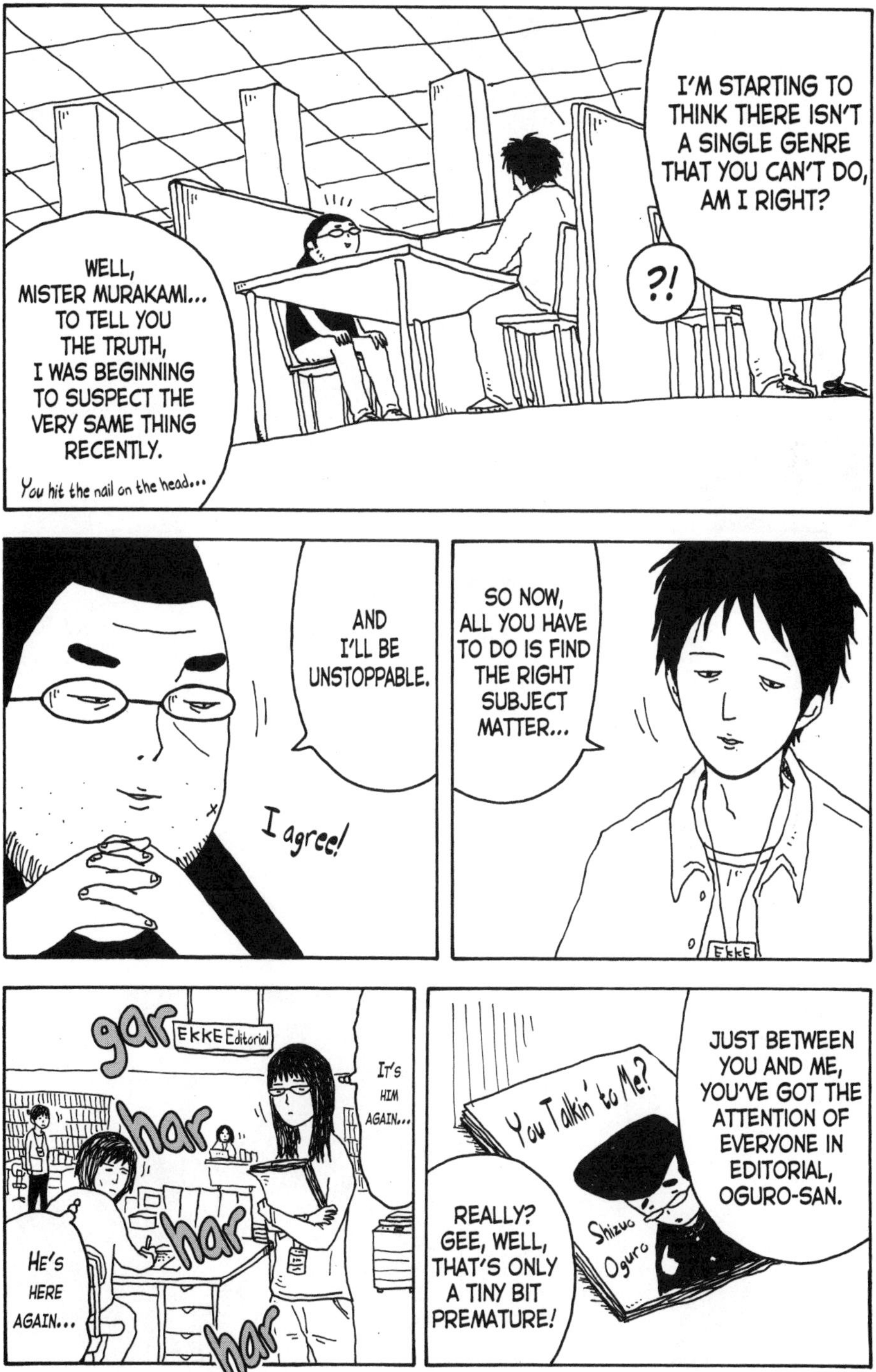
I'M STARTING TO THINK THERE ISN'T A SINGLE GENRE THAT YOU CAN'T DO, AM I RIGHT?
?!
WELL, MISTER MURAKAMI... TO TELL YOU THE TRUTH, I WAS BEGINNING TO SUSPECT THE VERY SAME THING RECENTLY.
You hit the nail on the head...
SO NOW, ALL YOU HAVE TO DO IS FIND THE RIGHT SUBJECT MATTER...
EKKE
AND I'LL BE UNSTOPPABLE.
I agree!
JUST BETWEEN YOU AND ME, YOU'VE GOT THE ATTENTION OF EVERYONE IN EDITORIAL, OGURO-SAN.
You Talkin' to Me?
Shizuo Oguro
REALLY? GEE, WELL, THAT'S ONLY A TINY BIT PREMATURE!
It's HIM AGAIN...
EKKE Editorial
gar
har
har
har
HE'S HERE AGAIN...

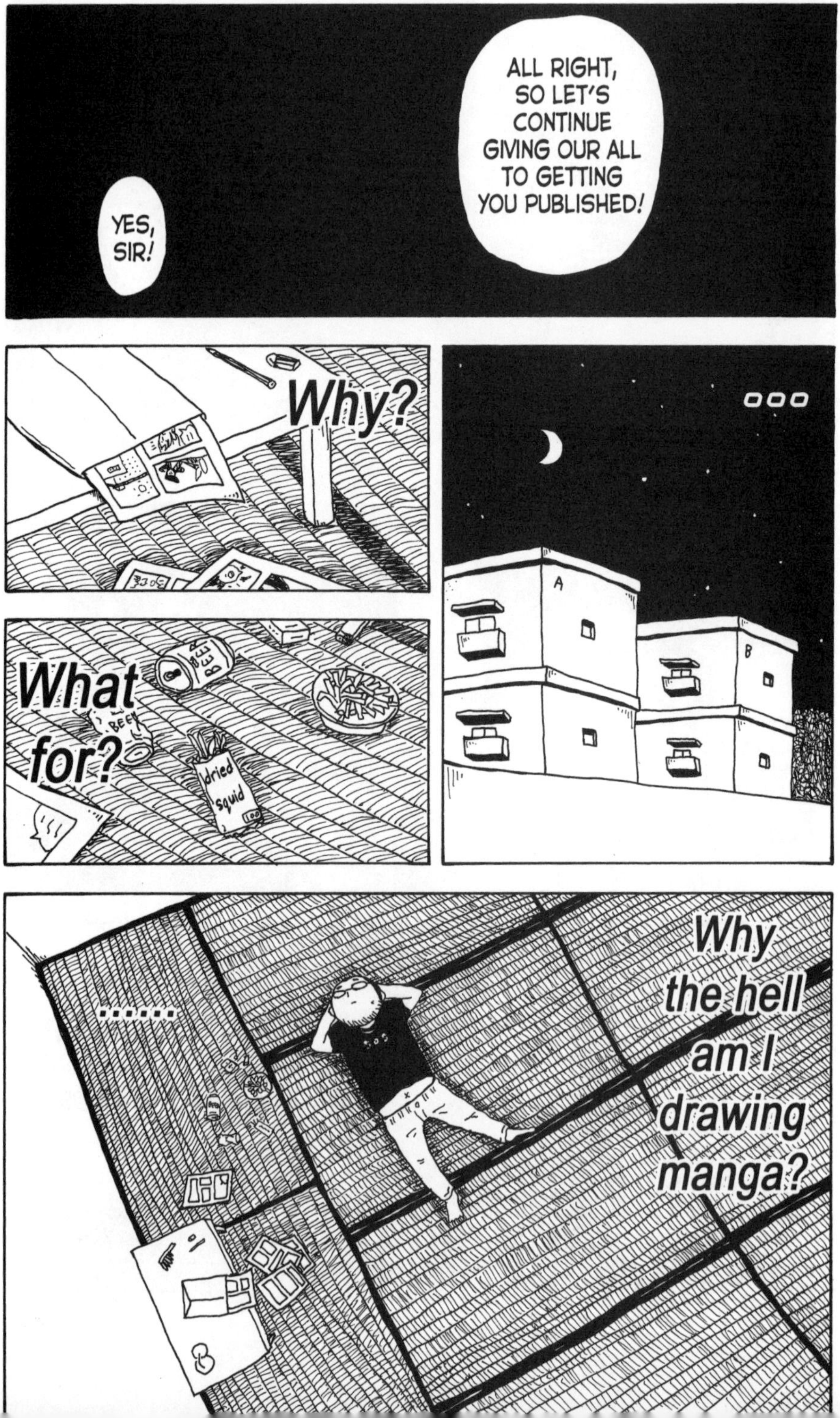
ALL RIGHT, SO LET'S CONTINUE GIVING OUR ALL TO GETTING YOU PUBLISHED!
YES, SIR!
Why?
What for?
dried squid
Why the hell am I drawing manga?
......

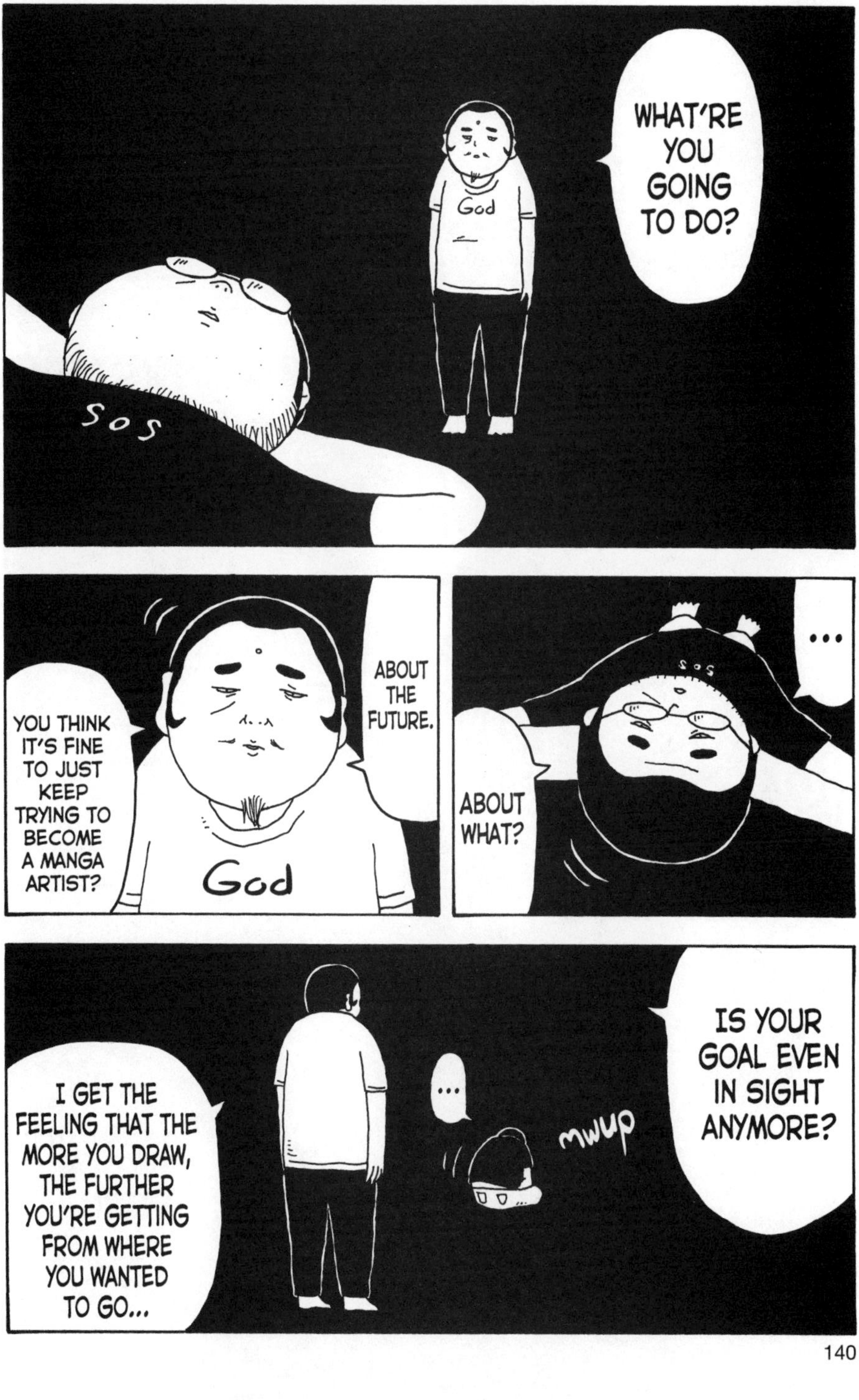
WHAT'RE YOU GOING TO DO?
...
ABOUT WHAT?
ABOUT THE FUTURE.
YOU THINK IT'S FINE TO JUST KEEP TRYING TO BECOME A MANGA ARTIST?
IS YOUR GOAL EVEN IN SIGHT ANYMORE?
...
mwup
I GET THE FEELING THAT THE MORE YOU DRAW, THE FURTHER YOU'RE GETTING FROM WHERE YOU WANTED TO GO...

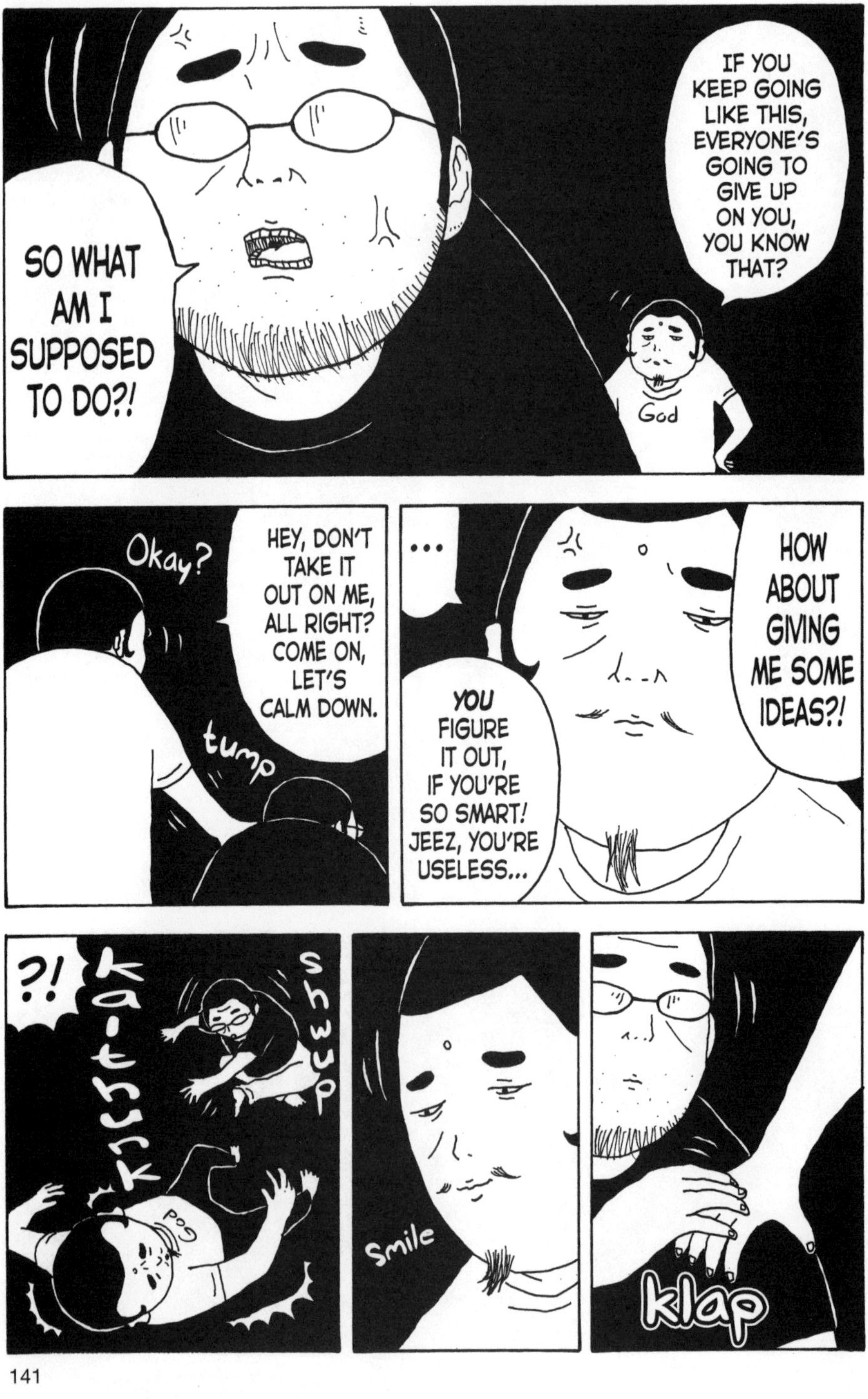
IF YOU KEEP GOING LIKE THIS, EVERYONE'S GOING TO GIVE UP ON YOU, YOU KNOW THAT?
God
SO WHAT AM I SUPPOSED TO DO?!
HOW ABOUT GIVING ME SOME IDEAS?!
...
YOU FIGURE IT OUT, IF YOU'RE SO SMART! JEEZ, YOU'RE USELESS...
HEY, DON'T TAKE IT OUT ON ME, ALL RIGHT? COME ON, LET'S CALM DOWN.
Okay?
tump
klap
Smile
shwup
ka-thunk
?!

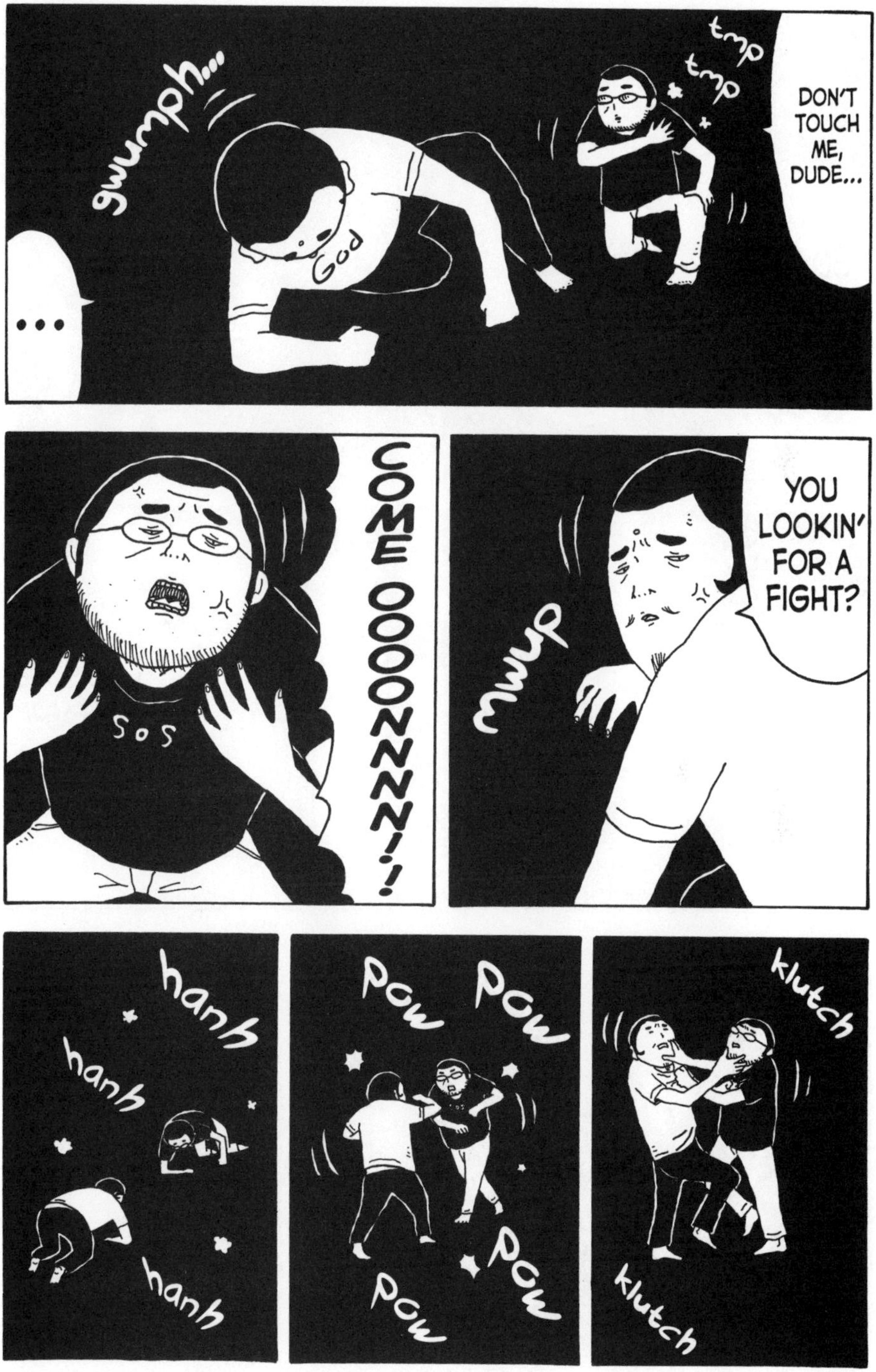

DON'T TOUCH ME, DUDE...
tmp tmp
gwumph...
...
YOU LOOKIN' FOR A FIGHT?
mwup
COME OOOOONNNN!!
klutch
klutch
pow pow
pow pow
hanh
hanh
hanh

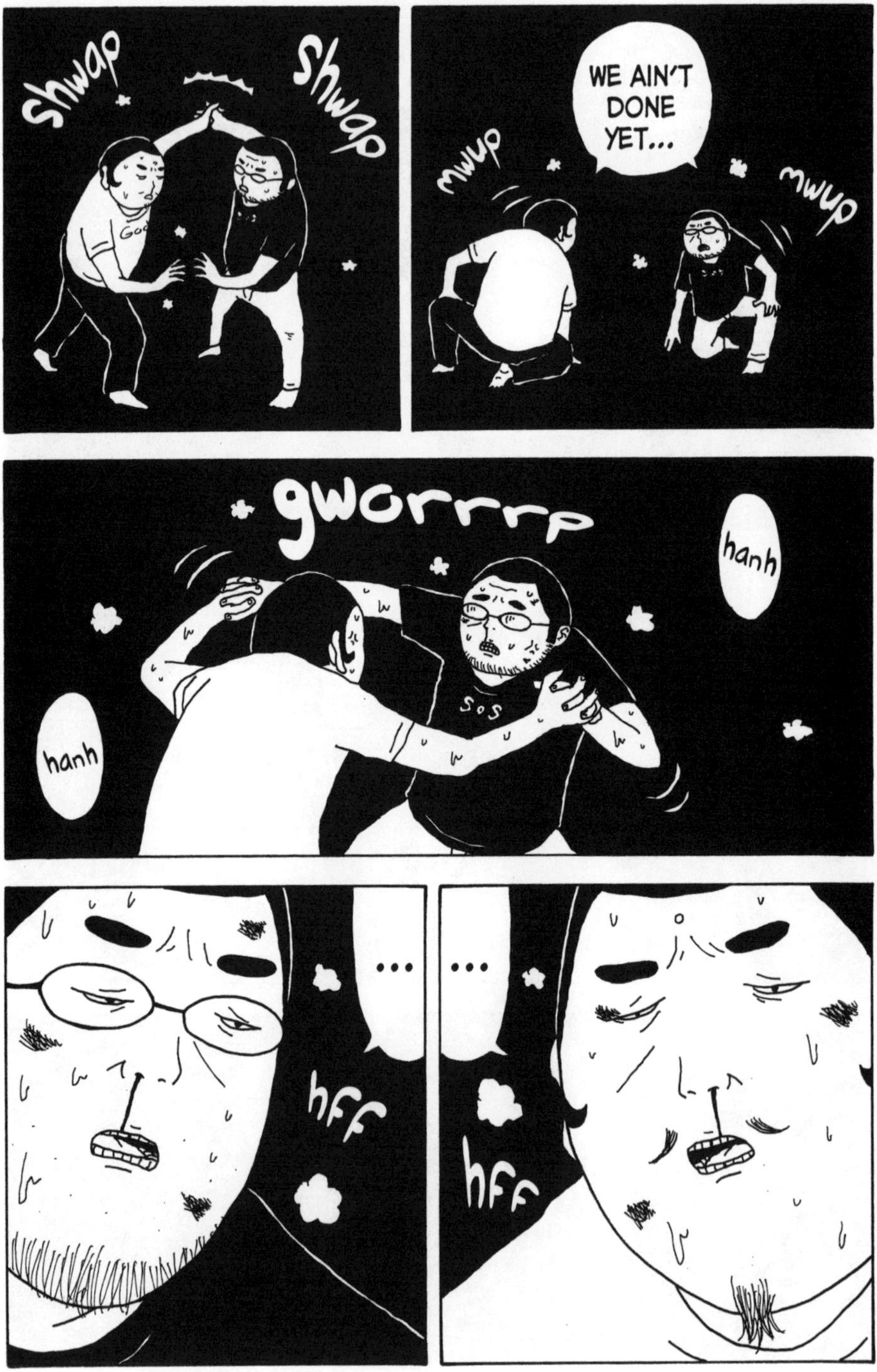
WE AIN'T DONE YET...
mwup
mwup
shwap
shwap
gworrrp
hanh
hanh
...
hff
...
hff

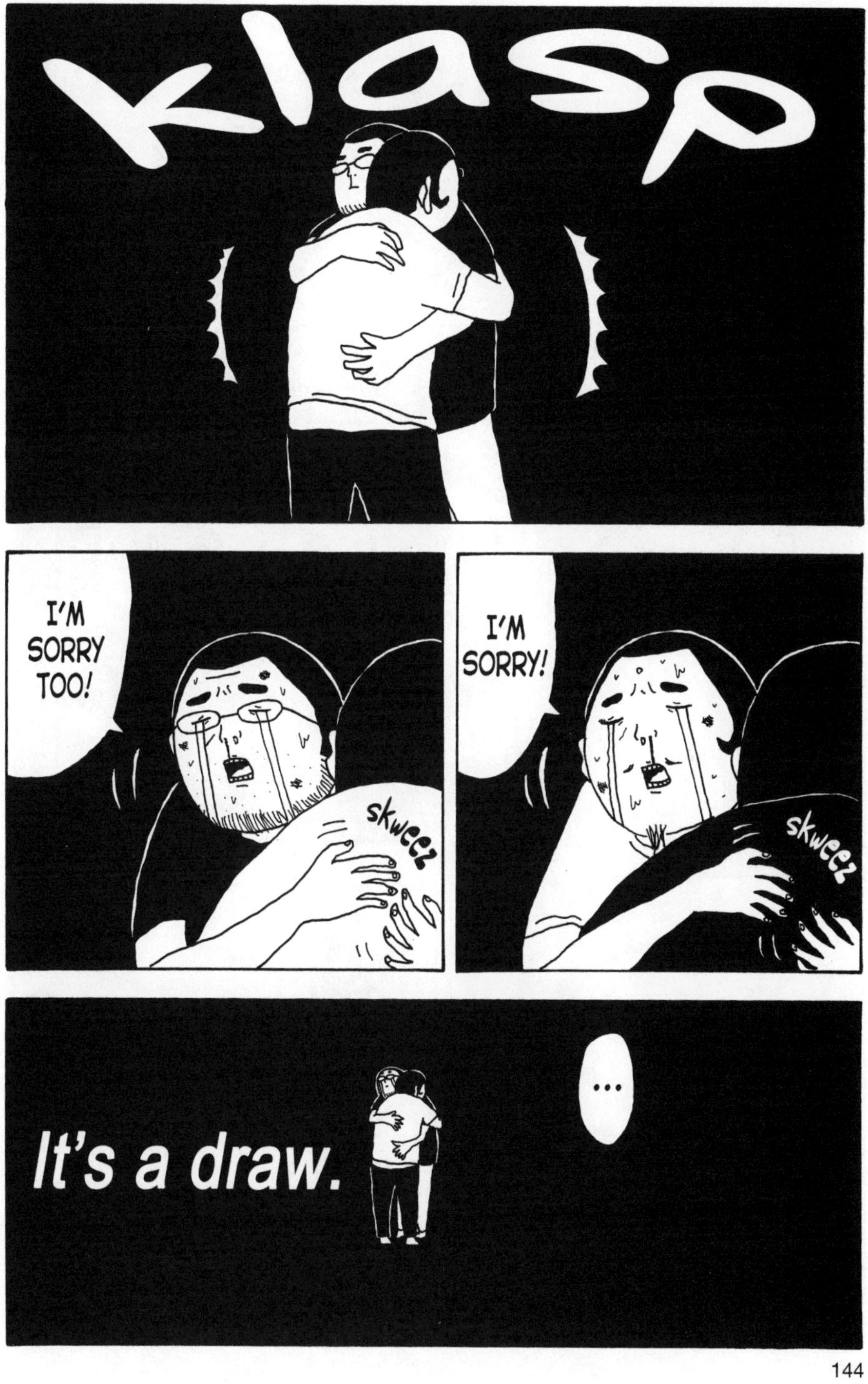
klasp
I'M SORRY!
skweez
I'M SORRY TOO!
skweez
...
It's a draw.

Chapter 4:

Give Me Wings

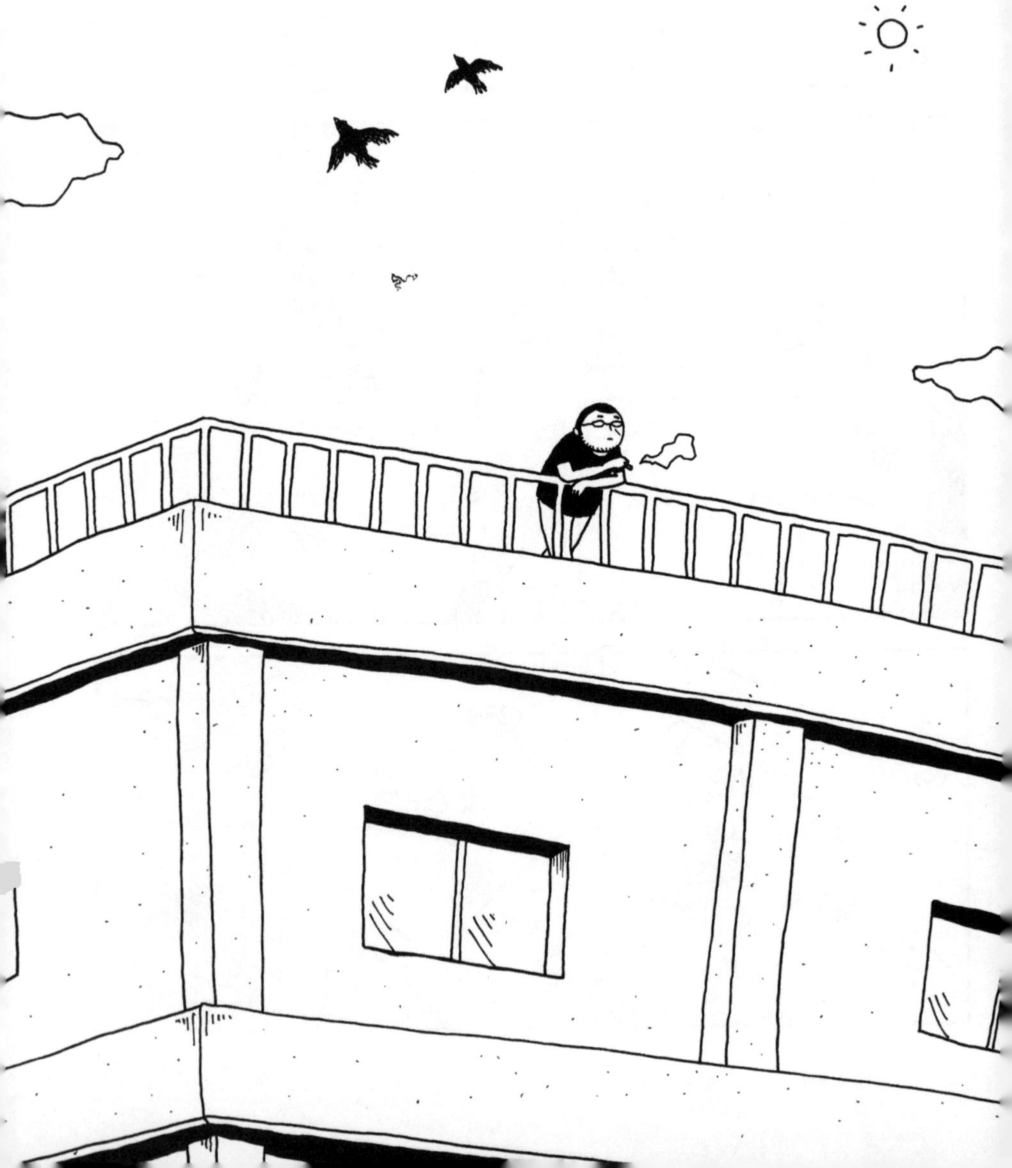

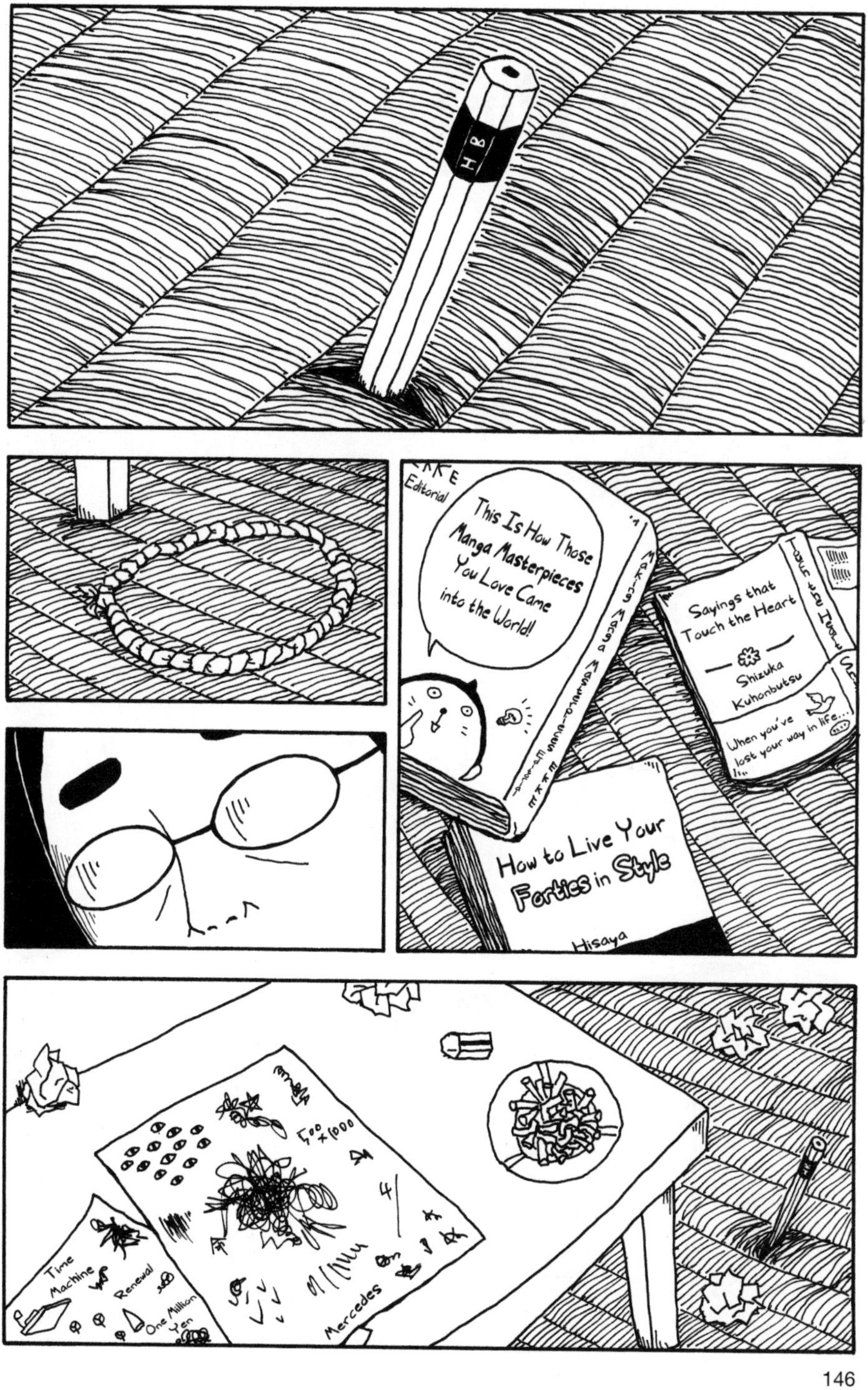
HB
Editorial
This Is How Those Manga Masterpieces You Love Came into the World!
Sayings that Touch the Heart
Shizuka Kuhonbutsu
When you've lost your way in life...
How to Live Your Forties in Style
Hisaya
Time Machine
Renewal
One Million Yen
Mercedes

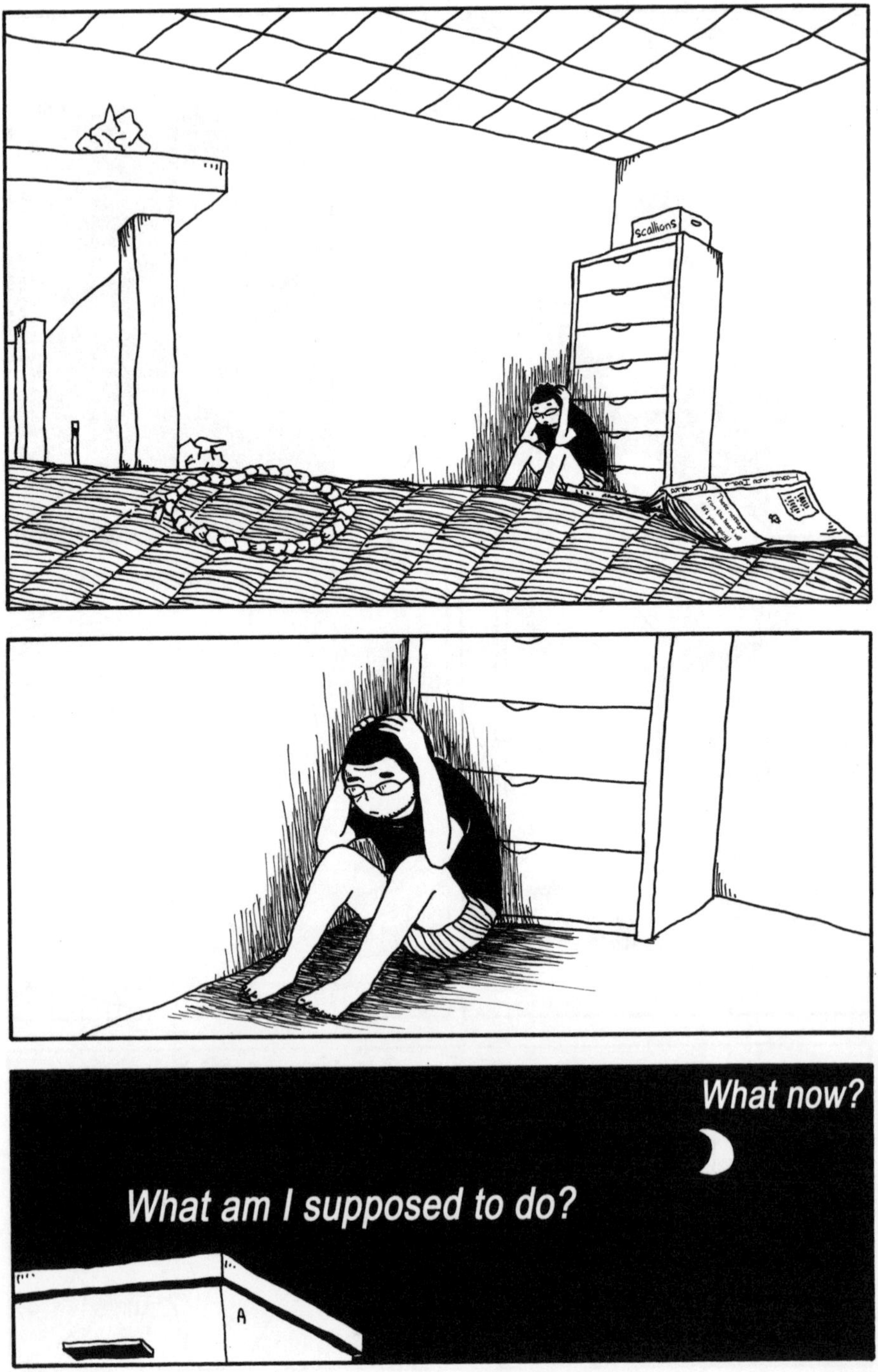
scallions
What now?
What am I supposed to do?

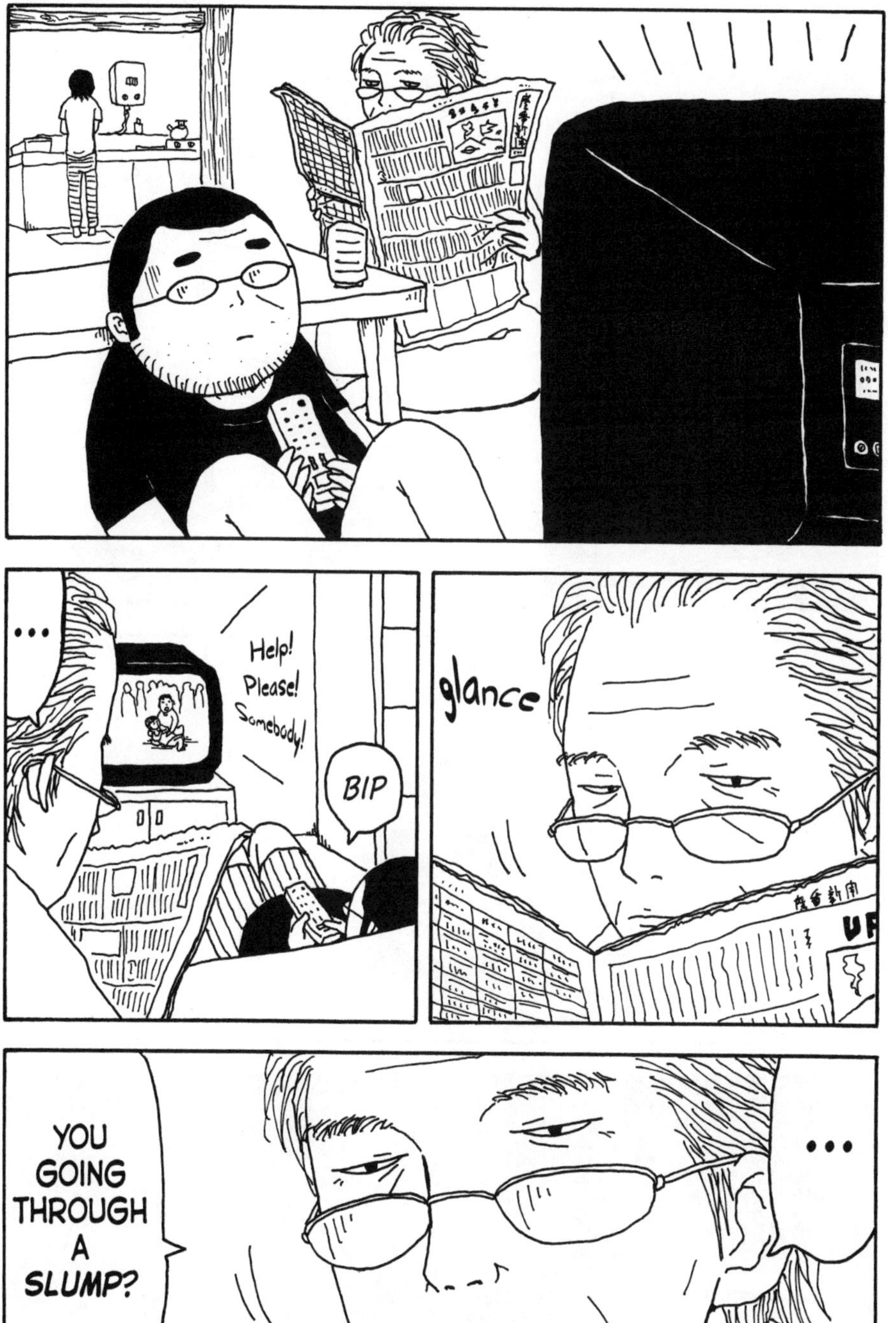
glance
Help! Please! Somebody!
BIP
...
...
YOU GOING THROUGH A *SLUMP?*

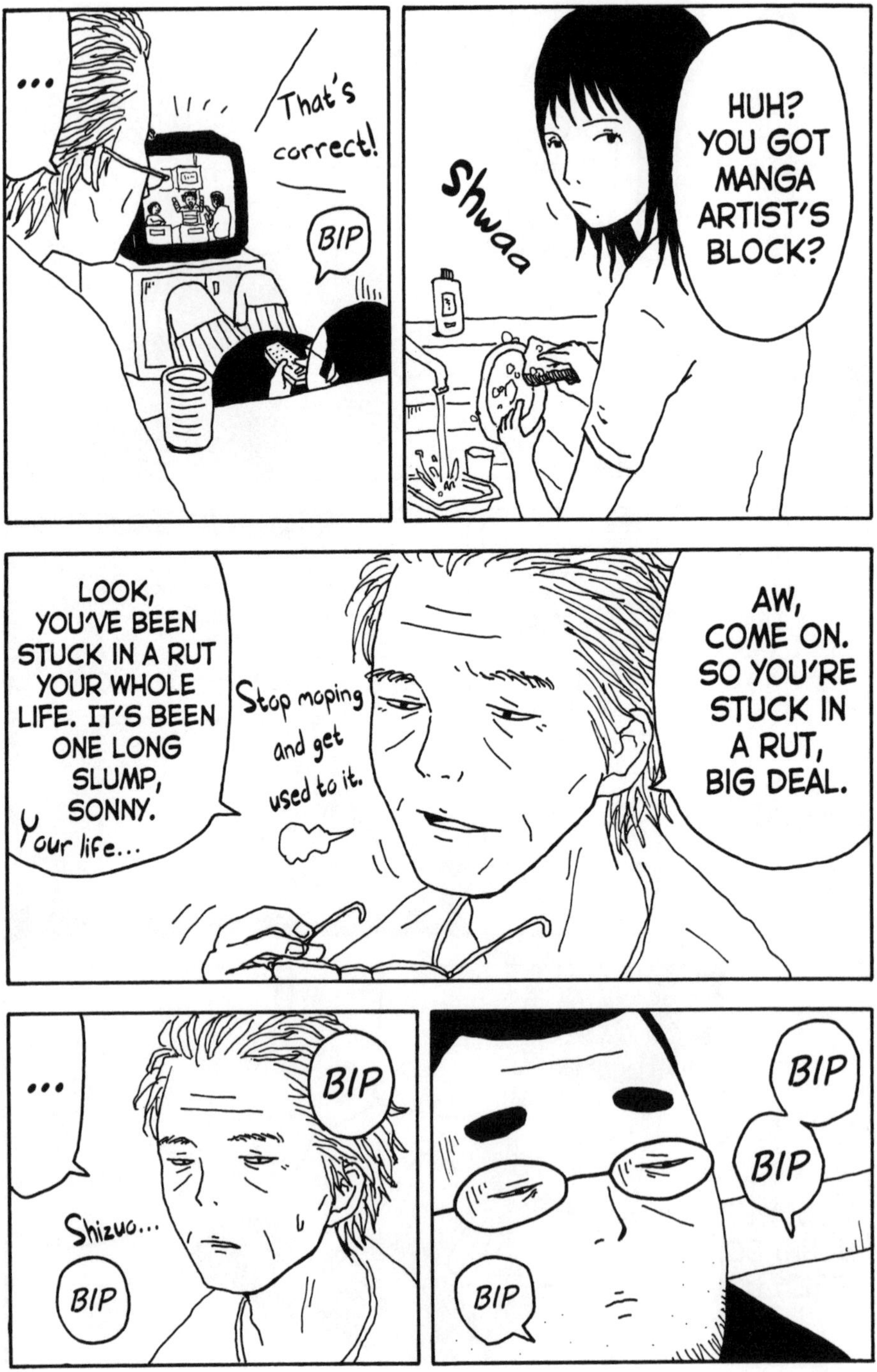
HUH? YOU GOT MANGA ARTIST'S BLOCK?
Shwaa
That's correct!
BIP
...
AW, COME ON. SO YOU'RE STUCK IN A RUT, BIG DEAL.
Stop moping and get used to it.
LOOK, YOU'VE BEEN STUCK IN A RUT YOUR WHOLE LIFE. IT'S BEEN ONE LONG SLUMP, SONNY.
Your life...
BIP
BIP
BIP
BIP
...
Shizuo...
BIP

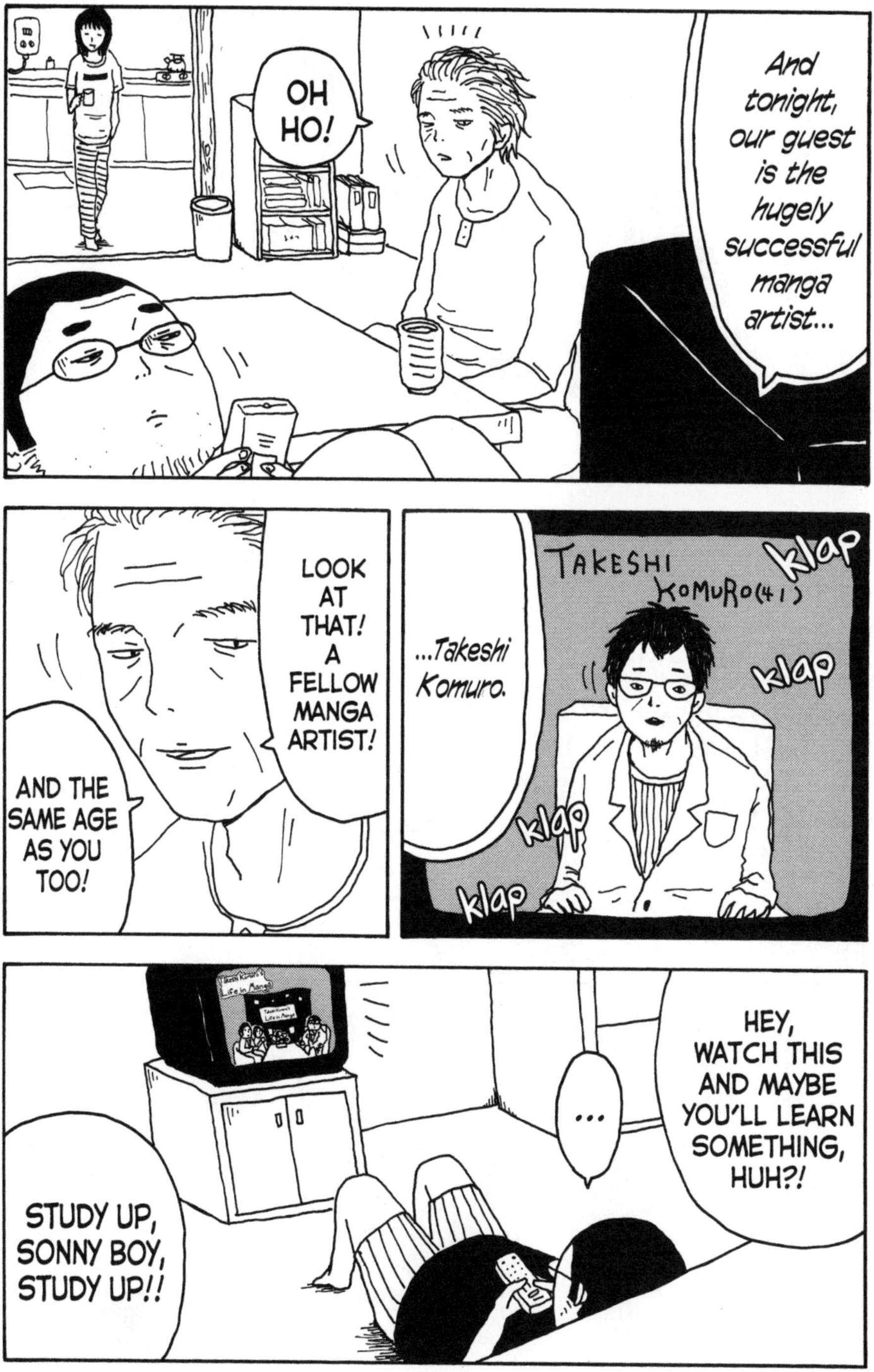
And tonight, our guest is the hugely successful manga artist...
OH HO!
klap
TAKESHI KOMURO(41)
...Takeshi Komuro.
klap
klap
klap
LOOK AT THAT! A FELLOW MANGA ARTIST!
AND THE SAME AGE AS YOU TOO!
HEY, WATCH THIS AND MAYBE YOU'LL LEARN SOMETHING, HUH?!
...
STUDY UP, SONNY BOY, STUDY UP!!

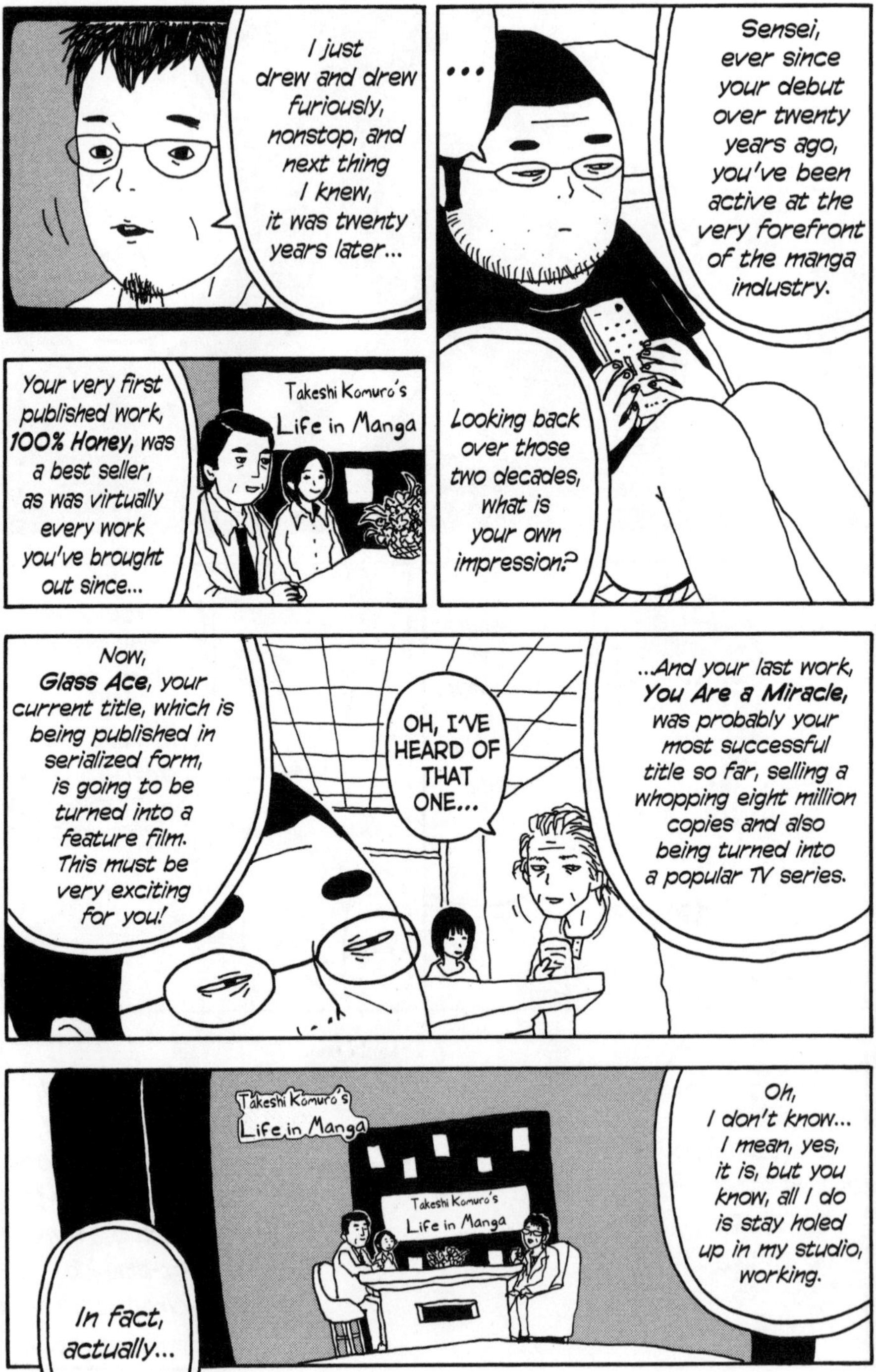
Sensei, ever since your debut over twenty years ago, you've been active at the very forefront of the manga industry.
...
Looking back over those two decades, what is your own impression?
I just drew and drew furiously, nonstop, and next thing I knew, it was twenty years later...
Takeshi Komuro's Life in Manga
Your very first published work, **100% Honey,** was a best seller, as was virtually every work you've brought out since...
...And your last work, **You Are a Miracle,** was probably your most successful title so far, selling a whopping eight million copies and also being turned into a popular TV series.
OH, I'VE HEARD OF THAT ONE...
Now, **Glass Ace**, your current title, which is being published in serialized form, is going to be turned into a feature film. This must be very exciting for you!
Oh, I don't know... I mean, yes, it is, but you know, all I do is stay holed up in my studio, working.
Takeshi Komuro's Life in Manga
Takeshi Komuro's Life in Manga
In fact, actually...

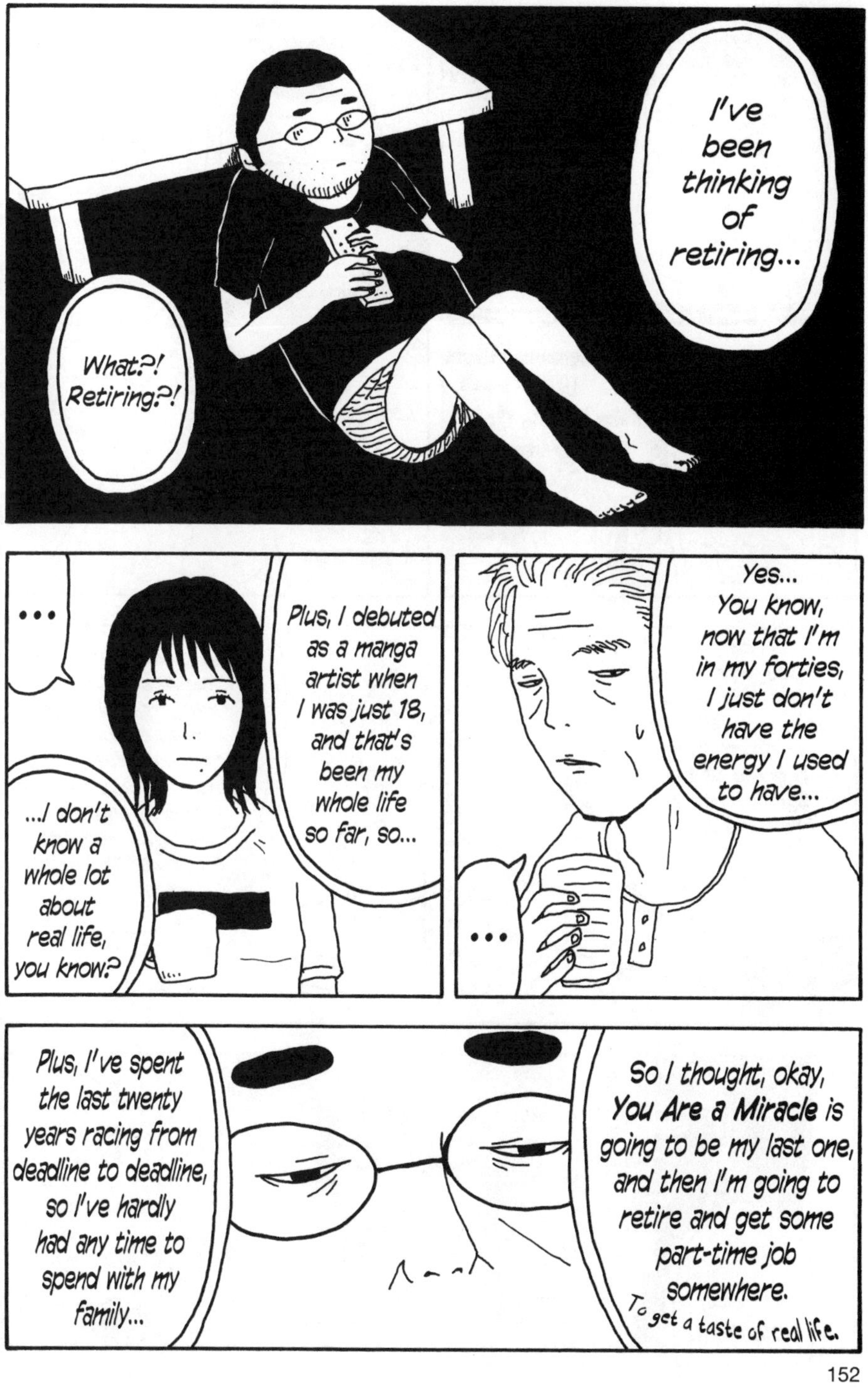
I've been thinking of retiring...
What?! Retiring?!
Yes... You know, now that I'm in my forties, I just don't have the energy I used to have...
...
Plus, I debuted as a manga artist when I was just 18, and that's been my whole life so far, so...
...
...I don't know a whole lot about real life, you know?
So I thought, okay, **You Are a Miracle** is going to be my last one, and then I'm going to retire and get some part-time job somewhere.
To get a taste of real life.
Plus, I've spent the last twenty years racing from deadline to deadline, so I've hardly had any time to spend with my family...

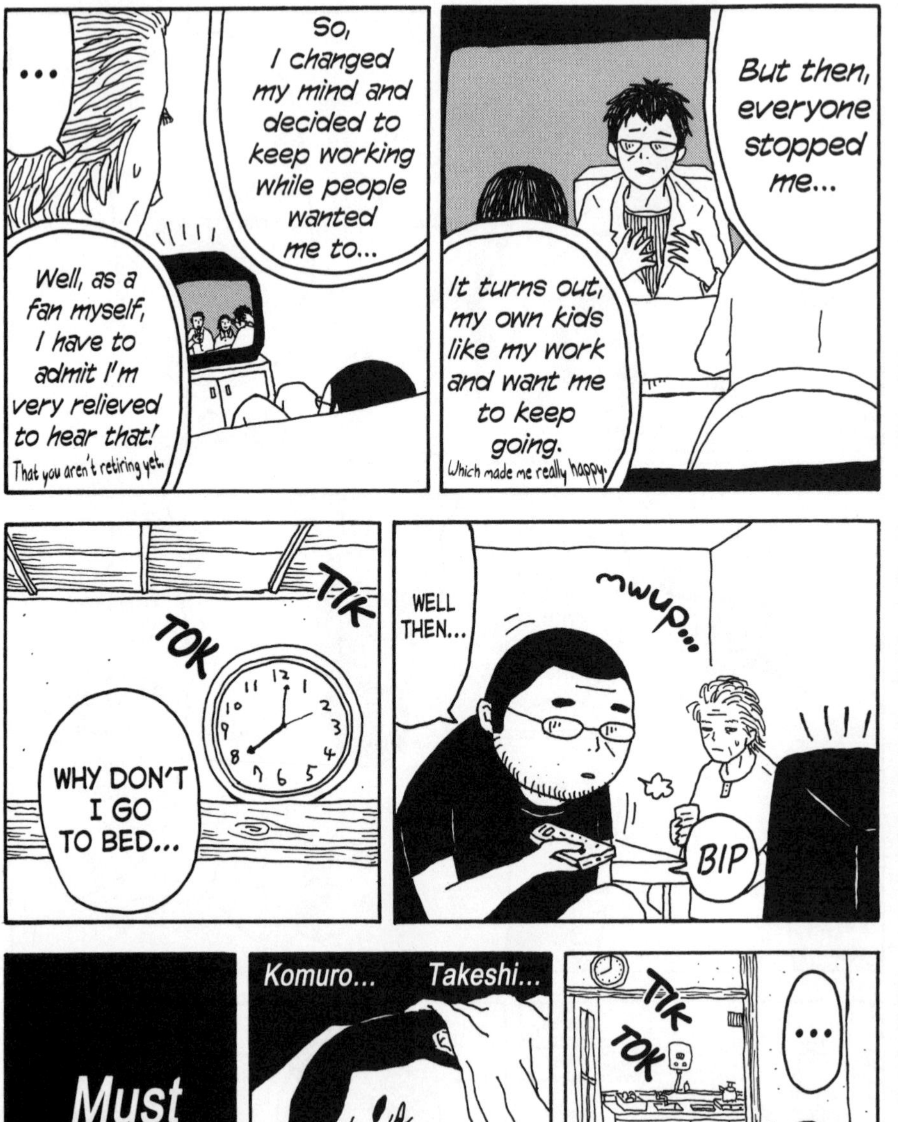

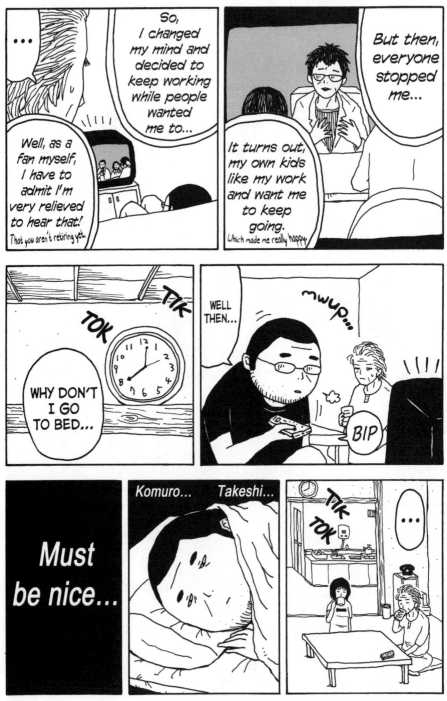

But then, everyone stopped me...
It turns out, my own kids like my work and want me to keep going.
Which made me really happy.
So, I changed my mind and decided to keep working while people wanted me to...
...
Well, as a fan myself, I have to admit I'm very relieved to hear that!
That you aren't retiring yet.
WELL THEN...
mwup...
BIP
TIK
TOK
WHY DON'T I GO TO BED...
TIK
TOK
...
Komuro... Takeshi...
Must be nice...

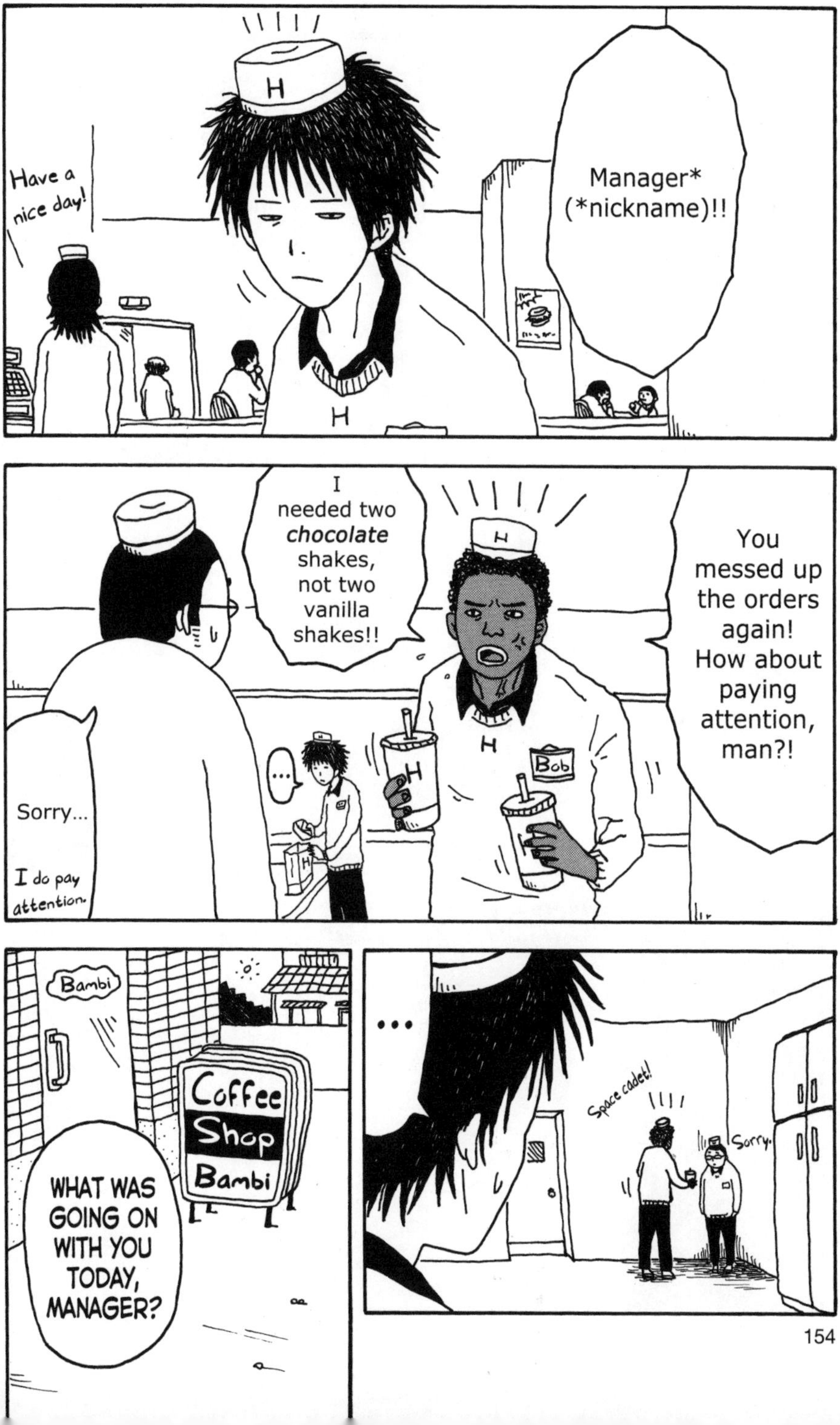
Manager* (*nickname)!!
Have a nice day!
You messed up the orders again! How about paying attention, man?!
I needed two chocolate shakes, not two vanilla shakes!!
...
Bob
Sorry...
I do pay attention.
...
Space cadet!
Sorry.
Bambi
Coffee Shop Bambi
WHAT WAS GOING ON WITH YOU TODAY, MANAGER?

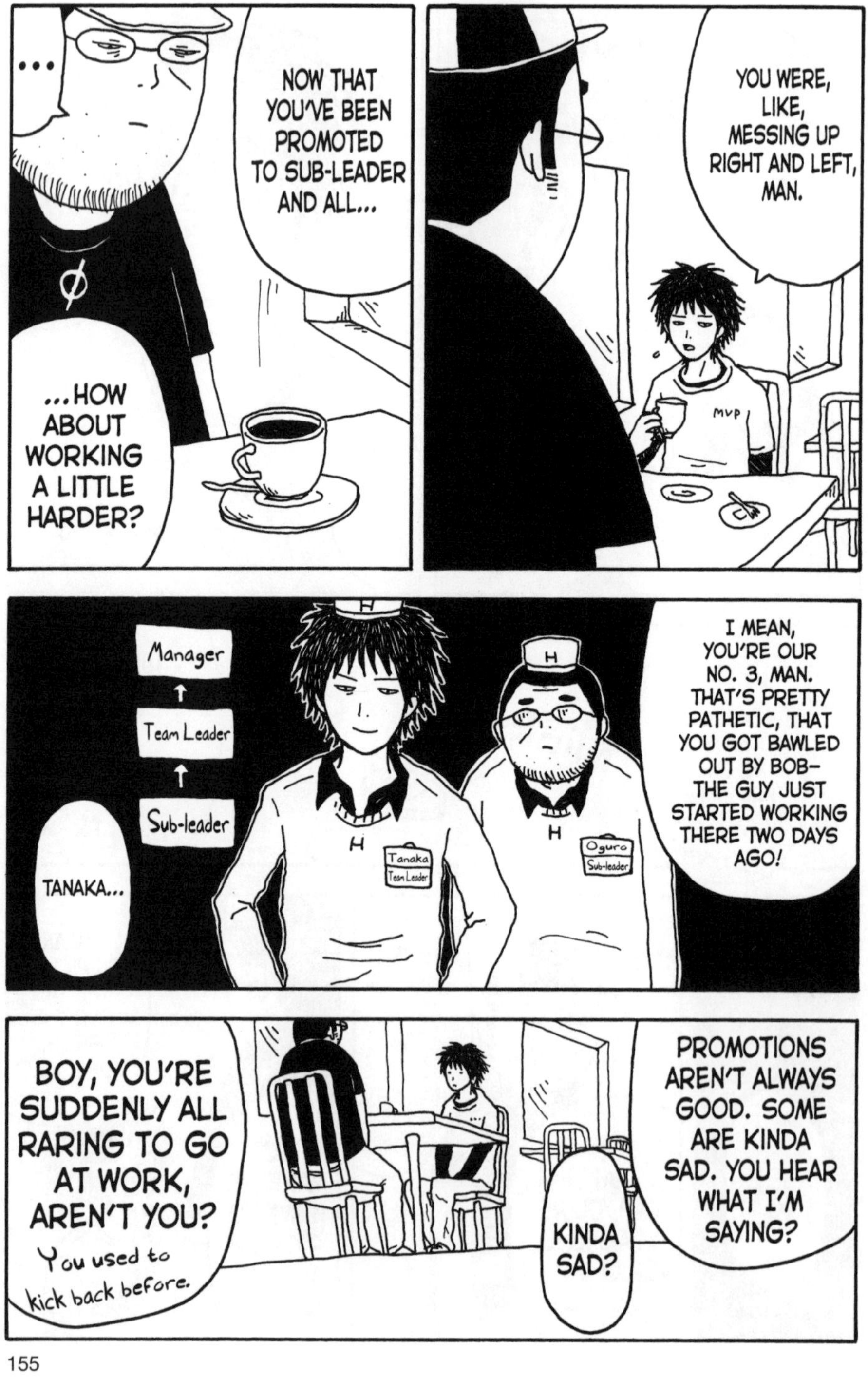
YOU WERE, LIKE, MESSING UP RIGHT AND LEFT, MAN.
MVP
...
NOW THAT YOU'VE BEEN PROMOTED TO SUB-LEADER AND ALL...
...HOW ABOUT WORKING A LITTLE HARDER?
I MEAN, YOU'RE OUR NO. 3, MAN. THAT'S PRETTY PATHETIC, THAT YOU GOT BAWLED OUT BY BOB– THE GUY JUST STARTED WORKING THERE TWO DAYS AGO!
Oguro Sub-leader
Tanaka Team Leader
Manager
Team Leader
Sub-leader
TANAKA...
PROMOTIONS AREN'T ALWAYS GOOD. SOME ARE KINDA SAD. YOU HEAR WHAT I'M SAYING?
KINDA SAD?
BOY, YOU'RE SUDDENLY ALL RARING TO GO AT WORK, AREN'T YOU?
You used to kick back before.

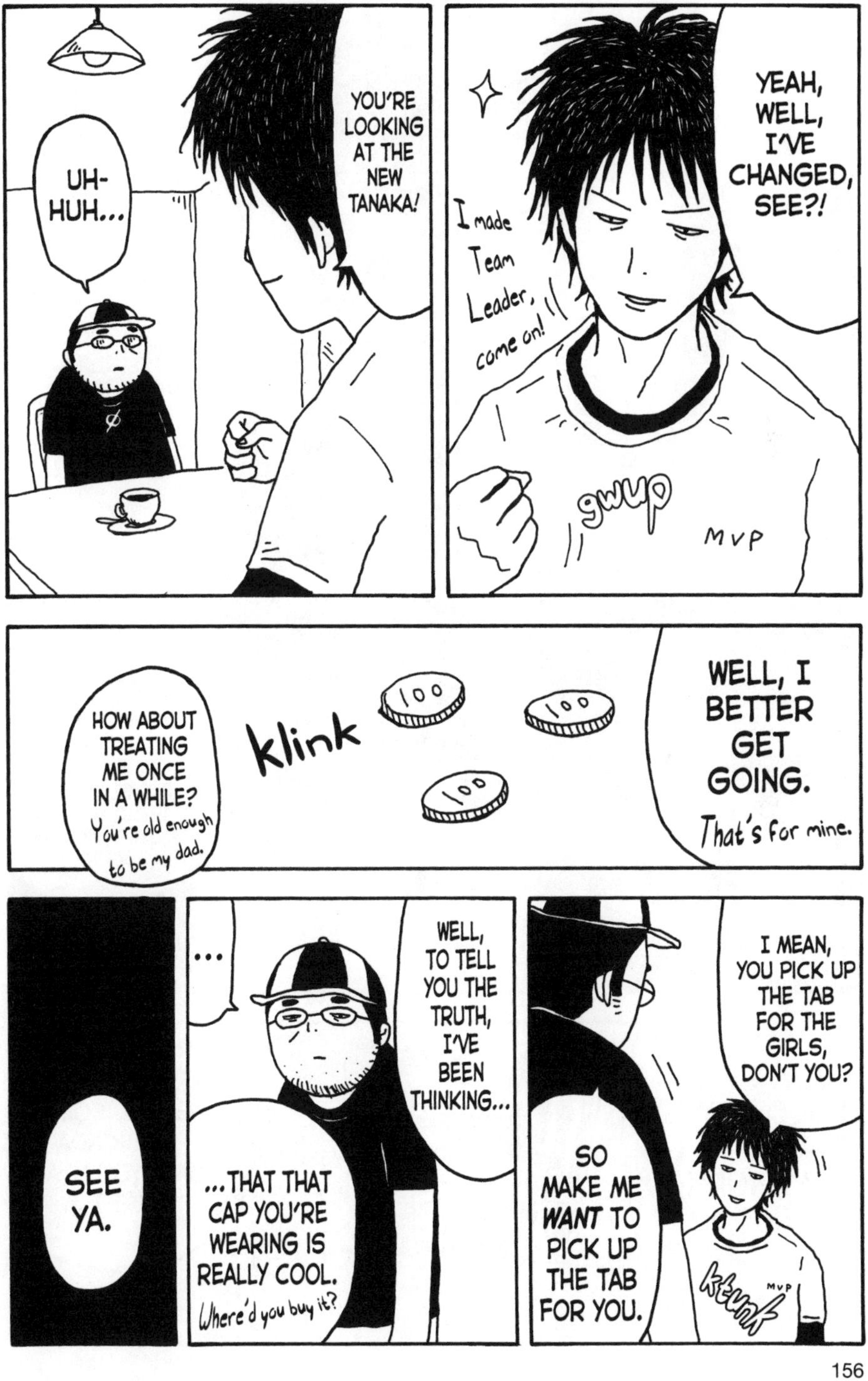
YEAH, WELL, I'VE CHANGED, SEE?!
I made Team Leader, come on!
gwup
MVP
YOU'RE LOOKING AT THE NEW TANAKA!
UH-HUH...
WELL, I BETTER GET GOING.
That's for mine.
klink
HOW ABOUT TREATING ME ONCE IN A WHILE? You're old enough to be my dad.
I MEAN, YOU PICK UP THE TAB FOR THE GIRLS, DON'T YOU?
SO MAKE ME *WANT* TO PICK UP THE TAB FOR YOU.
ktunk
MVP
WELL, TO TELL YOU THE TRUTH, I'VE BEEN THINKING...
...
...THAT THAT CAP YOU'RE WEARING IS REALLY COOL. Where'd you buy it?
SEE YA.

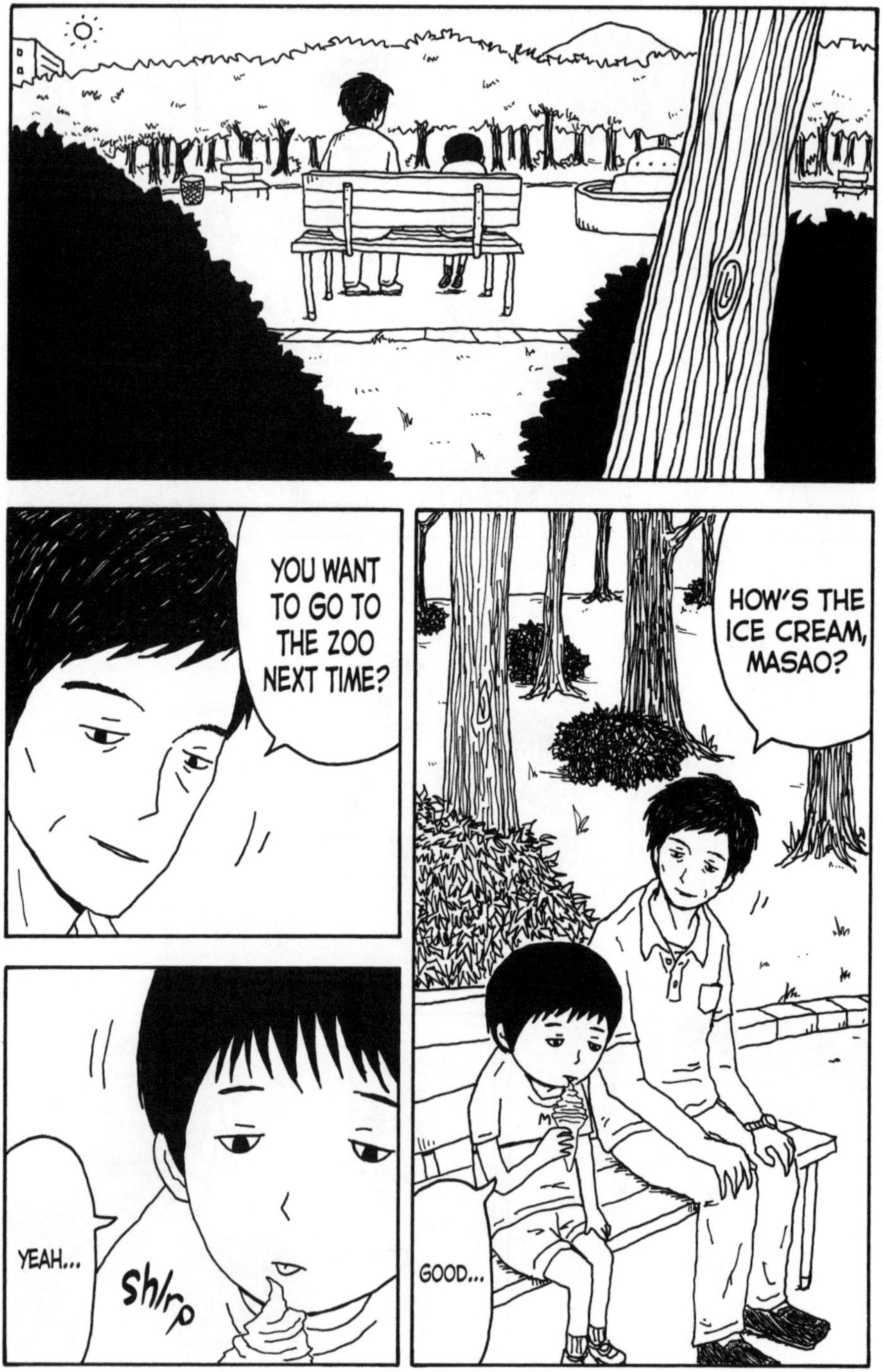
HOW'S THE ICE CREAM, MASAO?
GOOD...
YOU WANT TO GO TO THE ZOO NEXT TIME?
YEAH...
Shlrp

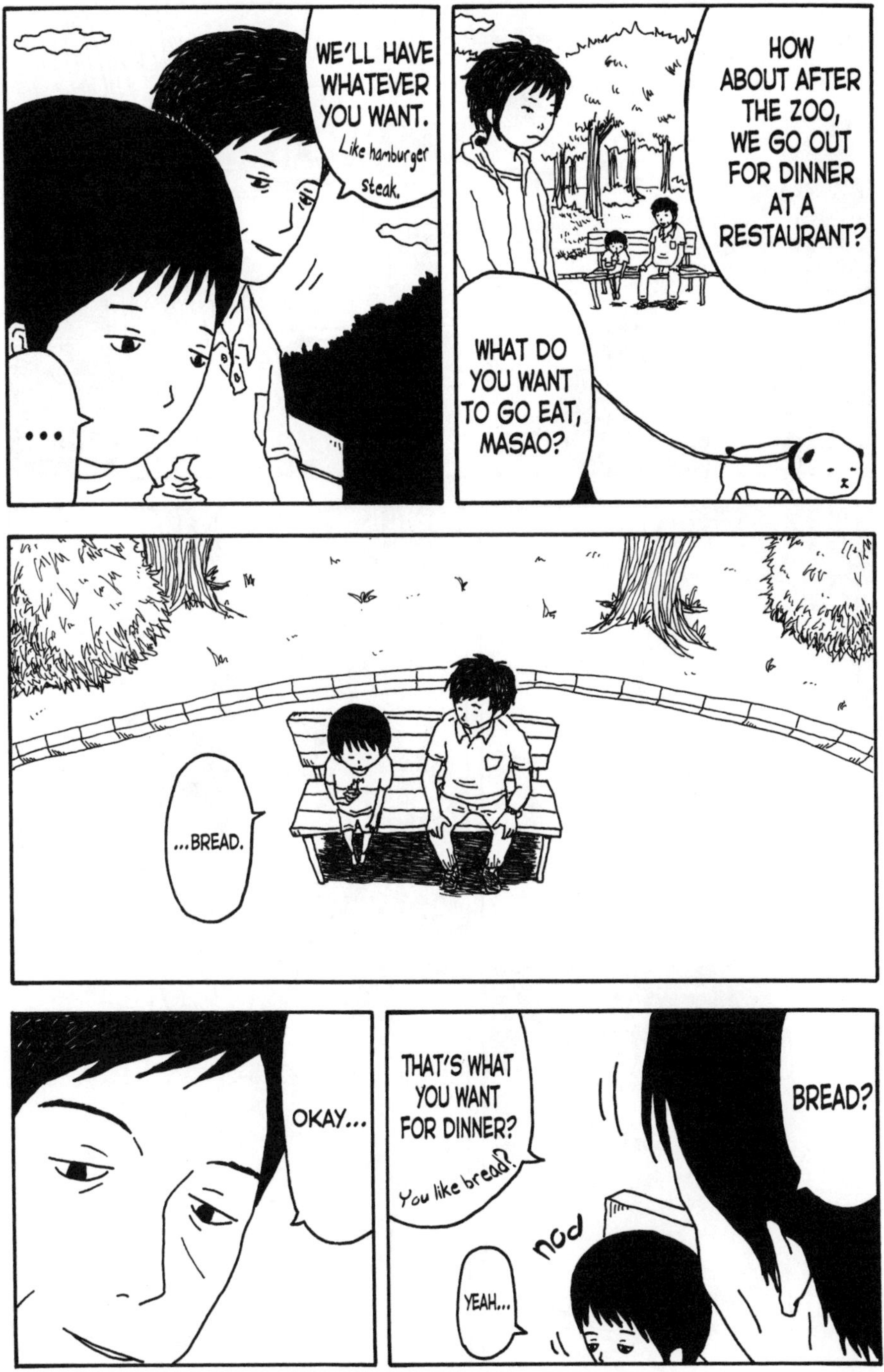
HOW ABOUT AFTER THE ZOO, WE GO OUT FOR DINNER AT A RESTAURANT?
WHAT DO YOU WANT TO GO EAT, MASAO?
WE'LL HAVE WHATEVER YOU WANT.
Like hamburger steak.
...
...BREAD.
BREAD?
THAT'S WHAT YOU WANT FOR DINNER?
You like bread?
nod
YEAH...
OKAY...

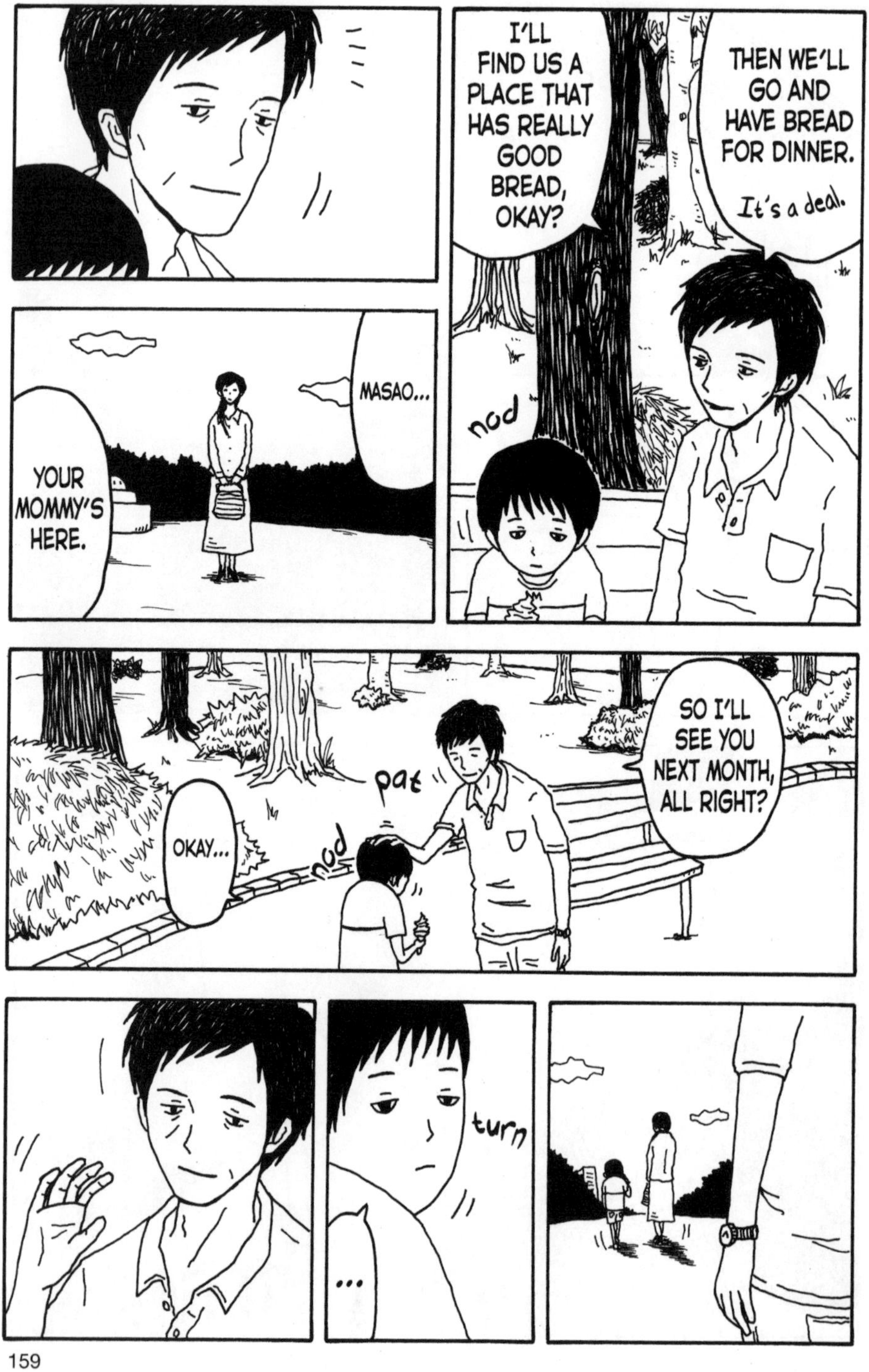
THEN WE'LL GO AND HAVE BREAD FOR DINNER.
It's a deal.
I'LL FIND US A PLACE THAT HAS REALLY GOOD BREAD, OKAY?
nod
MASAO...
YOUR MOMMY'S HERE.
SO I'LL SEE YOU NEXT MONTH, ALL RIGHT?
pat
OKAY...
nod
turn
...

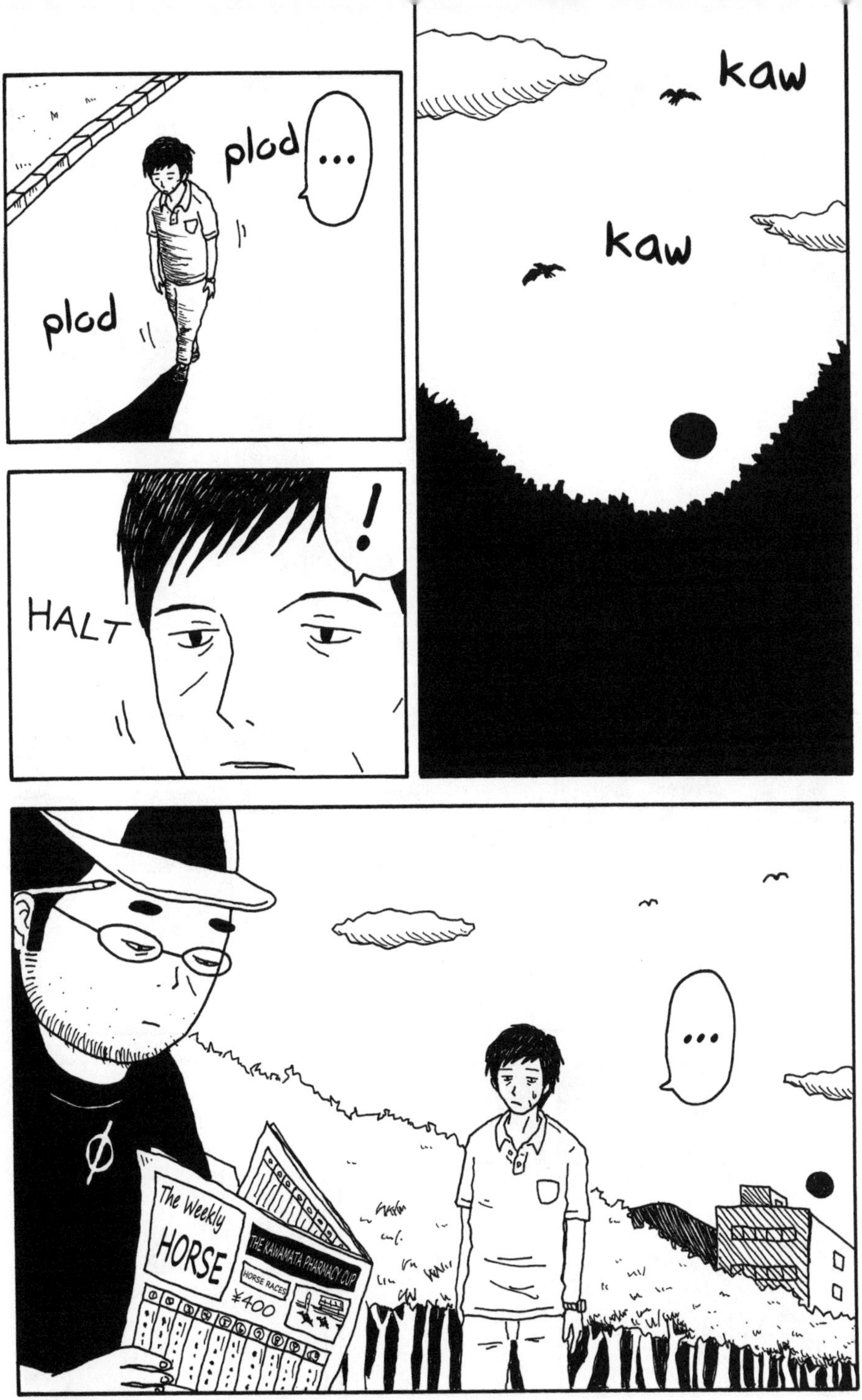
kaw
kaw
plod
...
plod
!
HALT
...
The Weekly
HORSE
THE KAWAMATA PHARMACY CUP
HORSE RACES
¥400

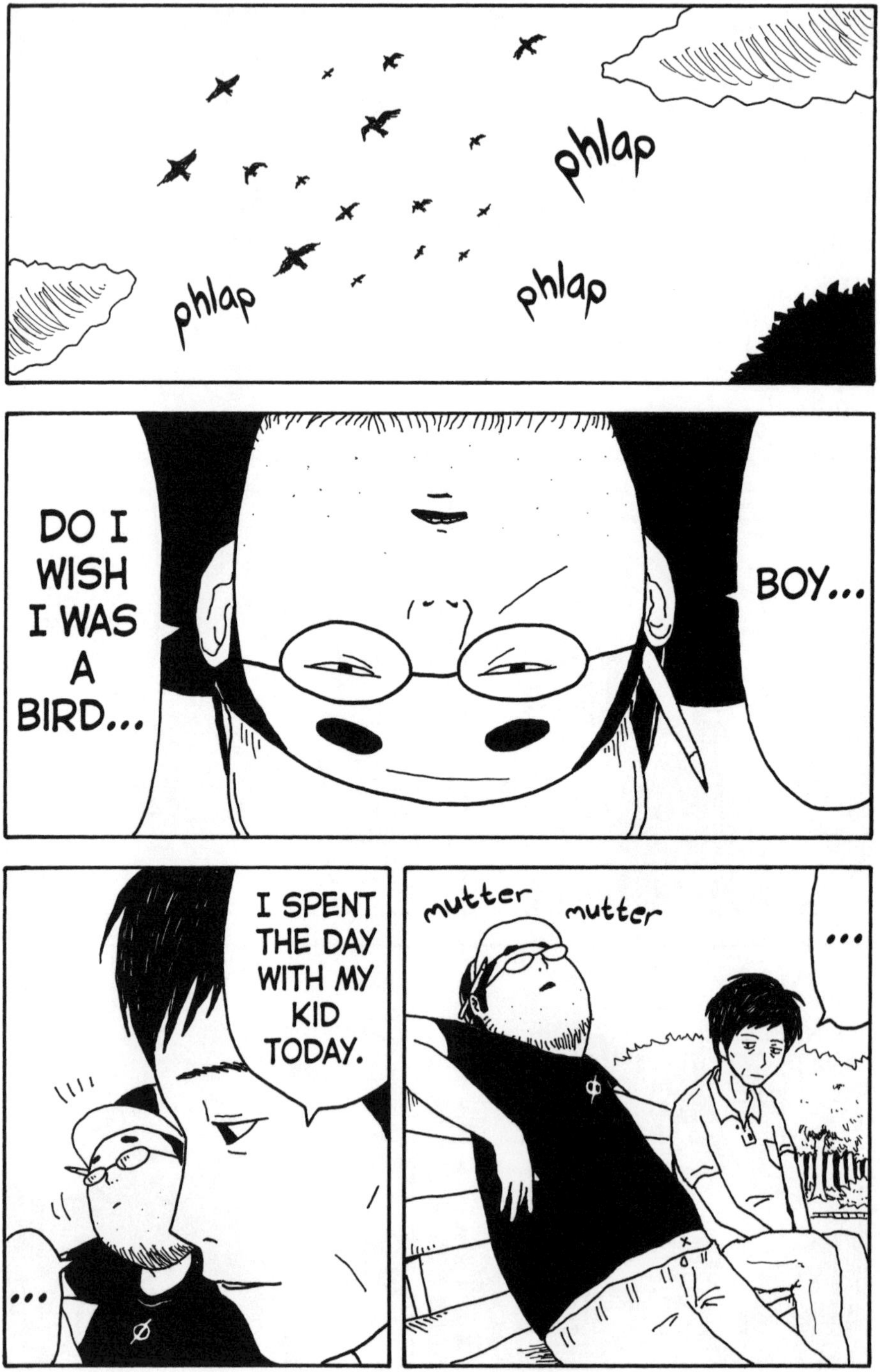
phlap
phlap
phlap
BOY...
DO I WISH I WAS A BIRD...
mutter
mutter
...
I SPENT THE DAY WITH MY KID TODAY.
...

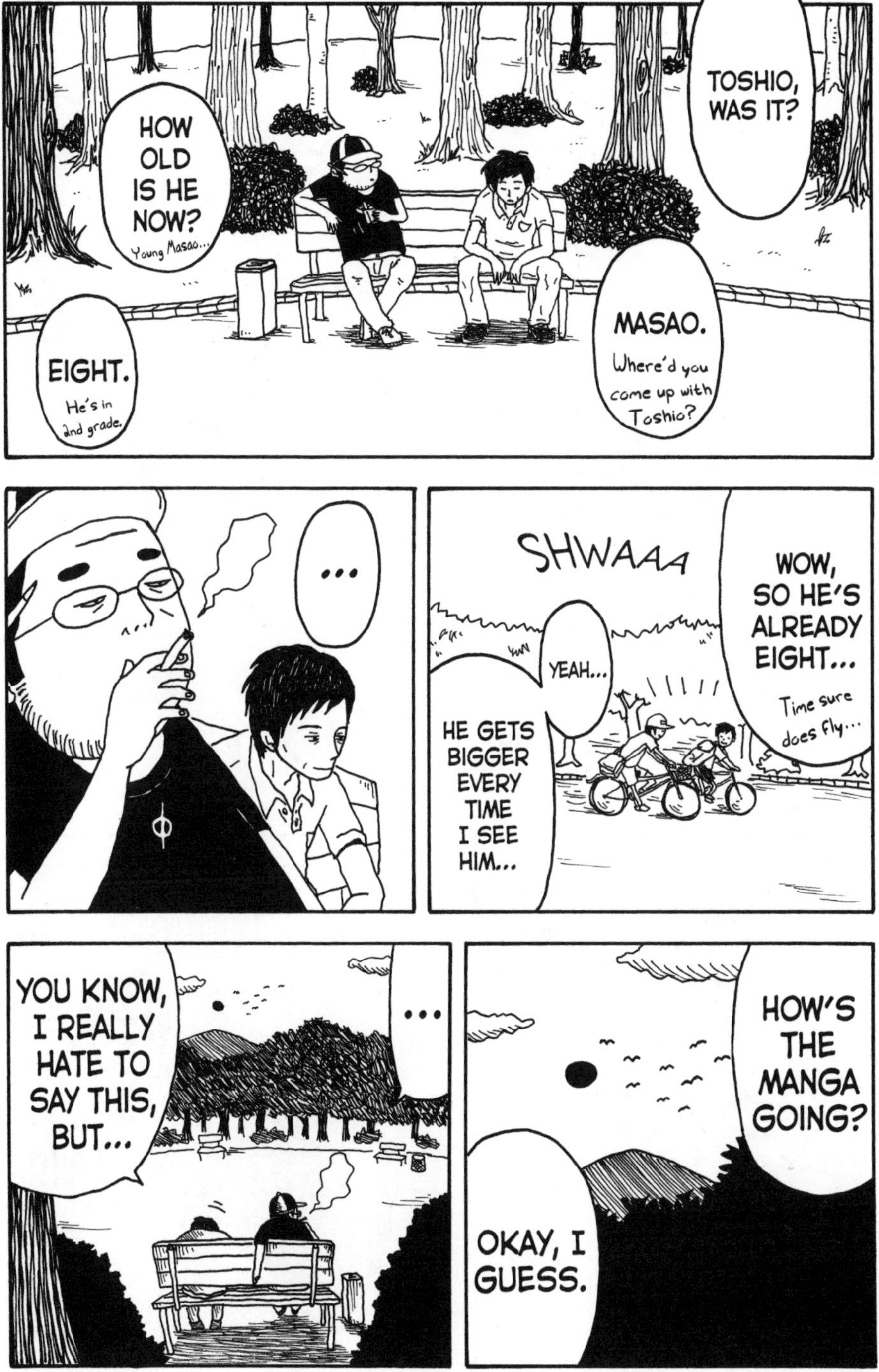

TOSHIO, WAS IT?
MASAO.
Where'd you come up with Toshio?
HOW OLD IS HE NOW?
Young Masao...
EIGHT.
He's in 2nd grade.
WOW, SO HE'S ALREADY EIGHT...
Time sure does fly...
SHWAAA
YEAH...
HE GETS BIGGER EVERY TIME I SEE HIM...
...
HOW'S THE MANGA GOING?
OKAY, I GUESS.
...
YOU KNOW, I REALLY HATE TO SAY THIS, BUT...

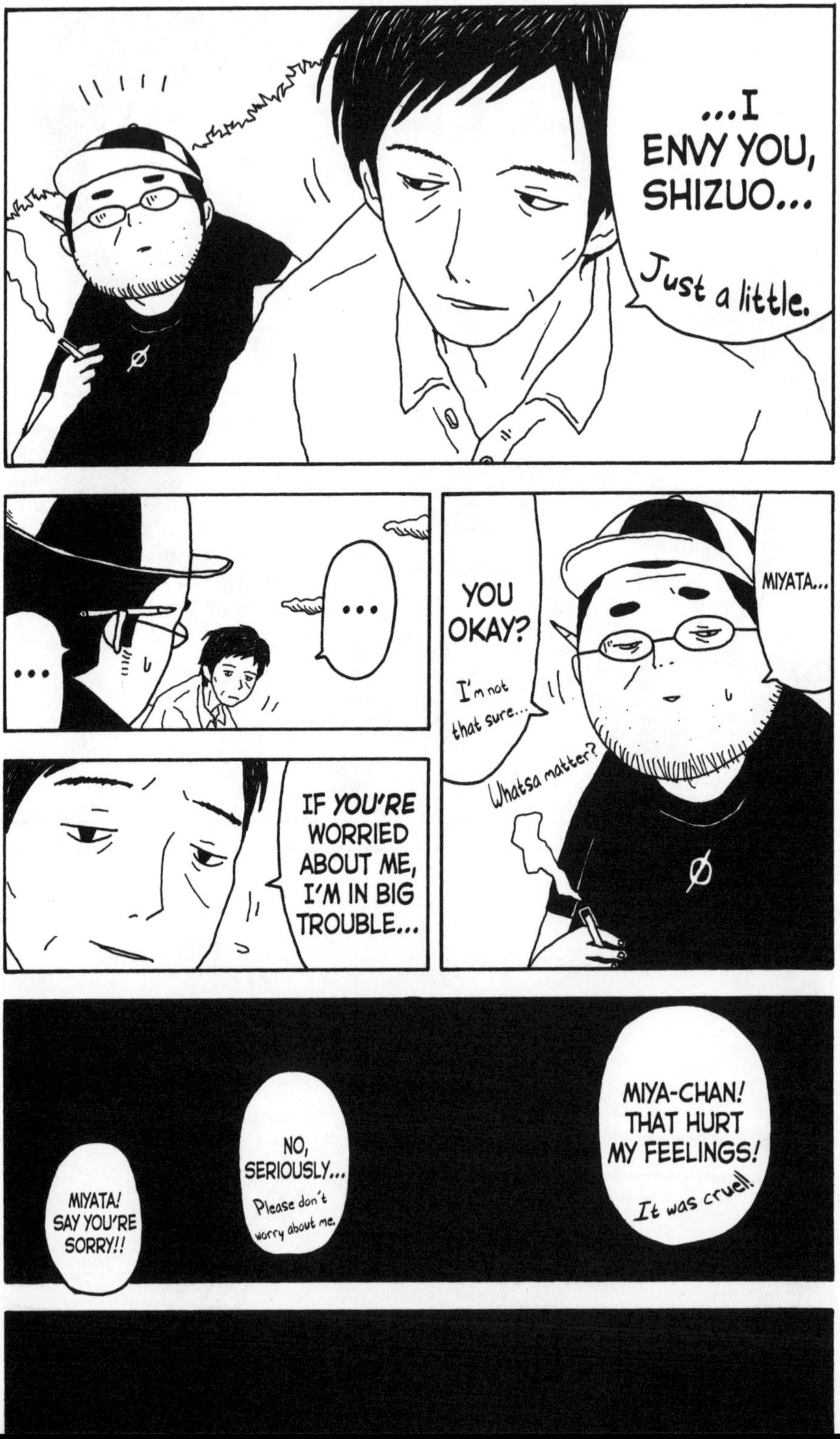
...I ENVY YOU, SHIZUO...
Just a little.
MIYATA...
YOU OKAY?
I'm not that sure...
Whatsa matter?
...
...
IF *YOU'RE* WORRIED ABOUT ME, I'M IN BIG TROUBLE...
MIYA-CHAN! THAT HURT MY FEELINGS!
It was cruel!
NO, SERIOUSLY...
Please don't worry about me.
MIYATA! SAY YOU'RE SORRY!!

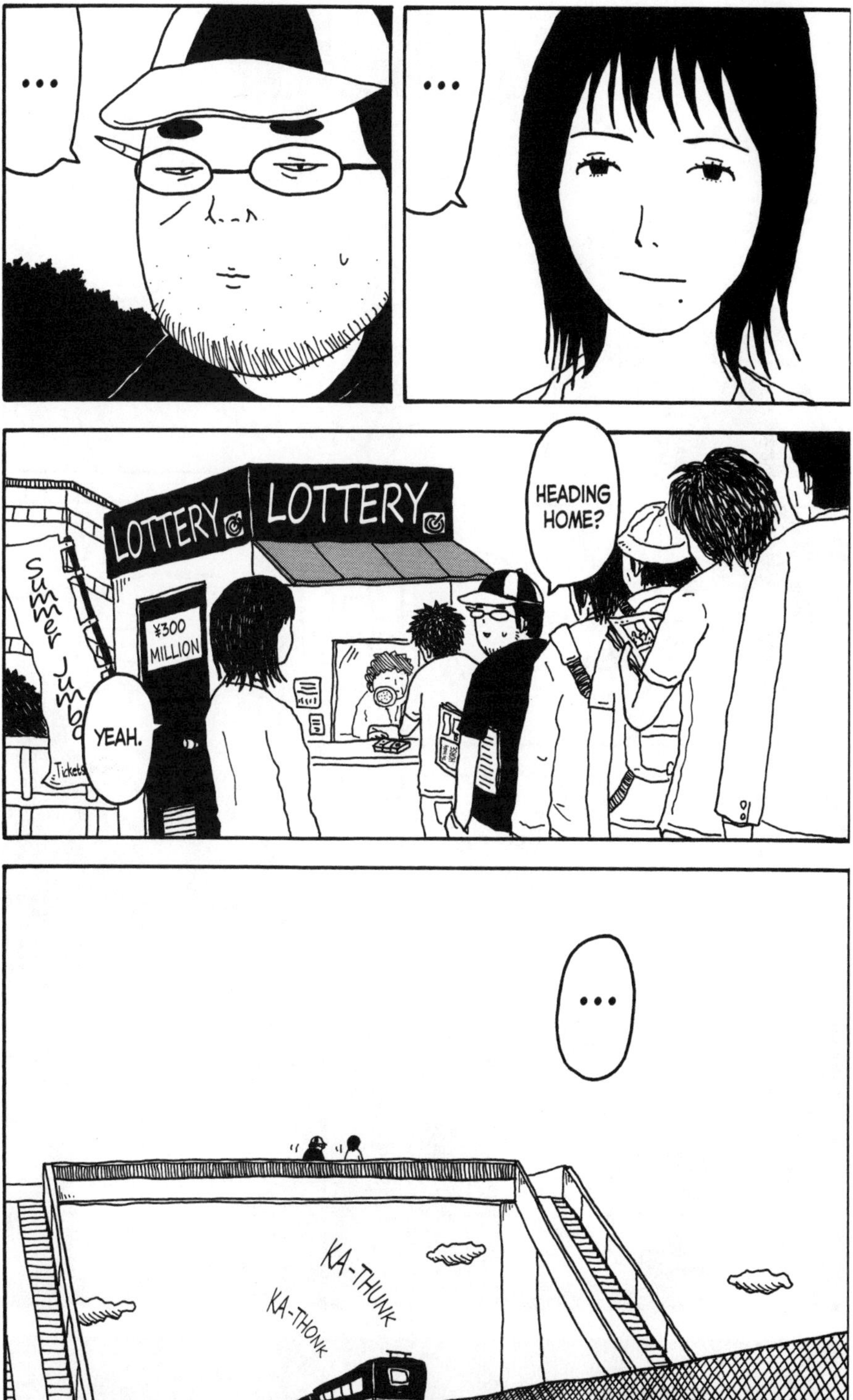
...
...
HEADING HOME?
LOTTERY
LOTTERY
¥300 MILLION
YEAH.
...
KA-THUNK
KA-THONK

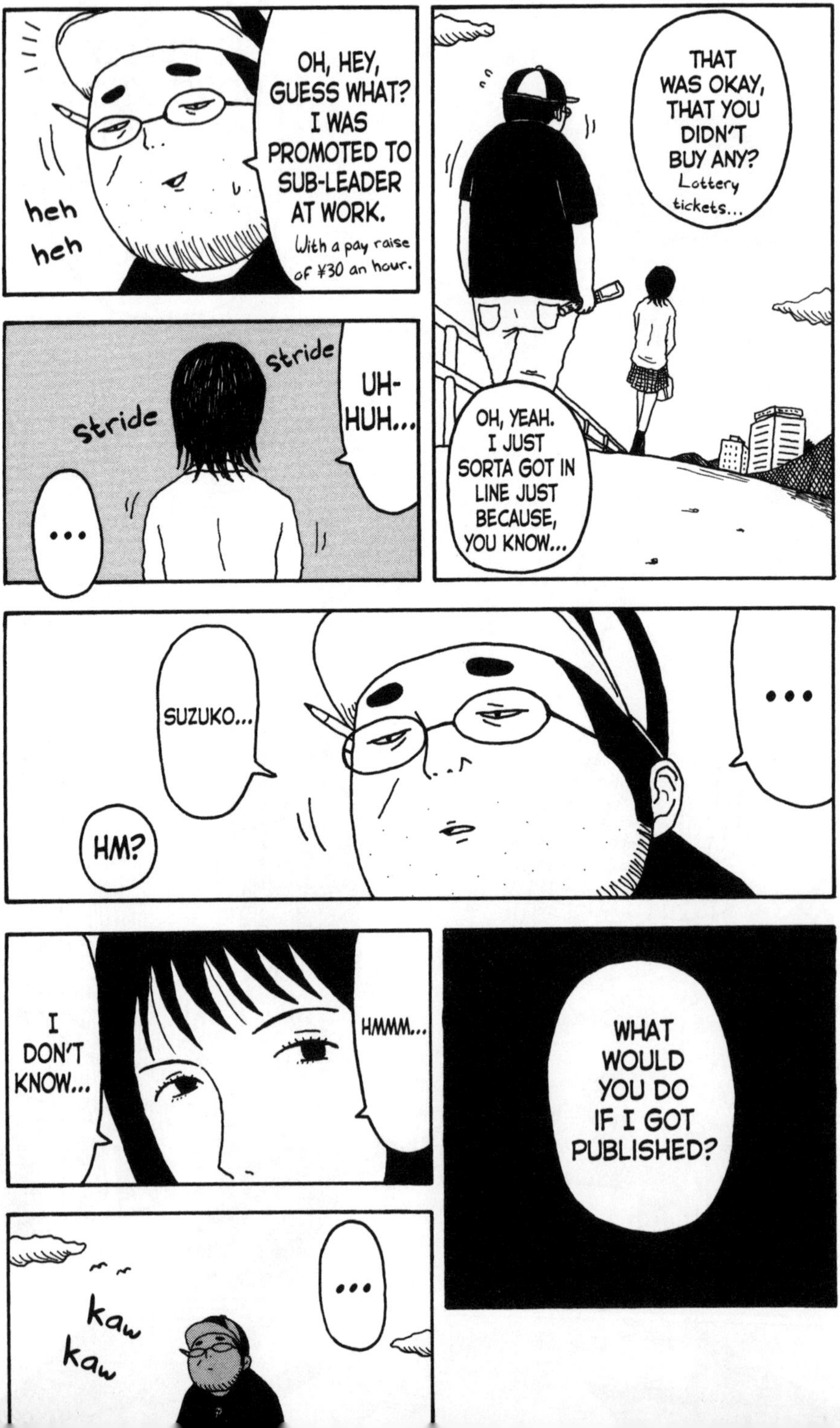
THAT WAS OKAY, THAT YOU DIDN'T BUY ANY?
Lottery tickets...
OH, YEAH. I JUST SORTA GOT IN LINE JUST BECAUSE, YOU KNOW...
OH, HEY, GUESS WHAT? I WAS PROMOTED TO SUB-LEADER AT WORK.
With a pay raise of ¥30 an hour.
heh heh
UH-HUH...
stride
stride
...
...
SUZUKO...
HM?
WHAT WOULD YOU DO IF I GOT PUBLISHED?
HMMM...
I DON'T KNOW...
...
kaw kaw

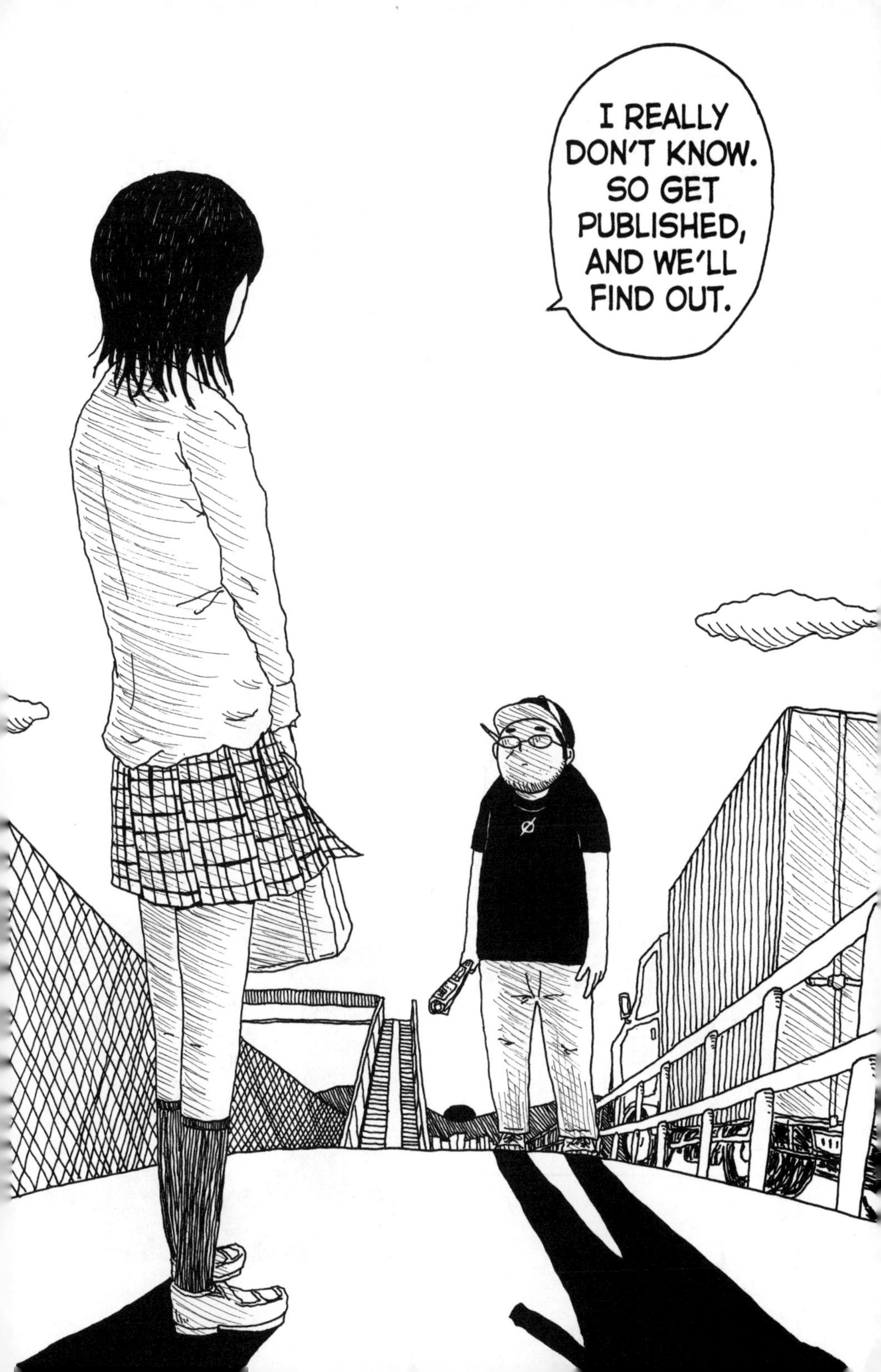
I REALLY DON'T KNOW. SO GET PUBLISHED, AND WE'LL FIND OUT.

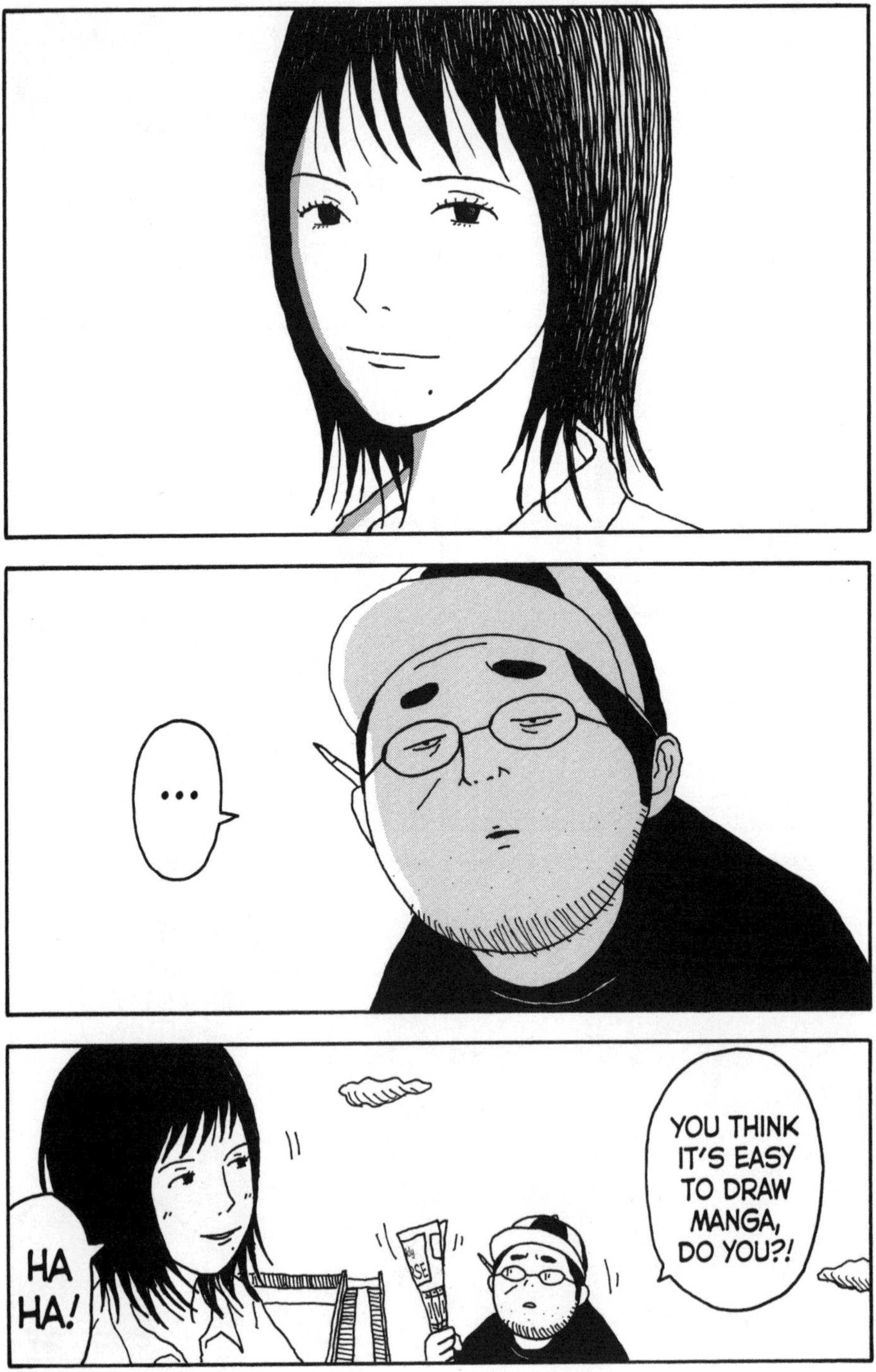
...
YOU THINK IT'S EASY TO DRAW MANGA, DO YOU?!
HA HA!

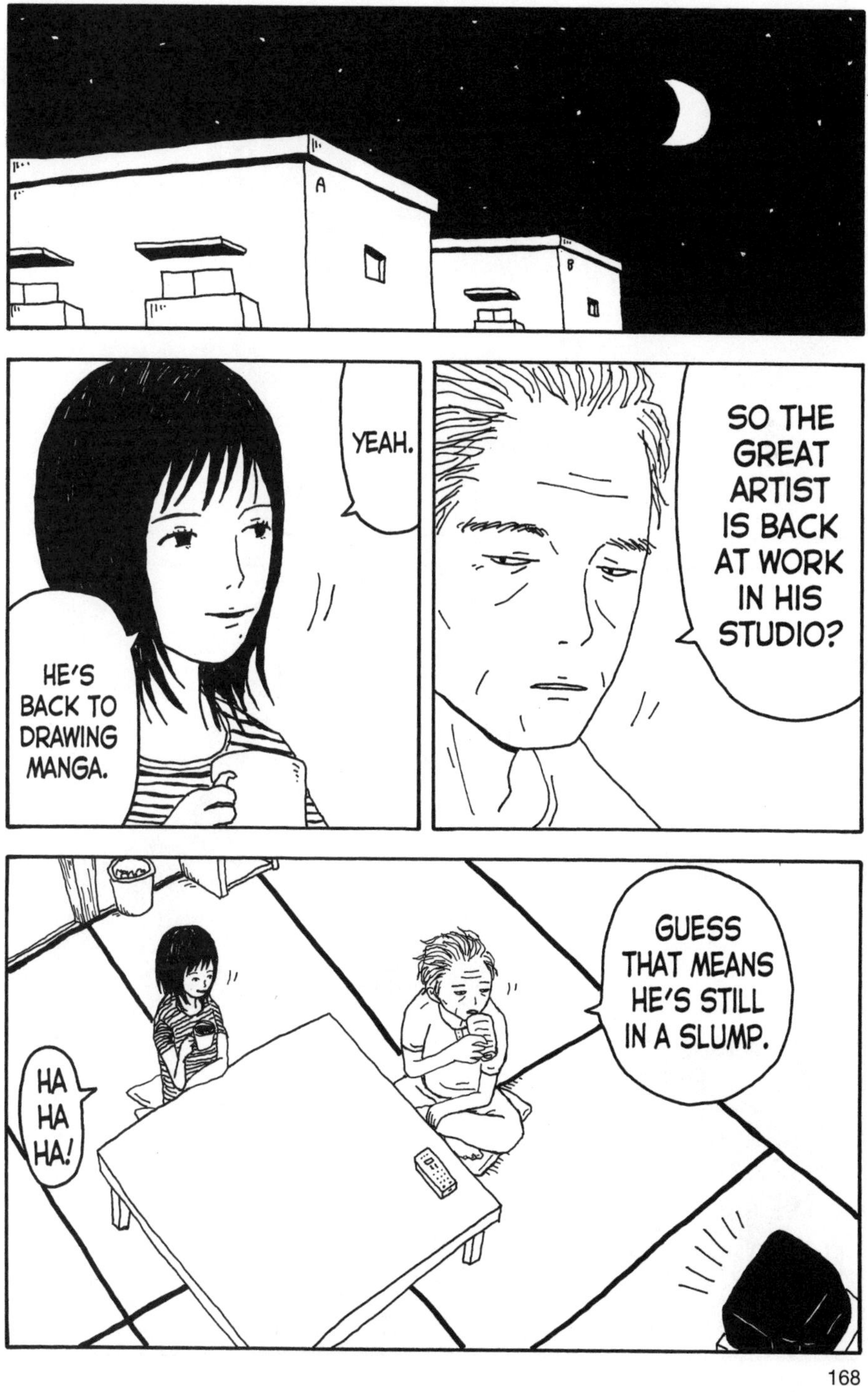
SO THE GREAT ARTIST IS BACK AT WORK IN HIS STUDIO?
YEAH.
HE'S BACK TO DRAWING MANGA.
GUESS THAT MEANS HE'S STILL IN A SLUMP.
HA HA HA!

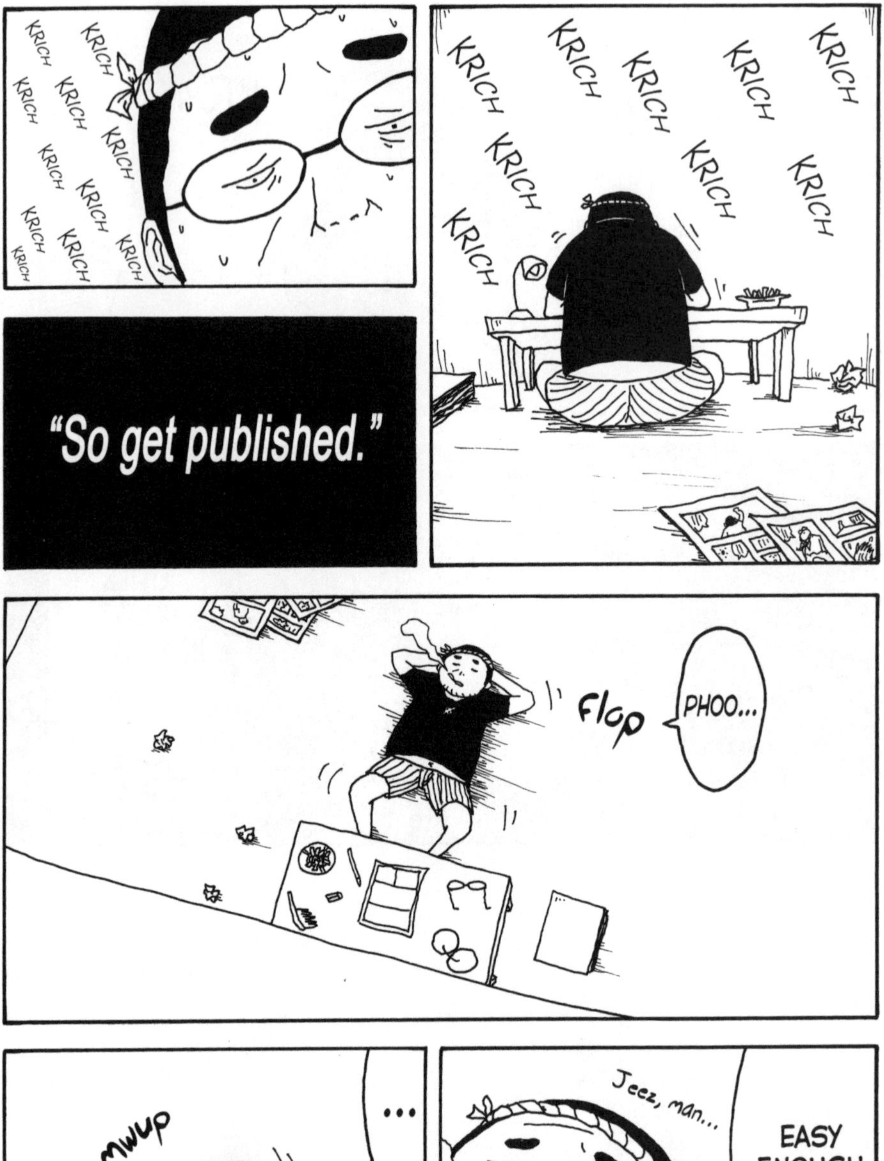
KRICH
KRICH
KRICH
KRICH
KRICH
KRICH
KRICH
KRICH
KRICH
KRICH
KRICH
KRICH
KRICH
KRICH
KRICH
KRICH
KRICH
KRICH
KRICH
KRICH
"So get published."
FLOP
PHOO...
Jeez, man...
EASY ENOUGH FOR HER TO SAY.
...
MWUP
OKAY...

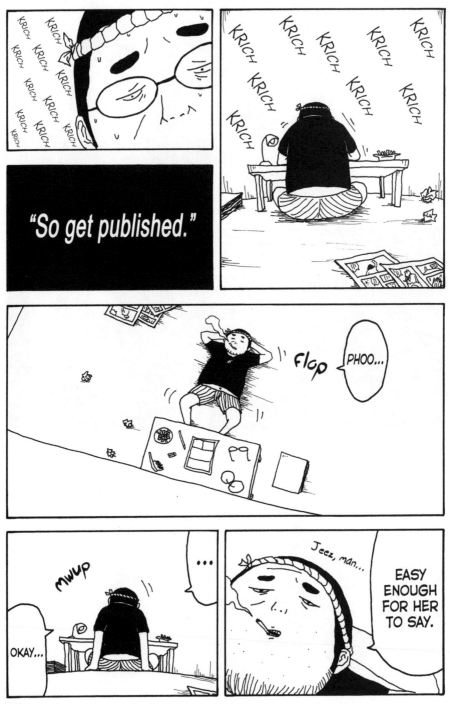

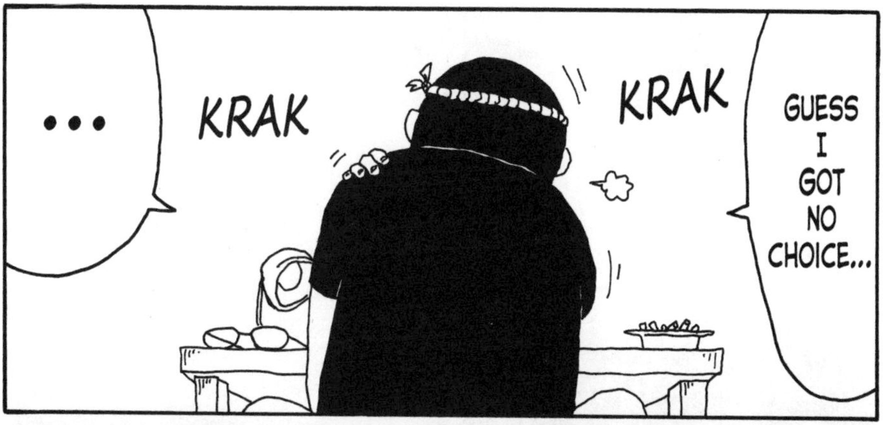
GUESS I GOT NO CHOICE...
KRAK
KRAK
...
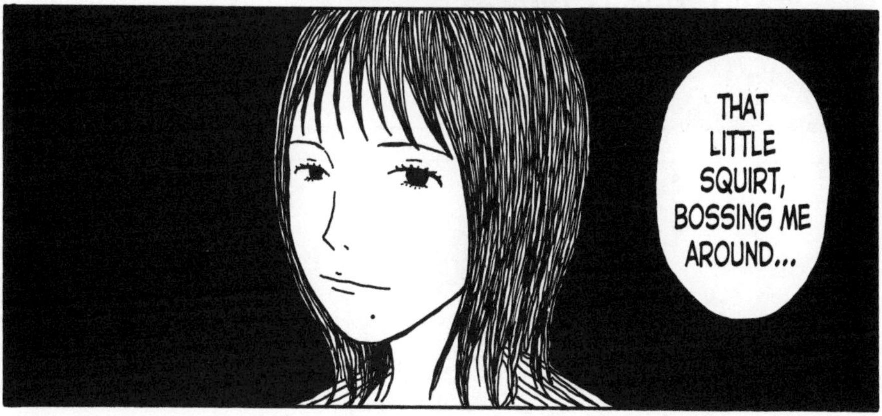
THAT LITTLE SQUIRT, BOSSING ME AROUND...
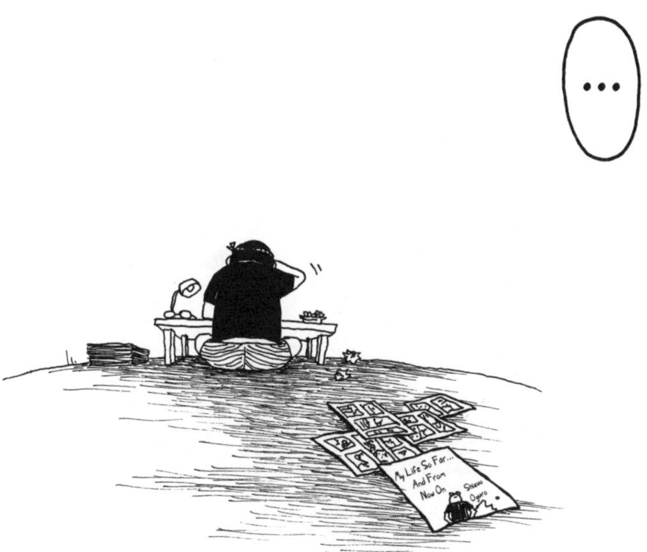
...
My Life So Far... And From Now On
Shizuo Oguro

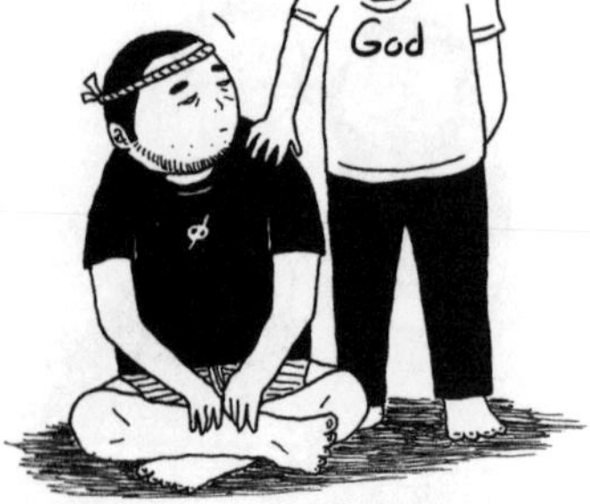
God

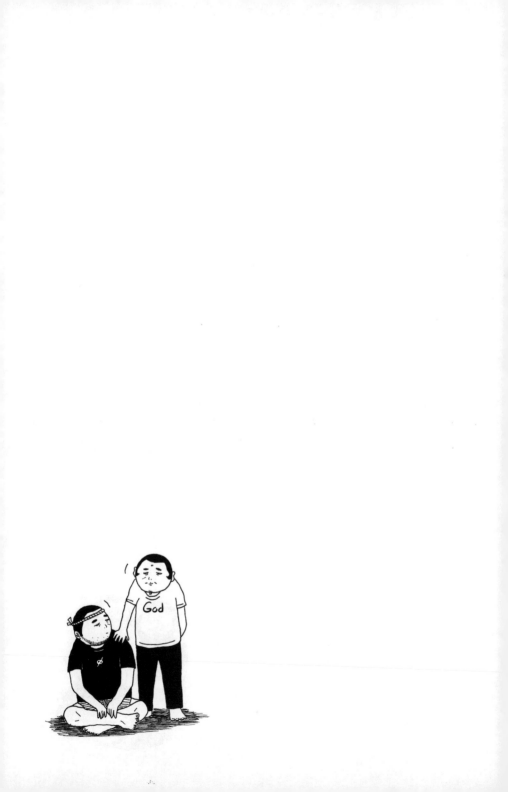

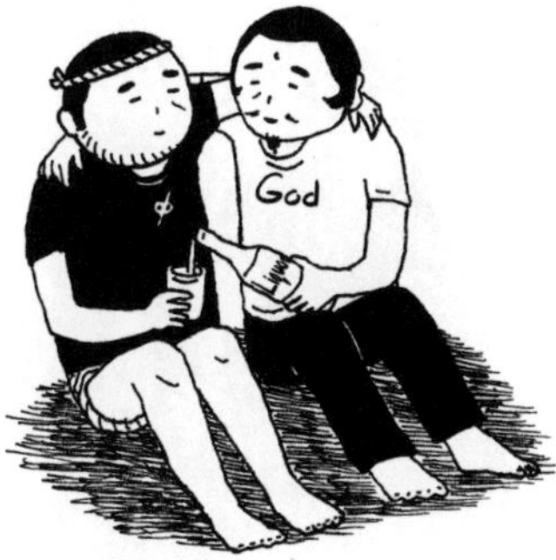
God

Bonus Story:

To Live

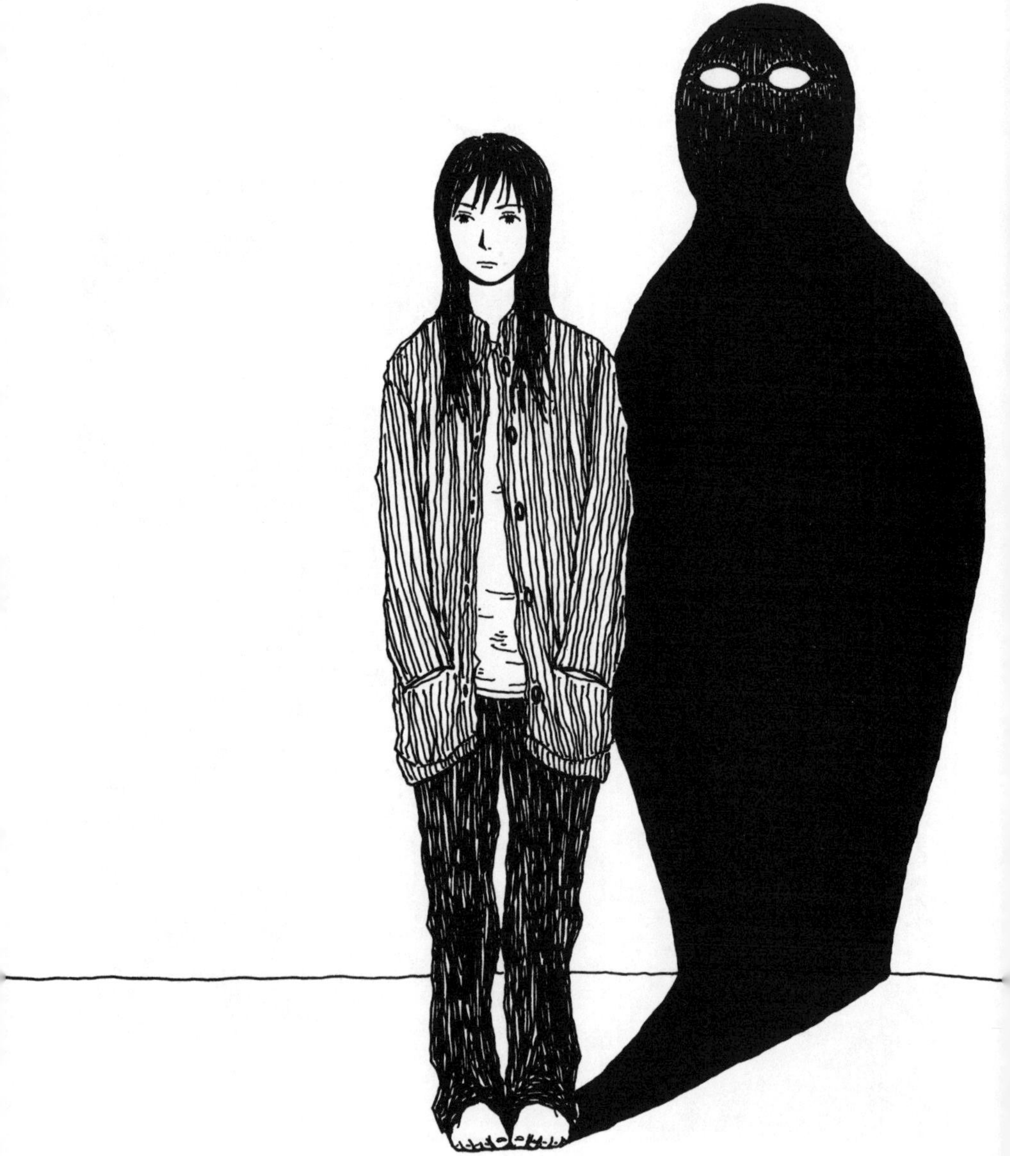

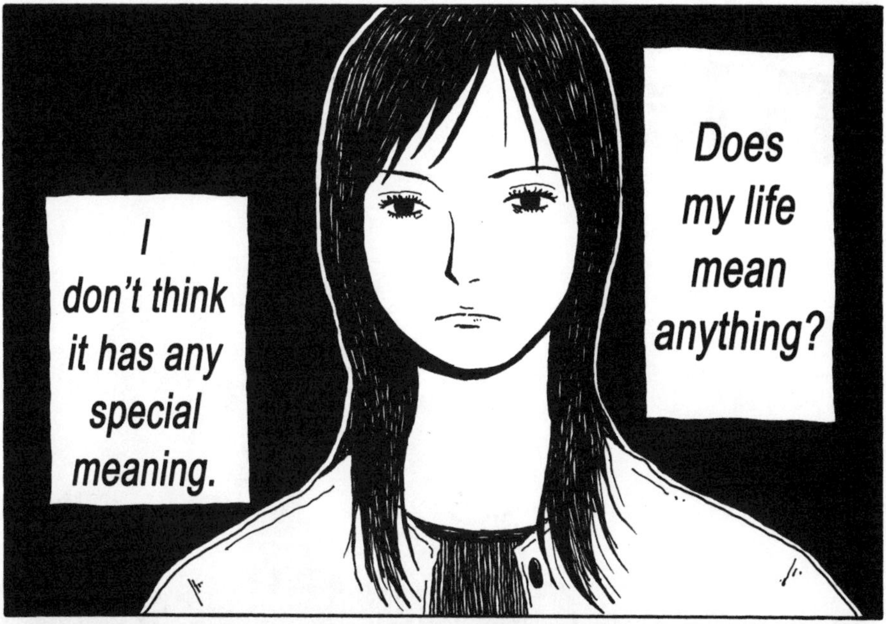
Does my life mean anything?
I don't think it has any special meaning.
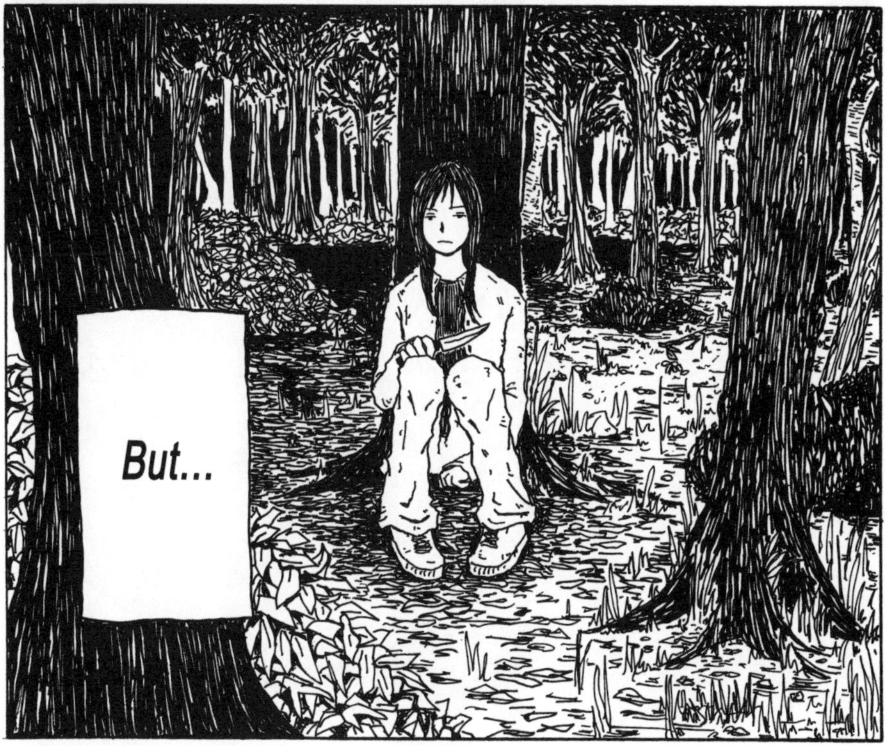
But...

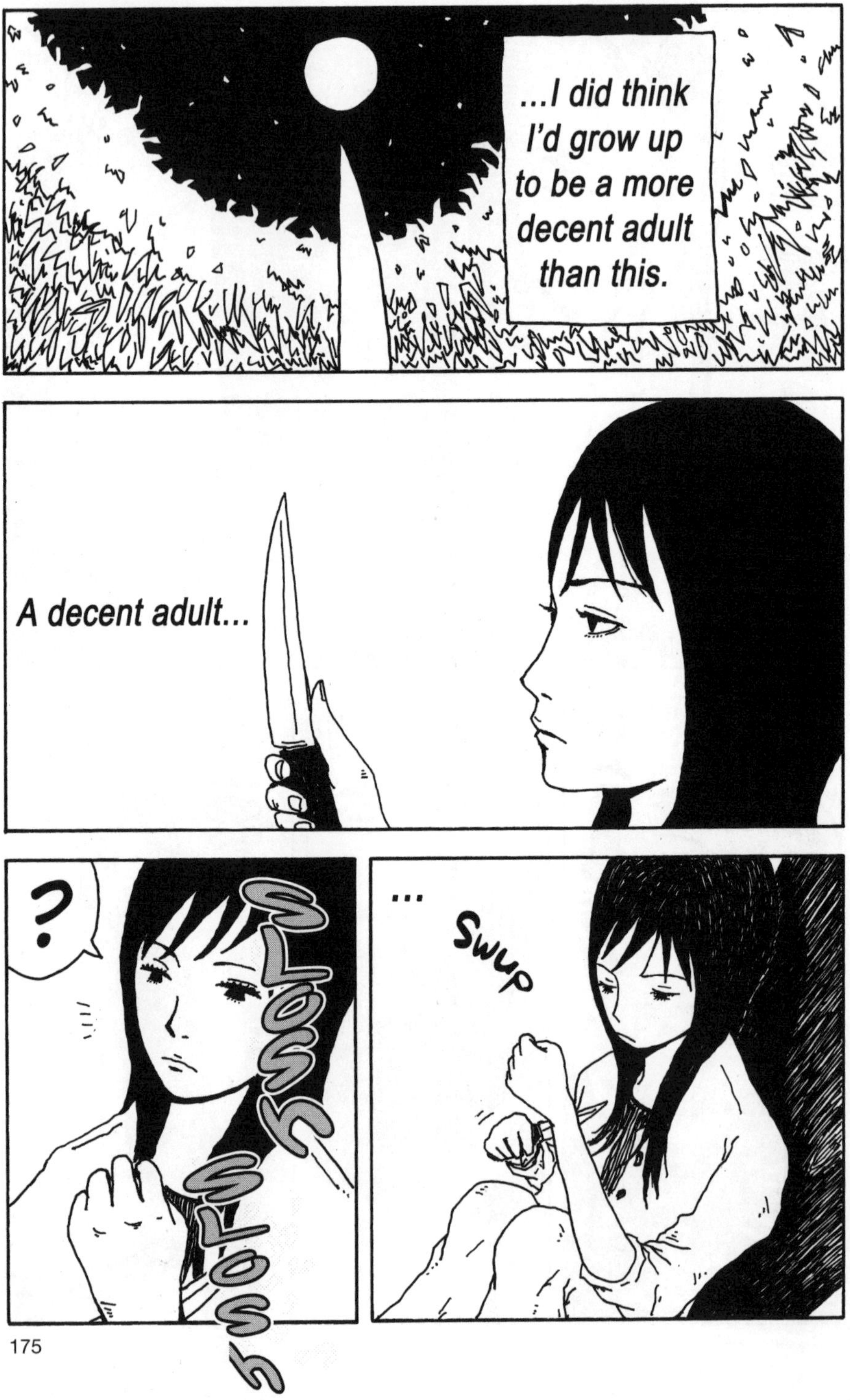

...I did think I'd grow up to be a more decent adult than this.
A decent adult...
...
Swup
?
SLOSH SLOSH

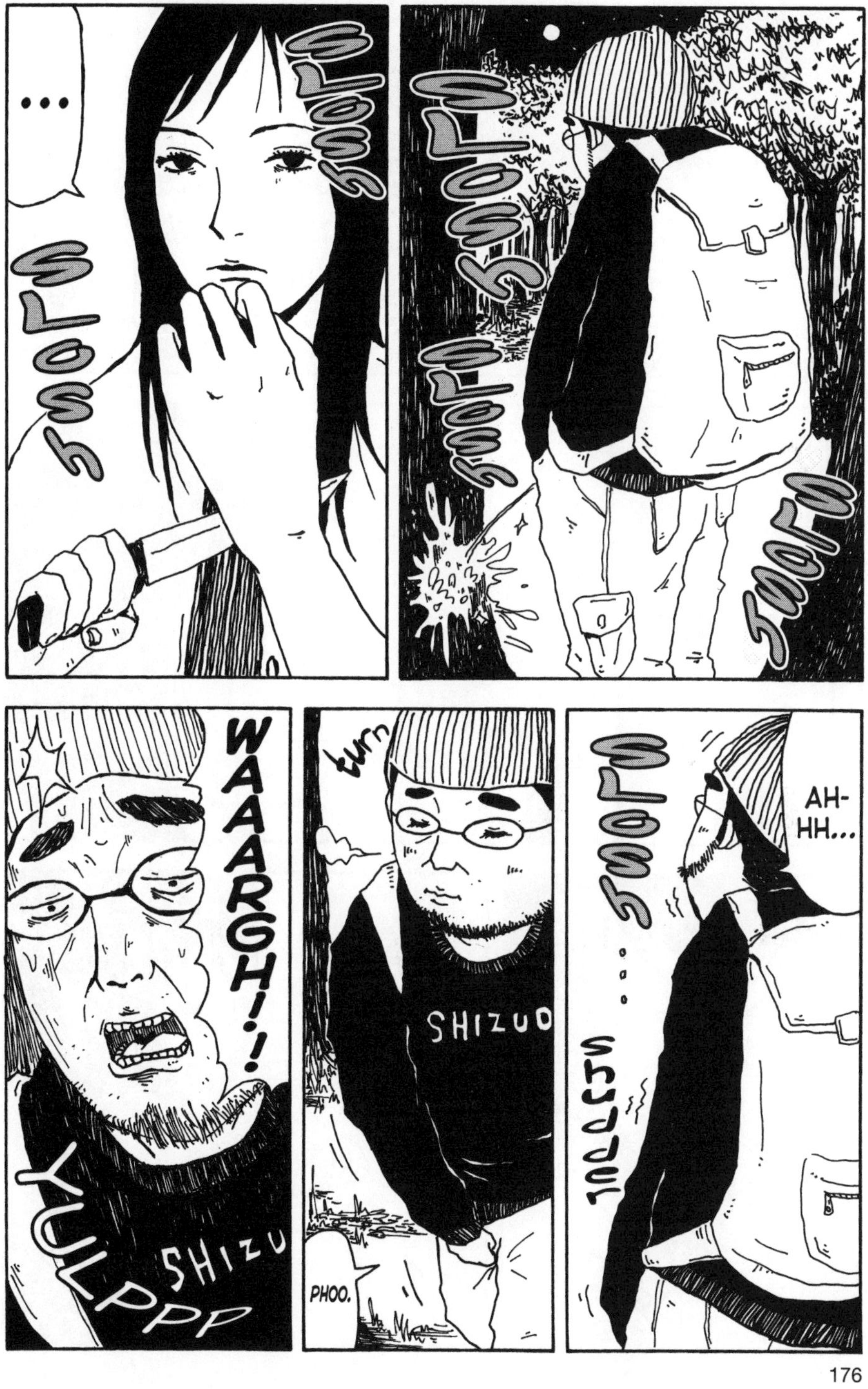
SLOSH SLOSH
SLOSH
SLOSH
...
SLOSH
SLOSH
AH-HH...
...
SHUDDER
turn
SHIZUO
PHOO.
WAAARGH!!
SHIZU
YULPPP

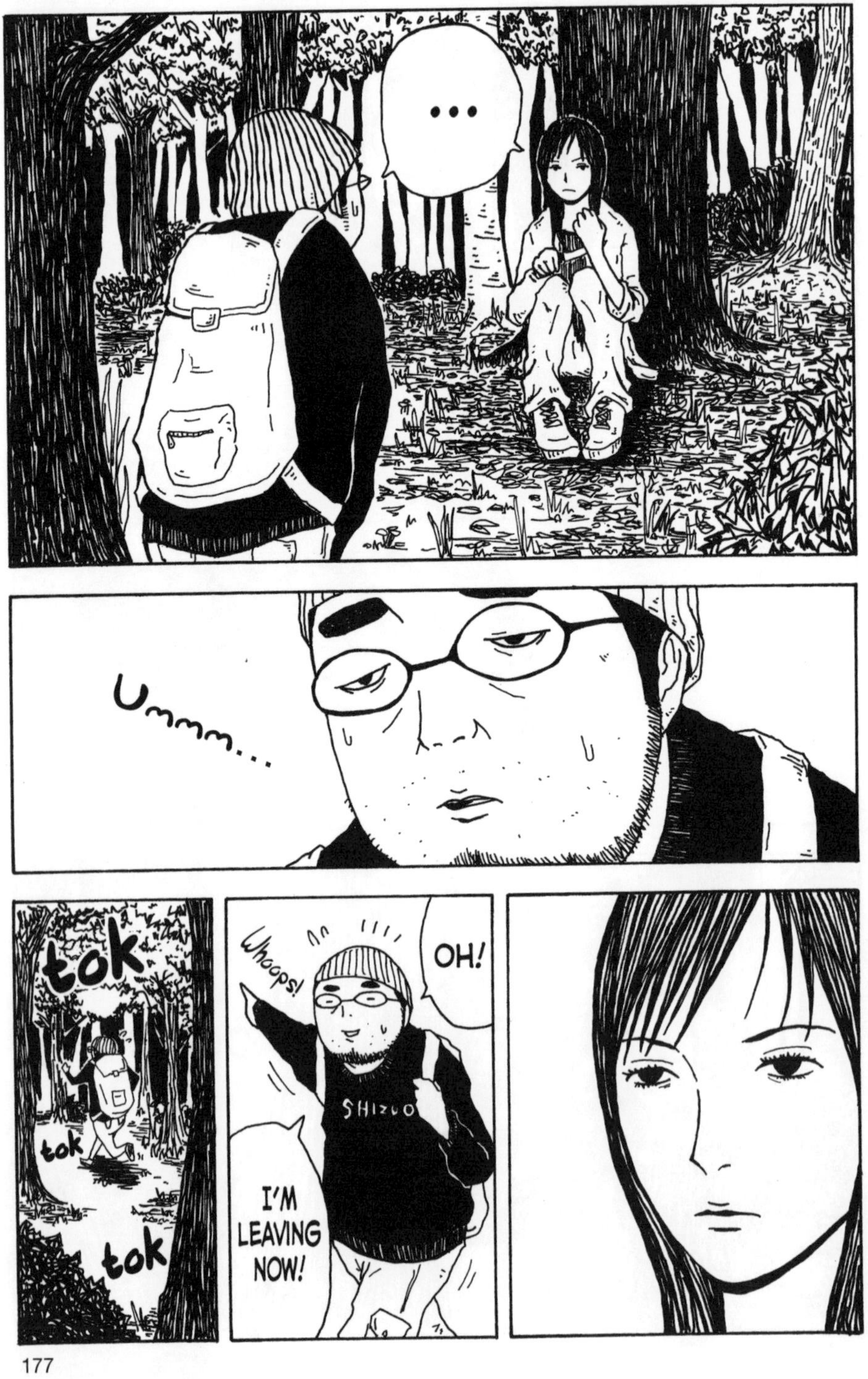
...
Ummm....
OH!
Whoops!
I'M LEAVING NOW!
tok
tok
tok

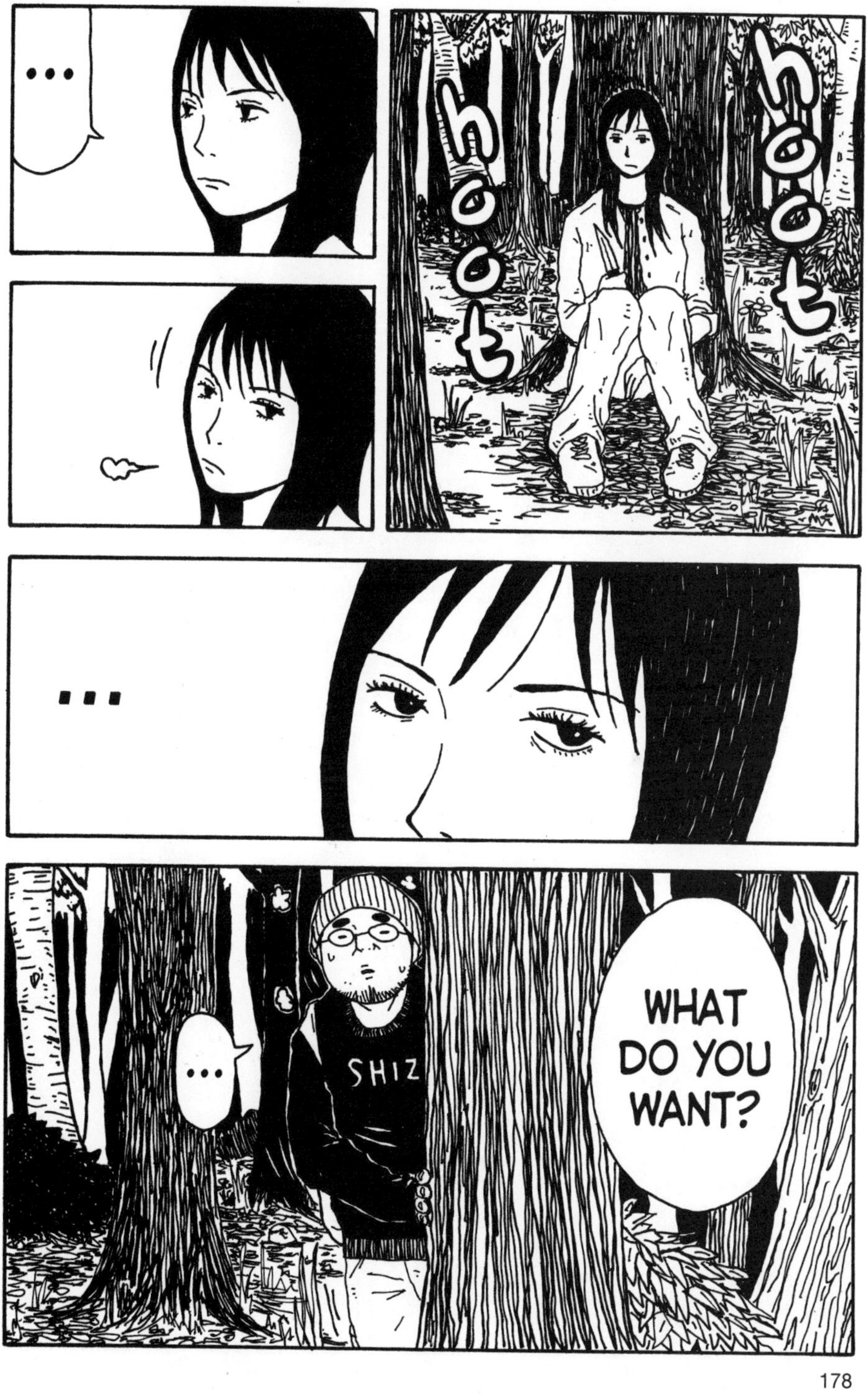
hoot
hoot
...
...
WHAT DO YOU WANT?
...

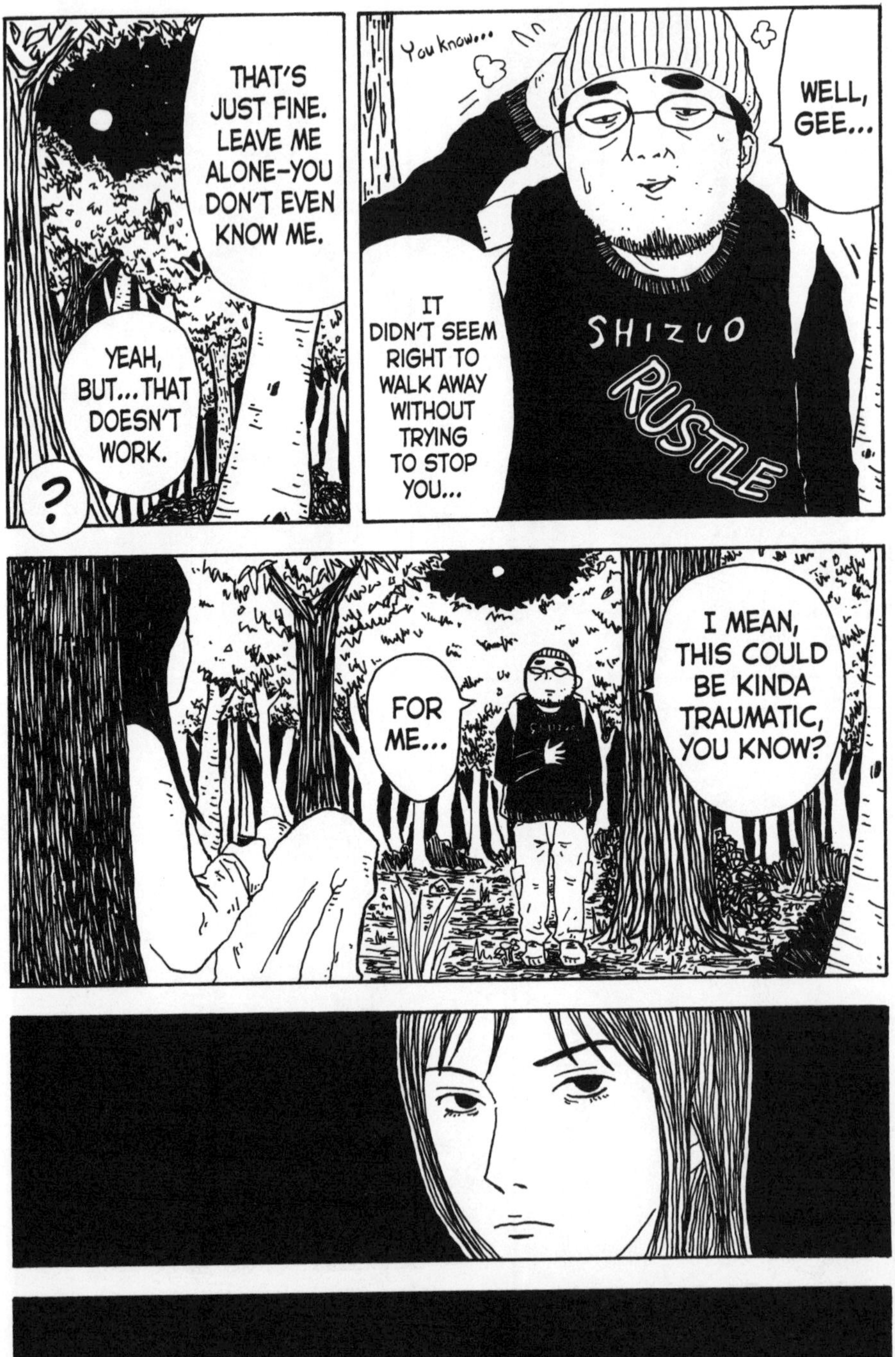
WELL, GEE...
You know...
IT DIDN'T SEEM RIGHT TO WALK AWAY WITHOUT TRYING TO STOP YOU...
SHIZUO
RUSTLE
THAT'S JUST FINE. LEAVE ME ALONE—YOU DON'T EVEN KNOW ME.
YEAH, BUT...THAT DOESN'T WORK.
?
I MEAN, THIS COULD BE KINDA TRAUMATIC, YOU KNOW?
FOR ME...

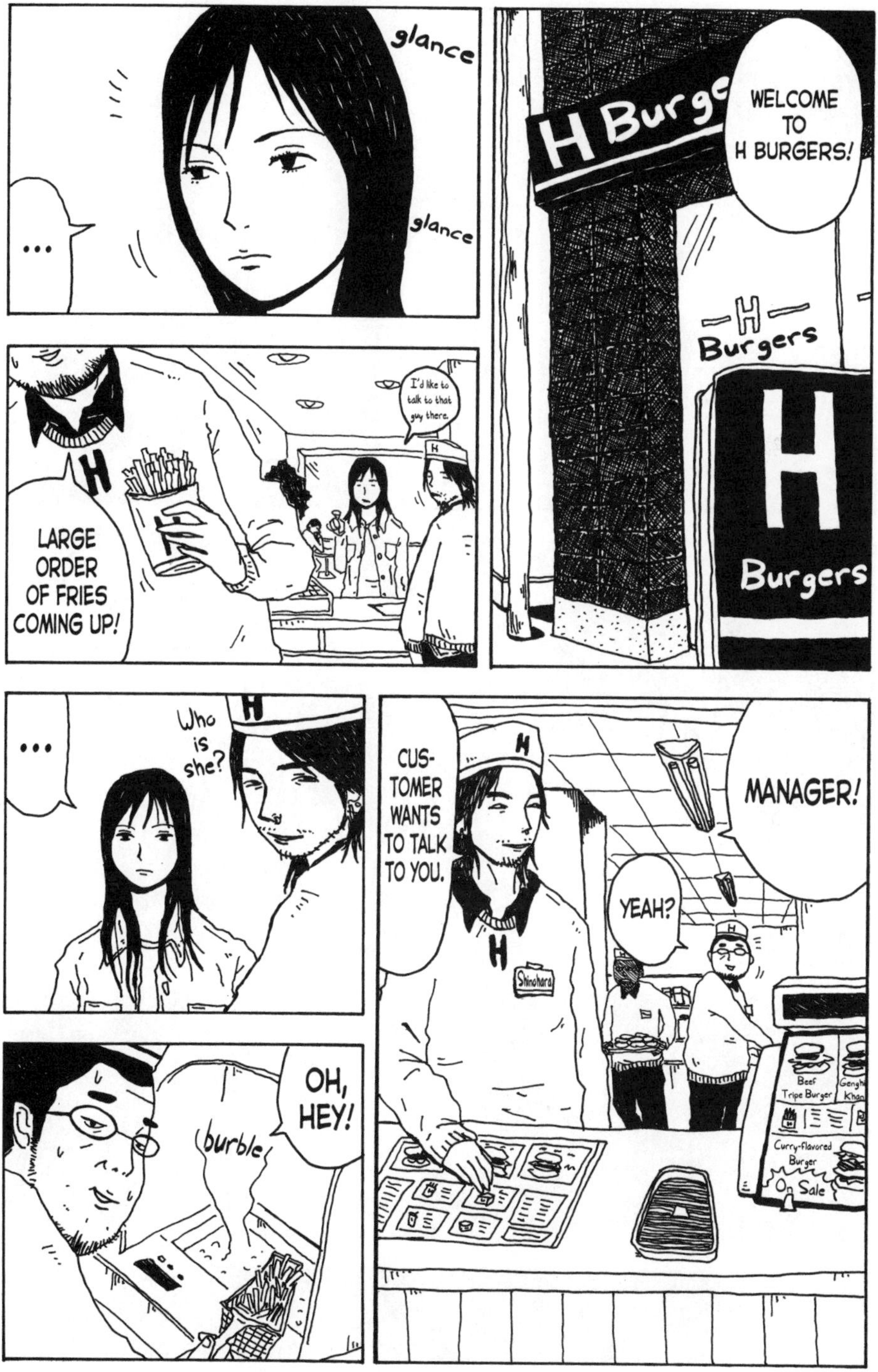
H Burge
WELCOME TO H BURGERS!
H Burgers
H Burgers
glance
glance
...
I'd like to talk to that guy there.
LARGE ORDER OF FRIES COMING UP!
MANAGER!
CUS-TOMER WANTS TO TALK TO YOU.
YEAH?
Shinohara
Beef Tripe Burger
Curry-flavored Burger On Sale
Who is she?
...
OH, HEY!
burble

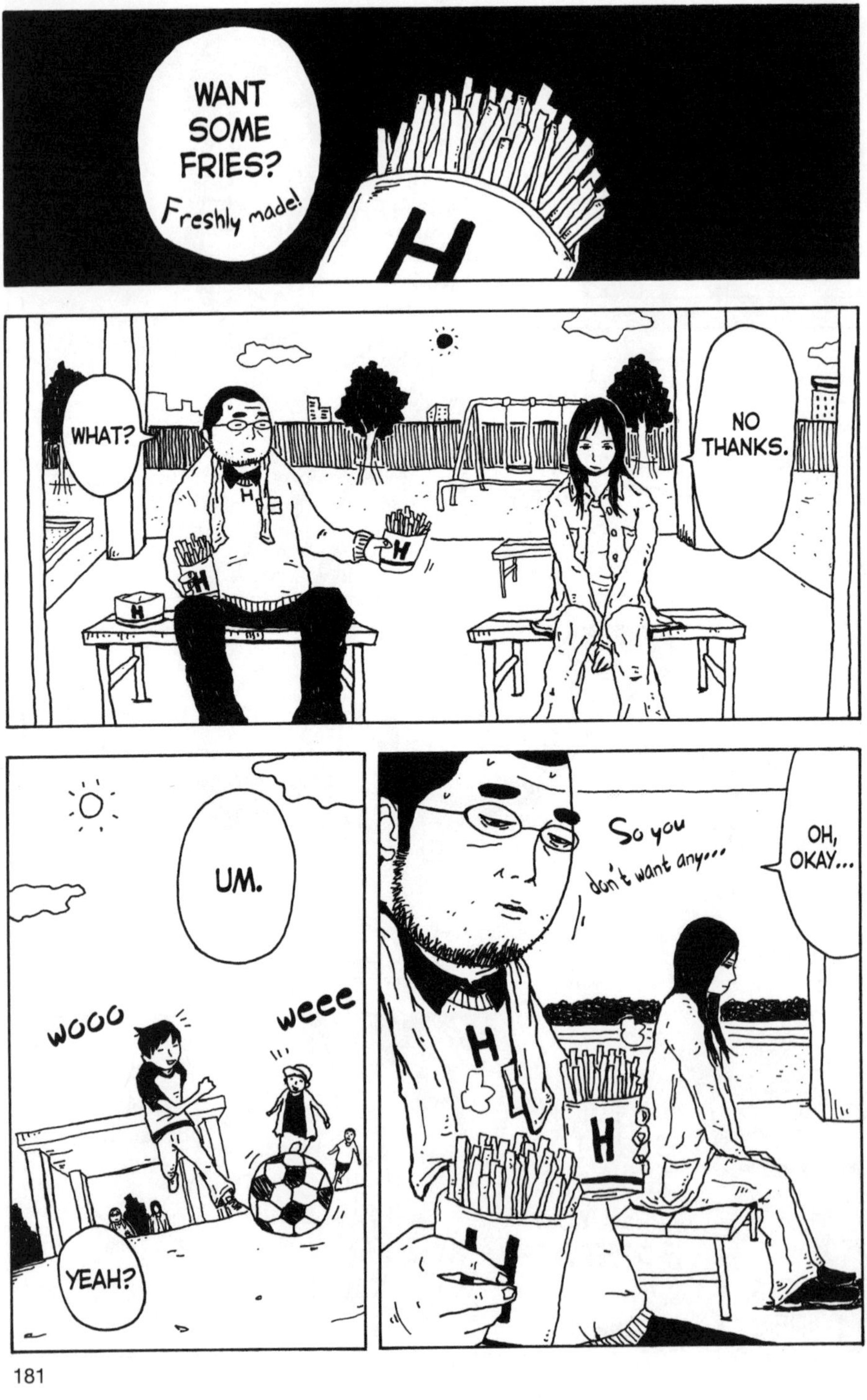
WANT SOME FRIES?
Freshly made!
NO THANKS.
WHAT?
OH, OKAY...
So you don't want any...
UM.
weee
WOOO
YEAH?

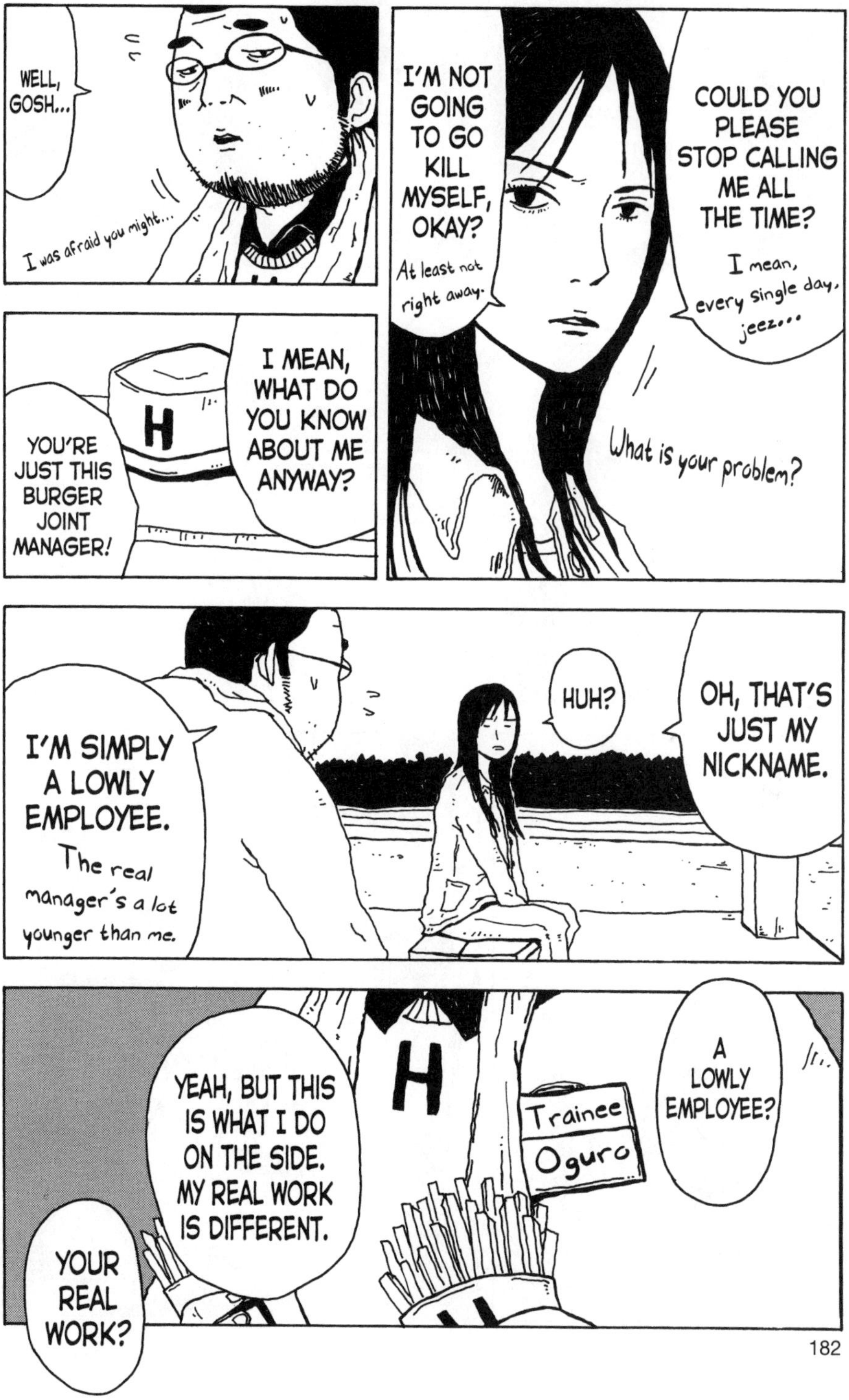
COULD YOU PLEASE STOP CALLING ME ALL THE TIME?
I mean, every single day, jeez...
I'M NOT GOING TO GO KILL MYSELF, OKAY?
At least not right away.
What is your problem?
WELL, GOSH...
I was afraid you might...
I MEAN, WHAT DO YOU KNOW ABOUT ME ANYWAY?
YOU'RE JUST THIS BURGER JOINT MANAGER!
OH, THAT'S JUST MY NICKNAME.
HUH?
I'M SIMPLY A LOWLY EMPLOYEE.
The real manager's a lot younger than me.
A LOWLY EMPLOYEE?
Trainee
Oguro
YEAH, BUT THIS IS WHAT I DO ON THE SIDE. MY REAL WORK IS DIFFERENT.
YOUR REAL WORK?

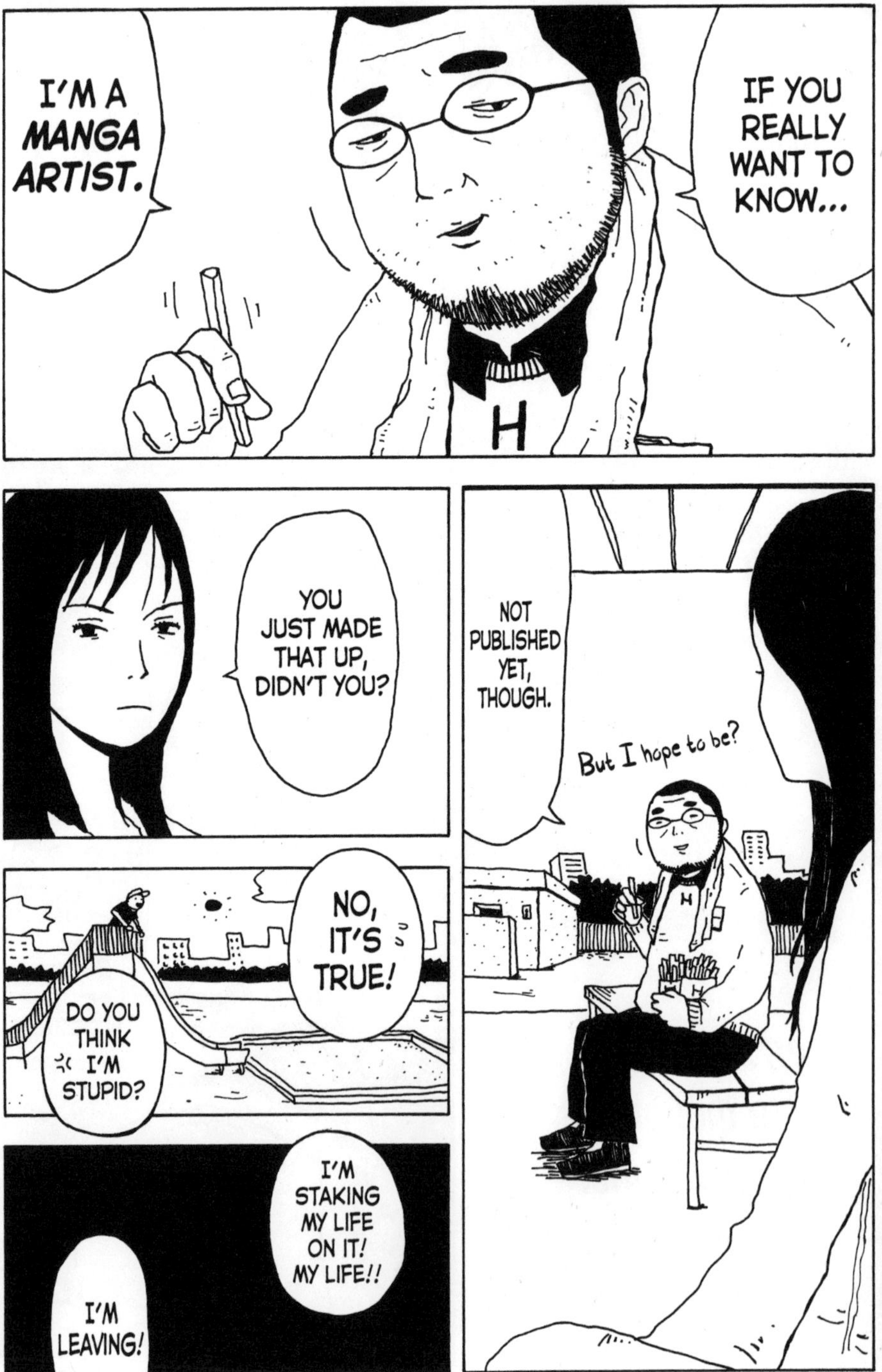
IF YOU REALLY WANT TO KNOW...
I'M A *MANGA ARTIST.*
NOT PUBLISHED YET, THOUGH.
But I hope to be?
YOU JUST MADE THAT UP, DIDN'T YOU?
NO, IT'S TRUE!
DO YOU THINK I'M STUPID?
I'M STAKING MY LIFE ON IT! MY LIFE!!
I'M LEAVING!

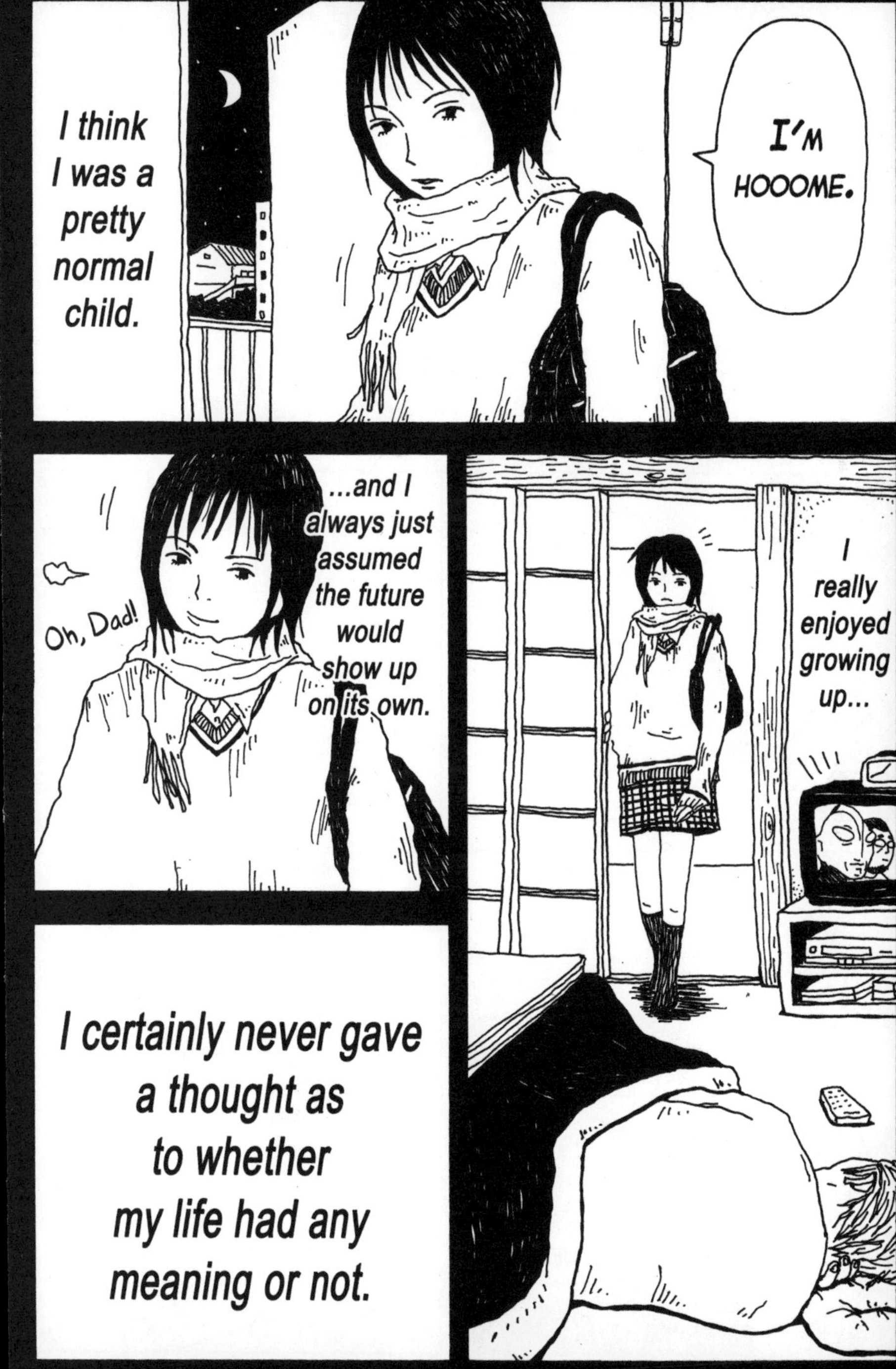
I'M HOOOME.
I think I was a pretty normal child.
I really enjoyed growing up...
...and I always just assumed the future would show up on its own.
Oh, Dad!
I certainly never gave a thought as to whether my life had any meaning or not.

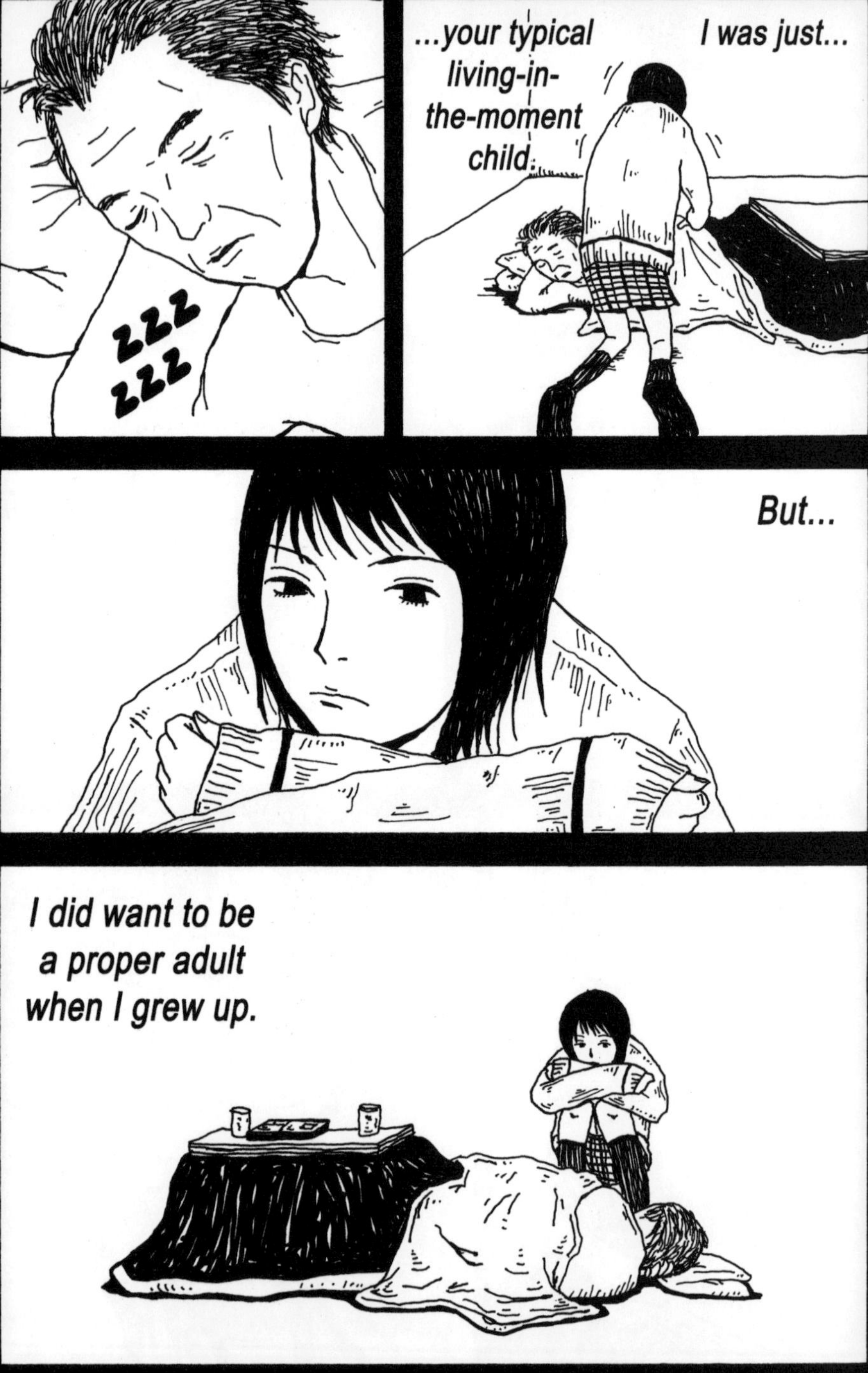
I was just...
...your typical living-in-the-moment child.
ZZZ ZZZ
But...
I did want to be a proper adult when I grew up.

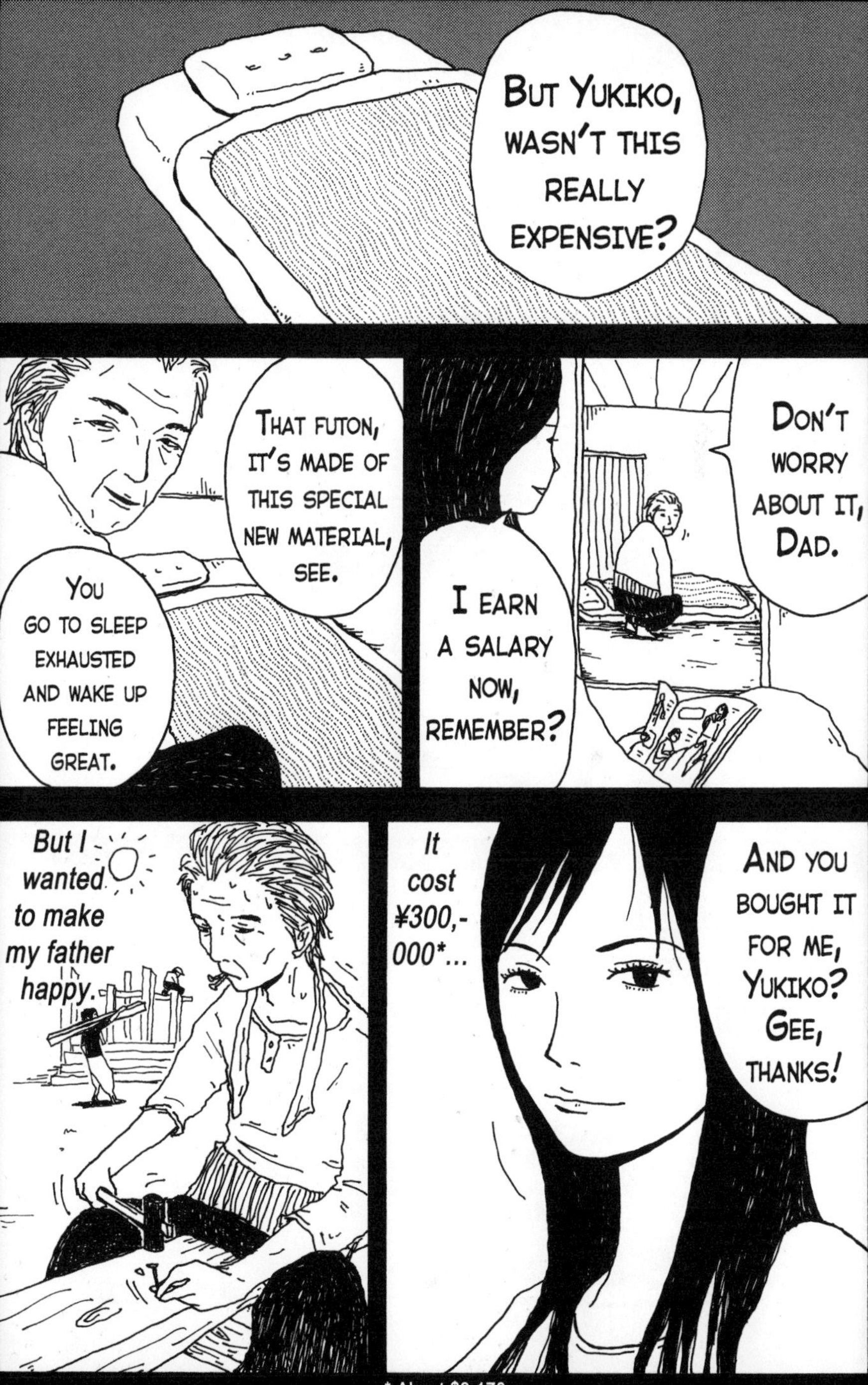
But Yukiko, wasn't this really expensive?
Don't worry about it, Dad.
I earn a salary now, remember?
That futon, it's made of this special new material, see.
You go to sleep exhausted and wake up feeling great.
And you bought it for me, Yukiko? Gee, thanks!
It cost ¥300,000*...
But I wanted to make my father happy.

* About $3,170.

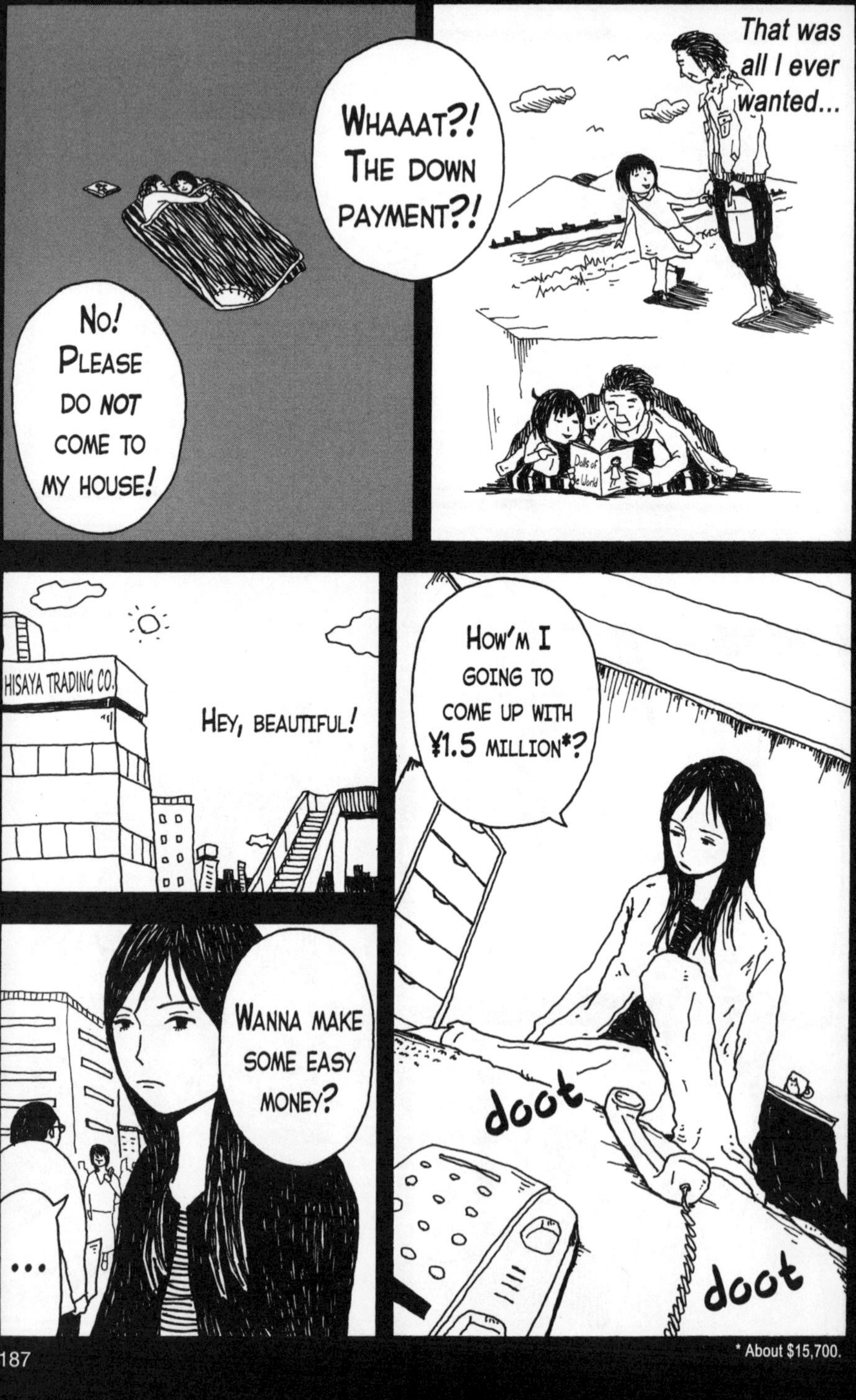
That was all I ever wanted...
Dolls of the World
WHAAAT?! THE DOWN PAYMENT?!
NO! PLEASE DO NOT COME TO MY HOUSE!
HOW'M I GOING TO COME UP WITH ¥1.5 MILLION*?
doot
doot
HISAYA TRADING CO.
HEY, BEAUTIFUL!
WANNA MAKE SOME EASY MONEY?
...

* About $15,700.

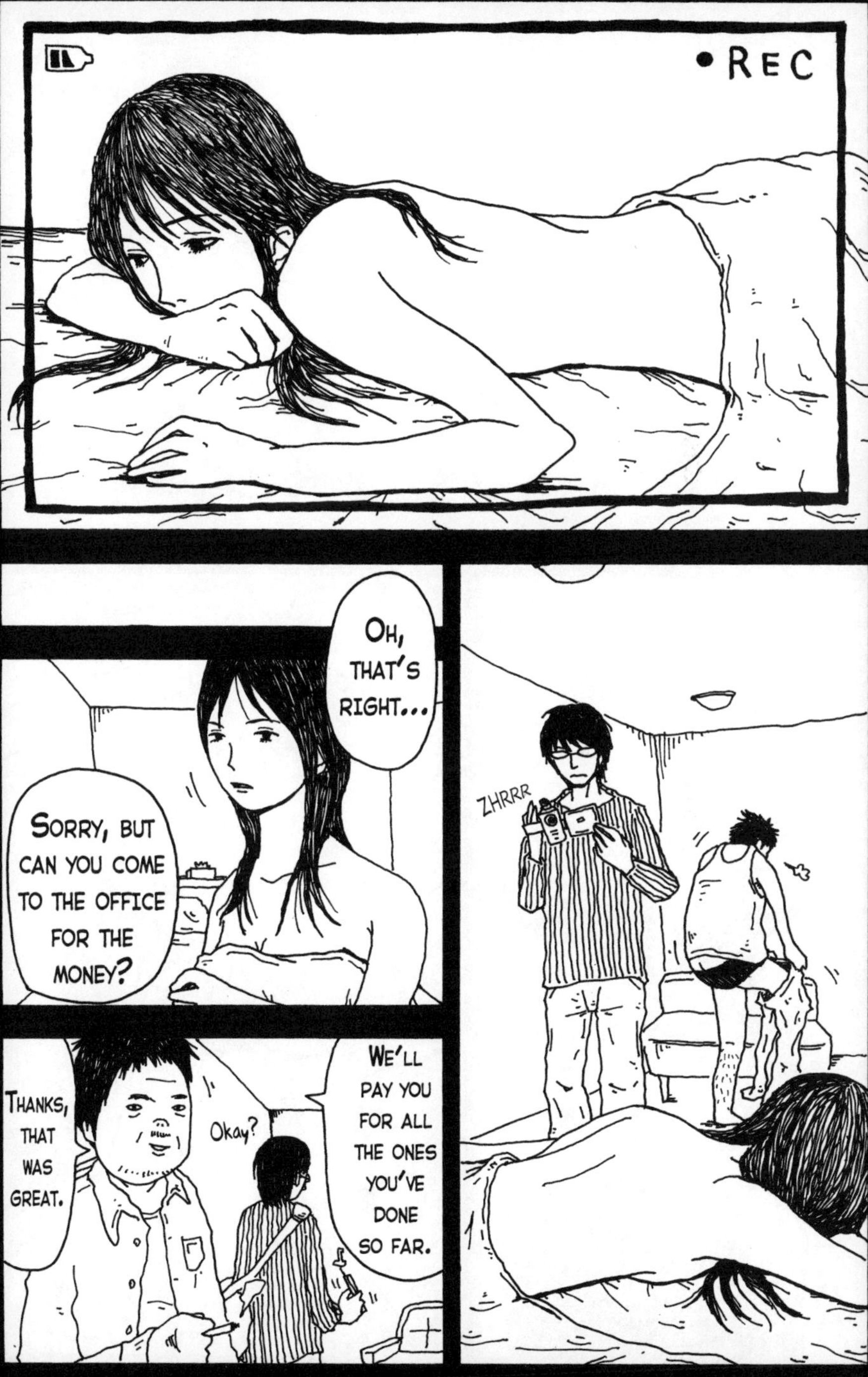
REC
ZHRRR
Oh, that's right...
Sorry, but can you come to the office for the money?
We'll pay you for all the ones you've done so far.
Okay?
Thanks, that was great.

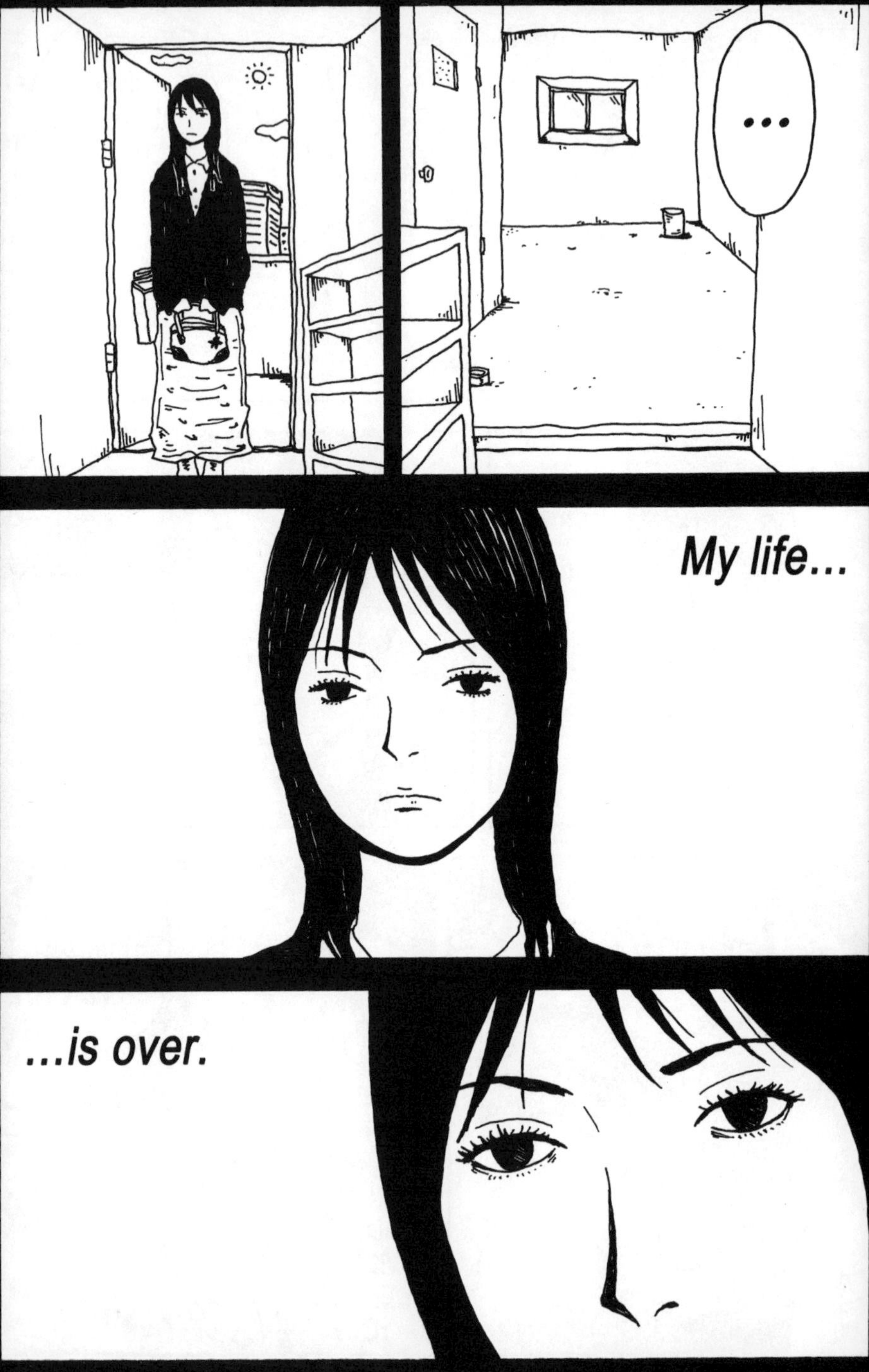
...
My life...
...is over.

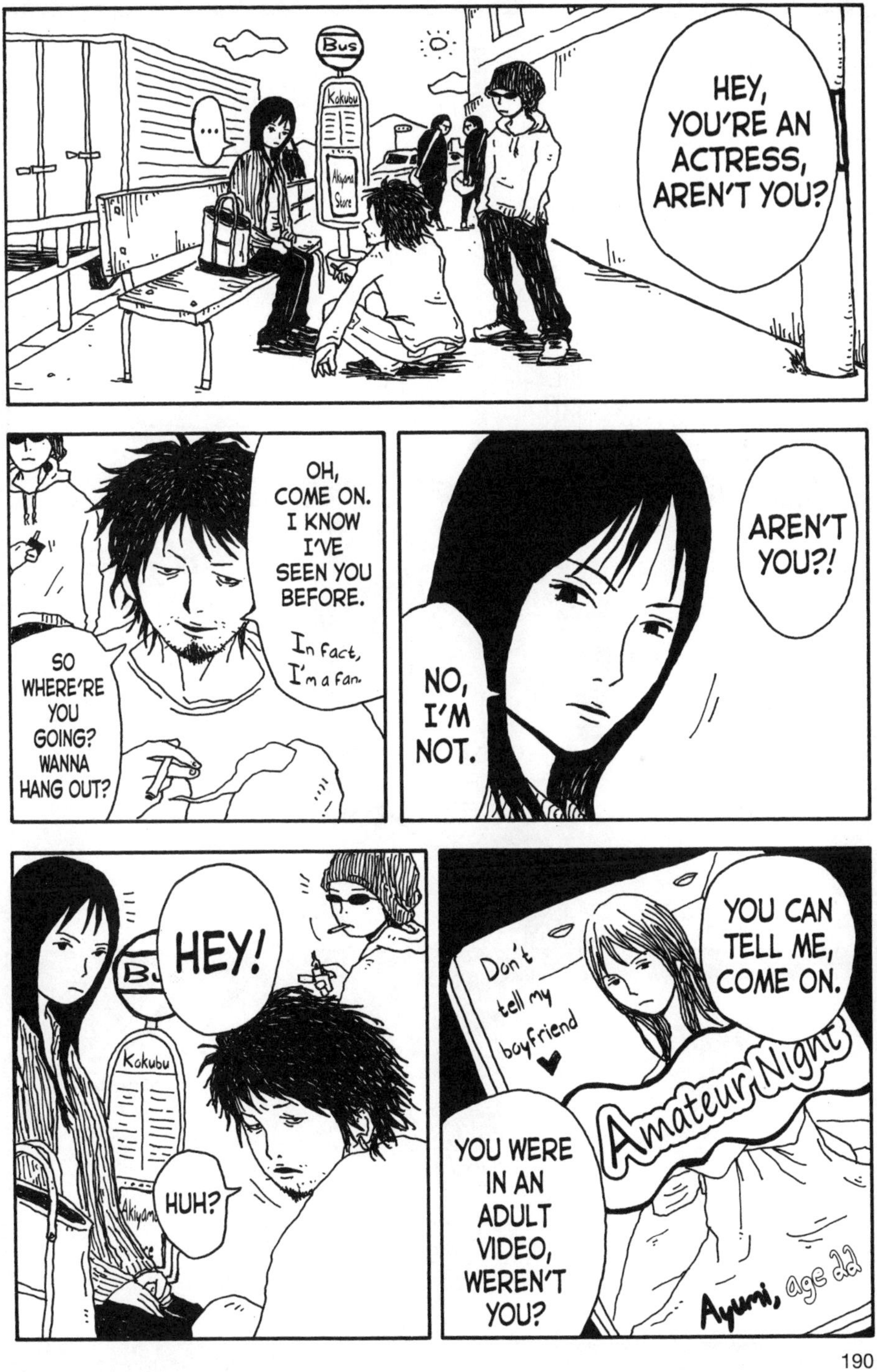
HEY, YOU'RE AN ACTRESS, AREN'T YOU?
Bus
Kokubu
Akiyama Store
...
AREN'T YOU?!
NO, I'M NOT.
OH, COME ON. I KNOW I'VE SEEN YOU BEFORE.
In fact, I'm a fan.
SO WHERE'RE YOU GOING? WANNA HANG OUT?
YOU CAN TELL ME, COME ON.
Don't tell my boyfriend
Amateur Night
YOU WERE IN AN ADULT VIDEO, WEREN'T YOU?
Ayumi, age 22
HEY!
Kokubu
HUH?

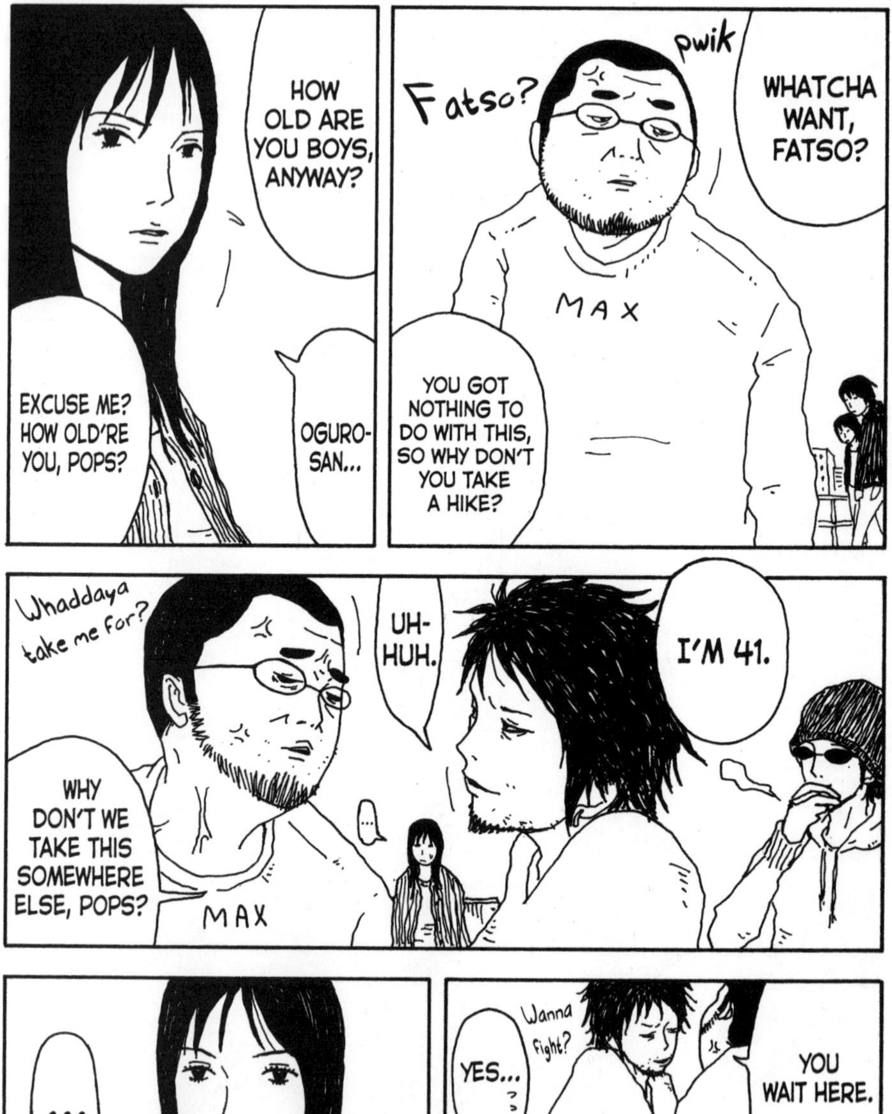
pwik
WHATCHA WANT, FATSO?
Fatso?
YOU GOT NOTHING TO DO WITH THIS, SO WHY DON'T YOU TAKE A HIKE?
HOW OLD ARE YOU BOYS, ANYWAY?
OGURO-SAN...
EXCUSE ME? HOW OLD'RE YOU, POPS?
I'M 41.
UH-HUH.
Whaddaya take me for?
...
WHY DON'T WE TAKE THIS SOMEWHERE ELSE, POPS?
MAX
YOU WAIT HERE.
Here, hold on to my glasses for me.
Wanna fight?
YES...
peh
...

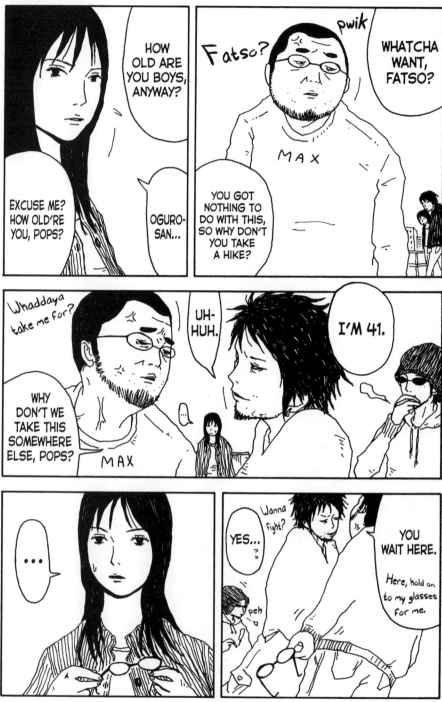

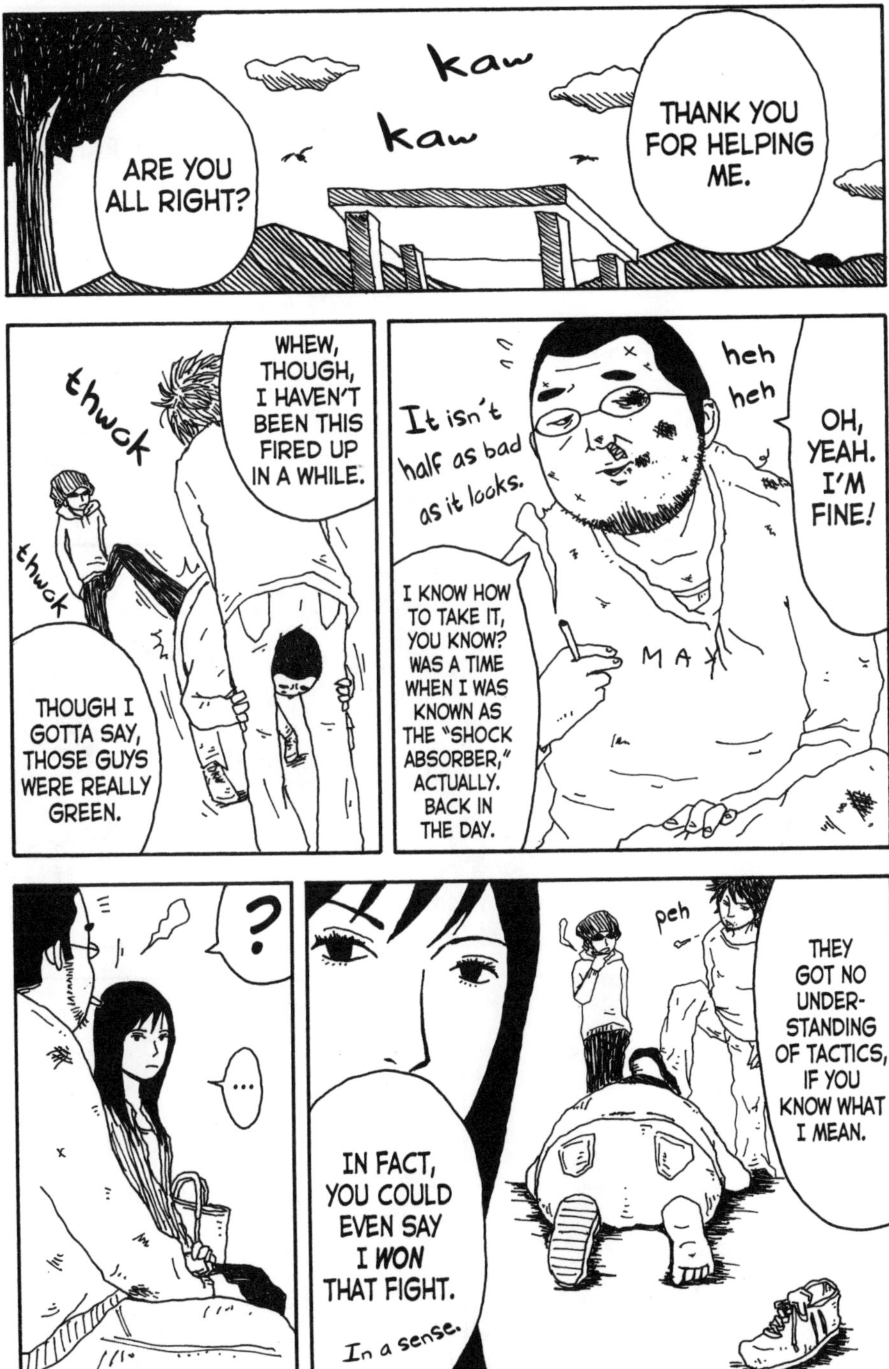
THANK YOU FOR HELPING ME.
kaw
kaw
ARE YOU ALL RIGHT?
heh heh
OH, YEAH. I'M FINE!
It isn't half as bad as it looks.
I KNOW HOW TO TAKE IT, YOU KNOW? WAS A TIME WHEN I WAS KNOWN AS THE "SHOCK ABSORBER," ACTUALLY. BACK IN THE DAY.
MAX
WHEW, THOUGH, I HAVEN'T BEEN THIS FIRED UP IN A WHILE.
thwck
thwck
THOUGH I GOTTA SAY, THOSE GUYS WERE REALLY GREEN.
THEY GOT NO UNDER-STANDING OF TACTICS, IF YOU KNOW WHAT I MEAN.
peh
IN FACT, YOU COULD EVEN SAY I *WON* THAT FIGHT.
In a sense.
?
...

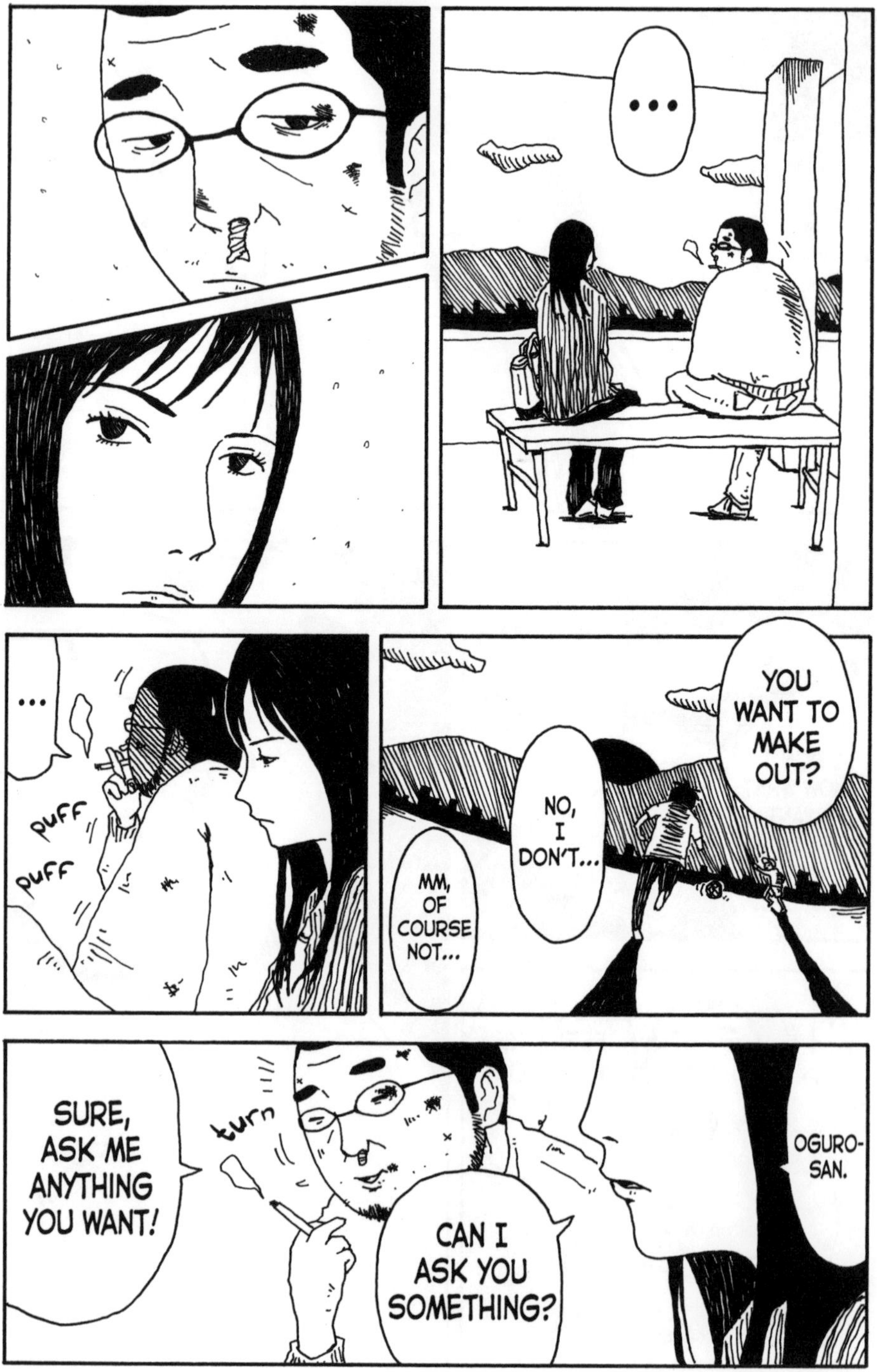
...
YOU WANT TO MAKE OUT?
NO, I DON'T...
MM, OF COURSE NOT...
...
puff
puff
OGURO-SAN.
CAN I ASK YOU SOMETHING?
turn
SURE, ASK ME ANYTHING YOU WANT!

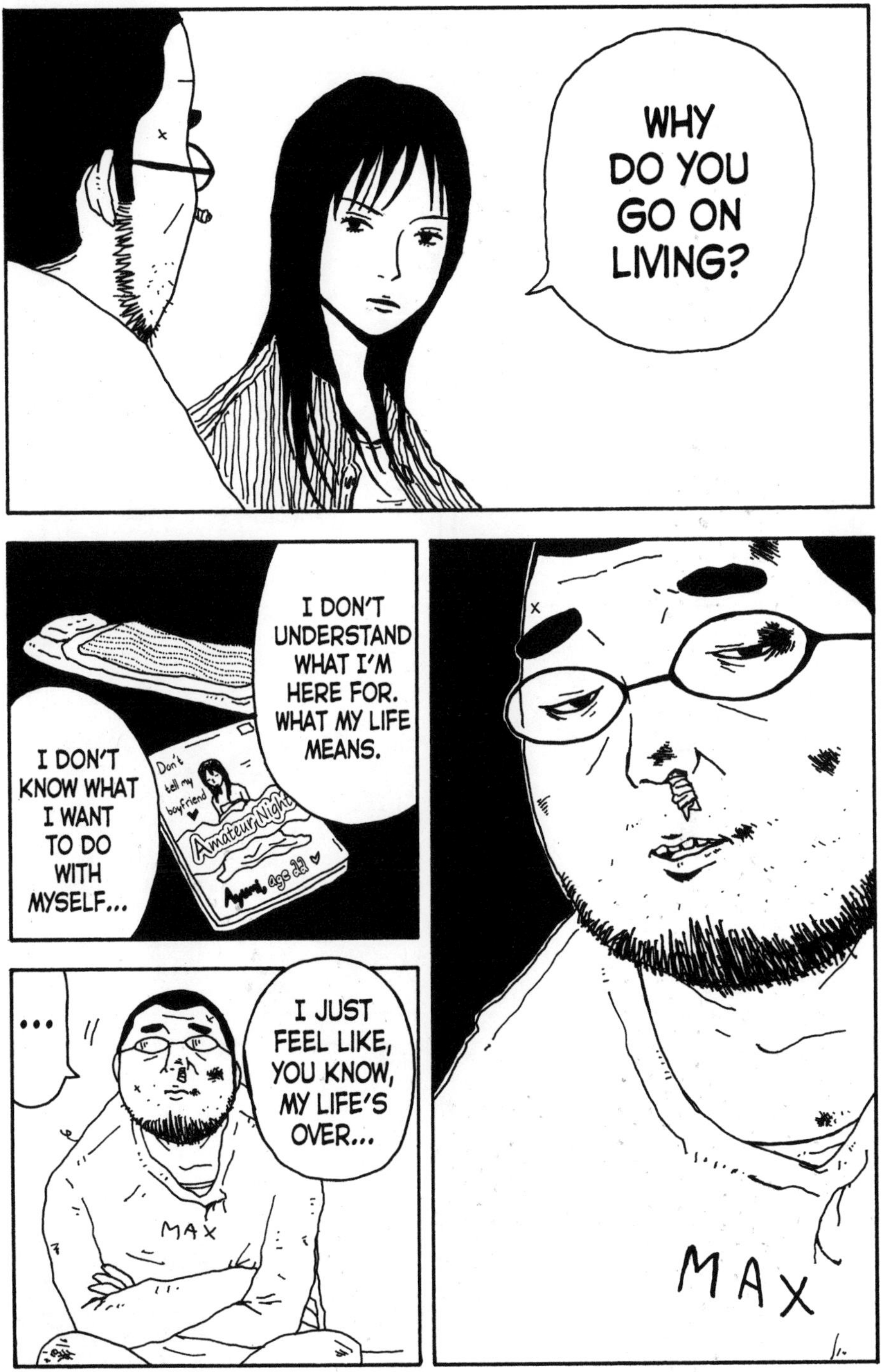
WHY DO YOU GO ON LIVING?
MAX
I DON'T UNDERSTAND WHAT I'M HERE FOR. WHAT MY LIFE MEANS.
I DON'T KNOW WHAT I WANT TO DO WITH MYSELF...
Don't tell my boyfriend ♥
Amateur Night
age 22 ♥
I JUST FEEL LIKE, YOU KNOW, MY LIFE'S OVER...
...
MAX

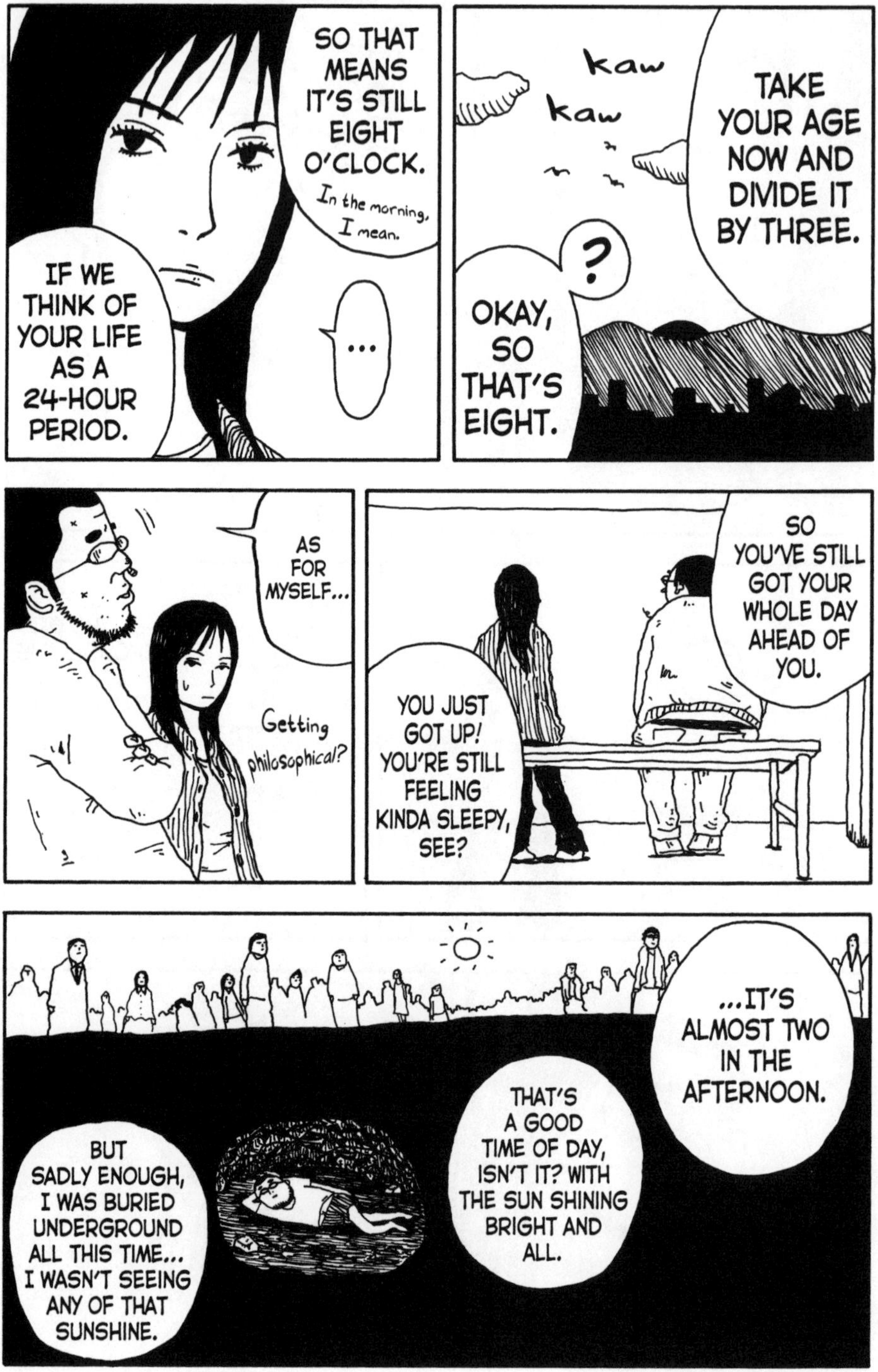
TAKE YOUR AGE NOW AND DIVIDE IT BY THREE.
kaw
kaw
?
OKAY, SO THAT'S EIGHT.
SO THAT MEANS IT'S STILL EIGHT O'CLOCK.
In the morning, I mean.
IF WE THINK OF YOUR LIFE AS A 24-HOUR PERIOD.
...
SO YOU'VE STILL GOT YOUR WHOLE DAY AHEAD OF YOU.
YOU JUST GOT UP! YOU'RE STILL FEELING KINDA SLEEPY, SEE?
AS FOR MYSELF...
Getting philosophical?
...IT'S ALMOST TWO IN THE AFTERNOON.
THAT'S A GOOD TIME OF DAY, ISN'T IT? WITH THE SUN SHINING BRIGHT AND ALL.
BUT SADLY ENOUGH, I WAS BURIED UNDERGROUND ALL THIS TIME... I WASN'T SEEING ANY OF THAT SUNSHINE.

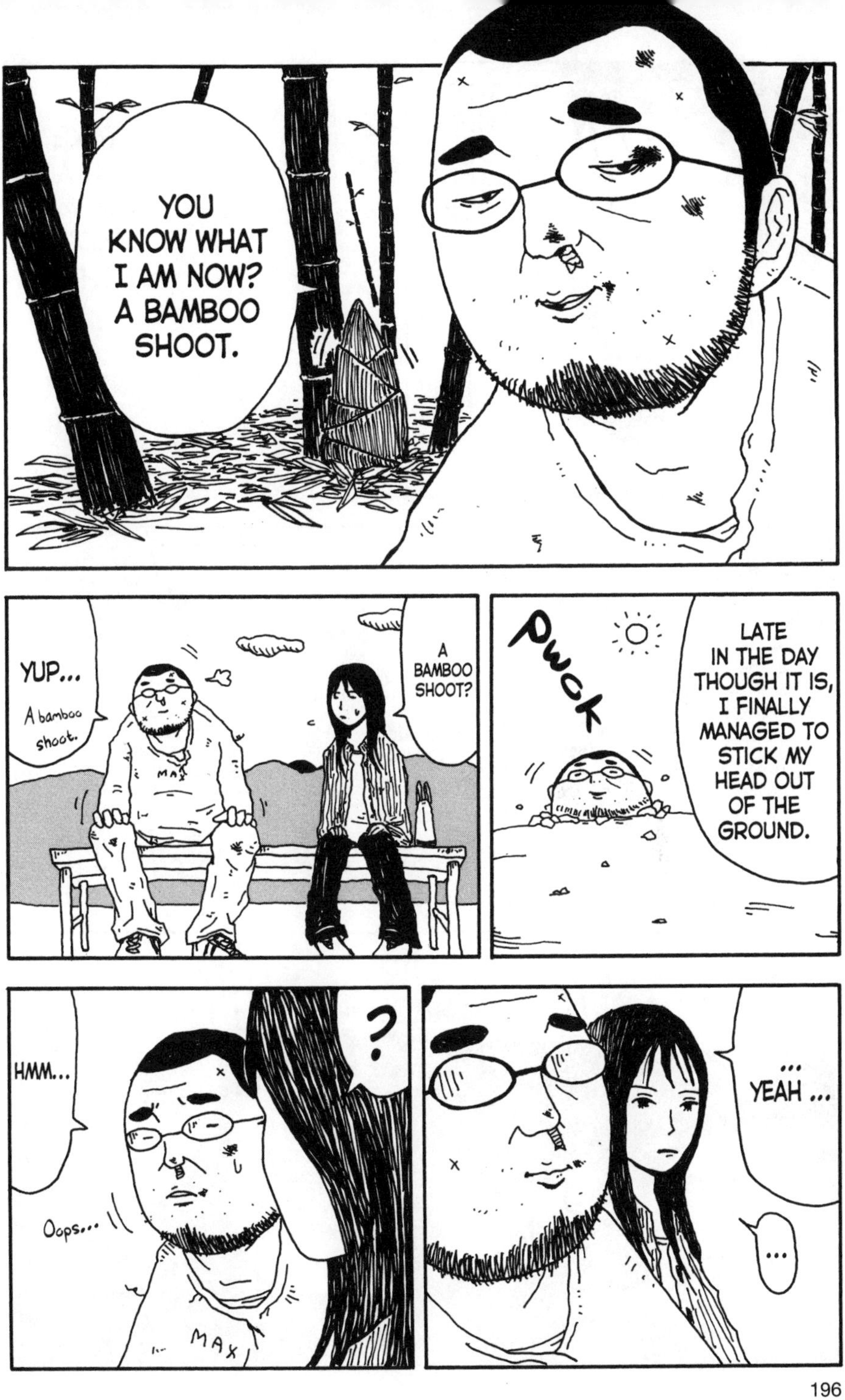
YOU KNOW WHAT I AM NOW? A BAMBOO SHOOT.
PWOCK
LATE IN THE DAY THOUGH IT IS, I FINALLY MANAGED TO STICK MY HEAD OUT OF THE GROUND.
A BAMBOO SHOOT?
YUP...
A bamboo shoot.
... YEAH ...
...
?
HMM...
Oops...

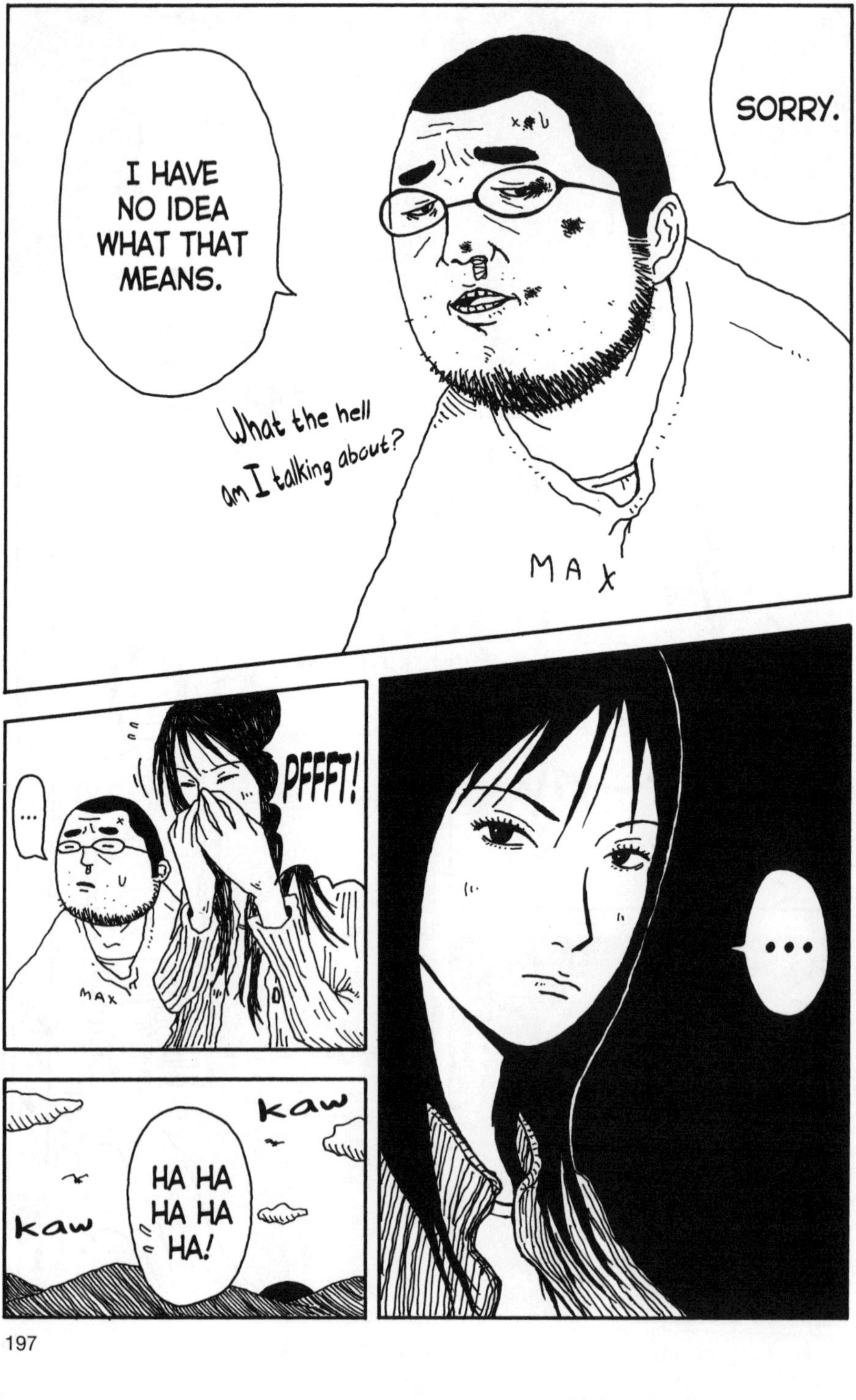
SORRY.
I HAVE NO IDEA WHAT THAT MEANS.
What the hell am I talking about?
MAX
...
PFFFT!
...
MAX
kaw
HA HA HA HA HA!
kaw

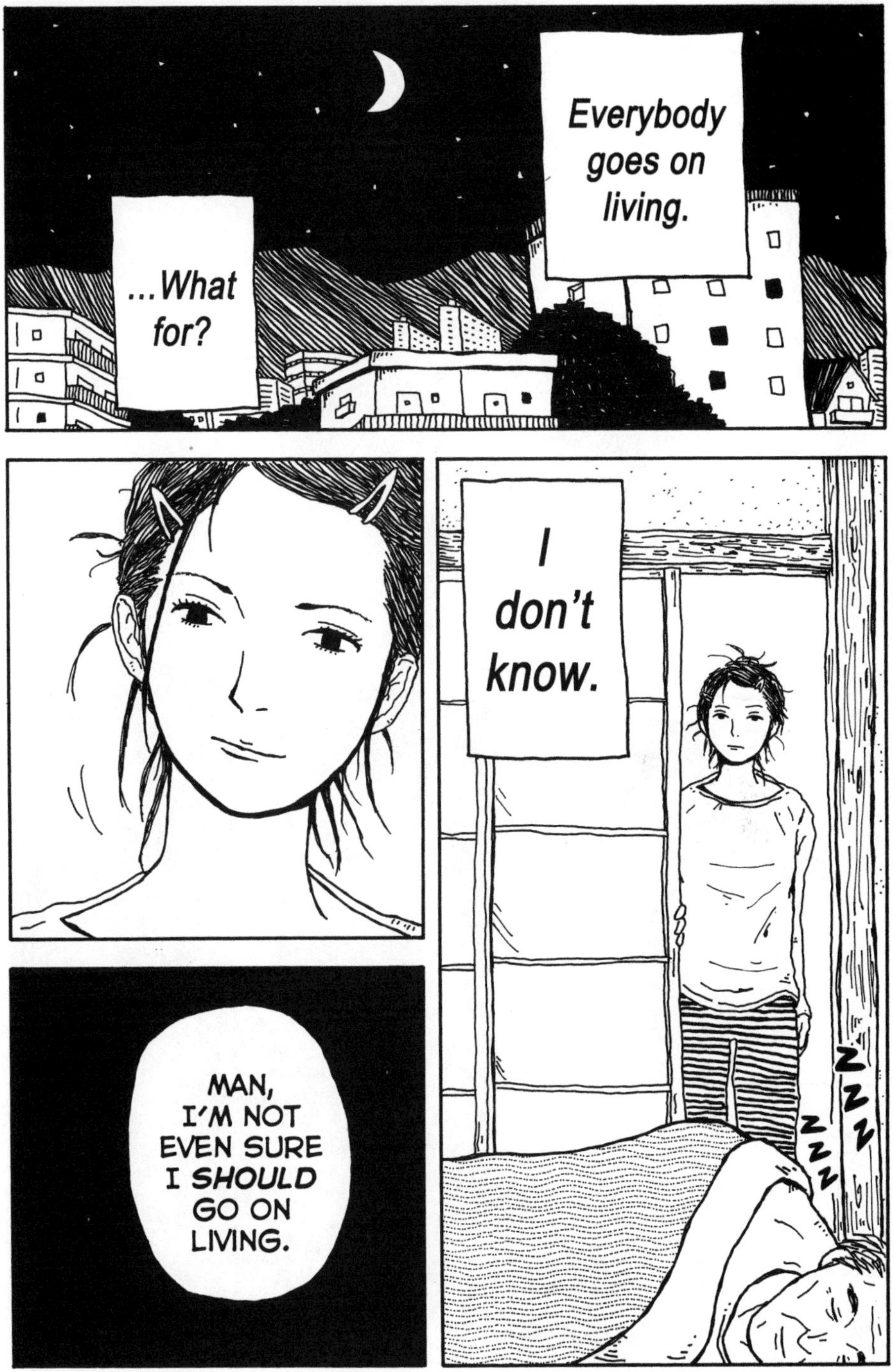
Everybody goes on living.
...What for?
I don't know.
ZZZ
ZZZ
MAN, I'M NOT EVEN SURE I *SHOULD* GO ON LIVING.

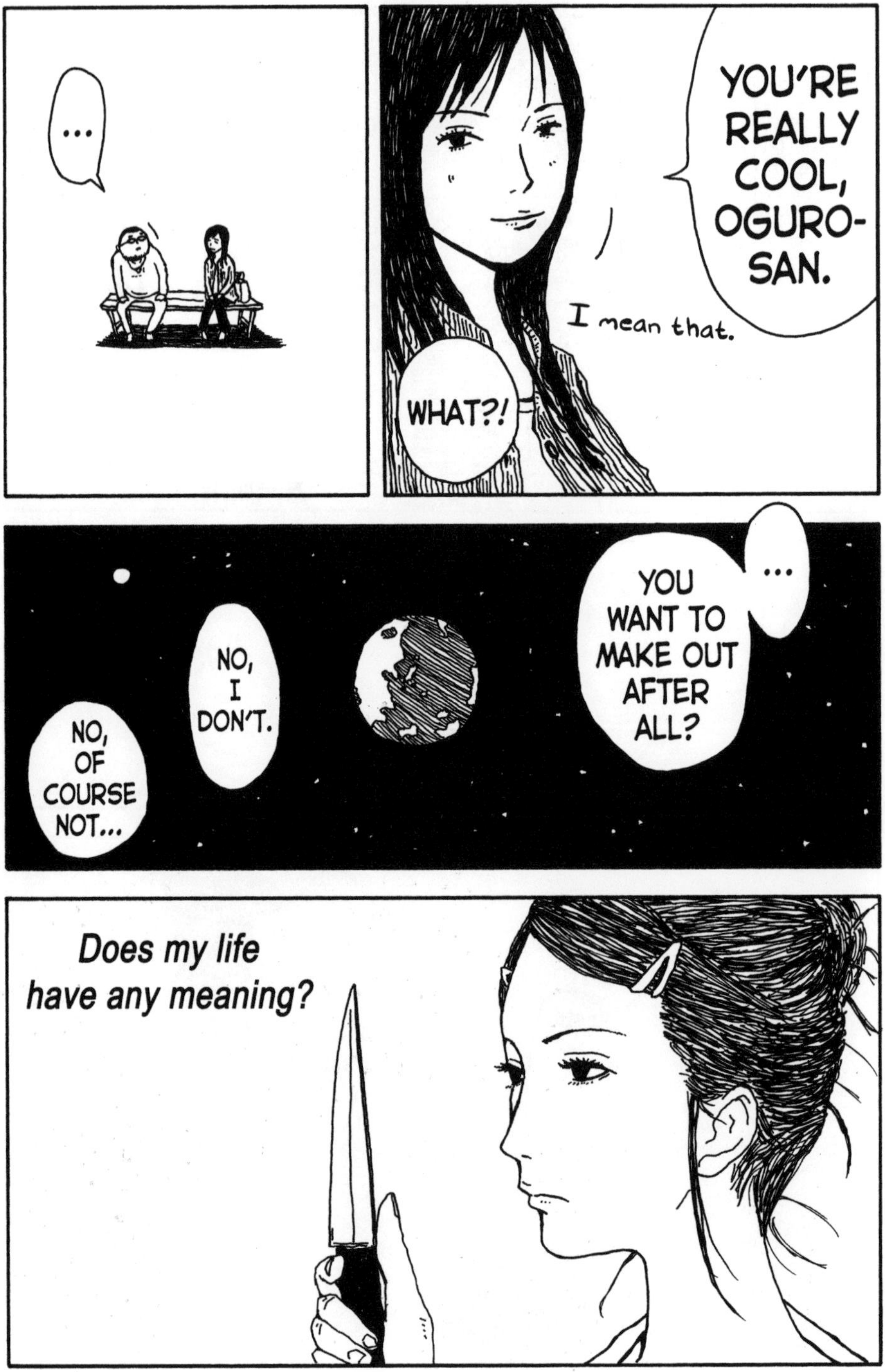
YOU'RE REALLY COOL, OGURO-SAN.
I mean that.
WHAT?!
...
...
YOU WANT TO MAKE OUT AFTER ALL?
NO, I DON'T.
NO, OF COURSE NOT...
Does my life have any meaning?

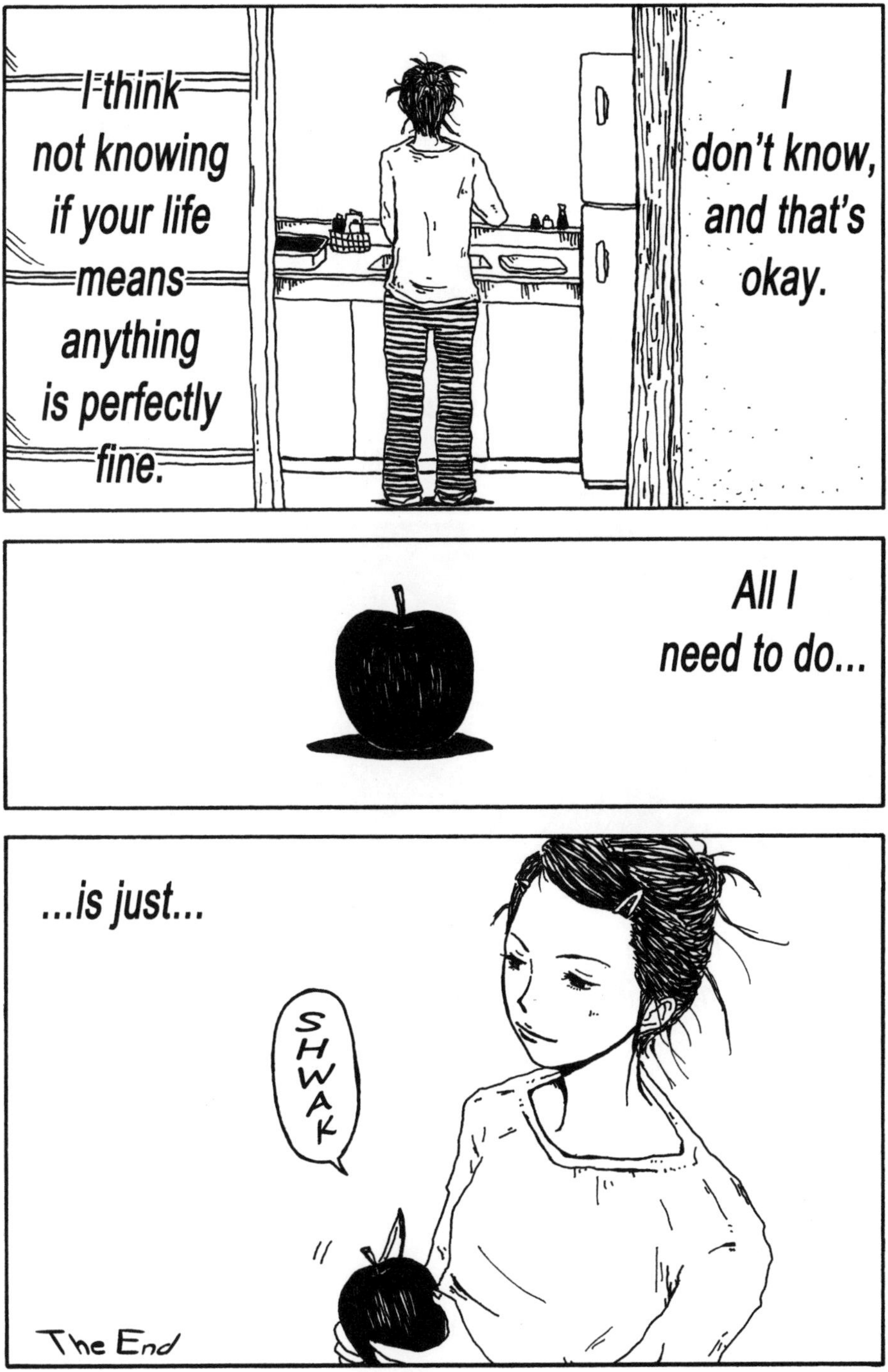
I don't know, and that's okay.
I think not knowing if your life means anything is perfectly fine.
All I need to do...
...is just...
SHWAK
The End

extra poem: "I'm Fine"

I've fallen down so many times, my knees are a mess
But I think I'm pretty good at falling down

People use strange nicknames for me
I think I'm really popular

I can't seem to make any friends
I think people are just holding back to be polite

People get so mad at me, they tremble
I think they see a lot of potential in me

I see a stranger in the mirror looking back at me
I think he looks like a nice guy

I have this numbness from my neck down my left arm
I think it's a temporary symptom

   I'm fine
   I pay my rent
      I eat my vegetables
            I laugh a lot
Look at how much I've grown!

            Thank you, Mom, for having me.

I'll Give It My All... Tomorrow
Volume 1
VIZ Signature Edition

Story & Art by Shunju Aono

© 2007 Shunju AONO/Shogakukan
All rights reserved.
Original Japanese edition "OREWAMADA HONKIDASHITENAIDAKE"
published by SHOGAKUKAN Inc.

English Adaptation · Akemi Wegmüller
Touch-up Art & Lettering · Steven Rhyse
Cover & Book Design · Frances O. Liddell
Editor · Kit Fox

VP, Production · Alvin Lu
VP, Sales & Product Marketing · Gonzalo Ferreyra
VP, Creative · Linda Espinosa
Publisher · Hyoe Narita

Printed in the U.S.A.

Published by VIZ Media, LLC
P.O. Box 77010
San Francisco, CA 94107

10 9 8 7 6 5 4 3 2 1
First printing, May 2010

www.viz.com

www.vizsignature.com

All My Darling Daughters

Story & Art by Fumi Yoshinaga

Eisner-nominated author and creator of *Antique Bakery* and *Ōoku*

As an adult woman still living at home, Yukiko is starting to feel a little bit… stuck. When her mother gets engaged to an ex-host and aspiring actor who's younger than Yukiko, will it be the motivation she needs to move on and out?

Follow the lives of Yukiko and her friends in five short stories that explore their lives, relationships, and loves.

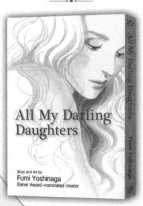

All My Darling Daughters

Story and Art by
Fumi Yoshinaga
Eisner Award–nominated creator

US **$12.99** | CAN **$16.99**
ISBN: 978-1-4215-3240-0

Manga on sale at **WWW.VIZSIGNATURE.COM**
Also available at your local bookstore or comic store.

VIZ SIGNATURE

Aisubeki Musumetachi © Fumi Yoshinaga 2003 /HAKUSENSHA, Inc.

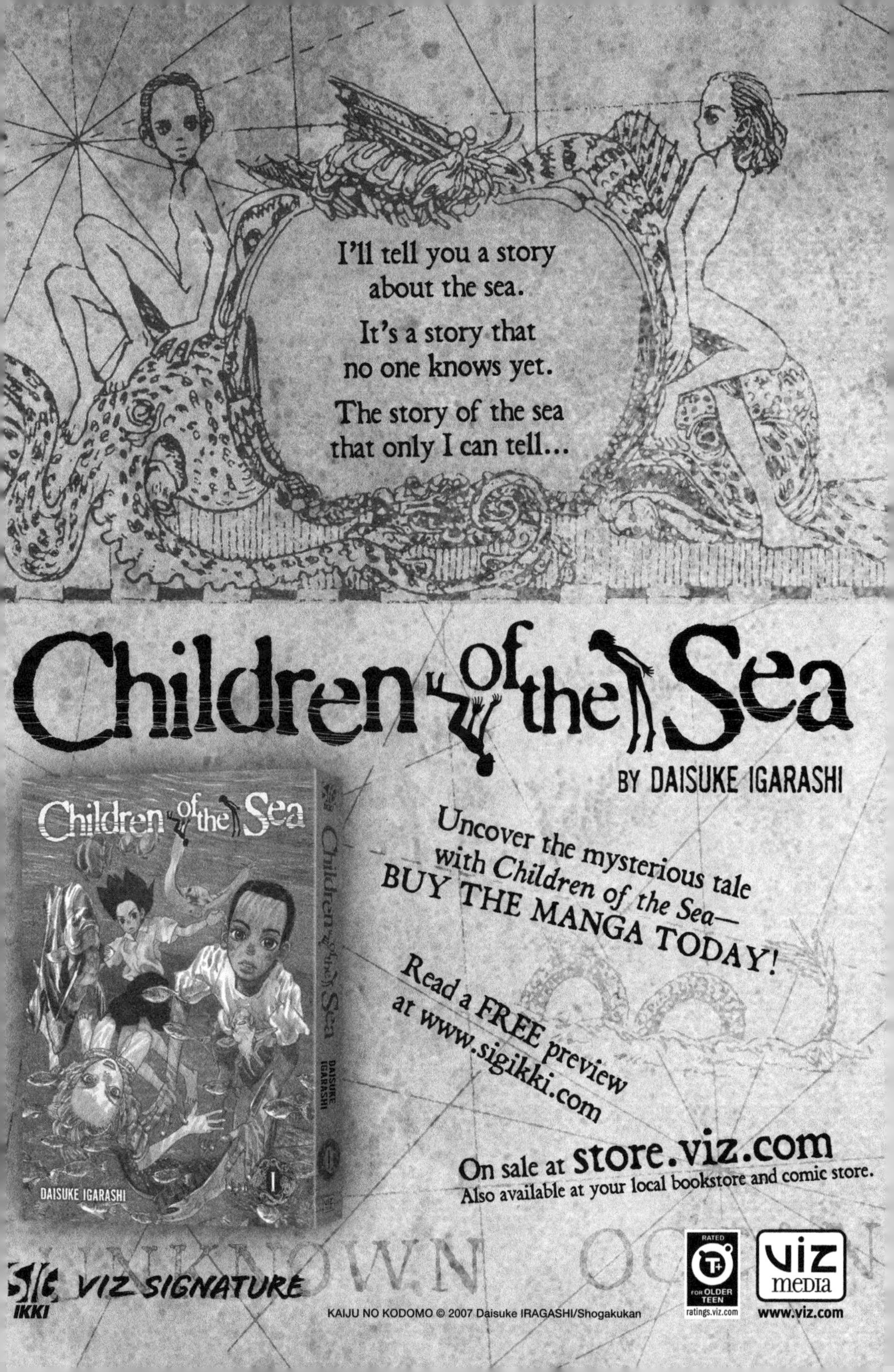
I'll tell you a story
about the sea.
It's a story that
no one knows yet.
The story of the sea
that only I can tell...
Children of the Sea
BY DAISUKE IGARASHI
Children of the Sea
DAISUKE IGARASHI
1
Uncover the mysterious tale
with Children of the Sea—
BUY THE MANGA TODAY!
Read a FREE preview
at www.sigikki.com
On sale at store.viz.com
Also available at your local bookstore and comic store.
UNKNOWN OCEAN
VIZ SIGNATURE
IKKI
KAIJU NO KODOMO © 2007 Daisuke IRAGASHI/Shogakukan
RATED T+ FOR OLDER TEEN
ratings.viz.com
viz media
www.viz.com

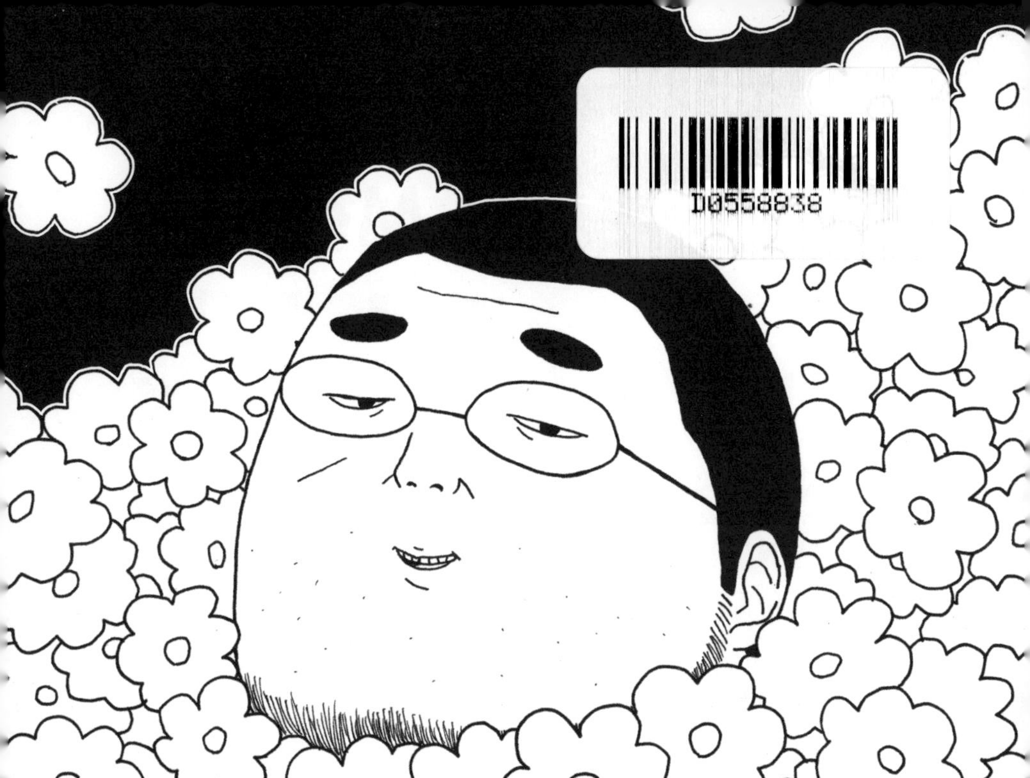

Will Shizuo finally get published?!

At long last he's out of his slump, thanks to his daughter's words. Now, in the warm bosom of his family, will he finally complete his masterpiece?! And...is something going to change?

ON SALE DECEMBER 2010